COHERENCE IN PSYCHOTIC DISCOURSE

COHERENCE IN
PSYCHOTIC
DISCOURSE

Branca Telles Ribeiro

New York   Oxford
OXFORD UNIVERSITY PRESS
1994

Oxford University Press

Oxford   New York   Toronto
Delhi   Bombay   Calcutta   Madras   Karachi
Kuala Lumpur   Singapore   Hong Kong   Tokyo
Nairobi   Dar es Salaam   Cape Town
Melbourne   Auckland   Madrid

and associated companies in
Berlin   Ibadan

Published by Oxford University Press, Inc.
200 Madison Avenue, New York, New York 10016

Oxford is a registered trademark of Oxford University Press, Inc.

Library of Congress Cataloging-in-Publication Data
Ribeiro, Branca Telles.
Coherence in psychotic discourse / Branca Telles Ribeiro.
p.   cm.—(Oxford studies in sociolinguistics)
Includes bibliographical references and index.
ISBN 0-19-506597-2—ISBN 0-19-506615-4 (pbk.)
1. Psychoses—Patients—Language—Case studies.
2. Discourse analysis—Case studies.
3. Cohesion (Linguistics)—Case studies
I. Title.
[DNLM: 1. Interview, Psychological—methods.
2. Physician-Patient Relations.   WM 141 R484c]
RC455.4.P78R53   1994
616.89—dc20
DNLM/DLC for Library of Congress   92-49156

1 3 5 7 9 8 6 4 2

Printed in the United States of America
on acid-free paper

To Zaida Costa
and Bianca Telles Ribeiro,
grandmothers.

To Jurema Cardozo,
whom I have never met.

SERIES FOREWORD

Sociolinguistics is the study of language in use. Its special focus, to be sure, is on the relationships between language and society, and its principal concerns address the forms and functions of linguistic variation across social groups and across the range of communicative situations in which women and men deploy their verbal repertoires. In short, sociolinguists examine discourse as it is constructed and co-constructed, shaped and reshaped, in the language of everyday interaction and as it reflects and creates the social realities of everyday life.

While some branches of linguistics examine the structure of sentences independent of who is speaking (or writing) and to whom, independent of what precedes and what follows in the discourse, and independent of the setting, topic, and purposes of the discourse, sociolinguistics aims to investigate language as it is embedded in its social and institutional contexts. Not surprisingly, among observers who are *not* professional linguists virtually all interest in linguistic matters likewise focuses on language in use, for it is there that language mirrors the intricacies of social structure and reflects the situational and strategic complexities that shape discourse.

In offering a platform for studies of language use in communities around the globe, Oxford Studies in Sociolinguistics invites significant treatments of discourse and of social dialects and registers, whether oral, written, or signed, whether treated synchronically or diachronically. The series hosts studies that are theoretical or descriptive, analytical or interpretive. While most volumes will report original research, a few will synthesize or interpret existing knowledge. All volumes will aim for a style accessible beyond linguists to other social scientists and to humanists examining human discourse.

Occasionally, a volume may appeal to students and other educated readers keenly interested in the everyday language of human affairs—for example, in the discourse of doctors or lawyers trying to engage clients with their specialist registers, or of women and men striving to grasp the sometimes baffling character of their shared interactions.

By providing a forum for innovative and valuable studies of language in use, Oxford Studies in Sociolinguistics aims to influence the agenda for linguistic research in the twenty-first century and, in the meanwhile, to provide an array of insightful and provocative analyses to help launch that agenda.

In the present volume, Branca Telles Ribeiro analyzes two extensive samples of discourse, comparing and contrasting the structures of coherence that characterize "deviant" talk between a patient and her psychiatrist when the patient first enters a hospital for treatment of an acute psychotic crisis and the "normal" talk used when she is discharged after treatment. Using frame analysis and topic analysis as central tools, Dr. Ribeiro untangles some of the confusion between assessment of language and assessment of thought, and she explains how psychotic discourse exhibits a coherence of its own. Focusing on the effect of frame and topic on establishing discourse coherence, Dr. Ribeiro describes the different forms that coherence takes in the admitting and discharge interviews. Her fascinating study also takes up significant methodological questions concerning the transcription of normal and deviant conversation and the representation of conversation in translation. We are pleased to have this valuable and pathbreaking study in Oxford Studies in Sociolinguistics.

Edward Finegan

ACKNOWLEDGMENTS

Many people have contributed to the development of this book. Most of all, the book is the direct result of strong encouragement on the part of Deborah Tannen, my professor and mentor while I was at Georgetown University, and a dear friend from then on. From the book's earliest stages up to its final form, Deborah has been a source of constant inspiration, guidance, and support. She has my deep appreciation and sincere thanks.

Also, I would like to thank my professors at Georgetown University, especially Deborah Schiffrin and Cléa Rameh, for their interest and generous time. My gratitude also goes to Frederick Erickson, a friend and a master, who has attuned my perception to the relevance of nonverbal communication in face-to-face interaction. His constant support has been most valuable.

My thanks to Drs. Eustáquio Portella and Jeremias Ferraz-Lima of the Psychiatric Institute, Federal University of Rio de Janeiro, for providing the tapes and material used in this study. The interviews that formed the subject matter of this study were conducted by a doctor who will remain anonymous; her interest and availability for discussion were most helpful to the study. And even though I have never met the patient, I remain indebted to her.

My special acknowledgment to Dr. Eduardo Rodrigues da Silva for having introduced me to the field of medicine, and specifically to psychiatry. I owe Dr. Carlos J. Doin more than words could ever express.

At later stages, colleagues and friends have contributed valuable time, suggestions, and references to this work. I thank, in particular, Lúcia Quental, Margarida Basílio, Malcom Coulthard, and Carmen-Rosa Caldas-Coulthard. Douglas W. Maynard's careful review of and suggestions on the initial manuscript oriented many of the changes made in the book, for which I am thankful. I am particularly indebted to Susan M. Hoyle for lengthy and stimulating discussions (over bitnet) and for her encouraging responses. She was, and is, an excellent reader. I would like to extend my appreciation to Susan Green for the fine drawings and her keen editorial remarks. Cynthia Read, Peter Ohlin, and Melinda Wirkus at Oxford University Press have provided me support and editorial assistance, and I am grateful for their help.

A grant from the Conselho Nacional de Pesquisa (CNPq), with a complementary grant from the Catholic University of Rio de Janeiro, provided the financial support that enabled me to study full-time during most of my graduate program in the United States. A preliminary version of this study constituted my doctoral dissertation at Georgetown University.

My love and gratitude to my parents, Maria and Milton—who, very often and in spite of myself, have encouraged me to listen "to different discourses." And finally, my love to Scott Philip Studebaker, who has provided me endless support and affection throughout this project. Without his presence this work would not have been accomplished. I am forever grateful for all that he is.

CONTENTS

TRANSCRIPTION CONVENTIONS

..	noticeable pause or break in rhythm, less than half a second
...	half-second pause, as measured by stopwatch
....	one-second pause
(1.5)	numbers within parentheses represent pauses in talk over one second, measured with a stopwatch
.	sentence-final falling intonation
?	sentence-final rising intonation
,	phrase-final intonation (indicating more talk to come)
˙	high pitch on word
⌐	pitch shift on phrase, upward, continuing until punctuation (several marks indicate progressively higher pitch)
ˌ	low pitch on word
∟	pitch shift on phrase, lowered, continuing until punctuation (several marks indicate progressively lower pitch)
-	glottal stop or abrupt cutting off of sound
:	lengthened sound (extra colons indicate greater lengthening)
underline	emphatic stress
CAPS	very emphatic stress, loudness, or shouting
/words/	spoken softly
//words//	spoken very softly
( )	transcription impossible
(words)	uncertain transcription
((words))	differences in the English version

Note: Most of these conventions are based on Tannen (1984).

\<words\>	spoken with articulatory problems (slightly slurred speech)
=	two utterances linked by = indicate no break in flow of talk (latching); = also links different parts of a single speaker's talk that has been carried over to another line of transcript
[hhh]	audible aspirations
['hhh]	audible inhalations
[talk]	various characterizations of the talk (such as singing, chanting) or tempo (such as staccato) are indicated one line above the segment of talk, in square brackets
[acc]	spoken quickly (appears over the line)
[dec]	spoken slowly (appears over the line)
[whining]	high pitch (half crying)
[creaky voice]	low pitch (half crying)
[nonverbal]	description of nonverbal behavior (changes in posture and orientation) is indicated one line below the segment of talk in square brackets
→	at the left of line highlights point of analysis
//	overlap in a parallel-column transcript; indicates that participants' utterances occupy the same line(s), with the double slash showing where the overlap begins (overlapping speech: two people talking at the same time)
[	a bracket between lines indicates overlapping speech, that is, two people talking at the same time

COHERENCE IN PSYCHOTIC DISCOURSE

1

Coherence in
Psychotic Talk

The process of entering into the other *world from this world, and returning to*
this *world from the other world, is as natural as death and giving birth or being*
born. But in our present world, that is both so terrified and so unconscious of the
other world, it is not surprising that when "reality," the fabric of this world,
bursts, and a person enters the other world, he is completely lost and terrified, and
meets only incomprehension in others.

R. D. Laing, *The Politics of Experience,* p. 103

Entering another world—the inner world—can be a lonely experience for
the traveler and a mystery to us who are left behind. Only by listening
to the voices of those who have stepped beyond can we come closer to
them. In listening we may find meaning and coherence.

Doctor:	Patient:
Dona Jurema!	[whining] **ma:ma::!** =
= **Dona Jurema!**	
	[whining] **ma:ma::!** .. /what is it, (my child)?/
Dona Jurema, **let's talk a little bit.** ..	
	[staccato and baby talk] **what-is-it-you-wish-to-know** =
// **O.K.?**	= **madam-my-mother,** **don't you already know** = = **everything?**
// /mmm/	// /has she not shown you = = (everything?)/

3

Doctor:	Patient:
⌐tell me your FULL name. =	
	[baby talk]
	= there is no need cause the =
	= doc, doc, doc, the doc-
	papapapapapapapapapapapa- ['hhh]
	[moving her face to the right]
	Pau-lo-de-A-ze-ve-do-Mur-ti-nho
	[looks up, looks down]
	[chanting and baby talk]
	you yourself know quite well,
	[left and right hand gestures,
	tapping on the armchair]
	better than I,
	better than anyone,
	when I get,
	to my ward,
	I'm gonna tell,
	I'm gonna tell,
//**DONA JURE:MA!**	//this was,
	[looking down]
	this was,
	this was,
	my secret,
	this was, ..
	this was,
	and this was,
Dona Jurema! =	
	= my secret. ..
[acc]	
DONA JUREMA!	
	[singing and baby talk]
	my dear husband,
	[looks down, face turns
	sightly to the left]
	knew very well,
	he did not come to help,
	his dear dear wife,
	but it does not matter, ..
	his good luck will not last,..
	that is all I can wish on him =
	with all my heart:::. (1.5)
	[face turns to the right,
	looks up at the doctor]
DONA JUREMA!	
⌐how long have you been =	
⌐= in the hospital?	
	[new tune: church hymn]
	⌐all dressed in white,/

Doctor:	Patient:
	[looks down, gestures not visible]
	[creaky voice, baby talk]
	she appeared,
	bearing ⌐round her waist,
	the colors of the sky,
	[whining]
	⌐Hail:, Hail:, Hail Ma:ry,
	Hail:, Hail:, ∟Hail ∟Ma:ry,
	∣raises both hands together, raises head, raises eyes]
	[creaky voice] [acc]
	what more do you want,
	[looks at the doctor]
	umh? ....
	[freezes position, right hand shaking and pointing]
[dec]	
Dona Jure::ma!	
[half smiling]	[creaky voice]
	umh:?
	you know that I can't::.(1.3)
	[freezes position, right hand shaking and pointing]

This is the opening of a psychiatric interview between a patient and a doctor. The interview takes place two days after sixty-one-year-old Jurema has been hospitalized in an acute psychotic crisis.[1] The most striking and repetitive aspect of the patient's behavior reveals a psychological regression as she assumes the role of a child and establishes with her real audience—the doctor—a mother-daughter relationship.

In the preceding segment the doctor repeatedly summons the patient to participate in the psychiatric interview. To this effect she repeats Jurema's name eight times. It is an attention-getting device. Dona Jurema does not respond to the summons. That is, she does not comply with a basic conversational requirement, that for every summons (from the doctor) there is an expected response part (from the patient). Locally, on a turn-by-turn basis, conversational coherence fails. However, Jurema's entire stretch of talk can be interpreted as an answer to the psychiatrist's underlying question "what's the problem with you?" After she has addressed her mother continuously, referred to her husband and put a curse on him, sung a religious hymn to the Virgin Mary, Dona Jurema closes this segment by asking the doctor in a half-crying voice: "what more do you want?" and by asserting, "you know that I can't."

This interview presents a different "state of talk" (Goffman [1967] 1982) from standard everyday medical interviews. That is, between the doctor and the patient there is only a small degree, if that, of jointly accomplished interaction. Speakers compete for each other's attention. The typical turn allocation in medical discourse of the type "doctor talks (and thereby asks question)" and "patient talks (and thereby responds to question)" seldom takes place. The doctor does sometimes ask a question (e.g., "how long have you been in the hospital?"), to which the patient may or may not respond (e.g., "there is no need [for me to tell you my name] because doctor Paulo de Azevedo Murtinho [already knows it]" and "you know it quite well, better than anyone"). More often than not, the patient's responses are indirect and inconclusive. They must be pieced together through entire segments of talk. The transcript attempts to capture this structure of participation by reproducing the patient's and doctor's discourses in a two-column format, representing them as relatively independent discourses (Ochs 1979). This format portrays the type of interaction that takes place in an interview where there is no expectation of sequential information.

The doctor is only one of the many characters with whom Jurema speaks and interacts. As the interview progresses, Dona Jurema brings a multitude of different addressees (her sister, her grandmother, her grandchild), of which "the mother" is the most salient. These addressees are not legitimated or ratified by the doctor. Discourse topics are also brought up idiosyncratically in Dona Jurema's talk. For the most part they are indefinite referents, partially developed. The doctor seldom pursues any of these topics. As a result, discourse coherence breaks down at different levels. The interview goes on as follows:

Doctor:	Patient:
[dec]	
Dona Jure::ma!	
	[creaky voice]
	umh:?
	you know that I can't::.(1.3)
	[freezes position, right hand
	shaking and pointing]
⌐[dec]	
=⌐**you can't**=	
// = **talk to me?**	//**totototototototo:.** ['hhh]
	[moves hand back to armchair;
	looks beyond the doctor]
	⌐**the tototô:::!**
	[gesture with right hand
	pointing straight ahead]
what's totô?	
	the totô totô::!
	[series of pointing gestures]
what's totô?	

Doctor:

Patient:
that totô:::! (1.5)
[pointing gestures]

what is it=
=you're saying?

[acc]
totodododododododododo
/dododododododdodo/ ...
[gesture with hands indicating
"who knows;" looks down]

you don't know, do you. ...
[hhh'] **Dona Jure:ma!** ..

[looks up at the doctor]
hi!

how old are you?

⌐HI! IVE::TE!! DE:TE!...
[calling her sister Idete:[2]
looks to the left, then looks further away,
smiles, and turns to the left, moving body backward, with back pressing against the right arm
of armchair]

[chest bent forward,
microphone on right hand,
pointing toward patient; left arm
down on the chair]

Deti::nha! ....
[looking to the far-left corner of the room, as if
someone was there]

[staccato and baby talk]
so-you-ma'am-will-do-like- this-later-so-
over-there at home-it-will-be-bad-oh-very-
bad-for you-it will-be. ..
[moves closer to the doctor; bends and leans
forward]

[baby talk]
but I won't allow (it),
I won't allow (it),

[slowly turns to the right; moves torso backward and then forward, looks down; moves
both hands backward and holds chair in a movement to get up]

[baby talk]
oh, so that's what you wanted to know ...
[keeps position]

[swings body forward; gets up halfway, sits back,
halfway in the armchair; faces the doctor; holds
body slightly up, pressing both hands on arm-
chair]

Doctor: Patient:
[camera focus moves
away from patient]

                                 [chanting]
                                 I've already said it,
                                 I've already said it,
[camera focus on   I've already said it,
patient]   said, said,
                                 [right foot plays with the doctor's feet; patient
                                 looks down at their feet]

                                 ['hhh] that now,
                                 that now,
                                 it is the foot of (Tuxa).
                                 [moves feet away; takes slipper off right foot;
                                 points with foot at doctor's left foot]

                                 ['hhh] I've already said,
                                 I've already said,
                                 [caresses doctor's foot with her foot]
                                 I've already said,
                                 it's a little caress,
                                 [looks up at doctor]
                                 ['hhh] a little caress,
                                 a little caress,
                                 a little caress,
                                 ['hhh] to the little tip of=
                                 =the little toe of my li::ttle=
                                 =grand:daughter.

                                 [hymn; baby talk]
                                 ⌐Malie:::ne:::,
                                 ⌐Sa:::cred Lie:ne,
                                 [moves feet away, searches for slippers, makes
                                 movement up and forward, looking down]

                                 to me she is:::is:,
                                 sanctifi::ed,
                                 [gets halfway up in the chair, sits at the edge of
                                 the armchair, looks down, and holds posture]

                                 [chanting]
                                 ['hhh] that's why,
                                 that's why::: y:::. ...
                                 ['hhh] that's why,
                                 that's why::: y:::. ...
                                 ['hhh] THAT'S WHY,
                                 THAT'S WHY::: Y:::. ...

                                 [whimpering, baby talk]
                                 ⌐aren't you going to=
                                 =ask me questions now?=

Doctor: Patient:
                                         [raises her head, holds her body halfway up,
                                         hands pressing on the chair, looks at doctor]

= I'm going to ask,
Dona Jure:ma. =

                                         [sighing]
                                         = what are you going to ask?
                                         [stands and holds her body halfway up]

[acc]
⌐WHERE DO YOU LIVE? ...

                                         [coarse voice, baby talk]
                                         I live over there with the pope,
                                         over there in the Lome.

[dec]
you live with the pope?

                                         = yes, over there in the Lome.

⌐what's your full name?

                                         will you believe me =
                                         = if I say it right? ...

⌊I'll believe you. =

                                         = you know why? =

= mmm? ...

                                         you don't know why. (1.2)

what is it =
= I don't know?

                                         let me speak because, ..
                                         because I know my full =
                                         = na:::::me =
                                         = Holy Mother of God. (see)

⌐so tell me your =
= full name. =

                                         = no, only if you have, (1.3)
                                         do you have?
                                         [acc]
                                         /oh, mother!/
                                         [bends over to get the slipper]

have what?

                                         [acc]
                                         ma:ma::! ...

Doctor: Patient:

mmm?

[acc]
ma:ma::! ma:ma::! ...
she says she has, ma:ma::...
she says we can leave,
ma:ma:: ...
[picks up slipper, pushes it away to the right,
moves torso and right leg to the right]
then ask to be excused,
my child. ..
[looks at slippers; puts slipper on right foot]
it's like this that we ask ..
[bending down and forward, bending right, slippers on]
so much curiosity, ['hhh] ..
they wanted to have,
didn't they child, ['hhh] ...
[acc]
to: know about you,
right child,
just because- ['hhh]
they saw you barefooted (out=
=of doors), right child,['hhh]
they thought that you had-

Dona Jure:ma!

popopodedededddddd
shssssssssssssssssssssssss
[raises head, looks up, raises left hand, brings
right finger to mouth to indicate silence, looks
beyond the doctor, points and nods, looks
straight ahead, wide-open eyes]

what's happening over there?

shssssssssssssssssssssss
['hhh] shsssssssssssss
['hhh] shssssssssssssss

[points and nods, turns sideways to the right,
moves left arm to the right, bends down, looks
down to the right]

Dona JuRE:MA!

[dec] [baby talk]
Thank God! ....
[interrupts movement, raises head, looks up,
turns to doctor and smiles]

Doctor: Patient:
[dec]
Thank God, for what?

                                     = it's all over. ....
                                     [holds the position and smiles]

[acc]
what is over?

                                     [dec]
                                     ⌐Jurema is a little dizzy y'know.
                                     [turns torso and head to face doctor, moves left
                                     hand down and grabs armchair]

mmm.

                                     could you give ⌐my little =
                                     = sister a glass of water,
                                     she didn't even know that =
                                     = this would happen to her. ..
                                     you are very polite. ..

                                     [acc]
                                     /⌐then, I only (knew), ...
                                     /⌐then, I only (knew),

                                     [moves forward, leans forward and down, looks
                                     down, then repeats a movement to get up]

                                     [coarse voice]
                                     see, mother! ['hhh]
                                     see, mother!
                                     she even forgot the glass of water,
                                     y'see, oh mother.

The interview goes on for another thirteen minutes. At different moments Doña Jurema requests to leave and thereby close the interview.
The doctor keeps restating that they need "to talk for a little while
longer."

Coherence in Psychotic Discourse

> Given [the] bizarre forms of ward behavior, one must come to see that after
> all they are not so extraordinary, for what seems to be involved are merely
> atypical framing practices. . . . Since realms are built up through the main-
> tenance of these conventions, realms can be attacked by declining to sustain
> these conventions. A frame perspective, then, allows us to generate crazy
> behavior and to see that it is not all that crazy. (Goffman 1974:246)

Speakers and hearers have multiple options for coherence as they
select candidates from different levels of talk (Schiffrin 1987a:23). In the
admitting interview the patient displays unexpected verbal and nonverbal

behavior. Consequently, coherence breaks down at various points in her discourse. Coherence breaks down within the exchange system. The patient does not follow turn-taking rules; that is, she does not alternate speaker and hearer roles. It also breaks down in the action structure. The patient does not provide the expected sequencing of actions that characterizes doctor-patient interviews; that is, the doctor's questions often remain unanswered as well as her summons unattended. Finally, coherence breaks down in the propositional content. The patient fails to refer to what is being talked about, ignoring the topics introduced by the doctor and often presenting unclear referents.

Psychotic talk, however, may have a coherence of its own. As one analyzes the discourse of a patient in a severe psychotic crisis, it becomes clear that her discourse may be segmented into several different frames. The concept of *frame* is central to the understanding of unfolding contexts through talk and interaction (Bateson [1972] 1981; Goffman 1974, 1981a; Gumperz 1982; Tannen 1979, 1984, 1986, 1990, 1993; Tannen and Wallat 1987). These may be transient contexts—inner realities—proposed by the patient. They are often embedded in outer contexts—proposed by the doctor, generating multiple frame embeddings. Within each frame of talk, the speaker signals a different metamessage that indicates the type of interaction she believes is taking place at that moment; interactive frames bring about particular schemas that represent the speaker's prior experiences and expectations about people, objects, and situations (Tannen 1985; Tannen and Wallat 1987). When this interweaving of particular schemas and interactive frames is patched together, Dona Jurema's discourse coheres.

This study analyzes two psychiatric interviews with the same two participants—a patient and a doctor. The first interview takes place two days after the patient has been hospitalized and has been diagnosed as being in an acute psychotic crisis. The second and last interview takes place nineteen days later. The patient was considered fully recovered and ready to be dismissed from the hospital.

While the admitting interview presents atypical framings, and thereby represents the deviation, the purpose of the discharge interview is to evaluate how coherent and well integrated into reality the patient is. This interview represents the norm, as during this interaction the patient performs according to the expected interactional rules for medical interviews. For example, she provides the second part of an adjacency pair (i.e., she gives a locally coherent response to the doctor's question), expands on the doctor's comments (by introducing entry talk), and stays on topic, addressing the topic agenda that the doctor brings to the interview. Therefore, if we look at the different interactional frames and at the topics that are introduced, developed, and negotiated, the discourse is coherent.

The following excerpt from the opening of the discharge interview illustrates this type of interaction:

[Nonverbal information: both participants are in baseline postures.[3]]

         [acc]
Doctor: ⌈**You were born on what <u>date</u>?** ..
Patient: **on January 11** ..
         [nods]
Doctor: ⌊**of what year?**
Patient: **of 1921.** ...
         [nods]
         I am sixty-one. =
         [nods]   [smiles]
               [acc]
Doctor: =**you have a son,** ⌈ **don't you?**
Patient: ⌊ **I have a son.**
                [nods]   [short smile]
Doctor: **what's his name?** =
Patient: =**Francisco Ferreira de Souza.** ...
               [dec]
Doctor: **and he is how old now?** ..
Patient: **he's- about forty-two.**
         [looks away, looks at doctor and smiles]
Doctor: /mmm/ ...
                    [acc]
         you also have a granddaughter, don't you? =
Patient: =**I have a ((little)) sixteen-year-old granddaughter.**(1.4)
         [raises head]   [smiles]
Doctor: //mmm//
Patient: **she's my li:fe.**
         [raises head, looks up, big smile]

This interview follows closely the principles of turn taking as the basic form of organization for conversation. In the frame of the medical interview, the doctor and the patient have complementary roles: The doctor introduces the discourse topics and requests information; the patient addresses the topics and provides information. A system of conventions and procedural rules for spoken interaction is at work. Goffman points out that "an understanding will prevail as to when and where it will be permissible to initiate talk, among whom, and by means of what topics of conversation" ([1967] 1982:34).

The focus of this study is twofold. First, it looks at how the participants jointly establish *referential meaning* and at how discourse coherence is achieved or breaks down. Second, it looks at how participants convey superordinate messages—*metamessages*—for what is taking place at that moment, and how the patient coherently signals and assesses the context of communication in both interviews.

    The study uses *frame analysis* to indicate "what is being done by talk, what activity is being engaged in, how a speaker means what s/he says"

(Tannen 1985:315). It uses *topic analysis* to indicate what a speaker does when she engages and collaborates in talk (as in the discharge interview) or when she disengages herself from the conversational topic (as in the admitting interview). For the discharge interview, a topic analysis is useful to describe the amount of work needed to jointly build a coherent on-topic discourse. For the admitting interview, frame analysis indicates the social meaning implicit in what was said and done.

The discussion will indicate that discourse coherence is apparent in Dona Jurema's talk in the interview during crisis as well as in the interview after crisis. The difference is that the surface forms of coherence in Dona Jurema's talk at the latter stage are consonant with the doctor's definition of the situation of talk as interview talk. In the former stage the patient refuses to participate in the interview frame, although her talk can still be seen as coherent, albeit in a bizarre way. It is a matter of participating or not participating in the socioculturally defined normal, unmarked speech situation. By refusing to participate in the conventional frame for the situation, one's behavior is regarded as crazy or deviant. In this case, "what seems to be involved are merely atypical framing practices" (Goffman 1974:246). By agreeing to participate, one is regarded as "normal."

Psychotic Discourse: Thought or Talk Disorders?

When one listens to Dona Jurema's talk in the admitting interview, terms such as a *thought-disordered patient* or a *psychotic speaker* often come to mind. As a speaker Dona Jurema presents several of the complex symptoms described in psychiatric textbooks: derailment (when patient shifts idiosyncratically from one topic to another); tangentiality (in reply to questions, patient offers elusive responses, which may not be related to the question at all); distractible speech (an abrupt change in reference triggered by nearby stimulus); clanging (where rhythmic relationships rather than pragmatic and semantic meaning direct word choice); and pressure of speech (amount of talk increases and pace of talk accelerates), among others. Most of these definitions of language and cognitive behaviors are indeed language-based. As Lakoff points out: "There are no physical correlates of cognitive activity. The only direct window to the functioning of the mind is linguistic" (1981:359).

Several issues may be raised when one applies to Dona Jurema labels such as thought-disordered patient or psychotic speaker. I will restrict my comments to two issues of relevance to this study. The first points to the complex discussion on *speech* (as a social phenomenon) and *thought* (as a cognitive phenomenon). In the past, psychiatrists, psychologists, psycholinguists, and linguists, among other theorists, have investigated the relationship between thought disorder and psychotic talk. Thought disorder is a broad diagnostic label associated with those psychiatric cases in which the patient's speech is "so confusing to the examining clinician that the [patient] is said to be unable to think clearly" (Rochester and Martin 1979:vi). Of course, what is implicit in this assumption is the link between thought and speech.

Rochester and Martin (1979) caution us about the fact that one assesses thought disorder *from talk*, rather than directly from thought, inferring disordered thought processes from the discourse of patients. Thus, clinicians diagnose thought disorders based on an inference from the speaker's utterance about the speaker's own cognition. Most research in psychosis has relied on cognitive categories that have emerged from clinical observations of language behavior.[4]

The problem may be in the two types of inferences that clinicians make from observations, as pointed out by Rochester and Martin (1979:3–4). In the first situation the clinician assesses "thought disorders" from talk; the main question is "Why is the thought of the schizophrenic patient so confused?" This is often transposed to "Why is the language of the schizophrenic speaker so confusing?" In the second situation the clinician infers "talk failures" from his or her own experience of confusion as a listener; then the main issue is "How (or why) does the schizophrenic speaker produce language that is so confusing to listeners?"

Psychiatrists have acknowledged the probable mismatch that may lie in this circular conception (from thought to talk and then back to thought), where linguistic analysis stands as an indirect way of assessing cognitive processes. Hence, Kasanin states that "fragmentary and otherwise disturbed associations may render the speech of the schizophrenic illogical or even unintelligible although in the mind of the patient the idea behind it may be connected" ([1944] 1964:x).

Often in the literature, thought-disorder phenomena have been presented in terms of "thought-based" descriptions rather than language-based variables (Rochester and Martin 1979:6). Hence, among the several diagnostic signs that the psychiatrist must pay attention to, Sullivan lists those that reflect "disturbance of verbal communication" (1954:189). Under this category, which he labels "more profound phenomena," he includes autistic processes such as "loss of thought," "blocking of ideas," "hallucinations," as well as language-related occurrences such as the use of "stereotyped verbal expressions" (1954:192).

Rochester and Martin point to the inconvenience of this circular definition to those who diagnose schizophrenia as a dysfunction of the left hemisphere (Flor-Henry 1976; Gruzelier 1978), to those who hypothesize that schizophrenia may involve an episodic aphasia (Benson 1973; Chaika 1974), and to clinical investigations in general.

Since thought disorder is a central concept for the study and diagnosis of schizophrenia, Rochester and Martin inquire: "Why . . . have we had no systematic descriptions of the discourse failures on which this designation is based? . . . Why has 'thought disorder' been described in terms of thought-based rather than language-based variables?" (1979:7).

Researchers have been addressing this question. In recent studies Andreasen, Tsuang, and Canter (1974), Andreasen (1979a, 1979b), Harrow and Quinlan (1977), and Harrow, Silverstein, and Marengo (1983) reviewed and specified diagnostic criteria for assessing psychosis that look into a clinical assessment of thought, language, and communication disorders (the disorders listed in Appendix A constitute a "checklist" for psychiatric interviews).[5] This discussion elucidates how psychiatrists and therapists view thought disorders as manifested in speech and language behaviors. For example, the traditional concept of "looseness of association" or "illogical thinking" (Bleuler [1911] 1950; Cameron [1944] 1964) has been replaced by five different categories: derailment, tangentiality, incoherence, illogicality, and clanging (Andreasen 1979a, 1979b).[6]

The preceding discussion points to some problematic issues commonly associated with the diagnostic concept of thought disorder. As indicated by researchers, it is indeed a misnomer. Regarding this study, the term does not apply. In part, this book addresses Rochester and Martin's request for research on the need for "systematic descriptions of the discourse failures" in terms of language-based variables. To this end, topic analysis will be used to examine the structure of the content of talk: how referents are introduced in the discourse and negotiated in interaction. It also addresses discourse failures in terms of communicative and interactive patterns. It looks at discourse as a joint production, where both the doctor and the patient are coparticipants and jointly establish the context of talk.

Turning to our second concern, what happens when one labels a patient in a psychotic crisis a "psychotic speaker"? Such a label seems to give the speaker a rather permanent psychotic status; the speaker would be expected to perform accordingly (i.e., psychotically) in any type of event or situation. One would also expect her to be in such a state of mind (or behavior) more or less continuously (i.e., she would be in a constant state of producing some kind of abnormal talk). As Laing asserts, once hospitalized and subjected to a "degradation ceremonial" (Garfinkel 1956) known as a psychiatric examination, "the 'committed' person labelled as patient, and specifically as 'schizophrenic,' is degraded from full existential and legal status as human agent and responsible person. . . . Once a 'schizophrenic' there is a tendency to be regarded as always a 'schizophrenic' " ([1967] 1974:100–101).

In fact, patients get in and out of crisis. In describing the behavior of Miss Frumkin, (a young woman who long struggled with schizophrenia), Sheehan ([1982] 1983:106) reports the following interaction between her and another patient: " 'What made your mind suddenly snap back?' Eileen O'Reilly asked. 'The medicine does it and prayer does it,' Miss Frumkin said. 'It just happens.' "

During a crisis the patient's behavior may shift dramatically. On being admitted to the hospital, under extreme tension and agitation,

Miss Frumkin says: "I'm not a nut. I have something wrong with my brain" ([1982] 1983:25).

In Dona Jurema's case, the really aberrant speech is to some degree under the patient's control—at least it is somewhat variable, as the analysis will demonstrate. At times Dona Jurema's conversation can be quite florid and at other times relatively sedate. She may turn to the doctor and engage in talk, or otherwise choose to ignore her and establish some private conversations of her own. Thus, referring to Dona Jurema as a "psychotic speaker" would not capture the transient nature of talk and interaction as it occurs in the admitting interview. Moreover, it would definitely not portray the fleeting nature of various worlds brought about by Jurema's talk, some of which outsiders would label "reality."[7]

Organization of This Study

This study reverses the chronology of the two interviews. The first part of the book discusses the discharge interview, which happened last. This is the interview in which the patient's and doctor's interactional behavior conforms to social and linguistic expectations for doctor-patient communication. It represents the norm. The second part of the book discusses the admitting interview, which happened first. It describes the disturbances that occur when the patient is in a psychotic crisis. The "normal" discourse (in the discharge interview) is then contrasted with the "deviant" discourse (in the admitting interview).

Chapter 2 provides the background scenario of the two interviews: who are the participants, what is the nature of the patient's illness, when and where did these interviews take place, and for what purpose. It also discusses the patient's speech patterns and variants. We see that in the admitting interview, while undergoing an intense psychotic crisis, the patient makes use of a simplified register, similar to a "child register." She also uses certain nonstandard linguistic variants that belong to a rural Brazilian dialect. Given her social background and family history, the patient had probably used one version of this dialect in her childhood. No such linguistic variants are used in the discharge interview. The second part of the chapter describes analytic and interpretive decisions in the process of transcription (from spoken discourse to written text) and translation (from the original text in Portuguese to the translated English version).

Chapter 3 brings to discussion particular issues in discourse analysis. *Frame analysis*—the analysis of the always-emergent contexts in talk—is considered crucial to the understanding of face-to-face communication and interaction. Definitions of frame and major frame functions are reviewed as they relate to the data. Multiple frame embeddings attest to the complexity of talk in interaction. So do the subtle ways whereby participants signal reframings (i.e., changes in the context of talk). The notion of *topic* is also discussed at length and related to participants'

knowledge schemas. It is argued that the analysis of topic structure provides a natural criterion for establishing coherence in discourse. Definitions of topic are examined as are problematic aspects of topic analysis.
This discussion lays the ground for a detailed study of the two interviews, where topic and frame analysis are related to *discourse coherence.*
Topic coherence is to be found (or not found) at the referential and
propositional level, while frame coherence is achieved through the
metacommunicative properties of language. The last part of this chapter
contrasts *institutional discourse* (i.e., medical interview) and *conversational
behavior* (i.e, personal talk). Issues of *power* and *deviance* are brought to
discussion. These relate to cultural definitions of framing: legitimate versus atypical framings, as well as institutional versus personal framings.
The interrelated nature of micro- and macroanalysis surfaces in the discussion.

The core of analysis is found in chapters 4 through 7. Chapters 4
and 5 discuss frame and topic coherence in the discharge interview, while
chapters 6 and 7 discuss topic and frame coherence in the admitting
interview. Chapter 4 describes the subtly conflicting frames that emerge
in the discharge interview. While the doctor proposes talk within the
institutional framings, the patient would rather shift to a more personal
encounter. This subtle interactional work has implications for the initial
distancing between the doctor and the patient (i.e., for the natural asymmetry in doctor-patient interaction). By successfully proposing reframings, the patient sometimes manages to establish a more personal relationship with the doctor and thus mitigate the asymmetry. The doctor,
however, invariably resists staying in the frame introduced by the patient.
Her resistance may be seen in many of the excerpts.

Chapter 5 is a topic analysis of the same interview: It discusses the
many ways in which topics are coherently assessed by the patient and
jointly negotiated in the interaction. It thoroughly examines the amount
of joint work needed for the participants to achieve topic coherence. The
topics introduced in this interview are the doctor's; these are cues to the
signaling of institutional framings. The patient's role within these contexts is restricted: She must address the doctor's topics and expand on
them, but she never introduces a topic from her own personal agenda.
Nevertheless, a complex interactional work is in place; it emerges as one
relates frames and topics and discerns the dynamic nature of frames in
interaction.

The next two chapters analyze the admitting interview, which represents the deviation. Chapter 6 examines the structure of discourse. A
topic analysis works to indicate where coherence breaks down: Competing topic agendas emerge, topics are hardly developed, and topics are
never concluded. The participants are clearly engaged in different and
often conflicting activities. Chapter 7 looks at the frames that emerge in
the admitting interview. Multiple frame embeddings take place, in which

both doctor and patient compete to install a prevailing frame. When the doctor succeeds, some reframings unfold within the institutional context of the doctor-patient interview. Most reframings, however, occur within the context of the psychotic crisis. Within each frame of talk (the institutional context of the doctor-patient interview and the context of the psychotic crisis), the patient's discourse is shown to be coherent.

The conclusion in Chapter 8 presents a discussion of the frames described in the two interviews, and of how topic and frame are particularly appropriate tools for analyzing coherence in this genre of discourse.

Notes

1. The patient's name is Jurema Cardozo. The most common formal address form in Brazilian Portuguese is title + first name (Dona Jurema = Mrs. Jurema). Since there is no such form in English, the translation would be Mrs. Cardozo. In the book I kept the original term of address.

2. Jurema starts out by calling "Ivete," her sister's maid. This form triggers "Idete," her sister. At different moments in the interview, Jurema summons either one of these two characters. Neither is present. She addresses her sister as "Idete," "Dete," "Deta," or "Detinha." The last three forms are nicknames.

3. In this interview the doctor and the patient keep their sitting positions and shift minimally from what Scheflen calls *baseline postures* (1973:29). For the discharge interview this corresponds to their initial postural arrangement. Chapter 2 provides a full description.

4. While most thought-disordered phenomena may not be language disorders per se (unlike, e.g., aphasia), they are manifested through linguistic behavior "and diagnosed almost wholly in terms of linguistic anomaly" (Lakoff 1981:359).

5. Andreasen and Powers (1974), Andreasen, Tsuang, and Canter (1974), and Andreasen (1979a, 1979b) expanded Bleulerian descriptions to characterize the features of "formal thought disorder." Both Bleuler and Kraepelin recognize that patients have disorders in their "form of thought" as well as their "content of thought" (Andreasen 1979a:1316). Andreasen created eighteen categories of language use (all subtypes of thought disorder that represent clinical categories) and used them in psychiatric interviews of manic, depressed, and schizophrenic speakers. She also added two language disorders that occur in aphasia—semantic and phonemic paraphasia—"to encourage clinicians to include aphasia in their differential diagnosis" (1979a:1316). Some language phenomena are common to various diagnostic groups. The disorders that occur most often are derailment (Bleuler's looseness of association), poverty of speech, pressure of speech, incoherence, illogicality, and poverty of content of speech (1979a:1317). Schizophrenic speakers can be differentiated by "the poverty of speech content" and the characteristic of "tangentiality" regarding replies to questions, while manics present derailment and pressure of speech (Bleuler's flight of ideas). There is considerable evidence, however, that in acute psychosis the Bleulerian categories describe behaviors that are common to schizophrenia as well as to mania or depression.

6. Andreasen recommends to psychiatrists that "the practice of referring

globally to 'thought disorder,' as if it were homogeneous, be avoided . . . and instead that the specific subtypes occurring in particular patients be noted in both clinical practice and research" (1979b:1325).

7. The implications of using the label "psychotic speaker" were pointed out to me by Douglas W. Maynard.

2

About the Psychiatric Interviews

[The prepatient] . . . starts out with relationships and rights, and ends up, at the beginning of his hospital stay, with hardly any of either. The moral aspects of [the prepatient's] career, then, typically begin with the experience of abandonment, disloyalty, and embitterment.

Erving Goffman, *Asylums*, p. 133

The loneliness of being sick is almost inexpressible. The doctor's power to reach through that loneliness and be with his patient for a while is one of his most mysterious, potent, and potentially curative tools Yet, finally, he leaves and the patient is alone. . . . There can be no doubt that illness means separation of a most profound and fundamental kind.

David Reiser and Andrea K. Schroder,
Patient Interviewing: The Human Dimension, p. 47

Definition of the Situation

Some Background Information

On the evening of December 14, 1982, Jurema Cardozo, aged sixty-one, was hospitalized at the Psychiatric Institute of the Federal University of Rio de Janeiro. Earlier that day her family had taken her to a general hospital for emergency cases. She was then transferred to the psychiatric institute, where she was hospitalized (an involuntary entrance). This was her fifth hospitalization in five years, the first one in this institution. No medication was given to her on admission. Doctor Edna Lopes, a recently graduated doctor, was assigned to take care of Jurema.

Two days later, on December 16, Doctor Edna and Dona Jurema had a meeting in which the doctor tried to evaluate Jurema's degree of response and awareness of her surroundings and of her clinical-psychiatric condition. According to her hospital records, Jurema was still off psychiatric medication (except for a symptomatic prescription).

The doctor reported having first seen Jurema on the patio of the ward. She was standing up, in a stereotyped posture, and her gestures followed ritual sequences (making a cross, kissing the tips of her fingers, bringing them closer to the doctor's face, moving her foot forward and backward, always in the same order). She seemed inattentive to her surroundings and did not relate to any other patient on the premises. She did not respond to any call, but mumbled unintelligibly and performed little rituals. She would sometimes turn to the wall and caress it, speaking incomprehensibly. When the doctor took her back to the ward, she offered some resistance and kept stopping along the way.

In the meeting that took place sometime later on the same day, Doctor Edna tried to follow the standard routine for medical-psychiatric interviews. She later reported that she had tried to do a regular interview by asking routine-type questions; however, "the patient's behavior conflicted with a pre-established interview format. I had to let her go her own way, and talk about topics she brought up." This meeting was videotaped, a common routine for in-training staff in a university hospital. In spite of Jurema's disruptive state, she was informed that the interview would be recorded. Her family was also informed and agreed.

Dona Jurema's stay in the hospital lasted twenty-eight days. In her first week she reacted poorly to the medication (mostly neuroleptics, which are antipsychotic drugs). She improved, however, in her second week, when the medication was suspended. The last two weeks were spent both at home (under medical surveillance) and at the hospital. She enjoyed being home, where she lived with two sisters: Idete and Tereza Rodrigues. Reports from the hospital attest to the fact that she often became quite depressed the evening before returning to the hospital. The second interview (the discharge interview) took place shortly after a homestay that lasted for five days (from December 30 through January 3). On January 4 Jurema returned to the hospital. The discharge interview was recorded at the suggestion of Doctor Edna, who thought the recording would provide interesting contrasting data when compared with Dona Jurema's condition nineteen days earlier. Consent for recording was again requested and granted. In the discharge interview Jurema was considered to have recovered, with complete removal of the psychopathological symptoms. She was dismissed from the hospital on January 11. (Appendix B presents a summary of the patient's stay in the hospital.)

The Participants in the Psychiatric Interviews

This study is a discussion of these two interviews, two video recordings with the same two participants—a patient and a doctor—separated by a nineteen-day interval.[1] Dona Jurema and Doctor Edna met several times during Jurema's twenty-eight-day stay at the hospital (they also met for a short time during her outpatient treatment). These meetings are part of what Reiser and Schroder ([1980] 1984:190) call the patient's *therapeutic data* (i.e., reports on medication and dosages, side effects, adverse reactions, regression of symptoms over the four weeks) and *objective data* (the "hard data," such as lab results and other measurable information).

(The hospital furnished the patient's clinical records, her medical history, and letters from her sister Idete to Doctor Edna.)

Background information provided by Idete—the patient's sister and caretaker—at the time of Jurema's admittance informs us that the patient was a divorced sixty-one-year-old woman. She was originally from the state of São Paulo and came from a large family of eight siblings (five males and three females). Her father died when Jurema was four, and her mother lived in good health until the age of eighty-six, when she died of "stomach problems." As a young woman Jurema moved to the city of Rio de Janeiro (in the state of Rio de Janeiro), where she married at the age of sixteen. A year later she had a son. Childbirth was painful, and Jurema avoided bearing any more children. In the discharge interview, Jurema states that she was married for twelve years, and then divorced when she found out that her husband was involved with another woman. After the divorce she worked as a civil servant for another twelve years and quit the job on the advice of a boyfriend. The relationship with this boyfriend lasted for ten years, against her family's wishes. During this time and afterward, she worked as a saleswoman off and on. Since her illness, however, she had stopped selling and had been living on a small pension. At the time of the interviews, the persons who were closest to her were her sister (Idete), her son (Francisco), and her granddaughter (Mariene). All the names and descriptive information have been changed to protect the patient's confidentiality.

Doctor Edna was a twenty-five-year-old woman from Rio de Janeiro. She was married and had two children. At the time the interviews took place, Edna was in her first-year internship in the psychiatric institute, having graduated from medical school a year before. Dona Jurema had been assigned to her as a patient. Five years later, after a viewing session held at the institute, Doctor Edna commented on her youth at the time of the recordings. She said she had felt close to the patient, who saw her as "a very young doctor, one who reminded Dona Jurema of her own granddaughter." These comments allude to what Reiser and Schroder describe as the developmental process of becoming a doctor, whereby one learns to be an expert and, through learning, is "transformed as a person" ([1980] 1984:28). These interviews capture the very beginning of what will be a lifelong process for Doctor Edna. We see her struggling in a double stance: the one of overidentification with the patient (to the point of "becoming" the granddaughter, Mariene) and the one of excessive detachment (the professional Edna). Reiser and Schroder tell us that no medical professional "is immune from these swings"; young doctors, however, are prone to dwell in the two extremes ([1980]1984:46).

In 1986 I exchanged letters with Doctor Edna on her feelings and opinions about the two interviews. She stated that Jurema's case was singled out for recording because of the difficulty of making a proper diagnosis. "It was a controversial case which raised academic debate." The doctor reported that Jurema's behavior for the first two weeks was "bizarre and difficult to describe. . . . In her own ways she somehow established contact with me. . . . She accepted me and asked for help." Assuming an extremely regressed stance, Dona Jurema would often call the doctor "little mother" or "mama". Doctor Edna added, "I was willing to help her and was also quite interested in her case; I used to discuss it with the medical staff."[2]

In 1987 Doctor Edna and I held a viewing session at the psychiatric institute. On watching the admitting interview, the doctor commented on Jurema's refusal to engage in talk as well as her wish to end the interview. "She is aware that this is an interview and that she is in a hospital. . . . She knows I am there, she knows who I am. . . . However, she remains seemingly oblivious of her surroundings. . . . She refuses any objective talk. . . . At times she seems out of it. . . . At times she seems to be acting out. . . . She wants me to say that the interview is over and to take her back to her ward."[3]

On viewing the discharge interview, Doctor Edna told me the patient responded strictly to what was asked: "She did not want to talk much, though she displays cooperative behavior. . . . This is a formal interview . . . a standard clinical interview." Doctor Edna had informed Dona Jurema that the interview would bring up information that was already familiar to both of them; these topics would be introduced anyway, for the sake of the video recording.

During the course of the interviews, both participants reveal what Erickson and Shultz (1982) call the "performed social identity." Although their study involved students and guidance counselors, the phrase is also applicable to medical interviews:

> *Performed social identity* refers to the composite social identity of [the participants] that actually was relevant in a given interview. It is an aggregate of officially and unofficially relevant attributes, particularistic and universalistic, which [the participants] revealed to one another during the course of their encounter. (1982:16)

Besides performing their official roles as doctor and patient, Doctor Edna and Dona Jurema also reveal some unofficial attributes: (1) their sex (both are women); (2) their socioeconomic status (Doctor Edna belongs to the educated middle class, while Dona Jurema did not complete secondary education and belongs to the low middle class); and (3) their relative age (a thirty-five-year difference between them).

There are only two participants in both interviews. However, one must also include the video camera operator as a third participant, an onlooker for both events. As a rule, patients are informed about the recording and its purpose. In the admitting interview, Dona Jurema addresses not only the doctor but also several other people; except for Doctor Edna none of them are "really there."

A few times Jurema refers and talks to the camera. There is one specific instance, toward the end of the admitting interview, where she signals her awareness both of the tape and video recording. First, Dona

Jurema turns to the doctor, looks at the microphone Doctor Edna holds in her hand, and speaks into the microphone. At this point she is looking at the doctor and stuttering; then, she turns to the right (where the camera is), looks up, smiles, and says:

docdoc ofofofofofofofofofof
ofofofofofofofofofofofofofof-
of te::levision.
ma:ma::. .... ma:ma:!

The following interaction takes place:

Doctor: Patient:
where is the television?

                             ma:ma::!
                             [looking at the mirror and the camera, address-
                             ing the camera]

uhm:?

                             ma:ma::!

is there a television there?
[turns face to the camera and
back to the patient]

                             so it's with you....
                             [facing the mirror and the camera]
                             so it's been since that=
                             =time, ma:ma::? ...
                             so now that I know,
                             ma:ma:: ....

Two situations co-occur: First, Jurema addresses the camera (the television) as the mother, the figure who has the highest authority over the child. To the mother, Jurema presents a series of vague complaints and concluding statements; second, she indicates that, as a patient, she is also aware of the presence of a camera (or the eye of a video operator) as well as of an audience (made up of those who will see the video on the television screen). In mixing these two contexts Dona Jurema signals her awareness of the video recording. She also alludes to the power that the television/camera has as it takes the place of the most prominent addressee in the psychotic discourse: the mother.

In the videotaping of the discharge interview, it is the doctor who acknowledges the recording: Twice in the interview she states explicitly that whatever the patient says will be addressed to a medical audience larger than herself (composed of interns, social workers, supervisory staff, etc.). The patient never addresses the camera or even acknowledges it. Here she talks to the doctor and to nobody else, a sharp contrast with the previous interview.

These two interviews took place in an annex to an inpatient facility belonging to the university. To reach this annex one must walk through a small patio, leaving behind the patients' wards, enter the building, and then go up the stairs to the second floor. The videotaping was done in a sparsely furnished room with no windows, where a chair and an armchair were placed sideways beside one another. There was an opaque glass wall facing the participants, behind which the cameras were located.

The Psychiatric Interview

Sullivan (1954) describes the psychiatric interview as a professional interview in which one party (the interviewer) has been defined as an expert and has the task of clarifying characteristic patterns of living of the subject/patient (interviewee). It is therefore an expert-client relationship where the expert has been defined by the culture (1954:4). The patient expects to find in the psychiatrist more than a friendly listener. The interviewer is never seen as a neutral figure in the therapeutic setting; on the contrary, she is an active participant and as such contributes to the context by her presence. Sullivan remarks that psychiatry is a field of "participant observation" and that "the data of psychiatry arise in participant observation of social interaction" (1954:3).

The purpose of the interview is to find out who the patient is by reviewing the course of events that he or she has gone through in order to be who he or she is (1954:19). The doctor thus aims at detecting patterns of affect relations that may trouble the patient (1954:14). The terms *affect* and *emotion* are often used interchangeably in psychiatry. A patient displays an "improper" affect when feelings contradict what is being said—for example, laughing when talking about a child's death.

The doctor has an active question-asking role and follows a series of preestablished steps that make up the diagnostic interview. In order to obtain relevant data from the patient, Sullivan suggests the following topics as major guidelines (1954:147–75):

disorders in learning toilet habits
disorders in learning speech habits
attitudes toward games and partners in them
attitudes toward competition and compromise
ambition
initial schooling
experience in college
puberty
unfortunate relationships in early adolescence
attitudes toward the body
sexual preference
attitude toward solitude
use of alcohol/narcotics
eating habits

sleep and sleep functions
sex life
courtship and marriage
parenthood
vocational history
avocational interests (recreational activities)

Topics such as these are part of the *anamnesis*—a procedure through which the doctor assesses the patient's situation.

Sullivan then proceeds to enumerate the diagnostic signs and patterns of mental disorder to which the psychiatrist must be sensitive. Among the various behavioral signs he lists "disturbances of verbal communication" and "disturbances in the gestural components of communication," both regarded as manifestations of "more profound phenomena" (1954:189). The first refers to autistic processes (with the consequence of provoking "loss of thought" on one hand and "blocking" on the other [*blocking* refers to an interruption before the discourse has been completed]). The language used by the patient is described as "stereotypical" with recurrent "tags of expression" (1954:193). "Peculiar misunderstandings" or "mistaken interpretations" may occur in answering the interviewer's questions, or there may be "hallucinations" when another reality prevails

The second category—disturbances in the gestural components of communication—points to the importance of stereotyped gestures that are often unrelated "to what is going on" (1954:193). There may also be "mannerisms," which are described as peculiar bodily movements that contradict expected social behavior patterns, and "tics," which stand as fragmented communicative gestures, apparently unrelated to the context (1954:193–94).

These disturbances are not unique to psychotics; that is, in the case of language use, the processes and deviances are not unfamiliar (Chaika 1974, 1977; Fromkin 1973, 1980). Rather, it is "the misapplication of these processes" that makes communication break down (Sullivan 1954:201). Any of these diagnostic signs may be part of a mental disturbance or may appear in a normal interviewee. However, in the case of a psychosis, they become "fixed parts of the person" (Sullivan 1954:195).

The Case of Dona Jurema

The following description is part of a letter from Idete, the patient's sister, to Doctor Edna:

> Jurema's present crisis began exactly like the ones before, according to what her son and other relatives have told me: laughter, long monologues, euphoria, restlessness, incoherent behavior (as if another being had possessed her), mild aggressiveness, convulsive crying. In these moments, she often doesn't want to get dressed; she smokes a lot; nothing can make her sleep

(our family doctor once gave her Valium, with no result). She answers our questions but displays no collaborative behavior. She does not complain about any pain and still recognizes people around her.

Dona Jurema was diagnosed as being in an acute manic crisis. However, according to her doctor and to the clinical reports, there were uncertainties related to the diagnosis throughout the patient's stay at the hospital. Although she was initially diagnosed as presenting a manic-depressive psychosis, her doctor pointed also to another possibility: an organic-transitory psychotic episode. The doctor's initial description stated that the patient presented "no cooperation during the clinical examination, a decrease of attention span, hypotenacity, hypovigilance, unstable affect [i.e., sudden mood shifts], indifference to the environment, childish behavior, pressure of speech [fast, frenzied, intense speech], excessive talkativeness, and perseveration [continuous repetition of words and expressions]." She added that the patient was in a state of "delirium" throughout the interview.

Disturbances in the use of language are exhibited in several psychiatric conditions, such as mania, severe depression, organic disorders, and schizophrenia (Andreasen and Powers 1974; Harrow and Quinlan 1977; Rosenberg and Tucker 1979; Rochester and Martin 1979; Wykes and Leff 1982, among others). The literature in this domain is vast. Mania and schizophrenia seem to present the same aberrant language phenomena (Andreasen and Powers 1974; Harrow and Quinlan 1977; Andreasen 1979a, 1979b; Harrow et al. 1982).[4] The fact is that clinicians seem to use similar set of symptoms to arrive at the two different diagnoses (Astrachan et al. 1972). (Appendix A describes a common set of language and cognitive disorders.)

Classic Definitions of Schizophrenia and Mania

At this point it is helpful to shift gears and briefly review some of the major premises in the classic definitions of *schizophrenia* and *mania*—the two major disorders in the field of psychiatry. This discussion serves two purposes: First, it provides a succinct background on schizophrenia versus mania psychosis; since Dona Jurema was diagnosed in a manic psychosis, a brief assessment of this type of pathology contextualizes the patient's illness. Second, in order to examine mania one must also examine schizophrenia; the discussion shows that differentiating the two psychoses can be problematic.

While Emil Kraepelin ([1919] 1925) was the first to differentiate the schizophrenic disorder from other psychiatric conditions and to subsume the symptoms under the term *Dementia Praecox* (early insanity), Eugen Bleuler ([1911] 1950) introduced the term *schizophrenia* (splitting of the mind) and further developed the typology presented by Kraepelin. Bleuler's *Dementia Praecox; or the Group of Schizophrenias* ([1911] 1950), the major descriptive study in the field, identifies schizophrenia as a cognitive disturbance where the crucial symptom is a "loosening" of associations, viewed as a psychopathological process. Owing to a constitutional weakness, the patient's affect gains "dominion over the train of thought," and "wishes and fears control the trend instead of logical connection" (1950:77–78). Whereas a normal adult forms "logical associations" that represent models of reality, a schizophrenic forms "autistic associations," dreamlike disturbances of association. According to Bleuler, when this mechanism repeatedly reoccurs:

> The mental stream becomes "distorted" and finally coherence disappears altogether. The individual thoughts then have no connection with one another from the point of view of the observer, and in most cases also from that of the patient. Indeed, it not infrequently happens that the patient never produces any coherent thought, as the concepts are piled together without any logical connection. (1950:79)

Hence, autistic thinking is characterized by random associations in experience or by partial similarities among ideas.

Both Kraepelin and Bleuler state that various patterns of disturbances are subsumed under dementia praecox or schizophrenia. However, the boundaries between the cases are quite difficult to establish, as often different types of schizophrenia are not mutually exclusive. As Bleuler comments, "Under schizophrenia are included many atypical melancholias and manias, [and] most hallucinatory confusions" (1950:436–37). Therefore, there may be a mixture of schizophrenic symptoms with those of other psychoses, such as the manic-depressive psychoses (Andreasen and Powers 1974; Harrow and Quinlan 1977; Harrow et al. 1982).

Both Kraepelin and Bleuler describe *manic psychosis* as presenting the following traits: (1) "exalted or depressive moods;" (2) "flight of ideas" or "retardation of the mental stream;" and (3) "abnormal facilitation" or "retardation of resolutions, of acting" (Bleuler 1950:465). Most manic crises show a cyclic change between euphoria, flight of ideas, and pressured activity, on one hand, and depression and melancholia, on the other hand.

The key concept for manic psychoses has been that of a "flight of ideas" associated with a disturbance of attention (Bleuler 1950:73). Bleuler describes this diagnostic trait as having the following characteristics: "The patients change their objective idea with abnormal frequency, and in the most serious cases it follows every thought uttered or indicated" (1950:71). There is a "lack of orderly arrangement" (1950:73); there is a weakening in "the resistance exerted by the leading thought [which] no longer suffices to inhibit associations which are unrelated to it" (1950:74). There is also a disturbance of attention, which demonstrates "a preponderance of external and world associations at the expense of inner associations" (1950:72).

The schizophrenic and manic pathologies were regarded by Kraepelin and Bleuler as two types of cognitive disruptions. What has been labeled by clinicians "the schizophrenic factor" relies heavily on thought disorder, delusions, and affect disturbances (Astrachan et al. 1972:535). Manics, on the other hand, were described as coherent but presenting a mood disorder. Following in Kraepelin and Bleuler's tradition, psychiatric studies (Feldstein and Jaffe 1963; Gottschalk and Gleser 1964; Chapman 1966) have concentrated on a better understanding of schizophrenic thinking, leaving other closely related psychoses—for example, mania—unexamined as to cognitive output.

It was only recently that the classic boundaries began to be questioned, as the difference between schizophrenia and mania has become the focus of intense debate. Recent studies in thought-disordered phenomena (Harrow et al. 1982) have discussed the possibility of a general psychosis factor that may cut across psychotic diagnoses. Hence, although thought pathology has been regarded as one of the primary symptoms of schizophrenia (Bleuler [1911] 1950; Chapman and Chapman 1973; Arieti 1974; Johnston and Holzman 1979, among others), disturbances in thinking and perceptions are now known to occur also in manic patients (Clayton, Pitts, and Winokur 1965; Winokur, Clayton, and Reich 1969; Lipkin, Dyrud, and Meyer 1970; Akiskal and Puzantian 1979; Harrow et al. 1982).

Psychotic Disorder in an Organic Brain Syndrome

Dona Jurema's symptoms did not fully fit into the category of a manic-depressive psychosis. The patient's written records point to an uncertainty in diagnosis: a manic-depressive psychosis or an organic transitory psychotic state? Toward the end of her stay at the psychiatric institute there seems to have been an informal consensus (never mentioned in her records) toward an organic psychosis.[5] This was partly due to Jurema's poor reaction to the neuroleptic medication and partly to her sudden improvement when the medication was suspended. Organic syndromes often have an acute onset and are reversible (MacKinnon and Michels 1971:340). Each one of Jurema's crises since the first one in 1976 followed this same pattern.[6]

A Controversial Diagnosis

In general, the major problems in poor diagnosis are erroneous medication and faulty treatment. Sheehan's report ([1982] 1983) on Sylvia Frumkin's long struggle with schizophrenia depicts a trial-and-error treatment in which Frumkin was diagnosed and medicated as a manic-depressive. In addition, she was undermedicated and, consequently, reacted poorly to the medication.[7] Commenting on her treatment, one of Frumkin's former psychiatrists said: "First, you turn a schizophrenic into a manic-depressive and then you fail to prescribe lithium [a common drug for manic patients] . . . [These] two wrongs may well be required to make a right" (Sheehan [1982] 1983:115). It seems that patients often know more about their own condition and what has worked for them than do doctors.[8] Frumkin told her doctor that the diagnosis was wrong: "I've never been a manic-depressive. I'm a schizophrenic. I've always been a schizophrenic" ([1982] 1983:113).

Dona Jurema reacted poorly to neuroleptics. On December 16 she was medicated with Haldol, an antipsychotic drug with great sedative effect. She also took nitrazepan and Fenergan. The medications made her drowsy, and her symptoms deteriorated. Jurema spent the next four days displaying rapid mood changes (lability), alterations of consciousness, and indifference to her surroundings and to her personal hygiene; she refused to eat and was agitated at night (she had to be "restrained in bed"). Until December 20 her overall state remained the same. She kept to herself, withdrawn, in silence, holding catatonic postures and performing ritual gestures. After the medications were suspended on December 21, except for a night drug (nitrazepan), Jurema progressively improved. She became more cooperative and aware of her surroundings; she talked to people, and what she said made more sense. Eight days later, on December 29, she was allowed to go home for a short stay. She returned to the hospital on January 3.

A letter from her sister Idete provides an account of Jurema's state of health during the time she spent at home:

> Jurema ate well (with someone's help), slept through the night and preferred to stay in bed during the day (she would feel tired with the least physical effort); she displayed a small neurological problem in walking (walked slowly) and while holding small objects (a fork or a spoon, pants zippers, cigarettes). This sort of impairment improved when she paid less attention to it (i.e., when she stopped monitoring). She did not complain about any pain except for the lack of energy which kept her in bed. She talked about her hospitalization and crisis, not knowing 'how it had happened' (in spite of the medical care she has had). On the eve of returning to the hospital Jurema started to get anxious and restless. She spoke of a roommate whom she fears (she had had a nightmare where this woman was strangling her). The prospect of being hospitalized again depressed and disturbed her. I did my best to distract and soothe her.

Dona Jurema's fast recovery surprised her doctor as well as the medical staff. It seemed that she "snapped out of the crisis" in the same way that she "snapped into it." Doctor Edna suggested taping a last interview to record the changes. This interview took place on January 4.

Speech: Patterns and Variants

The language in the interviews is Brazilian Portuguese. Brazilians from Rio de Janeiro speak the Carioca dialect; those from São Paulo speak the Paulista dialect. There are also dialectal nonstandard variations in rural São Paulo.

Doctor Edna speaks the standard Carioca urban dialect (she was born and raised in the city of Rio de Janeiro). Dona Jurema was born and raised in the state of São Paulo. Thus, as a child she spoke a variation of a nonstandard rural dialect; however, at sixteen she moved to Rio and has lived in the city for the subsequent forty-five years. Throughout these years she has acquired the Carioca urban dialect.

In the discharge interview there are no dialectal differences; for the most part, participants use the standard Carioca dialect. That is, in this interview, Dona Jurema does not use linguistic features (grammatical or phonological) typical of her original rural dialect. This may be accounted for by the formality of the interview situation.

The admitting interview displays an entirely different situation. Under the psychotic crisis, Dona Jurema shifts dialects: from the standard urban Carioca dialect to her original rural dialect from the interior of São Paulo. The most prominent indicator of this shift is a sound change. Throughout the interview, she uses the marked nonstandard phonetic segment—the phonetic retroflex form [ɻ]—for two different phonological segments: It is used in word-final position for the Carioca and the Paulista /l/, in words such as *mal* /mal/ "bad," *hospital* /oʃpi'tal/ "hospital," *tal* /tal/ "such"; she uses it again for the Carioca and the Paulista /R/ in preconsonantal midposition in words such as *certinho* /sɛR'tiño/ "O.K.," *verdinha* /veR'diña/ "green," *árvore* /'aRvore/ "tree," and in final position in *de cor* /de'kɔR/ "by heart," *melhor* /me'lɔR/ "better," among others.⁹ All of these occurrences are predictable in the nonstandard variations.

Dona Jurema uses these substandard forms exclusively in the admitting interview, although the dialect belongs to a time and place long past. Gumperz (1982:60) calls this type of shift a *metaphoric switching*—a code change used in a given situation carrying a specific meaning. In the psychotic crisis, Jurema "revisits the past" by code-switching from the urban Carioca dialect to the rural dialect of São Paulo.

Another type of codeshift also takes place in the psychotic crisis: The adult Jurema shifts to the talk of a very young child addressing her mother. This *child register* follows closely some of the well-known linguistic processes that take place in the speech of two to four year-olds. These processes—viewed as *simplifying processes*—are conventional and systematic.

There are a number of different forms in Jurema's child register.¹⁰ One of the most frequent phonetic changes occurs with the velar fricative [x], the alveolar flap [r], and the lateral [l]. The [r] sound retains the liquid sonorant quality but reduces the vibration of [r] to a lateral continuant [l]. Thus, the velar fricative [x] (in Rio) or the alveolar trill [r] (in São Paulo) changes to [l], in words such as *Terra* /'tɛRa/ → *Tela* ['tɛlʌ] "Earth" (where the → sign means "becomes," the form to the left of the arrow is the standard phonological adult form, and the form to the right of the arrow is the child phonetic form); *morrê* /mo'Re/ → *molê* [mo'le] "die;" *Roma* /'Roma/ → *Loma* [lõmʌ] "Rome." The [r] as an alveolar flap changes to [l] in words such as *era* /'ɛra/ → *ela* ['ɛlʌ] (forms of the verb "to be"); *por isso* /poR 'iso/ → *polisso* [polisu] "that's why;" *senhora*

/se'ɲɔra/ → *senhola* [sē'ɲɔlʌ] (formal address form for "you"); *Mariene* /mari'ene/ → *Maliene* [mali'eni] (the granddaughter's name); *maridinho* /mari'diɲo/ → *malidinho* [malijiɲu] "little husband;" *queria* /ke'ria/ → *quelia* [kiliʌ] "wanted;" *agora* /a'gɔra/ → *agola* [a'gɔlʌ] "now;" *moro* /ˈmɔro/ → *molo* [mɔlu] "live."

Another common linguistic process is fronting: The palatal fricative [š] is replaced by the dental fricative [s] in words like *chega* /šega/ → *sega* [sʸe'gaʰ] "arrive," *chove* /ˈšɔve/ → *sove* [so've] "rain"; the velar stop [k] is sometimes replaced by the alveolar stop [t] in words such as *casa* /ˈkaza/ → *tasa* ['tazʌ] "house," *aqui* /a'ki/ → *ati* [a'ti] "here"; the palatal lateral [ĺ] becomes the alveolar lateral [l] as in *melhor* /mɛ'lɔR/ → *melor* [mɛ'lɔr] "better"; the palatal nasal [ñ] becomes the alveolar nasal [n] as in *senhola* /se'ɲɔla/ → *senola* [sē'nɔla] "madam."

There is also a simplification of consonant clusters in initial positions in the following words: /pr/ *primeiro* /pri'meyro/ → *pimeiro* [pimeyru] "first," *prova* /ˈprɔva/ → *pova* ['pʷɔvʌ] "test," *pressa* /ˈprɛsa/ → *pessa* ['pɛsʌ] "fast," *presidente* /prezi'dente/ → *pesidente* [pezi'dēt'i] "president," *pra* /pra/ → *pa* [pa] "to;" /gr/ *graças* /grasas/ → *gaças* [gasʌs] "grace;" /tr/ *trazendo* /trazendo/ → *tazendo* [ta'zēⁿdʊ] "bringing"; in medial position in the following words: /pr/ *empregada* /enpre'gada/ → *empegada* [īmpe'gadʌ] "maid"; /pl/ *simples* /ˈsinples/ → *simpes* [s'ĩʸᵐpis] "simple"; /gr/ *segredo* /se'gredo/ → *seguedo* [se'gedu] "secret;" /kr/ *acreditar* /akredi'taR/ → *aqueditar* [akeji'tar] "believe." Some words drop the initial vowel (unstressed syllable), as in *acreditar* /akredi'tar/ → *queditar* [keji'tar] "believe" (together with the loss of a consonant cluster); *ajoelhar* /ažoelar/ → *zoela* [zoe'lar] "to kneel down" (together with fronting); *aparecer* /apare'seR/ → *palecer* [pale'ser] "show up" (together with a change of [r] to [l]). These processes (the simplification of consonant clusters, the reduction of frication or consonantality of the r-sound to a continuant and lateral sound /l/, the dropping of unstressed syllable, the fronting of consonants) are known as *simplifying processes*. They have been described in the speech of young children (language-acquisition studies) as well as in the speech of adults when addressing very young children ("baby-talk" register) (Snow and Ferguson [1977] 1979).

Throughout the admitting interview, Dona Jurema uses the formal address term—the Portuguese form *senhora*—to address either the doctor or the mother. This form is often transformed to *senola* with the variants [sĩɲɔla], [sĩɲɔlʌ], [sēnɔlɛ], (following a simplification process). Sometimes she avoids using the first pronoun (*eu* "I") or the address form (*senhora* "you"); instead she uses a personal name (Jurema), a kin term (*mãe* "mama"), or an indefinite (*a mocinha* "the young lady") to refer to the speaker or to the addressee. This strategy also mirrors young children's use of third-person nouns (Ferguson [1977] 1979:219; Wills [1977] 1979:277).

These linguistic variants occur only in the admitting interview. As Dona Jurema takes on different identities (speaking as a very young child, speaking as her sister Idete, as her own mother, etc.), she also distributes certain phonological variables. These variants do not occur categorically (for every role shift), nor systematically (every shift presents certain variables); however, they suggest the patient's preference to speak as a young child.

The doctor as well as the medical staff reported on Jurema's language: "Patient makes use of a young child's vocabulary, shifts sounds around, like a child learning to talk. . . . Also says unintelligible things. . . . She continuously repeats certain phrases or syllables . . . [and] uses contrastive voice pitches . . . shifting from speaking as an adult to speaking as a child."

In the admitting interview Dona Jurema also makes use of different modes of communication—nursery rhymes, church songs, or chanting. She often uses speech play that recalls the rhythm of children's lore and jingles. While the tunes are reminiscent of Brazilian children's songs, the lyrics are made up by the patient. Her speech shows gross changes in prosody. She may use a very high pitch in certain segments and alternate to a low pitch in another stretch of talk. Her pace may accelerate to a fast tempo, and then she may slow down and introduce statements at a very slow pace. Sometimes her talk gains different rhythms, often in a staccato beat.

Finally, in the admitting interview, Dona Jurema also presents certain phonological and articulatory disabilities. That is, in certain segments, she fails to initiate speech and stutters at the first syllable of a given word (for example, when she gives the name of her previous doctor, she says "pa-pa-pa-pa-pa-pa-pa-pa-pa-pa-pa-*Pau*lo de Azevedo Murtinho"). At other moments she stutters for a long stretch, whenever using bilabial or alveolar stops (alternating initial /t/ and /d/ or /p/ and /b/), until she is finally able to lexicalize a word—which could be nonsensical, as in the following:

> [creaky voice]
> Patient: **what else do you want,**
> **uhm:::?**
> Doctor: <u>**Dona Jure::ma!**</u>
> [creaky voice]
> Patient: **uhm:?**
> **you know that I can't:::.**
> ['hhh] (1.3)
> Doctor: **you can't talk to me?**
> Patient: **tototototototo.**
> **the totot<u>ô</u>:::.**

> [creaky voice]
> Patient: **que que senhora quer =**
> **= mais do que isso,**
> **hein:::?**

Doctor: **Dona Jure::ma!**
       [creaky voice]
Patient: **hein:?**
       a senhora sabe que eu=
       =não posso::: ['hhh]
       (1.3)
Doctor: **a senhora não pode=**
       =falar comigo?
Patient: **tototototototo.**
       o tototô:::.

In still other segments Dona Jurema begins to stutter and progressively changes to a range of sounds that are phonetically indistinguishable. These segments are suddenly interrupted as she engages in a different talk or type of activity. In contrast, the discharge interview presents none of the above. There is no trace of any language disability except for a small articulatory problem.

Analyzing Recorded Interviews

Transcribing Data

Both Ochs (1979) and Tannen (1984) discuss the selective process implied in the transcription of recorded data: "Just as the taped conversation creates an entity different from the interaction itself, so the transcript is yet another artifact" (Tannen 1984:36). This point is strongly discussed by Mishler (1984) in the study of clinical discourse.[11] In transforming speech into text, "each transcription is a rendering" (Garfinkel, cited in Mishler 1984:34).

The videotapes of Dona Jurema's two interviews were transcribed in conventional Brazilian Portuguese orthography, with modifications to reflect phonological variants or voice-quality changes used by Dona Jurema in the admitting interview. These variants are marked since they represent a departure from the norm.

Verbal Communication

For both interviews it was important to transcribe, as closely as possible, the occurrence of expressive paralinguistic and prosodic features. Together with other features (code-switching, formulaic expressions, lexical choice, etc.), they point to changes in the context of communication. Labov and Fanshel describe these paralinguistic and prosodic cues as "not easily coded in a discrete form" (1977:43). However, one can rely on the redundancy of certain patterns and on the co-occurrence of other similar cues to reinforce one's interpretation of the data.

The discharge interview presents a *dialogue* between Dona Jurema and Doctor Edna. The interview follows closely the principles of turn taking as the basic form of organization for conversation, where one party speaks at a time and turns recur (Sacks, Schegloff, and Jefferson 1974). Both participants collaborate on topic continuity and jointly negotiate topic change.

Two types of structure of participation tend to occur in the admitting interview. On one hand, the interview is partially a *monologue,* in the sense that one participant (Dona Jurema) speaks and holds the floor most of the time. Fewer turn takings occur (one-third fewer than in the discharge interview). There are frequent attempts by the doctor to interrupt the patient's discourse, but few successful interruptions. Dona Jurema holds the floor and, like a very small child, does not attend to the conversational norms for interaction (for example, in several segments there is chanting or singing in response to a question from the doctor).

On the other hand, this interview is also a *dialogue with those not present.* That is, Dona Jurema continuously addresses and talks to different participants (her mother, her grandmother Lena, her sister Idete) who are not there. In addition, she shifts roles and takes the "answerer" turn, providing the expected adjacency pair, as in the following:

                [whining]
Patient: **ma:ma::!**
                ma:ma::!
                → /what is it, my child?

These differences in participation structure are captured in the transcript, where two different formats are used to transcribe the data: a vertical format and a column format. The discharge interview follows the standard, linear, vertical format (where speakers alternate turns and the text is presented as a sequencing of utterances); the admitting interview, on the other hand, is displayed in a parallel-column format. There is no expectation of sequential information. Rather, it "encourages the reader to treat verbal acts more independently" (Ochs 1979:47). These two formats indicate that different interactive processes take place in the two interviews.

Nonverbal Communication

Nonverbal communication is complementary to verbal communication. Postural shifts, among other nonverbal behaviors, are one of the means to achieve a change in frame. Thus, they also constitute "contextualization cues" (Gumperz 1982; Erickson 1982; Streeck 1985). The transcription indicates interactional spatial and kinesic "maneuvers" by which a "frame attunement" or a change in frame is produced (Kendon 1979). Nonverbal behavior, therefore, will be coded only in those contexts where it indicates a switch in the discourse frame, a change in the speak-

Figure 2.1. Baseline postures assumed by the patient and doctor during the admitting interview.

er's alignment, or where it constitutes the communicative medium par excellence (as in a short segment during the admitting interview).

For each interview I describe the initial postural arrangement, which corresponds to the *baseline posture* (Scheflen 1973) assumed by the participants in each event. Scheflen says that participants tend to shift in and out of baseline posture (1973:29). This is relevant, since reframings may be accomplished as a departure from or return to the original posture.

The Admitting Interview. The following description presents the baseline posture assumed by Doctor Edna and Dona Jurema during the admitting interview. The chairs have been arranged so that the participants can sit diagonally to each other. However, Dona Jurema is sitting forward and bending sideways (toward her right), so that she actually faces the doctor. She sits at the edge of the armchair. Her legs and ankles are uncrossed, and her right foot slightly touches the doctor's right foot.

Doctor Edna is turned to the right, toward the patient. Her head leans forward, and her torso is slightly inclined to the right. She holds a microphone in her right hand, while her left hand rests on her lap. Her legs are slightly apart. She is close to Dona Jurema, as Figure 2.1 indicates. During the entire interview the doctor holds a microphone pointed toward the patient. In the playback session Doctor Edna said that Dona Jurema's unpredictable gestures and movements made it hard to attach a microphone to her gown. To a viewer, however, it looks as if the microphone stands obtrusively between the doctor and the patient. In the discharge interview no microphones were displayed.

During the admitting interview Doctor Edna shifts slightly from her baseline posture. She bends and leans over, closer to the patient, and she moves the microphone from one hand to the other, bringing it closer to the patient. Dona Jurema, however, constantly shifts postures: She moves backward and forward in her chair, turns sideways (to the left and toward the doctor; to the right and away from the doctor); she constantly bends down and tries to fix her slippers; she also moves to the edge of her chair in an attempt to get up.

Besides shifting from one posture to another, Dona Jurema assumes different body orientations and engages in a series of parallel activities. These activities fit into a group of acts classified by Scheflen (1973:70), who identified three types of kinesic behavior in a psychotherapy session: Type A presents activities that function to maintain the performer's orientation in the group; type B introduces physical tasks that stand as signals; and type C presents "representative elements in bond-servicing activities like courtship and mutual play" (1973:78). Type B and type C activities are particularly interesting. For example, at different moments during the admitting interview, Dona Jurema alternates between taking her slippers off and putting them on. Such a physical task seems to signal her ambivalent feelings about staying for the rest of the interview or leaving (she keeps saying to the doctor that she wants to leave, that "it's late," "it's time to go"). Type C subsumes activities such as "tactile play" and "quasi-courting activities;" for example, at one point, Dona Jurema takes off her slippers and with the toes of her right foot touches the doctor's foot, while chanting a tune. At another moment she raises her right hand toward the doctor, touches the doctor's face, and plays with her hair as she sings, "it's a little caress, it's a little caress."

Dona Jurema is overactive during this interview. Most of her movements are abrupt and rapid, and her nonverbal behavior parallels her prosodic features (i.e., her contrastive pitch heights and voice volume). Both types of information are described in the analysis whenever they indicate a shift of context.

The Discharge Interview. The following presents the baseline posture for Doctor Edna and Dona Jurema during the discharge interview. Although they shift in and out of this posture during the interview, the shifts that take place in this session are slight and subtle, confirming the general principle stated by Scheflen: "In a formal activity like psychotherapy . . . the posture and orientation of the position will be held stationary, fixed, relatively immobile, even rigid" (1973:25).

Dona Jurema and Doctor Edna are sitting diagonally to each other. Dona Jurema is sitting upright, slightly backward, in an armchair that

Figure 2.2.   Baseline postures of patient and doctor at the discharge interview.

has been placed to the right of the doctor's chair. Both hands are resting on the arms of the armchair; while the left hand is visible and its gestures can be observed, the right hand movements often cannot be described, as a high table partially obstructs the view. Both legs and ankles are uncrossed, with legs in a parallel position; her chest and head are slightly inclined to the left, so as to face the doctor. The patient keeps this "open position" (Scheflen 1973:44) throughout the session. This is her baseline posture.

Doctor Edna is sitting upright and slightly forward in a chair that is a bit higher than the patient's armchair. She bends forward as the interview progresses. In order to face the patient, her torso is slightly inclined to the right. Both legs and ankles are apart, and they get wider apart toward the end of the interview. Her hands, however, are folded together. She has a midopen position: Her body orientation, her proximity to the patient, and the position of the lower part of her body (legs and feet) are in an accordance with Scheflen's description of an "open position" (1973:44); however, she holds her arms and hands folded in a "closed position." There are no hand microphones.

During this interview the doctor and the patient keep complementary positions, as Figure 2.2 shows. Again the doctor and the patient are seated very close to each other. The right leg of the doctor almost touches the left leg of the patient.[12]

Finally, the camera recording must be mentioned. During the two interviews the camera does not keep a fixed focus on both participants. It may shift from an overall focus (on the doctor and patient) to a focus on either the patient or the doctor. Most of the time it shifts from the overall focus to concentrate on the patient. For example, at the opening of the discharge interview only the patient is in focus: She is nodding and smiling as she addresses the doctor's questions about her social history. Then, when the doctor shifts the topic (she requests information related to Dona Jurema's present illness), the camera shifts the focus to an overall perspective, with both participants in view.

There are two major problems with the video recording. First, when the camera focuses exclusively on one participant, it automatically removes the other participant from the picture. This is a serious disadvantage when one looks at discourse as a joint production. In this case one loses nonverbal information on how interactive discourse is being built at that moment. The second problem is the neutrality (or pseudoneutrality) of the camera perspective. In shifting focus (from the patient to the doctor and back to the patient) as well as in moving from a specific detail (a close-up on Jurema's hands) to an overall picture, the camera work creates an interpretation of the ongoing event. It segments, designates, and sets up the visual information it considers relevant in that event. The video recording will thus reflect this choice.

Translating Spoken Discourse

Since talk reveals the social attributes of the speakers—those attributes that are "performed" in a given interaction (their official as well as unofficial identities)—the question in translation is how does translated talk reinterpret these features? What kinds of information are modified? Which are lost? Since these social attributes surface in the Portuguese language, how can the English translation best reinterpret the original text?

The English version of both interviews is not a literal, word-for-word translation. Rather, it is a translation that portrays, as closely as possible, the sense of the talk that is taking place at that moment. In the process of translation, some information that exists in the original is inevitably lost.

One of the most problematic areas is prosody. For both interviews it was important to transcribe (from spoken to written Portuguese) instances of expressive prosodic features (such as the use of high or low pitch, vowel and consonant elongation, emphasis, etc.) and changes of pacing (faster or slower rate of speech, faster turn taking). Together with other features (discourse markers, lexical choice, etc.), these prosodic features indicate changes in the context of communication. The translated text, however, may often "sound" awkward if one does not take certain precautions. Thus, while trying to preserve the original stress and pitch so as to convey the original meaning to the English reader is desirable, it may not always be possible:

    [dec]
Doctor: **e assim:**, ...

cuida de <u>si</u>::, ..
/toma ba:nho/,
[acc]
faz tudo normalmente?

[dec]
Doctor: and let's see:, ...
you take <u>ca::re</u> of yourself,..
/you ba:the/,
[acc]
you do everything as usual?

In the Portuguese text, the stress is on the pronominal form *si* ("your-self"). In English, however, to preserve the original meaning of the doctor's question, the stress could only be on the verb. Marking the pronoun would indicate contrastive stress (yourself instead of others), a meaning not present in the original version. There is also a problem in indicating the stress through vowel lengthening of *si::* at the end of a tone unit; in English, the form "yourself" would not receive stress because it is in final position.

In the translation of spoken discourse, one of the most troublesome areas are "sound touch-offs" (Sacks 1971), where one sound triggers further occurrence of the same sound. These are frequent in the admitting interview, and contain interesting information on word analogy by sound association. In each occurrence the sound coordination among these forms is necessarily missed if they are translated.

[This segment takes place at the end of the interview; Dona Jurema has been talking for a while, and she concludes, saying the following:]

Patient:

 (1) ⌈ah::::, AH::::, AH::::, poli:::sso. ...
 (2) polisso que o Chico ontem a noite- ...
 (3) foi lá em <u>tasa</u>. .. me buscá:, ... pa levá:, ...
 (4) po hospita<u>r</u> .... po hospita<u>r</u> do Pener . ....
 (5) a senhora sabe o que é pene<u>r</u>? ... não é <u>peneu</u> ..
 (6) peneu. ..a senhora sabe o que é peneu?
 (7) não, é o caro do meu fio. ...
 (8) a senhora sabe quem é meu fio? .. não:,
 (9) é a coisa mais sagada desse mundo . ...
(10) eu posso ficá de pépépépépépépé?

---

 (1) ⌈oh::::, OH::::, OH::::, that's::: why. ...
 (2) that's why Chico last night, ...
 (3) came <u>home</u>. .. to get: me, ... to ta:ke (me), ...
 (4) to the hospital .... to Pener hospital. ....
 (5) do you know what "pener" is? ... not "<u>peneu</u>." ...
 (6) "peneu." .. do you know what "peneu" is?
 (7) no, it's my son's car. ...
 (8) do you know who my son is? .. no:,

(9) ((he's)) the most sacred thing in the world. ...
(10) Can I stand on my "pépépépépépépé"?

First Dona Jurema identifies the name of the hospital where she was taken—the Pinel hospital (in line (4) she uses the nonstandard variant [ɾ] for the Carioca [w], saying [penɛɾ] instead of [pinɛw]). Then, in line (5) she asks the doctor whether she knows what "penel" is. "Penel" here could refer back to the hospital Pinel, or to a more generic and popular term used in colloquial Portuguese to mean "crazy." In lines (5 and 6) the form "penel" triggers by sound association the form "peneu," which means "tire" (a car tire), and Dona Jurema makes a distinction between "penel" and "peneu" (/penɛɾ/ and /penew/), stating that one is not the other (line 5). At the end of this segment (which is also the end of the interview), she asks (in line 10): "Posso ficá de pépépépépépépé?" ("Can I stand up?"), where the form *pé* means "foot." The sound coordination among these forms is necessarily missed when they are translated.[13]

In such cases, which occur mostly in the admitting interview, I have kept the original Portuguese form within the English translation and provided explanations in the analysis. Hence, the translation preserves this information whenever it does not interfere with the communicative aspects of the discourse. Frequently, however, the original meaning may not be conveyed in its entirety, as in the first part of the same excerpt:

(1) ⌐ah::::, AH::::, AH::::, poli:::sso. ...
(2) polisso que o Chico ontem a noite- ...
(3) foi lá em <u>tasa</u>. .. me buscá:, ... pa levá:, ...
(4) po hospitaɾ .... po hospitaɾ do Peneɾ . ....
(5) a senhora sabe o que é peneɾ? ... não é <u>peneu</u> ..

(1) ⌐oh::::, OH::::, OH::::, that's::: why. ...
(2) that's why Chico last night, ...
(3) came <u>home</u>. .. to get: me, ... to ta:ke (me), ...
(4) to the hospital .... to Peneɾ hospital. ....
(5) do you know what "peneɾ" is? ... not "<u>peneu</u>." ...

Again we have a series of sound touch-offs starting with the repetition of the stressed front vowel /a/ in line (1), which in English finds its equivalent in the back dipthong /ow/; then, in lines (3) and (4), Dona Jurema goes on stressing the same sound in the words *tasa* ("house"), *buscá* ("get"), *levá* ("take"), and *hospitaɾ* (hospital). The English translation does not capture this sound play (except for the forms "home" and "know," no other form reproduces the sound [ow]).[14]

This segment presents other problems to the translator: The English version does not convey the phonological variants /l/ and /r/ used by the patient in forms such as /poliso/ instead of /poriso/ "that's why;" /t/ and /k/ in forms as /taza/ instead of /kaza/ "house/home;" and the absence of the consonant cluster /pr/ in *pa (levá)* instead of *pra (levá)* "to (take);" *po (hospital)* instead of *pro (hospital)* "to the (hospital)," and *sagada* instead of *sagrada* "sacred"; all of these signal variant forms used in child language. This sort of information will be indicated in the English transcript as "baby talk."[15]

Neither can the translation indicate dialectal variants that mark Jurema's place of origin, as in the case of *hospital*, where the patient uses [r] in [oʃpitar], a variant from the State of São Paulo. In the translation one misses the sound association in line (4) between two nonstandard forms [oʃpitar] "hospital" and [penɛr] "Pinel":

(4) po hospitar .... po hospitar do Penɛr . ....
(4) to the hospital .... to Pener hospital. ....

Dona Jurema uses the same nonstandard variant [r]: [oʃpitar] instead of standard [oʃpitaw] and [penɛr] instead of standard [pinɛw]. It is a metaphoric switch back to her home dialect from rural São Paulo. Again this same r sound is used in line (7), neutralizing an important distinction in standard Portuguese between [karu] "dear" and [kaxu] "car":

(7) nao, é o caro do meu fio. ...
(7) no, it's my son's car. ...

or

(7) no, it's my dear son

The nonstandard form [karu] is ambiguous: It refers back to the "car tire" *(peneu)* by introducing "the son's car," and it points forward to "the most sacred thing" (in line 9) by alluding to "the dear one." This type of information can only be conveyed in the analysis, and it will be mentioned whenever relevant to the discussion.

Another issue in translation is the type of answer form used for yes-no questions. In Portuguese one responds affirmatively to a yes-no question by repeating the verb form, as in the following:

Doctor: e assim:, ... cuida de si::, ..
/toma ba:nho,/ faz tudo normalmente?
Patient: ah, cui:do, tu:do direitinho,
tu:do direitinho.

Doctor: and let's see:, ...
you take ca::re of yourself, .. /you ba:the/,
you do everything as usual?
Patient: oh, yes:, ev:erything as usual,
ev:erything as usual.

In the Portuguese text the doctor asks a question using the verb *cuidar* *(cuida de si* "take care of yourself"). The patient answers by repeating the verb (*cui:do* "[I] take care"). In the English version, however, the affirmative answer is provided by the use of the particle "yes."

Next, I need to mention the terms of address and their translation. Both participants use address forms that in Brazilian Portuguese belong to a formal register. The doctor uses the form *Dona Jurema* ("Mrs. Jurema" = title + first name) when addressing the patient. The patient uses the analogous form *Doutora Edna* ("Doctor Edna" = title + first name). I decided to keep the Portuguese forms in the English text because there is no equivalent combination of forms in English. Both participants use the form *a senhora* (formal "you") to address each other. The T-form *você* (informal "you") is never used. Thus, in the English translation, "you" corresponds to the V-form in Portuguese.[16]

Finally, discourse markers—being language-specific—represent a difficult area for translation and an important area for contrastive studies. The Portuguese forms do not always have an equivalent in English, and they do not always work in the same way. One example can be seen in *não é* or *né,* the most frequent tag form in Brazilian spoken discourse. It has lost its original tag function (a request for confirmation); while it still functions to indicate phatic communication, its automatic usage in colloquial everyday talk signals, rather, the end of an intonational unit (Chafe 1986). The literal translation of this form would be "isn't it." The functional translation would be "y'know" and "right." In the English text I have used the form "y'know" (for the most part), "right" (a few times), or a tag question. Both "right" and a tag question work fine in the following question (where *não é isso?* would be translated literally as "isn't that?"):

Doctor: **mora a senhora e suas duas irmãs,**
          não é isso?
Doctor: **you live with your two sisters,**
          don't you?

or

          you live with your two sisters,
          right?

In most segments, however, *não é* is translated by the form "y'know," as in the following:

Doctor: **=o que é que aconteceu de repente?**
          explica pra gente.=
Patient: **=de repente, eu ⌜perdi o .. a razão,**
          os sentidos, não é, ...
          não vi mais nada,
          quando eu vi tava aqui no hospital, /não é./
          (1.7)

mas não vi nada do que se passou comigo,
/não é./

Doctor: = what happened all of a sudden?
explain to us. =
Patient: = all of a sudden ⌐I <u>lost</u> ah .. my mind,
my senses, <u>y'know</u>, ...
I didn't see anything anymore,
when I came to my senses I was here in the =
= hospital, /<u>y'know</u>./ (1.7)
but I did not see anything that happened to =
= me /<u>y'know</u>./

There are also instances where a discourse marker could be translated by the use of a verb form or by the closest English marker, as in the following:

Doctor: a senhora já teve outras internações, não é?
Patient: já doutora, infelizmente já, <u>viu</u>.

Doctor: **you have already had other hospitalizations, haven't you?**
Patient: **yes, doctor, unfortunately yes, y'see.**
(or) **yes, doctor, unfortunately yes, <u>I have</u>.**

The literal translation of the marker *viu* would be "see" (*viu* is the past-tense form of the verb "to see"). In Portuguese, this form seems to function as reinforcing an answer or reiterating the point a speaker has made. As such, it occurs only at the end of an utterance or a segment of talk. In English the marker "see" or "y'see" seems to be used either to announce an explanation or to refer back to one.[17]

In the preceding segment, the doctor asks a yes no question:

Doctor: **you have already had other hospitalizations, haven't you?**

This question gives Dona Jurema a choice between two answers—positive or negative; she gives a direct positive answer:

Patient: **yes, doctor, unfortunately yes, y'see.**
(or) **yes, doctor, unfortunately yes, <u>I have</u>.**

No further explanations are provided or needed. In this case a verb form is more adequate in conveying in English the speaker's original meaning.

In such segments I have used the most adequate form that keeps the functional meaning of the original text; I have also used double parentheses ((. . . ..)) to indicate a problematic translation. So the text would look like this:

Patient: **yes, doctor, unfortunately, yes. ((<u>y'see</u>.))**

Each of these issues and many others came up frequently during the processes of transcription, translation, and analysis of the data. My goal was to preserve most of the information presented in Portuguese while making the English text as close as possible to natural English discourse. Nevertheless, one must bear in mind the potential loss of information; when the loss was crucial I included the Portuguese text for clarification. As Becker, following Ortega y Gasset, points out, "The activity of language is in many ways utopian: one can never convey just what one wants to convey, for others will interpret what they hear, and their interpretation will be both exuberant and deficient" (1982a:124).[18]

Notes

1. The admitting interview lasts for seventeen and a half minutes. The discharge interview is eighteen minutes long.

2. MacKinnon and Michels report that "the bizarre behavior of a regressed patient has a disconcerting effect on most interviewers" (1971:256). Such behavior may range from conversing with a third nonexistent person in the interview scene to placing improper demands on the doctor.

3. Psychiatrists define *acting out,* in the narrow sense, as "behavior that is based upon feelings that arise in the transference relationship [with the psychiatrist] and are then displaced onto persons in the patient's every-day life. The purpose and result is to keep the expression of these feelings away from the therapist" (MacKinnon and Michels 1971:329). In the broader sense, *acting out* means to give overt expression to repressed emotions or impulses without full awareness or understanding.

4. Durbin and Marshall (1977) analyzed the discourse production of manic patients. They found that manics, like schizophrenics, keep a "basic linguistic competence as regards phonology, the retrieval of proper lexical items, and the generation of complex and grammatical sentences" (1977:217). Rochester and Martin (1979) compare their own findings with those of Durbin and Marshall and state that "language disorders seen in schizophrenic subjects may not be unique to schizophrenia, but rather may characterize an acute psychotic process general to mania and schizophrenia" (1979:201).

While most recent research agrees on the above premises, some scholars believe that the differences between manics and schizophrenics can be observed in longitudinal research. Wykes and Leff (1982) investigated whether the discourse of manic speakers is easier to understand, an assumption intuitively felt by most clinicians. Halliday and Hasan's (1976) cohesion analysis was used to measure the differences of performance in the discourse of manics and schizophrenics. Wykes and Leff state that "the concept of derailment seems to correspond quite closely to what the cohesion analysis measures" (1982:123). The results indicate that there is no difference in the frequency of occurrence of derailment in the two pathologies. However, there is a difference "in the severity with which the symptom occurs. . . . Manic patients provided the listener with more ties to relate his sentences together [*sic*] than the schizophrenics did." Nonetheless, Wykes and Leff add that "these ties were rated irrespective of logical relations between sentences so that cohesion analysis is not a direct measure of how understandable the text is. Rather it is a measure of the structure of the text . . . which can be independent of meaning" (1982:123). They also emphasize that their findings must be replicated in order to verify their basic assumption and the extent to which cohesion analysis can be useful as a diagnostic measure.

5. This syndrome, often referred to as *delirium* or *acute brain syndrome,* can be triggered by "any type of insult to the brain including trauma, infection, neoplasm, toxic or chemical agents, and metabolic changes" (MacKinnon and Michels 1971:340).

6. In many ways Dona Jurema's behavior patterns match the description for an organic psychotic disorder as provided by MacKinnon and Michels: "The patient is difficult to arouse and to interview. His awareness of his environment is decidedly dulled. . . . He is bewildered, confused, and disoriented. He has lost all sense of time . . . he may even have to peer at the window in order to decide if it is night or day. His sense of place is also disturbed, and he seems oblivious to the ward personnel and is unable to identify them. . . . Screaming and crying occur, as well as extreme states of excitement. . . . Perceptual disturbances are frequently part of the picture. At first the patient has illusory distortions and misidentifies other persons and objects. . . . The organic patient . . . [makes] the unfamiliar more familiar. . . . [He] often sees hospital personnel as relatives" (1971:342).

7. A psychiatrist and psychopharmacologist, familiar with Miss Frumkin's case, remarked on the complexity involved in administering antipsychotic drugs: "One trouble [in medicating] is that most psychiatrists simply don't know enough about psychopharmacology. With the exception of the field of allergy, there is no field in medicine with such a range of possible doses. Each patient metabolizes these medicines differently. You have to constantly make adjustments" (cited in Sheehan [1982] 1983:107).

8. Psychiatrists frequently report on patients' awareness about the "right" and "wrong" medication—the one that has and has not worked for them (Sheehan [1982] 1983:114).

9. This nonstandard phonetic segment [r] in Brazilian Portuguese marks a highly stigmatized rural dialect (equivalent to the "Brazilian hillbilly talk"). In Dona Jurema's speech, some of these forms are [mar], [oʃpitar], [tar], [sɛrˈt͡ʃĩnu], [verˈd͡ʒĩɲʌ], [arvori], [deˈkɔr], [meˈlɔr]. In American English the retroflex [r] is standard.

10. Every language and every speech community have different sets of registers. A register is defined by "the uses for which it is appropriate and by a set of structural features which differentiate it from the other registers in the total repertory of the community" (Ferguson [1977] 1979:212).

11. Mishler (1984) alerts researchers in the medical sciences to the problematic nature of transcription (1984:33). There are "distortions and inaccuracies" often ignored by researchers who read transcripts "as if" they were representations of actual speech (1984:33). Thus, studies based on medical interviews have not reflected significantly on the issue of "how speech is transformed into text." The analyst makes assumptions about what has been said. Mishler says that "essentially, these assumptions are those of common sense: the culturally-shared understandings of what persons 'mean' by what they say" (1984:33).

12. The physical closeness assumed by both participants is the norm in Brazilian settings (Harrison 1983:20). In the Brazilian culture, more often than not,

individuals stand only a few inches away from one another (in bank lines, bus lines, seating arrangements, etc.). Such proximity may result in some sort of physical contact (touching arms, thighs, or legs). It is usually the setting (a seat on the bus, a couch in a dentist office) that will determine whether a physical contact is considered intrusive or not.

13. Dona Jurema brings up sound association with the form /p/ throughout the interview. This is particularly interesting since there is a very common speech play among Brazilian children called *a lingua do p* (which means literally "the 'p' language"). The code is constructed in a way that every syllable in any given word is repeated using /p/ and the preceding vowel. Thus the name *Chico* /sĭku/ would be coded *Chipicopo* /šipikupu/.

14. Margarida Basilio pointed out the profusion of sound touch-offs in this short segment.

15. Ferguson uses "baby talk" to refer to the simplified register used by caretakers while addressing young children ([1977] 1979:216). In my study, however, "baby talk" refers to a simplified register used by the patient to signal "a child speaking."

16. Brown and Gilman ([1972] 1979) discuss the use of two pronouns— "T" (from the French *tu*) and "V" (from the French *vous*)—in the semantics of power and solidarity.

17. The discussion about the markers *viu* and "y'see" is intuitive. I am not familiar with any study on any of these forms. I asked native speakers in both languages, and they seemed to agree in the use of these forms.

18. Due to the process of translation, there may be some small inconsistencies between the full transcript included in the appendix and the excerpts. In this case, please refer to the full transcript. In either case, the original meaning was preserved.

3

Analyzing Discourse: Frame and Topic Coherence

The problem is not only that there is language, but that it is so complex. Using language involves doing several things at once, any one of which can go wrong. That is, in using language I am making sounds (or inscribing them), shaping structures, interacting with people, remembering and evoking prior text, and referring to the world—all at once.

Alton L. Becker, "Beyond Translation," p. 127

In language any one of these things can go wrong, since, as Becker adds, "it is at best an unstable integration" (1982a:128). When the integration is disrupted, an unsuccessful language and interactional experience results. People do many things through talk. They introduce topics for discussion that are eventually negotiated as conversational topics in the interaction. They convey requests, make demands, respond to summonses, and present statements, among a variety of different actions. Participants in a conversation also take turns, take and yield the floor, interrupt, and reveal their listenership verbally and nonverbally. In performing all this work, people continuously signal their relationship to one another, as well as to what they are saying, through talk.

Tannen's extensive work in discourse analysis (1984, 1986, 1990) investigates the basic question underlying discourse and interaction: How do people communicate and interpret meaning when they interact and speak to one another? Since talk, in any circumstance, is always meaningful, what are participants doing when they speak?

Sociolinguistic research in discourse indicates that the analyst does not have "rules" of language that are or are not satisfied; rather, as Levinson (1983) points out, "the analyst is in the position of the hearer who has interpretations of the discourse which do or do not make sense." Gumperz (1982) points out that speakers follow interpretive norms that are continuously revised as the interaction develops. In this process, participants are active predictors of "what will come next" in the interactive game. Speakers go back and forth, matching their prior knowledge against the unfolding discourse and predicting their next move.

The discourse analyst must, therefore, establish the message. Most of all, in order to determine the message, the analyst must determine the metamessage about how the communication has been intended, that is, the frame. No message (meaningful words or utterances) can be understood without a reference to the metamessage about the frame (Bateson [1972] 1981). According to Tannen:

> Whereas words convey information, how we speak those words—how loud, how fast, with what intonation and emphasis—communicates what we think we're doing when we speak: teasing, flirting, explaining, or chastising; whether we're feeling friendly, angry, or quizzical; whether we want to get closer or back off. In other words, how we say what we say communicates social meanings. (1986:30)

Given an interactional model for the analysis of talk (Goffman 1981a; Gumperz 1982; Erickson and Shultz 1982; Tannen 1984, 1986; Schiffrin 1987a), one may investigate what sorts of relationships are established through talk and how these relationships are negotiated in interaction. More specifically, one would ask "How do frames mold the ongoing discourse?" and "What do frames indicate about the way we communicate to one another?"

Analyzing Talk: Frame and Topic

This chapter discusses the notions of *frame* and *topic* in discourse. It reviews the theoretical assumptions underlying the use of these two concepts in this book. Frame and topic represent two ways of segmenting discourse—two different, but interrelated, principles of discourse and social organization. We will see that while topics are dependent on participants' prior and shared knowledge, framings are continuously being created (and recreated) in interaction. While topics address the discourse question "What is talk about?" framings establish a metamessage as "how this talk must be understood."

Framing: A Psychological Concept

The term *frame* was introduced into the social sciences by Bateson ([1972] 1981), who defines frame as a psychological concept that can be understood by means of two different analogies: the physical analogy of the "picture frame" and the more abstract analogy of the "mathematical set." The two analogies give contradictory instructions: "While the analogy of the mathematical set is perhaps over abstract, the analogy of the picture frame is excessively concrete" ([1972] 1981:187). Furthermore, Bateson adds that "the psychological concept which we are trying to define is neither physical nor logical" ([1972] 1981:187).

The picture frame refers to the literal way in which people mark events one from another by physical boundaries (where frames enclose pictures to indicate simultaneously the picture and that which is not picture, including the frame itself). According to Bateson, "the picture frame is an instruction to the viewer that he should not extend the premises which obtain between the figures within the picture to the wallpaper behind it" ([1972] 1981:189).

On the other hand, the mathematical set refers to logical implications of membership in a given category or set. Relationships between sets illustrate "a topological approach to the logic of classification" ([1972] 1981:186). Regarding communication, set theory helps enclose a group of messages. A frame "is (or delimits) a class or a set of messages (or meaningful actions)" ([1972] 1981:186).[1]

Bateson's illustration of frame has become classic. In observing the behavior of young monkeys at play, he says that a given behavior, such as a bite, which is typically associated with "combat activities," is interpreted in another context as "not combat." What makes this interpretation possible is a set of abstraction that recognizes (1) that the sign is only a signal and (2) that a signal may have more than one interpretation (i.e., in one situation a bite may denote "this is combat" while, in another situation a bite may stand for "this is play") ([1972] 1981:179).

Bateson proceeds by listing a series of common functions and uses of psychological frames ([1972] 1981:187):

1. "Psychological frames are exclusive" (by including certain messages within a frame, they exclude other messages).
2. "Psychological frames are inclusive" (by excluding certain messages from a frame, they include other messages).
3. "Psychological frames are related to . . . 'premises' " (i.e., the messages enclosed within the set are members of a class because they share common premises).
4. "A frame is metacommunicative" (any message, which either explicitly or implicitly defines a frame, constitutes instructions to the listener on how to understand the messages within the frame).
5. "Every metacommunicative . . . message defines, either explicitly or implicitly, the set of messages about which it communicates (i.e., . . . the psychological frame)".
6. There is a double framing (smaller sets are framed by larger sets, which are themselves enclosed in a frame. In this respect Bateson adds that "mental processes resemble logic": They need "an outer frame to delimit the ground against which the figures are to be perceived" ([1972] 1981:188).

In addition, the vast majority of metacommunicative messages remain implicit, and this aspect of metacommunication is quite relevant to the analysis of a psychiatric interview. Bateson observes that "in the psychiatric interview, there occurs a further class of implicit messages about how metacommunicative messages of friendship and hostility are to be interpreted" ([1972] 1981:178). This refers to the common indirect way of signaling frames, an issue that Gumperz (1982) and Tannen (1984, 1986) have addressed extensively in discourse analysis.

The preceding definitions establish how framing works. Two of these functions are particularly interesting. First, framing operates by inhibiting ground information and forwarding the perception of figure. In the present study the patient is admitted to the hospital during a severe psychotic crisis. In the admitting interview the doctor proposes talk as interview talk. However, for the patient, the frame of the psychiatric interview remains, more often than not, in the background, and she seldom ratifies this framing.

Second, the notion of double framing indicates that multiple contexts occur. These contexts may be simultaneous (juxtaposed) or embedded. For example, within the context of the psychotic crisis several framings emerge. While some are predominant (the framing of the child addressing the mother), others appear to be subsumed under the first one (the child addressing the grandmother, the [childlike] patient addressing the doctor [mother]). These subordinated contexts need the outer framing (the child addressing the mother) to establish the ground against which the inner framings are to be discerned.

Framing: A Situational Concern

Goffman borrows Bateson's term *frame* to address a situational concern: "My perspective is situational, meaning here a concern for what one individual can be alive to at a particular moment" (1974:8). He says that social life contains at least two kinds of understanding: a literal one (that addresses the question "What's going on here?") and a metaphoric one (that addresses the question "What is the meaning of what is going on here?"). People adjust their actions to their understanding of what the situation is. Frequently, they find out that "the ongoing world supports this fitting" (1974:247).[2]

A frame consists of principles of organization: "I assume that definitions of a situation are built up in accordance with principles of organization which govern events—at least social ones—and our subjective involvement in them" (Goffman 1974:10). Additionally, Goffman claims that organizational premises are something we arrive at, not something just created or generated in the mind (i.e., they are carried in the mind and in activity) (1974:247).

Goffman uses the concept of frame to indicate that simultaneous meanings are present in life as they are in language. There are multiple realities; however, each framing has its own realm of existence (1974:2). Following James (1950), Goffman points out that selective attention can make real several different worlds, and each one comes into being "whilst it is attended to" (1950:293).

Keyings and Fabrications

Transformed or framed activities are essentially of two types: a keyed activity or a fabricated activity (Goffman (1974). *Keying* is a transformation of basic experiential material—which Goffman calls a "primary framework."[3] He provides the following definition of keying:

> a. a systematic transformation is involved across materials already meaningful in accordance with a schema of interpretation . . . ;
> b. participants in the activity are meant to know and to openly acknowledge that a systematic alteration is involved . . . ;
> c. cues will be available for establishing when the transformation is to begin and when it is to end . . . ;
> d. keying is not restricted to events perceived within any particular class of perspectives . . . ;
> e. . . . the systematic transformation that a particular keying introduces may alter only slightly the activity thus transformed, but it utterly changes what it is a participant would say was going on. (1974:45)

Keying may take place with already transformed experience, as we must cope with retransformations as well as transformations (1974:80). Goffman states that there is no limit to the number of rekeyings in an activity, since multiple changes in context are possible (1974:80).

Multiple transformations result in a frame with different layers. The innermost layers are those where the dramatic (transformed) activity is at play. The outermost layer is the "rim of the frame" and identifies the sort of status the activity has in the real world. The adding of layers corresponds to a series of laminations that may progressively distance the core of the frame from the rim.

These distinctions are important to the analysis of the two psychiatric interviews, where different frames are at play. The shifts that take place may put the transformed activity closer to or further away from the rim of the frame. In the admitting interview, for instance, Dona Jurema sometimes requests permission to leave, and thereby terminate the encounter. Here a rekeying (or reframing) takes place. The patient's action brings the encounter closer to the rim of the interview frame (or real-world activities), where doctors propose closings to medical encounters (and patients agree) or patients request permission to close medical encounters (and doctors acquiesce). In another situation, Jurema's activities seem to be further removed from the outer rim of the frame; in these moments Dona Jurema engages in chanting and singing, addressing relatives who are not really present.

A *fabrication* is another type of transformation, where the fabricators make an intentional effort to manage activity so as to elicit a false belief (Goffman 1974:83). For the fabricators, the rim of the frame is a construction; for the "victims," what is being fabricated is what is "really" going on. While keying requires all the participants to have the same view about what is going on, a fabrication requires participants to have different views (1974:84).

Goffman distinguishes different types of fabrications: benign fabrications, exploitive fabrications, and deceptions and illusions. Concerning this last category, he says that "the individual may actively work against his own capacity for effective framing, setting himself against his own ability to realistically orient himself in the world" (1974:112). Specifically, he discusses *psychotic fabrications*, which are a form of self-delusion or self-deception, "here the individual presumably deludes himself . . . within the world sustained by other persons. Indeed, . . . he can convince others of his beliefs, at least temporarily" (1974:114). Thus, in psychotic fabrications, what seems to happen are "atypical framing practices" that, once adopted, "generate a continuous array of insane behavior" (1974:246).

"Frames," "keyings," "fabrications," "laminations," among other concepts, constitute a "framework of frameworks." We refer to these organizational principles to address the question "What is it that's going on here?" In the admitting interview, we will see that framed activities take on different statuses, ranging from real-world activities that match our expectations about medical interviews to fabricated activities that introduce a gamut of atypical framings. Framings that include micro frame embeddings (or laminations) are particularly interesting. They engender a variety of contexts that are consistent with the major framing of the psychotic crisis. Goffman's notion of frame lamination operates in much the same way as Bateson's psychological frames, where some situational contexts are brought to the foreground while others are inhibited (and become background). Distinguishing framings (as keyings) from (psychotic) fabrications provides meaningful information about the nature of reframings in the admitting interview. It also illustrates how typical and atypical framings operate in Dona Jurema's discourse and how transient they are.

Framing: An Interactive and Discourse Notion

There is no out-of-frame discourse. Participants in a social encounter are continuously reframing talk and thereby changing the ongoing interaction. To address specifically the issue of framing in conversation, Goffman (1981a) extends this notion to include participants' alignments vis-à-vis one another, which he calls *footings*. He says that during a conversation, participants are constantly engaged in shifting the frame of talk; that is, speakers change their alignment or footing vis-à-vis one another: "A change of footing implies a change in the alignment we take up to ourselves and the others present as expressed in the way we manage the production or reception of an utterance" (1981a:128).

These shifts may be closely related to *code-switching*, a phenomenon frequently investigated by sociolinguists.[4] In this case, however, the shifts may not include a code switch at all. Rather, these are changes of the participant's alignment, set, stance, or posture, frequently signaled through linguistic or paralinguistic cues. They vary from significant changes to the most subtle shifts in tone (1981a:128). In any case, a qualitative change in context triggers new interpretations about that discourse and/or interaction. This being the case, a reframing may alter only slightly the activity; however, it completely changes the participant's perception of the event (or what they would say was going on).

Tannen (1984, 1985, 1986) introduces the concept of *interactive frames* in discourse analysis to address an issue raised by Goffman (1981a:128): to look at language use in interaction and study the persistent changes in our frame for events. The notion of interactive frames shows that, in discourse, "activities which appear the same on the surface can have very different meanings and consequences for the participants if they are understood as associated with different frames" (Tannen 1985:318). Participants are constantly reframing their talk, and the process of reframing operates at various levels of conversation. It is precisely this work that makes conversation a complex activity. On one hand, there are different demands associated with the different frames (1985:319); on the other hand, most frames go unnoticed, since framing "can be done only indirectly, through metamessages" (Tannen 1986:83). Whenever someone names a frame, this very act brings about another frame. In a medical interview, for example, if the doctor turns to the patient and says "O.K., let's start this interview," she is no longer signaling an interview but, rather, attempting to reenter the interview frame.

Tannen (1986) states that footing identifies the relationship between speakers.[5] It conveys a metamessage about what kind of relationship is being enacted at that point in the interaction. Thus, in a standard psychiatric interview (as in the discharge interview), the footing between participants may shift from a more personal conversation (a "woman-to-woman talk") to a formal interaction in a professional stance. In each case a different metamessage is conveyed. These shifts in alignments indicate a contextual transformation. They also signal the amount of work involved in sustaining and shifting frames. The analysis of discourse must take into consideration this constant flux of context.

Frames and Schemas

Interactive frames can be distinguished from *knowledge schemas* (Tannen 1985)—"expectations based on prior experience about objects, events, and settings" (1985:315). A *knowledge schema* concerns stored, prior, or shared knowledge, and it relates to one's individual and prior experiences in the world.

Tannen (1979) points out that the notion of *schema* has been used largely in cognitive psychology (Bartlett 1932; Rumelhart 1975, among others) and in artificial intelligence (Winograd 1972; Minsky 1975;

Charniak 1975; Schank and Abelson 1977, among others). It is a cognitive notion that provides a metaphor for thinking about discourse understanding as "a process of fitting what one is told into the framework established by what one already knows (Charniak 1979, as quoted by Brown and Yule 1983:239). This mapping reflects a procedure of organizing a knowledge domain, of seeking regularities in repeated experiences (Mandler 1979).

A knowledge schema is another powerful principle for analyzing discourse and for understanding what people do in face-to-face interaction (Tannen and Wallat 1987). In a medical encounter, for example, the doctor and the patient may bring different schemas regarding the issues under discussion. Though both agree with the definition of the larger event (i.e., a medical interview), they may have different expectations about what is to be accomplished and mostly about what needs to be said. When this occurs and conflicting schemas result, Tannen and Wallat say that participants often have the feeling of frustration, of talking at cross-purposes (1987:213).

Frames and schemas interact as speakers are constantly forming, revising, and applying expectations about people, objects, and situations, including the signaling and interpreting of frames (Tannen 1985:316). Tannen and Wallat (1987) provide an example of how frames and schemas interact in a pediatric interview/examination. They describe how the doctor balances different frames when examining a child in the mother's presence and state that "an understanding of frames accounts for the exceedingly complex, indeed burdensome nature of the pediatrician's task" (1987:215). A mismatch in the pediatrician's and mother's schemas often accounts for the mother's discomfort and frequent questions, they add, requiring the doctor to interrupt an examination frame and shift to a consultation frame.

Contextualization Cues

Since frames are hardly ever explicitly stated, participants use a variety of more subtle cues to signal them. Gumperz (1977, 1982) calls these features *contextualization cues*. They may be paralinguistic and prosodic features of speech (Gumperz 1977, 1982), or they may be nonverbal cues (Scheflen 1973; Kendon 1979, 1981). Among the nonverbal cues, postural configurations appear to play a central role as embodiments of frames (Erickson and Shultz 1977:6). Streek says that "participants in face-to-face interaction assemble configurations and sustain them to frame phases of their joint activities. Changes in the activity, in topics of talk, or in the distribution of speaking and listening rights are commonly marked by major reorientations in each participant's posture" (1984:117).

A major point must be made regarding contextualization cues. These cues not only signal changes in contexts but also constitute these very contexts (Schiffrin [1988] 1989:260). We will see in the analysis of the two interviews that these verbal and nonverbal devices make up the building blocks of interactional frames. As such, contextualization cues are at the core of a discourse theory that derives its basic postulates from interaction (Gumperz 1982:29).

Framing and Coherence in Discourse

There are several approaches to the study of coherence in discourse. One can talk about coherence in terms of our cultural assumptions about what a text is and how it can be said to be meaningful (Becker 1979:216); in terms of participants sharing stylistic strategies (Tannen 1984:152); in terms of the concepts of connectivity and register that define a text (Halliday and Hasan 1976:23); in terms of local coherence, that is, coherence between adjacent units in discourse (Schiffrin 1985, 1987a); in terms of the communicative function of utterances and their relationship to actions (Labov 1972; Labov and Fanshel 1977); or in terms of the features that typify spoken and written discourse (Tannen 1984). Another way of analyzing discourse coherence is to situate the context where the discourse takes place: "To comprehend any utterance, a listener (and a speaker) must know within which frame it is intended" (Tannen 1985:314).

Coherence is problematic for a speaker undergoing a psychotic crisis; however, the notion of frame provides a natural criterion for establishing "chunks" of coherent discourse. In the admitting interview the patient's contributions, for the most part, do not make sense. She rarely addresses the doctor's questions, shifts idiosyncratically from one topic to another, and engages in noninteractional activities such as singing and chanting. However, the discourse analyst can isolate several contexts of communication that make sense by themselves. For example, within the context of the psychiatric interview at least two frames stand out. First, the patient acknowledges the presence and function of the doctor. Within this asymmetrical relationship, the patient acts out a "patient's schema." She uses language to complain, to request permission to leave, to request opinions, and to request attention from the doctor. At another point the patient reverses the asymmetry in the power relationship and reframes the situation as an elderly patient addressing a younger doctor. In this context she challenges the doctor as an interviewer ("Aren't you going to ask me anything?" or "What are you going to ask?"), by raising questions about her treatment and her health ("What do *you* know?"), by initiating leave-taking ("I must be going"), and so on.

Frame analysis provides a way of segmenting discourse. It displays an array of the metacommunicative properties of discourse: how participants engaged in talk and interaction express their relationship to their utterances, to other participants, and to themselves. In this study the analysis will demonstrate that within each interactive frame the patient's discourse can be functional and communicative, displaying a coherence of its own.

Topic Coherence: Being Attuned to the Message

Another way to address the issue of coherence in discourse is to look at *topics* and how participants in face-to-face interaction build a unified on-topic discourse. Following Goffman, any encounter presupposes a basic understanding among participants regarding when and where to initiate talk, among whom, and by means of what topics ([1967] 1982:34). Additionally, participants must share rules for topic development and topic shift. "A single focus of thought and visual attention, and a single flow of talk, tends to be maintained and to be legitimated as officially representative of the encounter" ([1967] 1982:34). This understanding corroborates participants' sense of coherence. It matches our knowledge schemas on how to conduct the business at hand. In psychotic discourse, however, some of these expectations are not met.

Psychotic talk often presents a "loss of goal directedness" (Bleuler [1911] 1950). The speaker ceases to contribute to the sequential (or cyclic) development of topics, thus thwarting topic continuity. Moreover, referents may be introduced with no meaningful relationship to each other. Often, the speaker gets farther and farther off the track. Word associations tend to be governed by rhythmic relationships (sound play) rather than by semantic and pragmatic ties.

Topic provides a natural criterion for distinguishing instances of a speaker's deviant discourse from a discourse that matches our expectations about coherence. The complex step-by-step process of topic introduction and topic development reveals the amount of effort that participants must undertake in interaction to assure topic continuity. This very process is crucial to one's feelings of reciprocal ratification in face-to-face interaction. In Goffman's words, "The persons so ratified are in what might be called a *state of talk*" ([1967] 1982:34). When topic continuity breaks down and speakers cease to ratify one another, participants often have the feeling of being alienated from the interaction. At this point, divergent knowledge schemas may trigger different expectations about what needs to be said. There arises a sense of strangeness, of being in different worlds.

Knowledge Schemas and Topics

Becker (1982a:127) points out that in using language, people are "remembering and evoking prior texts and referring to the world" at the same time. In evoking prior texts, speakers recycle background knowledge, which participants in an interaction may or may not share. When this knowledge is shared, scholars often refer to it as sharing a presuppositional pool (Venneman 1975), intersubjective knowledge (Keenan and Schieffelin 1976), or expectations about stored, prior, or shared knowledge (Tannen and Wallat 1987). Schiffrin points out that the concept of topic may help us "understand the role of shared knowledge in discourse," in spite of its inherent difficulties (1987b:12). This is particularly significant in instances of pathological discourse where social norms and linguistic rules are in many ways violated.

In Dona Jurema's admitting interview, we will see that discrepant knowledge schemas on the part of the doctor and patient result in reciprocal distancing. In each case the speaker's topic selection follows divergent expectations regarding "what this talk needs to be about." While the doctor proposes talk exclusively as "interview talk," the patient proposes talk as a "family encounter." She projects an addressee (e.g., the mother), while the doctor remains mostly as an unratified participant (Goffman [1967] 1982:34]. In this context the patient introduces personal topics that belong to prior family schemas. Frequently, the referents lack specificity (i.e., they are mostly encoded by pronouns that presuppose a high degree of topic accessibility [Givón 1983]).

Differing topic agendas brought about by the doctor or the patient indicate a substantial hiatus in background knowledge. In each case we hear a separate (individual) discourse, where both participants equally distance themselves from the interaction. There seem to be no listeners

In Dona Jurema's discharge interview, background knowledge is shared. It orients topic selection by promoting certain topics and inhibiting others. Above all, it exclusively assigns to the doctor control over content: She is the one who proposes new topics and introduces topic transitions. Thus, talk focuses on the development of "official topics." The patient's role is confined to addressing the doctor's topics. A joint discourse results, where speaker's and listener's roles alternate following strict social and institutional norms.

A Topic Analysis

The following discussion reviews concepts that will be developed in the topic analysis of both interviews. When speakers remember and evoke prior texts and refer to the world, discourse topics emerge. These may be "labels" or "titles"; they may be "participants" (subjects or agents); they may be encoded in the discourse as noun phrases or propositions. They carry "old" or "given" information: information that has been previously introduced in the discourse. Topics, therefore, convey the sort of information that integrates speakers' knowledge schemas.

Five approaches to topic analysis are reviewed here as they relate to the concept of prior and shared knowledge. First, there is Venneman's notion of topic as a label based on a pragmatic-semantic model of language (1975:317); second, there is topic as given information, derived from a functional sentence perspective (Bates and MacWhinney 1982); third is Givón's notion of topic continuity, based on a functional discourse analysis (1983); fourth, there is the concept of topic as a proposition addressing the "question of immediate concern" (Keenan and Schieffelin 1976); and finally there is Schiffrin's discussion of topic from a sociolinguistic perspective (1987b).

Topic as a "Title"

Venneman defines the topic of discourse as "a discourse subject on which the attention of the participants of the discourse is concentrated. Such concentration of attention is usually, though not always, brought about by an immediately preceding textual mentioning of the discourse subject" (1975:317). Venneman uses the expression *discourse subject* to mean the referent of a given discourse, mostly grounded in real-life experiences— "some individual phenomenon, such as a physical object, a set of physical objects, a process, or an event, that is uniquely determined relative to a discourse" (1975:315).

These topics are "message-centered," encoded by a noun phrase, as pointed out by Schiffrin (1987b). They are a very small part of the message. Semantically, they are mostly agents, and syntactically, they are often subjects. Frequently, they appear in clause-initial position.

Essential to Venneman's definition is the concept of a "presuppositional pool" constituted from the speaker's general knowledge, the situative context of the discourse and the previous discourse. Each speaker has her own presuppositional pool that develops as the discourse unfolds, and each speaker also behaves as if her own presuppositional pool were common to all participants. This pool can be characterized as "the set of all assumptions relevant to the discourse which [she] believes are shared by all the participants" (1975:314). This seems to be the underlying principle that accounts for the assumption of coherence that people bring to the interpretation of linguistic messages in a given situation.

New and Given Information

Various studies in topic analysis take a functional sentence perspective (Vachek 1966; Chafe 1976; Li and Thompson 1976; Pontes 1981; Bates and MacWhinney 1982, among others). For these scholars, topics are propositions encoded at the clause or sentence level. Sentences (or utterances) are analyzed from the viewpoint of the information conveyed. Thus, every sentence has two parts: a *topic* and a *comment,* or a *theme* and a *rheme.* This distinction is based on a notion of "communicative dynamism," where topic or theme receives the lowest communicative force (because it is encoded as "old" information), while comment or rheme has the highest communicative force (because it is encoded as "new" information). Vachek (1966) provides the following description:

> The *theme* is that part of the utterance which refers to a fact or facts already known from the preceding context, or to facts that may be taken for granted, and thus does not, or does only minimally, contribute to the information

provided by the given sentence-utterance. The other part, now usually called the *rheme,* contains the actual new information to be conveyed by the sentence-utterance and thus substantially enriches the knowledge of the listener or reader.

Thus topics are typically viewed as "given" or "old" information (Bates and MacWhinney 1982:180): "Topic selection is strongly associated with the givenness or oldness of information in a particular conversation," though they are not to be defined as such. Topics are also viewed as background information. All of this refers to information that is shared by both speaker and hearer.

The study of topic as old information has gained different perspectives from studies in discourse cohesion, topic prominence versus subject prominence, and topic-comment structures. However, as Bates and MacWhinney point out, the topic-comment system involves "elusive internal states, the speaker's ideas about how to structure discourse, 'stage' utterances, foreground and background information" (1982:198). To this point, Bates and MacWhinney convey a word of caution to linguists who must deal with "psychological structures and mental states that are not well understood even by the psychologists" (1982:199). Nevertheless, certain discourse genres, such as interviews and narratives, seem to favor the occurrence of such structures. They work to indicate that new information is being introduced and that old information has been attended to. As we will see in the analysis of the interviews, these structures also work to organize and shape the two most salient parts of an interview: the interview opening and its closing.

Topic Accessibility

The third concept is Givón's topic accessibility in discourse (Givón 1983), which is related to degrees of backgroundiness and predictability. Again, topic as shared knowledge is conflated with topic as background information (Schiffrin 1987b:10).

In measuring the degree of topic accessibility, Givón says that any speaker has available a certain number of strategies to maintain (or not) the continuity of a given topic noun phrase in the discourse. In Brazilian Portuguese, for instance, a speaker may use different linguistic forms when contributing to topic continuity. Both zero pronoun and full pronouns seem to alternate in written and spoken language.

Givón presents topic accessibility as a scalar phenomenon, where some of the possibilities are the following:

(1) (0) is forty-two years old
(2) He is forty-two years old
(3) **He** is forty-two years old
(4) He is forty-two years old, Francis/my son (is)
(5) Francis/my son is forty-two years old
(6) Francis/my son, he is forty-two years old

The Portuguese equivalent is as follows:

(1) (0) tem quarenta e dois anos
(2) Ele tem quarenta e dois anos
(3) **Ele** tem quarenta e dois anos
(4) Ele tem quarenta e dois anos, Francisco/meu filho (tem)
(5) Francisco/meu filho tem quarenta e dois anos
(6) Francisco/meu filho, ele tem quarenta e dois anos

Option (1) would indicate that the speaker chooses the most continuous topic utterance (and the highest degree of topic accessibility). That is, in answering the doctor's question: "How old is your son?" the patient may respond in Brazilian Portuguese with zero anaphora ("is forty-two years old"/*tem quarenta e dois anos*), indicating that the referent is the same in a closely knit discourse (as in an adjacency pair of the type question/ answer). Option (6) would indicate the least predictable response (and the least degree of topic accessibility). Thus, to render the topic accessible, utterance (6) presents a high degree of redundancy (a left-dislocated definite noun phrase "Francis" or "my son" plus the introduction of an unstressed co-referential pronoun "he"). Option (6) would not be a probable answer to the doctor's question "how old is your son?" Such option could be explained by the extralinguistic context (distance between the doctor and the patient, background noise, impairments related to speaker's production or hearer's interpretation) or the previous discourse context (a response to a new topic, recently introduced by the doctor). The principle underlying Givón's topic accessibility scale is quite simple: "The more disruptive, surprising, discontinuous or hard to process a topic is, the more coding material must be assigned to it" (1983:17).

Topic continuity and topic accessibility in discourse are particularly interesting in Dona Jurema's discharge interview, where the patient and doctor's discourse satisfies our expectations for doctor-patient interaction. It provides a framework for identifying the ongoing topic and speakers' expansions, which successively result in topic transition and topic change.

Topic as a Proposition

The fourth concept in topic analysis is Keenan and Schieffelin's notion of discourse topic as a proposition that addresses "the question of immediate concern" (1976). In their analysis, as in others (e.g., Atkinson 1979; Scollon 1979; Maynard and Zimmerman 1984; Button and Casey 1984), the process of establishing referents is a *prerequisite* for a successful talk exchange on a discourse topic (1976:338). The model adopted is a dynamic one that proceeds with alternative steps until a discourse topic has been either dropped or jointly constructed by both participants.

In this interactional model, the notions of "topic" and "point" may be used as equivalents. Keenan and Schieffelin propose that a topic analysis requires an explicit assessment of each utterance in terms of its purpose or reason: Why did the speaker say what he did? (1976:343).

The notions of "topic" and "point" may also be viewed as embedded within one another. Brown and Yule state that in an ongoing conversation, speakers often judge differently "what is being talked about." However, people "report regularly on what a conversation was about" (1983:73). Apparently, this has to do with the fact that during a conversation participants are constantly monitoring at least two things at the same time: "*What* is the talk about?" and "*Why* that now and to me?" The former addresses the "topic" and the latter the "point." The former addresses the linguistic message and works on the semantic-referential level, while the latter addresses the discourse metaquestion and operates on the pragmatic-interactional level. A participant, in a given piece of conversation, may well know "what's being talked about," as she may understand the referential meaning of an utterance; however, the same participant may not be able to see "why" this talk is taking place at all (Brown and Yule 1983:92). A familiar example in doctor-patient interaction is the doctor's use of "known-answer questions" (where the doctor often has the information and simply wishes to evaluate the patient through her response). As in a "test" situation, the doctor may ask the patient for her date of admittance: "Do you remember the day you came to the hospital? to this hospital?" The patient understands the topic (i.e., "date of admittance"); she may fail, however, to understand the point (since the doctor already knows the answer to this question): a standardized procedure? an exercise in control? or the opening of an interview?

A related aspect of the "why question" has been discussed by Sacks (1971) when considering what speakers actually tell one another. He establishes as a general rule that "it is your business not to tell people what you can suppose they know." This concept of "newsworthiness" is related to the degree of saliency (interest) that a given topic will likely have for the listener (Coulthard [1977] 1981:75; Polanyi 1979). However, in asymmetrical relationships such as medical interviews or classroom lessons, topic selection and decisions concerning newsworthiness are most often unilateral moves (Shuy 1974; Fisher 1984; Mehan 1979; Gonçalves 1984). It is the doctor who brings a topic agenda to the interview. The adequacy of this agenda—its degree of "newsworthiness"—to trigger newsworthy reports from the patient can only be evaluated in the analysis of the interaction that takes place in the interview situation.

An Integrated Approach

Schiffrin (1987b) discusses a sociolinguistic approach to topic analysis that would integrate different types and levels of topic. Thus, a sociolinguistic analysis "can add to the analysis of topics, and by so doing, expand the range of what can be explained as a process which is both social and linguistic" (1987b:7).

Topics relate to different aspects of communication: They can be viewed as "message-centered," "code-centered," "speaker-centered," or "interaction-centered" (1987b:7). When topics are analyzed as message-centered, they are viewed in three ways as to their size and as to what part of language encodes the topic. First, topics are "entities," encoded by a noun phrase. They are a very small part of the message. Semantically, they are mostly agents, and syntactically, they are often subjects (as discussed by Venneman 1975). Frequently, they appear in clause-initial position (as discussed by Givón 1983). Second, topics are encoded at the clause or sentence level. This is the level on which topics gain the status of propositions (as discussed by Keenan and Schieffelin 1976). Here the distinction of "background information" (related to topic) versus "foreground information" (related to comment) is often used, and clause topics (background information) are said to precede clause comments (foreground information) (as discussed by Bates and MacWhinney 1982). Third, topics are viewed as "macropropositions" or "themes." This is an overall framework where topics are *reflected* in the text, in its cohesive devices. Though themes may not always be explicitly encoded in the text, the entire discourse would be "about" the underlying theme (1987b:9). Schiffrin points out that these three definitions are difficult to unify, as each one focuses on a different level of the message (i.e., the noun phrase, the proposition, the text). Yet all three have something in common: It is the message that defines the topic (1987b:9).

A different perspective on topics focuses on communication instead of on the message per se. While in a conversation, participants have an intuitive notion of "what I think we're talking about" (Brown and Yule 1983:93) and enter negotiation to reestablish the topic whenever they feel that "what I think *you*'re talking about" differs from "what I think *we*'re talking about" (1983:93). Brown and Yule distinguish between "speaker's topic" and "conversational topic." The former refers to the "point," to the metamessage "why I am telling you this"; the latter refers to the interaction. It indicates that topics are not only subjective (i.e., "speaker-centered") but also "intersubjective" (i.e., "interaction-centered"), as pointed out by Keenan and Schieffelin (1976).

The preceding discussion indicates the degree of complexity involved in a topic analysis. Schiffrin argues that the analysis becomes even more complex because of the relation between topics and shared knowledge. Shared knowledge is difficult to define (Schiffrin 1987b:10): First, it derives from a great number of sources (personal knowledge, cultural knowledge, social knowledge, knowledge about prior text, etc.); second, the concept lacks objectivity, and leaves the decision to the speaker; third, the relation between knowledge and language is reflexive and dynamic, and therefore participants must constantly change their assumptions about each other's knowledge; fourth, in linguistic studies, different categorizations stress different aspects of the process by which the speaker and hearer come to assume shared knowledge. Schiffrin argues for an integrated view of topic to account for topic as encoded in the message, in the code, in the speaker's intentions, in the interaction. "Topic is an important concept that can help us relate different aspects of communication to one another and help us understand the role of shared knowledge in discourse" (1987b:12).

Conversational versus Institutional Topics

As already discussed, the notion of topic in discourse, and specifically in conversation, is an elusive one (c.g., Sacks 1971; Schegloff 1972a; Shuy 1981; Brown and Yule 1983; Tannen 1984; Jefferson 1984; Schiffrin 1987b). There are no straightforward definitions of the term *topic* or clear-cut ways of identifying a topic. Shuy states that "the dynamic, functional nature of a topic makes it difficult to categorize topics neatly, or to find fixed boundaries" (1981:69). Tannen says that "trying to identify instances of that phenomenon in actual interaction yields more equivocal than clear cases" (1984:41), and that it is equally difficult to identify who raised a particular topic. The pretheoretical notion of topic is "the most frequently used, unexplained term in the analysis of discourse" (Brown and Yule 1983:70). Essential to the study of coherence, but difficult to pin down, topics seem to "drift imperceptibly" in successful conversations (Sacks 1971, as cited in Coulthard [1977] 1981:77). The difficulties are twofold: They are content-related and dependent on the degree of explicitness of the topic; and they are form-related and dependent on the amount and combination of cues that constitute topic boundary markers (Brown and Yule 1983).

As Fisher points out, however, in the institutional context of a doctor-patient interview, practical concerns on the part of the doctor and the patient orient the selection of topics (1984:212). It is understood that the interviewer (doctor) requests information from the interviewee (patient). In so doing, the doctor introduces and shifts topics (e.g., Fisher 1984; Frankel 1984). The doctor, therefore, controls the sequential organization of the interview and brings to the interaction a set of "necessary topics" (Fisher 1984) to be discussed. These necessary topics include talk about "the patient's history and future plans, about her life, about her well-being" (1984:213). As a consequence, it is fairly simple to identify topics in the medical interview because the doctor follows a standard agenda; furthermore, it is usually the same participant, the doctor, who initiates topics.

Analyzing Talk in Interviews

The first part of this chapter dealt with two principles in discourse organization: frame and topic. The remaining sections will discuss talk in interviews. Particular issues in the analysis of everyday conversation will be raised as they relate to the analysis of institutional discourse, specifically to medical interviews. Issues of power in discourse as well as deviance will be examined. Finally, a few points will be made on the contributions of a detailed microanalysis to societal macro studies.

Institutional Discourse and Conversational Behavior

The study of medical (psychiatric) interviews brings to discussion issues related to discourse genre. Shuy (1974) and Fisher (1984), among others, compare the structure of doctor-patient communication with the structure of everyday conversation. While these events share features in common, discourse in institutional contexts differs essentially from discourse in everyday life. As Fisher describes it: "Medical interviews, like classroom lessons, are social events—structured in predictable ways, organized toward specific ends, and jointly accomplished in the spoken interactions of participants within the organizational constraints of particular settings" (1984:202).[6]

Differences and similarities in ordinary everyday conversation as they relate to medical interviews will be examined in chapters 4 and 5. Given the primacy of conversation in face-to-face communication, it is clear that conversation analysis lays the groundwork for the study of the two psychiatric interviews. Some basic assumptions in the field of conversation will be briefly reviewed in the following discussion.

Conversation Analysis

Conversation prevails in most face-to-face encounters, where one shares with other participants a world and a reality. The encounter has principles of organization, as Goffman points out: "We must . . . see that a conversation has a life of its own and makes demands on its own behalf. It is a little social system with its own boundary-maintaining tendencies; it is a little patch of commitment and loyalty with its own heroes and its own villains" ([1967] 1982:113).

Interest in face-to-face communication has pointed the way to the study of conversation as a way of understanding essential processes in language use (Levinson 1983). Other types of discourse may be described "in terms of their deviation from such a base" (Fillmore 1981:165). Conversation is viewed as the prototypical kind of language usage and the matrix for language acquisition (Fillmore 1974; Bates and MacWhinney 1979; 1982; Ochs and Schieffelin 1979; Levinson 1983; Tannen 1984), and it is often equated to or subsumed under discourse analysis (Coulthard [1977] 1981; Gumperz 1982; Levinson 1983; Tannen 1984; Fasold 1990).[7]

Research in conversation encompass a substantial number of studies that have branched out into two major fields (Fasold 1990:65): *ethnomethodological conversation analysis,* as practiced by Sacks and his collaborators (Garfinkel [1972] 1986; Sacks 1972b; Schegloff 1972b; Sacks,

Schegloff, and Jefferson 1974; Maynard 1980, and others); and *sociolinguistic (interpretive) conversation analysis,* as practiced by Labov and Fanshel 1977; Gumperz 1982, 1984; Erickson 1982; Tannen 1984, 1986, 1989; Schiffrin 1984, 1987a; Almeida 1987; Hoyle 1988; Grimshaw 1990b, among others. The two fields share basic theoretical and methodological assumptions, such as the interest in microanalysis of extensive segments of actual spoken discourse, inductive research methodology, rigorous and interpretive transcription, emphasis on speakers' inferential processes and their choice between alternative utterances, primacy to listeners' interpretation and understanding of speaker's utterances.[8]

Referring to one of Sacks's key contributions to conversation analysis, Gumperz states that the listener's and speaker's interpretations "take the form of preferences rather than obligatory rules"; in conversation there are "many possible alternative interpretations, many more than exist at the level of sentence grammar" (Gumperz 1982:159). There are certain constraints on choice, however, which have to do with speaker's intentions and expectations about hearer's reactions and assumptions. Gumperz tells us that "once a particular interpretation has been chosen and accepted it must be followed" (1982:159). A specific interpretive strategy will work until participants signal the need to change strategies. Thus, interpretations are to be "negotiated, repaired and altered through interactive processes rather than unilaterally conveyed" (Gumperz 1982:160).

An essential tenet in both traditions proposes that the linkage between language use and particular social activities is to be extracted from the conversational practices of speakers themselves. It is to be arrived at and not to be imposed a priori (prespecified categorizations) by the analyst (Goffman [1967] 1982, 1974; West and Zimmerman 1982; Gumperz 1982, 1986). Also, both speaking and listening are viewed as intertwined activities: First, the very act of speaking entails projecting the act of listening, which in turn is not a passive skill (Tannen 1989:12); and second, an act of speaking "is directed to and must be ratified by an audience" (Duranti 1986:243).

These two research traditions differ, however, in the following concerns. Ethnomethodological conversation analysis aims at discovering "the systematic properties of the sequential organization of talk, and the ways in which utterances are designed to manage such sequences" (Levinson 1983:287).[9] Some of the key words in this field are *membership, organization, orderliness, systematic properties,* and *sequences.* Research is sociological in nature. Its major interest lies in achieving a "naturalistic observational discipline" so as to deal with social interaction in a rigorous, empirical, and formal way (Schegloff and Sacks 1973:233). Ethnomethodological conversation analysis has successfully demonstrated that all kinds of casual talk are rule-governed. Research has focused on how participants accomplish particular conversational tasks, such as openings and closings (and (pre)preopenings and (pre)preclosings), turn taking, semantic pair sequences called *adjacency pairs* (e.g., greeting/greeting, summons/response), insertion (or side) sequences, repair mechanisms (such as false starts, repetition, or recycling information), and "bits" of talk such as "continuers." These studies indicate that there are specific rules that regulate everyday talk and allow for the predictability of social behavior in conversation. The nature of such rules allows for variation. The system is locally managed; that is, it is operated on a turn-by-turn basis where turn size and turn order vary. It is also interactionally managed since it fosters an interactive construction of the turn. Sacks, Schegloff, and Jefferson point out that "any party's contribution to turn order determination is contingent on, and oriented to, the contributions of other parties" (1978:42).

Sociolinguistic conversation analysis—a field also known as interactional sociolinguistics—proposes a "comprehensive theory of conversational inference" (Gumperz 1982:161). Its basic concern is a semantic one (Tannen 1984:7). It seeks to describe the linguistic bases of conversational cooperation by focusing on participants' sharing of contextualization strategies (Gumperz 1982:160) or conversational styles (Tannen 1984; 1989:11). Data gathering and data analysis typically follow an anthropological and linguistic perspective.[10]

The primary concern of sociolinguistic conversation analysis is a description of participants' communicative and interpretive strategies in interaction. This has been discussed at length elsewhere (see pp. 54–58). Research in this field aims at "specifying the linguistic and socio-cultural knowledge that needs to be shared if conversational involvement is to be maintained" (Gumperz 1982:3).

The notion of involvement is crucial to Gumperz's and Tannen's discussion of spoken discourse. Gumperz believes that "understanding presupposes conversational involvement" (1982:2): participants' ability "to attract and sustain others' attention" (1982:4). When participants share familiar strategies in discourse, Tannen says that a sense of coherence and involvement results (1989:13). Tannen's sense of conversational involvement encompasses Gumperz's but also includes "an internal, even emotional connection individuals feel which binds them to other people as well as to places, things, activities, ideas, memories, and words" (1989:12).[11]

When participants are engaged in talk, they may display more or less involvement in what they are saying or in the relationship they establish with one another. In Dona Jurema's discharge interview, at certain points the doctor and the patient share a strong sense of involvement. This feeling of being "connected" produces a more conversational discourse (i.e., there are shorter pauses between turns, the pace accelerates, turns may latch or even overlap, topics are introduced by both participants). In chapter 4 we will see how involvement is displayed in the patient's and doctor's discourse and interaction. At certain moments it seems to blur the considerable difference that otherwise prevails between the doctor and the patient.

This discussion lays the foundation for the analysis of the two interviews that are the object of this book. Ethnomethodological conversation analysis provides a theoretical framework for looking at how interaction is locally managed and organized (i.e., how turns are accomplished, questions are answered, listenership is signaled); sociolinguistic conversation analysis provides a way of interpreting "what participants are doing while they speak to one another." Crucial to my analysis, this research tradition provides a way of establishing the context of talk, what Goffman calls "our frame for events" (1981a:128).

Institutional Discourse: Medical Interviews

Medical (and psychiatric) interviews are a form of discourse that Mishler calls "meaningful talk": "It is not 'mere' talk, but the work that doctor and patient do together as an essential and critical component of clinical practice" (1984:8).

In doctor-patient face-to-face communication, certain framings—institutional ones—prevail over others. As pointed out by Mishler, talk that derives from medical concerns overshadows a more personal talk. In the psychiatric interview, for instance, participants display mostly their official roles of doctor and patient. They are viewed as "social agents, located in a network of social relations, in specific places in a social structure" (Kress [1985] 1989:5). As social agents, doctor and patient exhibit their official social attributes, which mirror and personify the institution.

Goffman (1961), Laing ([1967] 1974), and Foucault ([1975, 1977] 1987) discuss the workings of "total institutions" such as jails, penitentiaries, concentration camps, as well as mental institutions. There are common features among total institutions, one of them being that activities strictly follow a preestablished routine, "imposed from above by a system of explicit formal rulings, and enforced by "a body of officials" (Goffman 1961:6). Thus, the psychiatric institution, as a medical institution, has an articulated social behavior, a set of cultural values and forms of discourse (Foucault [1975, 1977] 1987; Laing [1967] 1974). Turning specifically to discourse, we will see that the institutional meanings are linguistically and interactionally revealed in the institutional framings of the psychiatric interviews. These contexts correspond to what Mishler calls "the voice of medicine" in doctor-patient encounters (1984:63), which displays a " 'technical' interest and expresses a 'scientific attitude' " (1984:104).

Patients, however, often propose a departure from the institutional contexts (Mishler 1984:107). They attempt to interrupt the voice of medicine by bringing up salient topics from their world of experience

(Mishler 1984:118). Doctors seldom accept (or realize) this shift. Mishler indicates that, more often than not, doctors interrupt patients' talk, ignoring information that may otherwise have been important (1984:120). The ensuing conflict is often the result of mismatched expectations on what needs to be talked about and how talk is to be constructed: "Discourse is revealed as a dialectic between the voices of the lifeworld [mostly done by patients] and of medicine [mostly done by doctors]; it involves conflict and struggle between two different domains of meaning" (Mishler 1984:121).

This discussion portrays a difference in the doctor's and the patient's knowledge schemas concerning events (such as a medical encounter or a psychiatric interview) in institutional settings. Indeed, it reveals a mismatch in expectations regarding participants' roles, ways to interact, topics, and topic management, among other things. This mismatch often accounts for the participants' discomfort in the medical interview. As Tannen and Wallat (1987) point out, differences in knowledge schemas place an extra burden on the interaction and certainly explain some of the frustrations that frequently characterize this type of encounter.

Power and Framings

Power relations in doctor-patient communication, an important part of institutional discourse analysis, have been the focus of a considerable number of studies. Power has been described in the sequential organization of medical discourse (West 1983; Frankel 1984; Fisher 1984); in topic control (Paget 1983; Frankel 1983, 1984; Fisher 1984); in the management of talk and interruption of patients' accounts (Fisher 1983, 1984; Mishler 1984); and in patients' and doctors' belief systems (Cicourel 1983; Frankel 1984; Mehan 1990; Mishler 1984; Tannen and Wallat 1987). These studies show that difference and role asymmetry characterize the doctor-patient relationship.

The inquiry on power relations closely follows an inquiry on context, particularly the ever-changing alignments between doctors and patients in the frames that come to play in an interview situation. Which framings trigger a more asymmetrical relationship? How is this relationship conveyed through discourse? Under which framings do participants work together to establish a more symmetrical relationship? How does discourse indicate this somewhat more balanced cooperation?

Two major framings emerge in the psychiatric interviews: the *institutional frames* (mostly proposed by the doctor) and the *personal frames* (mostly proposed by the patient). Both doctor and patient shift in and out of these framings. While participants may build talk in either of these contexts, each context has different sequential rules, different constraints on what talk should be about, and different underlying assumptions as to who controls the ongoing activity. The contextual transformations that take place follow the patterns described by Goffman (1974:41; 1981a:128).

The institutional framings of the psychiatric interview are by their very structure asymmetrical, as role distribution indicates. This asymmetry can be seen in the sequential constraints of the interview procedure, which may involve a type of *"sequential deference"* (Frankel 1984:165). Frankel says that by asking a question, doctors "impose the obligation of a response" (1984:165). This places a constraint on the patient's next move. Moreover, it also places the responder on a secondary role, "since responses always occur second and are limited in their appropriateness by the actions which preceded them" (1984:165).

This difference in role relations is also captured by the use of address form. In medical encounters in Brazil, participants use the reciprocal ceremonious address form (equivalent to the French V-form)—the *senhora* form—which makes participants "equal and not solidary" (Brown and Gilman [1972] 1979:259). However, the social asymmetry of the medical encounter works against this equality. In the institutional framings, "doctors are active while patients are more passive. Patients describe symptoms, but it is doctors who make a diagnosis and recommend treatment. Patients react. They can agree, disagree, or negotiate" (Fisher 1984:205). We see that questions and evaluations place the doctor in the active, inquirer, first role, while responses (to questions and evaluations) place the patient in the passive, respondent, second role.

Things get even more complicated. Mishler points out that doctors' contributions in the medical encounter (mostly questions) may be disruptive in at least two ways. First, doctors' questions often interrupt patients' flow of talk, that is, the patients' accounts of their problems. This kind of talk represents the patients' spontaneous information about their own lifeworld concerns. Doctors, however, tend not to consider such contributions. They interrupt patients by introducing new questions, thereby depriving them from introducing important lifeworld contexts of meaning (1984:121). Second, Mishler indicates that patients seldom confront a doctor's question. In the patients' schemas for the medical encounter (where doctors have more power than patients), doctors' requests for information are not to be challenged. Thus, patients "respond to any and all questions as legitimate and appropriate, even when they do not seem to understand their purpose" (1984:120).

A somewhat more balanced, conversational interaction is attempted in the personal framings. It is mostly the patient who proposes these framings and who strives to remain in these contexts. Shifting to personal framings introduces a more symmetrical relationship where the roles of patient and doctor remain largely in the background while a woman-to-woman relationship fleetingly emerges in the foreground. As noted in chapters 4 and 5, these shifts in frames have implications for the larger context of the interview. They alter the initial distance between the doctor and the patient. The doctor, however, shows resistance. She signals this underlying disagreement by shifting back to the institutional framings of the psychiatric interview.

Tannen (1986) discusses the power of frames. Reframings, for instance, may signal shifts in power among participants. When a frame changes, alignments of participants and ways of interaction change too. Goffman observes that an entire different reality comes into being (1974:45). The one who proposes the frame (and has it ratified) establishes how talk is to be understood in that context. It is not surprising, therefore, that often the person who controls the frame resists another participant's change in frames. Conflicting frames may thus result whenever someone resists staying in the prevailing framing or proposes some change.

One cannot call a frame into question as "they do their work off the record" (Tannen 1986:91). The indirect nature of frames adds to the complexity of power relations in spoken interaction. It also constrains one's effort to change the ongoing context as one has the natural impulse to "sail with the framing winds" (Tannen 1986:92). Nevertheless, participants shift frames as talk develops. In an asymmetrical situation such as a medical interview, these subtle contextual transformations alter the initial asymmetry. In the discharge interview, reframings mitigate the natural asymmetry that is established in the beginning of the interview.

Social Deviance

Power relations are increasingly more complex in encounters where one of the participants has the institutional power to establish and declare standard from deviant behavior (or socially approved versus socially condemned demeanor). The consequences of such evaluation may deprive the other individual of "a liberty that is regarded both as a right and as property" (Foucault [1975, 1977] 1987:11).

A person admitted to a mental institution generally suffers several losses (Goffman 1961). To perform the official role of patient, the individual has his or her rights as a person suspended. Goffman's work on asylums describes this ongoing process, in which the individual gains (sometimes forcibly) not only a new social role but actually begins a *career of patient* (Goffman 1961:14; Laing [1967] 1974:100). The end result is *role dispossession* (Goffman 1961:14), since personal roles are suspended while the individual remains in the institution. At this point the individual's self is provided by the institution. A "personal defacement" (1961:20) takes place. The institution supervises the individual, "neutralizes his dangerous state of mind" (Foucault [1975, 1977] 1987:18).

It comes, therefore, as no surprise to hear the sort of responses provided by patients in a psychiatric setting. In most cases the fabric of reality—the institutional framings—is attacked. "Realms are built up through the maintenance of [social, cultural, interactional] conventions;

[therefore] they can be attacked by declining to sustain these conventions" (Goffman 1974:246).[12]

In the admitting interview analyzed in this study, the patient refuses to participate in the institutional framings of the psychiatric interview. She refuses, therefore, to perform the role of patient. When she does ratify the official framings, she conveys explicit requests to leave or to terminate the interview (questions such as "Can I leave?" and "Can I go?" occur throughout the interview). Challenges to the doctor's competence and authority also represent a way to question the doctor's power over the patient's suspended rights as a person. Finally, complaints convey the patient's disapproval at the compliance or lack of compliance of a given act on the doctor's part (e.g., the doctor not having remarked on the patient's presence on a given day).

Psychosis, Goffman says, is an infraction of the social order ([1967] 1982:146), a type of deviance.[13] To act psychotic is, quite often, "to associate wrongly with others in one's immediate presence" ([1967] 1982:143). Such a situation can also be described as "atypical framing practices" (Goffman 1974:246).

Laing corroborates Goffman in saying that the psychotic journey inward may be perceived in different ways according to the prevailing social and cultural understanding of the event (Laing [1967] 1974: 92 93). In Western society the person labeled as psychotic (or schizophrenic) "is degraded from full existential and legal status" ([1967] 1974:100). Thus, the process of "immersion in inner space and time tends to be regarded as anti-social withdrawal, a deviancy, invalid, pathological *per se*, in some sense discreditable" ([1967] 1974:103).

Micro- and Macroanalysis

The issues of framing and power lie midway between sociolinguistic microanalysis and societal macroanalysis. Frame analysis resides in the domain of microanalysis and microsociology (Goffman 1974:13). It addresses "the organization of experience—something that an individual actor can take into his mind—and not the organization of society" (1974:13). So does most of the work undertaken by interpretive conversationalists. Researchers look closely at small-group interactions (mostly dyads) and produce meticulous transcripts. They portray what participants are doing through talk while a particular event unfolds. However, the questions that these sociologists, discourse analysts, and sociolinguists have been investigating have important implications for larger societal studies (Gumperz 1982, 1986; Erickson and Shultz 1982; Tannen 1986, 1990; Mishler 1984; Erickson and Rittenberg 1987; Mehan 1990; Grimshaw 1990a; Chenail 1991). While focusing attention on the microstructure, they also reveal its relation to institutional structures.

If this discussion is restricted to issues of deviance and resistance, for instance, extensive research in sociolinguistics and ethnography has described the behavior of those who refuse to operate within the legitimate societal-cultural frames, and, as a consequence, are perceived as deviant: native Americans (Basso [1970, 1972] 1979; Philips 1976), who are seen as too indirect; speakers who ask questions in a machine-gun conversational style (Tannen 1984), who are seen as too intrusive; resistant working-class British youth to school authority (Willis [1977] 1981), who are seen as befitting only working-class jobs; "gatekeeping encounters" in college counseling sessions, where the "counselor as the gatekeeper" has the authority to direct students away from certain career tracks (Erickson and Shultz 1982).

A microanalysis as used in the present study permits examination of issues of power as they relate to the cultural definitions of framing. Laing ([1967] 1974) points out that deviant behavior in psychiatric settings may be culturally defined. What is then regarded as legitimate behavior is often accompanied by the social and cultural support for frame definition. The institution defines the frames that are considered legitimate (it also appoints the actor with the power to declare these frames appropriate). In a mental hospital, for example, the institutional framings are proposed by doctors, nurses, working staff, and so on. Attacks on these framings would produce what may be considered deviant behavior—unexpected responses.

When one examines the relationship that binds the psychiatrist and the patient, some false assumptions spring up. For example, when a patient is committed to an institution unwillingly, the psychiatrist finds herself in a peculiar position: She must provide a type of assistance that has never been requested by the patient. Goffman observes, then, that "each party . . . is destined to seek out the other to offer what the other cannot accept, and each is destined to reject what the other offers" (1961:368). A false and unstable relationship results. This difference in expectations is often aggravated by the institution, which encourages staff and inmate to view themselves as "profoundly different human types . . . and the more profound the drama of difference between staff and inmate, the more incompatible the show becomes with the civilian repertoire of the players, and the more vulnerable to it" (1961:111).

This discussion leads us to chapter 4—the analysis of the discharge interview. This interview marks Dona Jurema's "release" from the hospital, her transition from "patient" to "person." We will see how the prevailing institutional frames proposed by the doctor provide the context against which other activities come into being. We will also see how personal reframings on the part of the patient represent a necessary contextual transformation in bringing about "a sense of self," of whom Jurema is, of the person beyond the patient.

Notes

1. Embedded activities are of a different kind. Bateson points out the paradoxical nature of the framing format, which uses a message of one logical type (Russell's logical types) to enclose a message of another type. In this respect, Bateson states that "the picture frame then, because it delimits a background, is here regarded as an external representation of a very special and important type of psychological frame—namely a frame whose function is to delimit a logical type" ([1972] 1981:189).

2. Goffman's comprehensive research in frame analysis (1974, 1981c) stands out as a major reference for sociological and sociolinguistic studies in interaction. He is concerned with close-up human interaction as it occurs in natural settings. The concepts that he develops for such a study derive from observations and descriptions.

3. Not all activities are transformations of other activities. An untransformed activity is a "primary framework"—an activity that is meaningful in its own right (Goffman 1974:21) In a primary framework, the "rim" of the frame (equivalent to its status in the real world) and the "innermost core" of the frame are the same.

4. *Code* refers to language or dialect. In a bilingual community such as Montreal, a speaker may switch codes, using either French or English at different times.

5. Bateson also points out that in metacommunicative messages "the subject of discourse is the relationship between the speakers" ([1972] 1981:178).

6. Lessons and medical interviews are structurally similar but differ in that they have different goals (Frankel 1984:157): While the classroom event aims at the "correctness" of an answer, the medical interview aims at the "completeness" of the information that is being sought. Thus, in analyzing how coherent Dona Jurema is, the doctor seeks "completeness" of information.

7. There are opposing views to this perspective (Maynard p.c.; Schiffrin [1988] 1989, among others). These researchers view conversation as a field of study in its own right, not to be subsumed under discourse analysis. Some issues (and some solutions to problems) are specific to conversation analysis (Schiffrin 1990:253). In my study, however, *discourse* refers to actual spoken discourse. I will be using the terms *discourse* and *conversation* (as well as *text* and *talk*) interchangeably.

8. Conversation analysts do not exhibit, however, a consensus on how to proceed on some of these issues. Schiffrin ([1988] 1989:254–55) discusses agreements and disagreements over data transcription and corpus for analysis.

9. *Ethnomethodology* is a compound term: *ethno* meaning members' proper (participants' own) and *methodology* referring to "the study of the collective use by members of society of systematic procedures for assembling [i.e., producing] and assessing [i.e., interpreting] social activities and events" (West and Zimmerman 1982:512).

10. Gumperz names this field of study *interactional sociolinguistics* (1982, 1986). It aggregates research from different domains: cultural and cognitive anthropology, educational linguistics, social and cognitive psychology, sociology, and linguistics. Interactional sociolinguistics represents the qualitative and interpretive branch of sociolinguistics that originated with Hymes and Gumperz in the ethnography of communications in the early sixties. At least three major re-

search traditions contribute to this field of studies: (micro)ethnography of communication, ethnomethodological conversation analysis, and pragmatics.

11. Tannen (1989) examines "linguistic strategies" as they occur in everyday conversation and literary discourse. These strategies are "pervasive, spontaneous, and functional" in ordinary conversation; they are "shaped and elaborated" in literary discourse (1989:1). She calls them "involvement strategies" because "they reflect and simultaneously create interpersonal involvement" (1989:1).

12. Goffman (1974) provides various examples of patients' shifts of behavior in mental institutions, indicating that behavior is somewhat under the patients' control. He cites, for example, the patient "who is mute in all daily interactions and steps off the sidewalk to avoid confrontation with the staff, yet at the patient dance becomes verbally facile and behaviorally full of address" (1974:246).

On the same note, a Brazilian intern reports that a sixty-five-year-old woman was admitted to the hospital under what was diagnosed as "conversion hysteria." She remained mute, in a semi-coma, pretending to be dead. For the next twenty-four hours the staff was unable to remove her from this behavior, though many approached her in a friendly way. The next day, there was a shift in staff. The doctor supervising the new team heard of the patient's behavior as he walked through the ward. Upon approaching her, he informally tapped her shoulder saying out loud, "Had too much to drink last night, ye gran'ma!" to which she immediately responded, "Keep your mouth shut, young man; y'd better have more respect for your elders!".

13. Goffman says that "much psychotic behavior is, in the first instance, a failure to abide by rules established for the conduct of face-to-face interaction—rules established, that is, or at least enforced, by some evaluating, judging, or policing group" ([1967] 1982:141).

4

Conflicting Frames in
the Discharge Interview

Participation in social scenes requires that members play into each other's hands, pushing and pulling each other toward a strong sense of what is probable or possible. . . . In such a world, the meaning of talk is rarely contained on the "inside territory of an utterance"; proposition and reference pale before the task of alignment, before the task of sequencing the conversation's participants into a widely spun social structure.

Ray P. McDermott and Henry Tylbor, "On the Necessity of Collusion in Conversation," p 278

One of the main accomplishments of total institutions is staging a difference between two constructed categories of persons—a difference in social quality and moral character, a difference in perceptions of self and other. Thus every social arrangement in a mental hospital seems to point to the profound difference between a staff doctor and a mental patient.

Erving Goffman, *Asylums*, p. 111

Introduction

Goffman's extensive research in face-to-face encounters masterfully demonstrates the subtle ways in which context is constantly being recreated in interaction. It has stimulated inquiry into the variety of roles and alignments that come into play when people engage in face-to-face interaction. Investigating how subtle changes in participants' stance or position vis-à-vis one another may alter or influence the direction of the ongoing talk is a fruitful approach to the understanding of different types of discourse.

This chapter will address these concerns while focusing on a psychiatric interview. It analyzes the patient's and doctor's discourse in the discharge interview and its appropriateness to the context of a medical encounter. This is the reference point for what is "expected" or considered "normal" talk from an interviewee. Shortly after this interview took place, the patient was discharged from the hospital.

Two major contexts can be identified in the interview. First, there are the *institutionally defined frames of the medical interview,* where the participants follow the prescribed social roles of interviewer-doctor and interviewee-patient. The encounter is characterized by the asymmetry that is typical of this sort of interview. The participants jointly create the asymmetrical context of the psychiatric interview: They abide by its rigid turn-taking system, make predictable moves, use formal address terms, and follow an official topic agenda. Second, there are the *noninstitutional frames.* In these frames the patient performs (and is ratified in) her non-official social identities. At times the patient-interviewee stance fades into the background, giving way to a rather assertive older woman talking to a younger woman; at other times we hear a gentle grandmother address-ing a friendly listener; at yet other times we hear an animated salesperson explaining sales activities.

The institutional frames are controlled by the doctor. She introduces questions, acknowledges responses, and presents topics for discussion: In sum, she proposes talk as interview talk. She gives the interview a direc-tion and a structure. The patient for the most part stays in the official frames set by the doctor. Nowhere in the interview, for instance, does the patient ask any clarification questions, nor does she introduce any follow-up questions that could redirect talk, thus reframing the interac-tion. The patient's role in the institutional frame is limited to addressing the doctor's requests as well as she is able.

However, shifts in footing do occur throughout the interview, intro-ducing subtle changes in the interview structure. Hence, "interview talk" may be reframed as a "chat" or an "animated conversation." Here it is the patient, Jurema, who controls the reframings that take place in the noninstitutional contexts. That is, she proposes a transformation of the situation in which she finds herself: from interview talk to a personal talk. The doctor sometimes ratifies these shifts. When this happens, the patient succeeds in inserting a personal frame into the official frame. Talk then continues until a new reframing occurs, this time proposed by the doctor.

Conflicting Frames

A major frame tension arises from the doctor's resistance to staying in the personal frame created by the patient. While Doctor Edna does, on occasion, ratify Dona Jurema's shifts from the medical encounter to the social encounter, the doctor rarely remains for long in this frame of talk. We often see her progressively working her way out so as to close that segment of talk and shift back to the medical encounter.

This conflict reveals a basic difference between the participants. Both are aware of the task that is to be accomplished: They must jointly create a medical encounter. However, each participant views her own role somewhat differently. While Dona Jurema approaches the encounter from a personal stance, one that says "be friendly," "be involved," Doctor Edna approaches it from a strictly professional stance, one that says "keep to the point [of the interview]," "be brief." Hence, while Dona Jurema introduces unofficial footings, seeking a more personal relationship, the doctor responds by reasserting her previous stance and shifting back to the official footings.

This conflict gains even more relevance if one considers the frames of the institutional context: a medical-psychiatric interview held at a mental hospital. Goffman (1961) discusses the work that patients do to manage the tensions between the outside world and the institutional world. To play the official role, the role of a patient, Dona Jurema must take on what Goffman calls "a disidentifying role" (1961:23)—that is, she must let go of each one of her social identities: the mother, the grandmother, the retired saleswoman, and so on. These unofficial roles are lost, says Goffman, given the barrier that separates the patient from the outside world (1961:16).

It is therefore quite moving to see the work that Dona Jurema accomplishes in the discharge interview. Here we see her timidly taking on her "unofficial roles" (if one views them from the institutional perspective), or her "social roles" (if one views them from the outside-world perspective). These reframings represent a necessary step for Dona Jurema to accomplish her transition from patient to person. These reframings represent Dona Jurema's effort toward what I call "expansion of self." Goffman (1961:130–31) says that institutionalized mental patients go through three main phases: prepatient (the period prior to entering the hospital), inpatient (the period in the hospital), and ex-patient (the period after discharge from the hospital. Jurema's discharge interview takes place when she is about to complete her inpatient career and begin her transition to being an ex-patient. Hence, to coherently perform her unofficial social identities, and thereby regain control over them, is a step in the direction of the ex-patient phase.

The Progressive Symmetry

Another type of social work that takes place in this interview has to do with a subtle and progressive symmetry between the two participants that is initiated by the patient. I will argue that in the first part of the interview, there is more deference on the part of the patient and less involvement between the doctor and the patient. As the interaction progresses, however, the patient introduces some changes in this situation. The sequencing in turn structure, floor management, performance of moves, terms of address, and topic change all reflect this ongoing social work. While the institutionally defined frames mirror one end of the continuum (i.e., less involvement, more deference), the noninstitutional frames are alternative alignments—brought about by the patient— toward the other end of the continuum (more involvement, less deference).

Involvement and deference are not always mutually exclusive; in this interview, however, Dona Jurema marks deference by adhering to the patient's role and staying in the frame created by the doctor. She marks involvement when she shifts footing and reframes the situation as a personal encounter (rather than an official encounter).

The institutional frames reveal deference patterns that are part of the role differentiation between the doctor and the patient. While discussing staff and inmate behavior in total institutions, Goffman (1961:7) says that the staff tends to feel superior and righteous, while inmates tend to feel inferior and blameworthy. There is no place for social mobility, and social distance is often formally prescribed.

In the discharge interview Dona Jurema attempts to place the interaction on a more symmetrical level by shifts of power and reframings. She is the only participant who performs unofficial social identities, which surface in her "ways of speaking" and "ways of listening" (Erickson and Shultz 1982:21)—that is, being a mother, a grandmother, a salesperson, a woman. The metamessages that underlie these frames are "I am grandmother and a nurturing person"; "I am a sixty-one-year-old woman, and I am in control"; "I enjoyed being a saleswoman"; "I am a woman who has gone through childbirth." Each one of these reframings will be analyzed in turn as they signal different contexts within which the patient operates and within which she is communicatively competent. Each takes place at different moments in the interview.

The Dominant Frames

In the discharge interview both participants remain mostly in the institutionally defined frames. These are powerful framings for at least three reasons. First, they are proposed by the "gatekeeper" (Erickson and Shultz 1982:4): the one who has the official status to structure talk and give it a direction. Thus, Doctor Edna sets the institutional frames by assuming the role of the interviewer, and she is careful never to embed any other alignments. Second, Dona Jurema—in the patient role—is compelled to participate in the frame proposed by the doctor, for fear of being evaluated incompetent or, worse, incoherent. Hence, she joins in by accepting the role of the respondent, the "disindentifying role" of patient (Goffman 1961:23). She lets go of other possible alignments, so as to be favorably evaluated by the doctor. Third, as Tannen says, most of us feel constrained to "sail with the framing winds" (1986:92). Jurema, like everyone, would rather yield to a frame than react, since resisting a frame or reframing talk takes an additional effort.

The institutionally defined frame of the discharge interview is made up of two contexts of communication: the psychiatric evaluation frame and the medical examination frame. The former occurs throughout the interview and represents what this interview is about. The latter occurs toward the end of the interview, when the patient complains about a medical (as opposed to psychiatric) matter. It is outside the psychiatric evaluation frame.

The Psychiatric Evaluation Frame

The purpose of the discharge interview is to evaluate Dona Jurema's coherence—her interpretation of reality. The metacommunication (Bateson [1972] 1981:178) of this frame is the following: Doctor Edna requests information from Dona Jurema so as to perform an evaluation of the patient's degree of awareness and responsiveness to the immediate context of communication. Sullivan (1954) observes that in the psychiatric interview the doctor plays a very active role in introducing questions "to make sure that he knows what he is being told" (1954:21).

The psychiatrist's task is viewed as the "official task"; that is, regarding the institution, she has the final and official say. Erickson and Shultz (1982:4) describe an analogous situation concerning counseling interviews, where the counselor is the "gatekeeper." In a psychiatric interview the doctor is the "institutional gatekeeper." That is, she has the responsibility and the authority to make decisions about the social mobility of the patient within the organization. And the interview is an important occasion on which the patient's "future is at stake, contingent at least in part on the decisions being made at that moment" (1982:5). Dona Jurema addresses the doctor's request for information (it is in her best interest to satisfy this request since she wishes to leave the hospital soon). She provides adequate responses and thereby signals cooperative behavior.

The evaluation frame stands as the most unmarked activity; that is, the activity that formally structures this interaction and provides for the official social identity of the psychiatrist and of the patient. The evaluation frame is signaled through sequencing of turns and moves,[1] floor management, and the use of address forms. I will discuss each of these elements in turn.

The Gatekeeper Sets the Frame

Within the evaluation frame, the social roles are asymmetrical and the discourse interaction is shaped by the institutional authority of the doctor. Sullivan (1954:11) talks about the "expert-client relationship" where the role of the psychiatrist-interviewer is to establish who the client is; that is, she "must review what course of events the client has come through to be who he is, what he has in the way of background and experience" (1954:14). Thus, the doctor is the one who establishes the topics, asks questions, and controls the floor, as the following example indicates:

(1)

             [acc]
(1) Doctor: ⌐**you were born on what date?** ..
(2) Patient: **on January 11th** ..
             [nods]

                            [acc]
(3) Doctor: ⌐of what year?
(4) Patient: of 1921. ...
                          [nods]
                I am sixty-one. =
                [nods] [smiles]
(5) Doctor: [nods]
                              [acc]
                = you have a son, don't you?

This segment, a short question/answer/question/answer (Q/A/Q/A) sequence that takes place at the beginning of the discharge interview, illustrates the rules set up for interviewing. Such rules as "the chaining rule"
(Sacks [1972b] 1988:343) rarely apply in long sequences in everyday
conversations, but they are typical of doctor-patient interviews, as Coulthard ([1977] 1981) has pointed out.

    In the discharge interview, many segments follow the pattern shown
in this example. There are, however, some instances in which the doctor
keeps pursuing a different type of answer from the one provided by the
patient in order to elicit new or additional information, as in the following:

(2)

  (1) Doctor: ⌐and sleep, .. do you have any problem sleeping? =
  (2) Patient: = no.
  (3) Doctor: never had?
  (4) Patient: I sleep very well. =
  (5) Doctor: = not even during these times? =
  (6) Patient: = I always slept very well, y'know.
                  [short nod]|
  (7) Doctor: └really?
  (8) Patient: yeah. =
  (9) Doctor: = you never had any-
 (10) Patient: └actually, after my illnesses,
 (11)   I started to take medicine, (1.1)
                          [short nod]
 (12) Doctor: mmm, mmm.
 (13) Patient: to sleep, ...
                  [short nod]
 (14) Doctor: mmm, mmm.
 (15) Patient: y'know ....
 (16) Doctor: which medicine, do you remember?

The doctor introduces a new topic in line (1) ("and sleep") and asks the
patient whether she has any sleeping problems. Dona Jurema's negative
answer (in line 2) triggers a series of questions about her denial. Two
opposing assumptions seem to be at work here. On one hand, the doctor
has been informed (by the staff and by the patient's sister) that Dona
Jurema has been complaining about not sleeping well at the hospital, so

she wants to check on the problem. On the other hand, Dona Jurema is eager to demonstrate that she is well and able to leave the hospital. Hence she answers negatively a question about "having problems." The questions that follow introduce a series of different requests to the patient. In lines (3), (5), and (7), Doctor Edna insists on double-checking the patient's answer. She requests confirmation (lines 3 and 5) and challenges the patient (line 7). Finally, (lines 9 and 10), as the doctor reintroduces her question another time, Dona Jurema overlaps with her and corrects the status of the information she has been providing. She prefaces her statement with "actually," which introduces a repair, and provides information about some sleeping medicine she has been taking, thereby implicitly admitting sleeping problems.

As a response to the doctor's requests, the patient fulfills her role by performing all the moves expected by the interviewer: She addresses the questions and provides the information requested ("on January 11") or confirmations that are sought ("I sleep very well"); she reasserts previous information that she had given ("I always slept quite well") or introduces repairs ("actually, after my illnesses, I started to take medicine"). By making the adequate moves and providing the expected second pair part of the adjacency pair, Dona Jurema is participating in the evaluation frame, demonstrating how coherent and in control of her communicative performance she is. Within this frame of communication, Dona Jurema is Doctor Edna's patient and addresses all responses to her.

A Frame Embedding: The Informant as a Narrator

In addition to being Doctor Edna's patient and answering the doctor's requests, Dona Jurema also assumes the role of a generic patient, the hospital patient, a patient who is being interviewed and recorded for the didactic purposes of the institution. This context of talk was described by Tannen and Wallat (1987), in whose research a doctor uses a reporting register to present an account of her examination for a video audience of pediatric residents. During the discharge interview under discussion here there are no changes of register.[2] However, there are changes in the type of activity that takes place, as the following example indicates:

(3)

Doctor: ⌐=well, what was the last thing that you=
         =remember? ...
         [raises head slightly]
         from- from- from- the beginning of- of-=
         =your illness,
         [gestures with right hand]
         what is it that you remember?
         [gestures with right hand]
         /what did you have-/

Patient: └I didn't have anything, doctor =
              [gesture with left hand]
Doctor: =/you weren't feeling anything./
Patient: it was all of a sudden.
           I wasn't feeling anything, anything,
           anything. =
           [series of head shakes]
Doctor: =what was it that happened all of a sudden?
           [gestures with both hands]
           explain it to us. =
           [folds both hands]

In this segment there is a departure from the standard role assumed by
the patient in the evaluation frame: Dona Jurema shifts from an
interviewee-informant to an interviewee-narrator. This is triggered by
her assertion "it was all of a sudden" in answer to a question from the
doctor. This assertion establishes the ground for a narrative to take place
and sets the time of a story (Labov 1972). Doctor Edna responds to and
aligns with this shift as she introduces a request through the metalin-
guistic verb *explain*. Hence, the patient's next contribution must provide
some sort of explanation.

But there is more to this frame break, as Doctor Edna conveys a
request that brings forth another frame, larger than the doctor-patient
encounter. The doctor requests that Dona Jurema explain "to us" instead
of explaining "to me." In doing so, she makes it explicit that whatever
Dona Jurema says will be, from then on, addressed to a larger audience
(made up of doctors, students, nurses—whomever her potential audience
might be). She brings about a change in the participation structure to
address the pedagogical situation: the recording of the event for teaching
purposes.

In performing the role of the narrator, Dona Jurema provides the
following information:

(4)

Doctor: =what happened all of a sudden?
           [gestures with both hands]
           explain to us. =
           [folds both hands]
Patient: =all of a sudden I lost ah .. my mind,
                        [turns both hands outward]
           my senses, y'know, ...
                        [begins to turn hands inward]
           I didn't see anything anymore,
           [hands back to baseline position]
           when I could see again I was here in the =
           =hospital, y'know. (1.7)
           [series of nods from doctor]

but I did not see anything that happened to=
=me (y'know)

Her story presents the narrative sequencing and structure described by Labov (1972:363):

Orientation	"it happened all of a sudden"
Complicating action	"I lost ah .. my mind, my senses"
	"when I could see again I was here in the hospital"
Complicating action and evaluation	"I didn't see anything anymore"
	"but I did not see anything that happened to me"

A sequencing in nonverbal behavior makes the entire episode highly cohesive.[3] As Doctor Edna requests an explanation, she makes the following shift from her baseline posture:

Doctor: =what happened all of a sudden?
          [gestures with both hands, body orientation toward the patient]
          explain it to us.=
          [folds both hands and leans slightly]

The patient responds with an open three-part gesture:

Patient: =**all of a sudden I lost ah .. my mind,**
                      [turns both hands outward]
          my senses, y'know, ...
                  [begins to turn hands inward]
          I didn't see anything anymore
          [hands back to baseline position]

Dona Jurema performs the following moves (departing from her baseline posture, where both hands have been resting on the arms of the armchair):

1. With her arms still resting on the armchair, she turns both hands outward (in a slow movement) as she utters, "I lost ah .. my mind";
2. With her arms still resting on the armchair, she starts turning both hands inward (in a slow movement) as she pauses after having said "my senses, y'know ...";
3. she returns to the baseline posture, with her hands resting on the armchair, after stating, "I didn't see anything anymore."

It is interesting to note the synchronicity of nonverbal behavior between Doctor Edna and Dona Jurema, as well as their complementary positions: Doctor Edna's hands are in a "closed position" (Scheflen 1973) (folded on her lap), while Dona Jurema's hands are in an "open position" (turned outward). Further, Dona Jurema indicates her highest degree of "openness" simultaneously in the verbal and nonverbal channels: She departs from her baseline posture (by turning both hands outward) and also verbally communicates her loss of control, her loss of self:

Patient: = all of a sudden I lost ah .. my mind,
                          [turns both hands outward]
              my senses, y'know, ...

Dona Jurema recycles this story three times during the discharge interview. The first time she tells her story, the doctor had been asking about her present hospitalization; she later reintroduces the same story when the doctor asks her about what happened during her past hospitalizations:

(5)

Doctor: **and do you remember <u>why</u> you were =**
              = hospitalized there?
              [slight body movement toward the patient; gesture with left hand]
              /what was happening?/
Patient: **the same thing,**
              [hands open outwardly]
              all of a sudden, I'm fine, fine,
              all of a sudden, right away ...
              I lose my mind, I lose my senses,
              doctor y'know ....
              and that's what happens to me. (1.3)
              [hands resume baseline position]

Thus, in the second instance, to answer a request from the doctor, she recycles her story, both verbally and nonverbally, without adding new information. The doctor probes into and insists on trying to clarify what type of behavior was occurring then:

(6)

Doctor: ⌐**do you remember, let's see:,**
              [torso inclination toward the patient;
              gestures with left arm and hands]
              if you begin to feel different,
                               [gestures with hands;
                               looks at the patient]
                                            [acc]
              you begin to feel something different =

=than usual?=
[hand gestures]

In response, Dona Jurema repeats her story a third time:

(7)

Patient: =no, nothing, nothing, nothing.
      [shakes head]   [looks down]
      the thing is all of a sudden, doctor.=
      [looks up]   [looks at doctor]
Doctor: =what happens all of a sudden with you? ..
           [gestures with both hands]
Patient: ⌐all of a sudden ⌐I .. lose my mind, ...
      I don't see anything anymore,
           [turns hands outward; turns head to the left, toward the doctor]
      by the time I can see I'm hospitalized.
      [turns hands inward, in a closing movement; nods]
Doctor: //mmm, mmm// ...
      [series of nods]

Three times (in examples 4, 5, and 7) the patient repeats her story about the experience she had. In doing so, she repeats highly fixed forms, with just some variation in tense:

1st time: (4)

(1) all of a sudden, I lost ah ..
(2) my mind,
(3) my senses, y'know, ...
(4) I didn't see anything anymore.
(5) when I could see (again) I was here in the hospital, (y'know.)
(6) but I did not see anything that happened to me,

2nd time: (5)

(1) the same thing,
(2) all of a sudden,
(3) I'm fine, fine,
(4) all of a sudden,
(5) right away ...
(6) I lose my mind,
(7) I lose my senses,
(8) doctor, y'know,
(9) and that's what happens to me.

3rd time: (7)

(1) the thing happens all of a sudden, doctor.
(2) all of a sudden 'I ..

(3) lose my mind, ...
(4) I don't see anything anymore,
(5) by the time I can see I'm hospitalized.

In retelling an often-told story, a speaker tends to repeat over and over again prepatterned forms that "encapsulate for [the speaker] what was memorable and reportable about this experience" (Tannen 1987b:228). What Dona Jurema is doing here is repeating a pattern of how she habitually tells her story to herself and to an audience (made up of doctors, and probably family and friends). One must remember that this is Dona Jurema's seventh crisis. In her account the patient produces a schema for her psychotic episode. She says and repeats: "I lose my mind, I lose my senses." Schemas account for the routinized nature of talk in interaction and for the identification of interactive frames. In Jurema's case a schema represents her knowledge of a particular recurring event. Enactment of this schema co-occurs with a change in frame: from being an informant (answering questions) to telling a story. The second frame is subsumed within the first one.

The evaluation frame is composed of two footings, one embedded within the other. The dominant footing is that of "informant," who answers the doctor's questions. The embedded footing is that of "narrator." In each footing Dona Jurema performs according to the doctor's expectations: She answers the questions by providing the requested information and reporting personal facts. As a patient and interviewee, she knows that only a certain range of moves is appropriate to the interaction. In following the sequential constraints of the interview, Dona Jurema demonstrates that she is oriented to the ongoing talk, taking her turn while "locating in what is said now the sense of what it is a response to" (Goffman 1981b:33). Hence, she successfully addresses the institutional context of communication by contributing to adjacency pairs, by providing an adequate response move, and by embedding narratives in her talk.

The Gatekeeper Controls the Floor

The two basic types of turn exchanges in the discharge interview reflect the control that the doctor has over the process of turn allocation: Type 1 is the minimal pair question/answer, and type 2 is the three-part structure question/answer/comment (Q/A/C). Type 1 can be expanded to Q/A/Q/A/Q/A as in example (2), repeated here:

(2)

(1) Doctor: ⌜and sleep, .. do you have any problem sleeping?=
(2) Patient: =no.
(1) Doctor: never had?

(2) Patient: **I sleep very well.** =
(1) Doctor: **not even during these times?** =
(2) Patient: **= I always slept very well, y'know.**

Type 2 is illustrated in the examples below:

(8)

(1) Doctor: **and how old is he now?**
(2) Patient: **he's about forty-two.**
(3) Doctor: **/mmm/ ...**

(9)

(1) Doctor: **you live with your two sisters, don't =**
        = you?
(2) Patient: **yes, ... the =**
        = three of us live together. ..
(3) Doctor: **/mmm./**

The question/answer/comment pattern has often been reported in studies of doctor-patient discourse (e.g., West 1983; Fisher 1984; Frankel 1984). The comment takes the form of an assessment or acknowledgment (Frankel 1984.155); that is, it allows the doctor to evaluate or signal understanding.[4] However, the comment also signals to the patient a transition slot between the end of one topic and the beginning of another topic, as in examples (10) and (11), which immediately follow (8) and (9), respectively:

(10)

Doctor: **/mmm/ ...**
        you also have a granddaughter, don't you?

(11)

Doctor: **/mmm./**
        ⌐Dona Jurema, .. do you remember the day =
        = that you came to the hospital? to this hospital?

Hence, the two-part interchange (Q/A/Q/A/Q/A) is often transformed into a three-part structure (Q/A/C), through which the doctor secures both the initial and the third turns. This enables her to regain control of the floor and start over with a new question.

Schegloff (1982:81) discusses the use of the same forms ("mmm" or "mmm, mmm") as "continuers." Doctor Edna uses a series of back-channels, repetitive statements, or nods to show that she is "with her patient," to encourage talk. These bits of talk are evidence of attention and interest on the listener's part and keep the conversation flowing smoothly (Schegloff 1982:78), as in the following:

(12)

    Patient: **actually, since my illnesses,**
            I started to take medicine, (1.1)
            [short nod]
→ Doctor: **mmm, mmm.**
    Patient: **to sleep, ...**
            [short nod]
→ Doctor: **mmm, mmm.**
    Patient: **y'know ....**

In medical interviewing, as Reiser and Schroder ([1980] 1984:128) indicate, "simple nods of the head, quietly saying 'uh-hum,' or just an attentive, concerned silence" can be quite effective in getting the patient's collaboration. Equally effective, they say, is the technique of repeating the last few words of what a patient says, as in example (13):

(13)

    Doctor: **=that did not use to happen before?**
    Patient: ⌐ **no:. ...**
                           [shakes head]
            I would wake up around .... six o'clock,
            [looks straight ahead, looks at doctor]
            seven o'clock in the morning ...
                [nods]   [nods]
    Doctor: **mmm. ....**
→   **you would sleep and wake up around six,**
          seven=

Repetition, which have many functions, is also relatively automatic in conversation (Tannen 1987a:581). When the doctor repeats the patient's words, she signals comprehension and listenership; she also signals to the patient to go on. These "continuers" provide a natural slot for the patient to propose a reframing of the situation in which she finds herself. Since she is encouraged to "go on talking," she may also feel encouraged to shift footing and to take on a more projecting role, a role where she would have the upper hand. In part II we will see how this may happen.

Deference and Address Forms

Goffman (1961:22) tells us that patients are frequently forced to display verbal acts of deference when they interact with doctors. Terms such as "sir" or "doctor" have obvious implications for role differentiation between staff and patients.

In the discharge interview, both the patient and the doctor use address forms that in Brazilian Portuguese belong to a formal register. The patient addresses the doctor as *doutora* "doctor," *Doutora Edna* (title + first name) "Doctor Edna," *a senhora* (formal second-person singular form); the doctor addresses the patient as *Dona Jurema* (title + first name), literally Mrs. Jurema, and *a senhora*.

In power/solidarity semantics these address forms represent the deference that derives from the two axes of age and status, where the two participants are "equals and not solidary" (Brown and Gilman [1972] 1979:259). The patient, Dona Jurema, is older than the doctor. There is a large age difference (over thirty-five years) between the two; in fact, the doctor is a very young woman (twenty-five years old). In Brazilian Portuguese it is customary for a younger woman to address an older woman as *dona* + first name, and/or *a senhora*. Hence, the patient has the upper hand in matters of age, while the doctor has the upper hand in matters of professional status. This makes them "equals."[5]

The address form *Dona Jurema* occurs only in the first (opening) and last (closing) parts of the interview. There may be two reasons for this. First, the doctor may be introducing the name on the tape recording for pedagogical use. Second, terms of address are used to signal the opening of the interview session and, then, eighteen minutes later, the closing of that session. In the development of the interview the form *a senhora* (formal "you") is used and alternates with zero pronoun.[6]

The patient addresses the doctor as *doutora* or *Doutora Edna* = title + first name. Two distinct considerations must be made regarding the occurrence, frequency, and distribution of the form *doutora*. First, Dona Jurema does not use this form of address in the admitting interview. It occurs frequently, however, in the discharge interview, signaling an acknowledgment from the patient of the participants' roles in the psychiatric-medical interview. It conveys a metamessage: "You are the doctor (and, therefore, I am the patient)." Its most common usage in the "answer slot" is in sentence-final position, right after the doctor has introduced a new topic (or subtopic), as in the following:

(14)

Doctor: ⌐Dona Jurema, .. do you remember the day=
        =that you came to the hospital?
        to this hospital?
Patient: =no, I don't remember <u>doctor</u>.

(15)

Doctor: do you stop eating? =
Patient: =no, I even eat very well, <u>doctor</u>. =

The second consideration is that the form *doutora* occurs in different answer slots during the development of a topic. This indicates that it is either unmarked or it accomplishes different things. Out of a total of 174 turns, Dona Jurema uses this form forty-five times, in 26 percent of her turns. She uses this form increasingly as the interview progresses. In the first half of the interview, she uses it in 18 percent of her turns, while in the second half the form occurs in 33 percent of the turns. In many of these instances, the form *doutora* seems to function as an emphatic particle, stressing the answer provided by Dona Jurema. Here no topic shift necessarily occurs. As an emphatic particle, in addition to being a marker of deference, this form reinforces the speaker's stand vis-à-vis the point she wants to make. This is particularly true in negative responses, as example (16) illustrates:

[In this segment Doctor Edna is trying to elicit information concerning the patient's general health prior to her first crisis.]

(16)

(1) Doctor: **you never felt any:thing before?**
(2) Patient: **nothing, nothing, nothing, nothing.** =
           [series of short head shakes]
(3) Doctor: = **there wasn't anything unusual** =
       = **(happening)?**
(4) Patient: **ne:ver had,**
       [looks down]
(5)   **ne:ver doctor, /never/.**
       [shakes head, looks at doctor]
(6) Doctor: **not e:ven .. physical problems?**
(7)   **/did you feel something physical/?**
(8) Patient: ⌊**ne:ver, never had an** =
           [shakes head]
       = **operation, doctor.** =
       [raises head, looks at doctor]

In answer to the doctor's yes-no questions, Dona Jurema provides a series of very strong negative answers (in lines 2, 4, 5, and 8), and she uses the form *doutora* twice, in final position, as a closing to her negative statements (lines 5 and 8). Her nonverbal behavior matches her verbal communication. She looks at the doctor, makes eye contact, and uses the address form (lines 5 and 8). In both cases the use of this form, as well as the other cues, signals a strong stand.

The other address form that the patient uses—*Doutora Edna* (title + first name)—is also pragmatically loaded and seems to indicate that some social work along the solidarity line is taking place. What seems to be the norm in Brazilian Portuguese doctor-patient communication is that a patient initially uses the address form *doutora* (title). As the relationship progresses and some social work is done toward more solidarity, a patient might start to alternate the forms *doutora* (title) or *Doutora Edna* (title + first name).

In the discharge interview the patient uses the address form *doutora* most of the time. However, in four instances, halfway through the interview, she makes also use of the form *Doutora Edna*. She uses this form three times while she is talking about her job as a saleswoman, a topic that is expanded by both participants; the fourth occurrence happens almost at the end of the interview, when the doctor reintroduces the patient's son, apparently a difficult topic for Dona Jurema.[7] The significant point here is that the form *Doutora Edna* is symmetrical to the form *Dona Jurema* that was used by the doctor in the opening of the interview. They are both title + first name forms. The patient uses this symmetrical form only in the second half of the interview, when other interactional microshifts are also taking place.

Thus, in the discharge interview, the form *senhora* is used throughout, showing deference on the part of both participants within the institutional frame. The patient and the doctor use two other types of address forms—(title) and (title + first name). With both forms participants show deference for age and status, but they seem to have different functions. The use of *Dona Jurema* by the doctor seems to address the pedagogical situation and the video recording. The doctor makes use of this form twice at the beginning of the interview, and then once as a closing to the interview.

The patient uses the form *doutora*, which seems to operate at different levels. On one hand, *doutora* signals deference and indicates that the addressor acknowledges the addressee's professional status, and thereby also acknowledges the institutional frame. On the other hand, it also functions as an emphatic particle, stressing Dona Jurema's stand regarding the answer she is providing and her involvement in the topic of conversation. The form *Doutora Edna* also occurs in the second part of the interview. Although the patient uses this form only four times, it seems to constitute another cue for the progressive symmetry that Dona Jurema is seeking. It indicates a more personal relationship to the doctor—a shift from (title) to (title + first name).

Summary of the Evaluation Frame

The evaluation frame stands as the unmarked situation—the one that matches our knowledge schemas (Tannen and Wallat 1987) for what a psychiatric interview is all about. The first two components analyzed here—the sequencing and moves, and floor management in the interview—define the participation structure and satisfy expectations about this frame. Both participants, therefore, comply with the social marking of roles defined by the institution and their official performed social identities (Erickson and Shultz 1982:16). The third component, the use of address forms, seems to have different functions, one of them being a marker for deference. Hence, the asymmetry is maintained in the sequencing of the discourse, turn allocation, and deference in the use of address forms.

The Medical Examination Frame

An examination frame[8] occurs when the doctor shifts from the psychiatric interview to a medical encounter and performs a short physical examination of the patient's arm and hand movements. Doctor Edna prefaces this action by asking the patient about a complaint that she has had: a weakness in her arms and hands:

(17)

                    [dec]

(1) Doctor: **you had complained .. of a weakness in =**
            =your arms /remember? =

(2) Patient: **=yeah, in my hands, doctor, in my hands.**
              [raises head slightly and nods]

(3) Doctor: ⌐ **what's it like,**
            this weakness? ..
            [acc]

(4) Patient: ⌐ **it's it's that I don't feel much in my hands**
            [looks at both hands, raises hands,
            closes hands inward]
            .. see. =
            [looks at the doctor, opens and
            shuts hands]

(5) Doctor: **=you can't make any movements?**
              [moves hands, rests hands on armchair]

(6) Patient: **yeah. I can't (   )**
              [shakes head, looks⌐ at doctor]

(7) Doctor: └ **what do you =**
            =feel when you're about to make a =
            =movement?

(8) Patient: └ **I have difficulty,**
            doctor. =
            [raises head and nods]

At this point the doctor asks the patient about her ability to move her hands and to eat by herself. Dona Jurema states that "these days my sister has been helping me," and she reasserts her "difficulty": "I have difficulty," she says. When Doctor Edna presents a specific question ("but is the difficulty in the strength to raise the spoon, or can't you reach your mouth?"), Dona Jurema finally states that she has problems lifting the fork. After this response move the doctor tells the patient to perform a specific gesture:

(18)

Doctor: **/make this movement, like this./** (3.8) (NV)
        [The patient raises both hands, turns arms outward with hands closed; the
        doctor touches the patient's left arm; the patient looks at her left arm, the

doctor takes her hand away, and the patient opens both hands, looks at them]

[acc]

Doctor: **are you feeling ... you are not feeling=**
=anything now, are you?=
Patient: **=no.** (1.5)

[looks at doctor, places hands back on armchair, and resumes baseline position]

As a closing to this frame, the doctor checks Dona Jurema's ability to move her hands and perform her bathroom routines. She requests specific information and Dona Jurema states that she needs help to zip up her pants. At this point Dona Jurema pauses and initiates a shift out of the physical examination and into the psychiatric-evaluative frame. She does this by assessing her present state of health and asserting how much better she feels:

[camera with focus on both participants; both of them are in baseline position]

(19)

(1) Doctor: **and to go to the bathroom, do you also=**
=need someone to help? ....
[dec]
(2) Patient: **yes. to zip up my pants,** (y'know /not
very/)
[series of nods]
(3) Doctor: | **/you also can't=**
=do it yourself./
(4) Patient: **yeah, I can't.** (2.0)
but I think I'm <u>much</u> better now,
[series of nods]
y'know doctor, thank God. ....
(5) Doctor: **you think you're better than you were=**
=a few days ago?
(6) Patient: **oh:, I AM.=**
[long nod]
(7) Doctor: **=yeah:?=**
(8) Patient: **=I think I'm <u>much</u> better.** =
[series of long nods]

In turn (4) Dona Jurema introduces a shift and presents her own assessment of her present state of health. There is a shift in frame and in the participant who controls it. The turn sequence (1–3) could have been a standard Q/A/C sequence in which the doctor would regain the floor and introduce another question; instead, Dona Jurema (line 4) takes the floor and echoes the doctor's comment by saying, "yeah, I can't." She then pauses and says, "but I think I'm much better now." The discourse marker "but," in initial position (after a pause), marks a contrast and introduces a shift in Dona Jurema's alignment, a reframing of the situation. She is now the one who performs an evaluation, and, in doing so, she switches back to the evaluation frame:

Patient: **yeah, I can't. (2.0)**
              but I think I'm <u>much</u> better now,
                 [series of nods]
              y'know doctor, thank God. ....

To get away from a topic that made her feel uncomfortable and helpless in that it revealed basic levels of dependency (in eating, in getting dressed), Dona Jurema shifts the topic and provides her own self-evaluation. In her next turn (turn 5), Doctor Edna ratifies the shift. She repeats Dona Jurema's answer and requests confirmation ("you think you're better than you were a few days ago?"). Dona Jurema very emphatically states:

Patient: **oh:, I AM. =**
                 [long nod]

She repeats:

Patient: **= I think I'm <u>much</u> better. =**
                 [series of long nods]

Dona Jurema uses increased stress to emphasize the way she feels about herself; she uses the marker "oh" (Portuguese *ah*) to display involvement and an expressive orientation to the topic; and her nonverbal behavior matches her statements as she provides long nods. She successfully accomplishes a shift out of the examination frame as Doctor Edna engages in the evaluation that Dona Jurema had introduced.

Summary of the Institutional Frames

Both the medical examination frame and the psychiatric evaluation frame represent the types of activities that are expected to take place in a medical-psychiatric institution. The psychiatrist's task is viewed as the "official task"; that is, from the point of view of the institution, she has the final and official say. She is the gatekeeper, and the interview is an important occasion that may largely determine the patient's future. In performing her official role, Doctor Edna faces a situation of inherent tension similar to the counseling sessions discussed by Erickson and Shultz (1982:18): She is the patient's evaluator (or judge) and as such has to be objective and distant (manifesting less involvement in the interaction). However, she is also the helper (or the advocate) and as such shows proximity and rapport (manifesting more involvement in the interaction). The first stance (less involvement) is present in both of the institutional frames, but it is the second stance (more involvement) that allows Dona Jurema a space to break frame and introduce unofficial footings that are extracted from the interaction. While the first part of this chapter analyzed the framings proposed by the doctor, the following sections will discuss frame breaks introduced by the patient.

Dona Jurema, as the patient, responds to the doctor's requests and addresses them. She seems to be working with at least two different strategies. On one hand, she stays in the frame presented by the doctor, and within this frame she does not say more than necessary. On the other hand, Dona Jurema uses a second strategy in which she provides as much information as necessary. In doing so, she reframes the interaction and shifts the control of the talk that goes on.

Negotiating Alternative Frames

In the discharge interview the participants perform the official framing in accordance with rules and norms set out by the institution; that is, they fulfill their prescribed roles. The doctor, as the gatekeeper, has the primary responsibility for the progression of the interview. Dona Jurema's contribution is restricted to providing the required information and no more.

However, there are instances of frame breaks, where the unofficial identities of the doctor and the patient are revealed to one another. The patient and the doctor shift from the institutional frame to the personal frame. In all of these instances, it is the patient (interviewee) who reframes the situation, and in doing so shifts the control of the interaction. While Dona Jurema proposes reframings in the direction of the social encounter, the doctor shifts in the opposite direction, toward the medical encounter. These shifts are similar to those described by Mishler (1984), who differentiated "the voice of medicine" from "the voice of the lifeworld." While the voice of medicine is "shown to control the organization and content of interviews," the voice of the lifeworld is "less well-defined and tend[s] to refer to statements by patients that depart from the 'normative' voice of medicine, occasionally disrupting the fluent flow of an interview" (1984:103).

In the following sections I describe four frame shifts, all proposed by Dona Jurema, which take place as follows: two at the opening, one halfway through the interview, and one at the closing. I have selected them in this way to illustrate the progressive symmetry that the patient seeks during the eighteen minutes of interaction. In each of them Dona Jurema gets the floor and establishes a new metamessage about what is going on. In doing so, she tries to shift the power toward a more symmetrical relationship. Doctor Edna, however, resists the symmetry that the patient seeks.

Reframing: "I am a nurturing grandmother"

The following segment occurs at the opening of the interview. It illustrates two frame breaks: The patient shifts from the institutional to a
noninstitutional frame, and the doctor ratifies this shift; a few turns later,
the doctor reframes the situation and shifts back to the institutional context.

(20)

```
                              [acc]
 (1) Doctor:  ⌈you were born on what date? ..
 (2) Patient:  on January 11th ..
                              [acc]
 (3) Doctor:  ⌊of what year?
 (4) Patient:  of 1921. ...
                           [nods]
               I am sixty-one. =
               [nods]      [smiles]
 (5) Doctor:  [nods]
                              [acc]
               =you have a son, don't you?
 (6) Patient:                   ⌊I have a son.
                           [nods] [short smile]
 (7) Doctor:  what's his name?
 (8) Patient:  Francisco Ferreira de Souza.
 (9) Doctor:  and he is how old now? ..
(10) Patient:  he's- about forty-two.
               [looks away, looks at doctor and smiles]
(11) Doctor:  /mmm/ ...
               you also have a granddaughter, don't=
               =you?
(12) Patient:  =I have a ((little)) sixteen-year=
               =old granddaughter. (1.4)
               [raises head and smiles]
     Doctor:  //mmm//
     Patient:  she's my li:fe.
               [raises head, looks up, big smile]
(13) Doctor:  do you- really? =
(14) Patient:  =really. I'm crazy (about her).
               I like (her) ve-
               [smiling]  |
(15) Doctor:             |you take care of her? =
(16) Patient:  =I don't take care of her because my=
               =daughter-in-law takes very good care,
               y'know ....
               [short smile]
               I just see her, and all that.
               (I don't     )
```

(17) Doctor: do you always <u>keep in touch</u> with them?
(18) Patient: oh, yes, <u>always</u>. ...
               [nods]
               well, as much as possible I do, y'know =
               = doctor. ...
               [nods and smiles, looks at doctor]
(19) Doctor: ⌐where do you live, Dona Jurema?
(20) Patient: what? =
               [lips tighten and frowns]
(21) Doctor: = //you-//
(22) Patient: └I live with my sister. (1.2)
                         [series of short nods]
               Dona Ide:te, Dona Tere:za,
               [series of short nods]
               161 Alvorada Avenue apartment 1001
               [series of short nods, smile]
(23) Doctor: you live with your two sisters,
               don't you?
(24) Patient: yes, ...
               [nods and serious]
               the three of us live together. ..
               [nods, tighten lips, and frowns]
(25) Doctor: /mmm./

In analyzing this segment I take into consideration the turn-taking system and the moves that are accomplished in each turn. A *turn at talk* refers to holding the floor, not to "what is said while holding it" (Goffman 1981b:23), while a *move* refers to the speech action taken during one's turn at talk. I also measure the amount of talk that goes on by the number of "intonational units" (Chafe 1986) produced by the speaker.

The following sequence that opens the discharge interview starts with the patient saying strictly what is required and no more. Thus, each turn has only one move. In the first ten turns, each move has only one intonational unit (one move = one intonational unit); the only exception for this is in turn (4):

(1) Doctor: (1) you were born on what <u>date</u>? ..
(2) Patient: (1) on January 11th. ..
(3) Doctor: (1) of what year?
(4) Patient: (1) of 1921.
               (2) I am sixty-one.
(5) Doctor: (1) you have a son, don't you?
(6) Patient: (1)   └I have a son.
(7) Doctor: (1) what's his name?
(8) Patient: (1) Francisco Ferreira de Souza.
(9) Doctor: (1) and he is how old now? ..
(10) Patient: (1) he's- about forty-two.

But a change of topic in turn (11) triggers a change in this pattern. After requesting information about Dona Jurema's son, the doctor asks the patient about her granddaughter:

[In the following excerpts, the intonational units are numbered to indicate the number of contributions from the participants]

(11) Doctor: (1) **you also have a granddaughter, don't you?**
(12) Patient: (1) **I have a ((little)) sixteen =**
               year-old granddaughter. (1.4)
               [raises head, smiles]
     Doctor: //mmm//
     Patient: (2) **she's my li:fe.**
               [raises head, looks up, big smile]

In response to the doctor's request for information, Dona Jurema provides more than what is minimally required. First she says that she has a granddaughter and states her age; she conveys involvement with the topic as she smiles and refers to her granddaughter by the Portuguese form *netinha* "little granddaughter" (where the *-inha* suffix expresses affection). Then she presents an evaluation: "she's my life." Dona Jurema's use of expressive communication (both verbal and nonverbal) and her evaluative statement ("she's my life") trigger a change in the doctor's question-asking routine, which can be seen in turns (13) through (18):

(13) Doctor: (1) **do you-**
          (2) **really?**
(14) Patient: (1) **really.**
          (2) **I'm crazy (about her).**
          (3) **I like (her) ve-**
(15) Doctor: (1)   ⌐**you take care of her?** =
(16) Patient: (1) **=I don't take care of her because =**
               =my daughter-in-law takes very =
               =good care, y'know. ....
          (2) **I just see her,**
          (3) **and all that.**
          (4) **(I don't)**
(17) Doctor: (1) **do you always <u>keep in touch</u> with=**
               =them?
(18) Patient: (1) **oh, yes,**
          (2) **always.**
          (3) **<u>well</u>, as much as possible I do,**
               y'know doctor. ...

In turns (12) through (18) Dona Jurema's contributions become more informative than they were in turns (2) through (10). She presents a series of evaluations in her four consecutive turns. She also makes use of expressive language through a variety of lexical and syntactic forms and nonverbal cues:

1. She uses adverbs and adverbial clauses: "my daughter-in-law takes very good care, (I) always (keep in touch)"; "always, as much as possible."

2. She uses discourse markers, which were absent in the preceding segment (turns 1–10) to indicate different aspects of communication. The marker "y'know" in (16) and (18) signals an appeal to the hearer for cooperation (Schiffrin 1985, 1987a), and in the latter case "y'know" gains stress as it is followed by the form "doctor." Also in (18) ("oh, yes, always. well, whenever it's possible I do, y'know doctor"), as a response to a yes-no question, we see the patient doing three things: (a) she uses the marker "oh" to indicate familiar information and an expressive orientation (Schiffrin 1985, 1987a) to the new topic—family contacts—that the doctor has introduced. She then reinforces her positive answer with "always"; (b) she uses the marker "well" to change the status of her prior contributions (Schiffrin 1985), and modifies her previous assertion; and (c) she closes her turn, using "y'know doctor" as a transitional device.[9]

3. The pace of talk accelerates for both speakers as turns latch (13/14 and 15/16) and overlap (14/15); there is joint use of emphasis (in turn 17 for the doctor) "you always *keep in touch* with them?" and (in 18 for the patient) *"always"*; and in Dona Jurema's talk there is vowel elongation in (turn 12) "she's my li:fe." These prosodic signals indicate the attitudinal aspects that underlie expressed emotions. So does Dona Jurema's nonverbal behavior. One sees the patient providing a series of nonverbal cues, such as raising her head, looking up to the doctor, smiling, and nodding at different moments in this interaction. These verbal and nonverbal devices seem to cluster to signal a change of alignment by the patient toward her doctor.

It is small wonder, therefore, that when the doctor suddenly changes the topic of the interview and resumes the question-asking agenda, a misunderstanding occurs:

(19) Doctor: ⌐**where do you live, Dona Jurema?**
(20) Patient: **what?**

Here the doctor switches from a series of questions that deal with relationships to a referential, factual request for information. As a consequence, a new alignment must be negotiated. The doctor signals this shift by a rise in pitch. The patient, however, is taken by surprise. In turn (20) she responds with what Goffman (1981b) calls a "rerun signal," which indicates that she is addressing "the process of communication, not what was communicated" (1981b:34). The doctor, then, starts to restate her question and overlaps with the patient, who provides an answer:

(21) Doctor: //you-//
(22) Patient: └I leave with my sister. (1.2)
                 Dona Ide:te, Dona Tere:sa,
                 161 Alvorada Avenue apartment 1001

There is a lack of clarity in Dona Jurema's answer: She refers to one sister and then mentions two names. As a result, the doctor reformulates the patient's answer and requests ratification: [10]

(23) Doctor: **you live with your two sisters,**
             don't you?

The patient provides confirmation and accepts the doctor's reformulation:

(24) Patient: **yes, ... the three of us live together.**

The doctor calls an end to this segment by acknowledging her response (25): "mmm."

This interaction (example 20, turns 1–25) presents changes in the participants' alignments with each other. Although both the doctor's and the patient's roles have been formally established by the official framing, changes in footings nevertheless occur. The initial doctor-patient interaction is one of less involvement; this situation changes when a new alignment between participants takes place, with the emphasis of communication being placed on evaluative devices and expressive language. This reframing triggers more talk from the patient while signaling a higher degree of cooperation, with the listener (the doctor) reinforcing the speaker's point, offering information, and providing evaluation. From that point on, the conversation changes in strategy, until a new shift occurs in turn (19), when the doctor returns to her official topic agenda. In changing the topic, the doctor regains control of the interview and reframes the interaction.

The preceding segment is particularly interesting since it opens the interview. From the very start we observe an underlying conflict between the way the doctor structures talk (as a medical interview) and how the patient views the encounter (as a personal talk). Dona Jurema proposes reframings in the direction of the social encounter; the doctor shifts in the opposite direction, toward the medical encounter. The following excerpts confirm the doctor's resistance to staying in the frame proposed by the patient.

Reframing: "I can take care of myself"

Other nonofficial social attributes surface in the interview. The following segment reveals Dona Jurema taking the stance of a self-assured person who can take responsibility for herself. We see the patient taking a stand and negotiating the topic of discourse according to the position she holds. We also see the doctor taking a different position. As a result, a confrontation occurs.

(21)

```
                    [dec]
(1) Doctor: ⌐do you:: remember, let's see,
             if you ((had already)) had periods of being very sa:d,
             for no rea:son, =
(2) Patient: = I have, yes, doctor.
             [nods] |
(3) Doctor:         | of being depressed? =
(4) Patient: = I have, yes.
             [nods]
(5) Doctor. you have? =
(6) Patient: = I have, yes. ....
             [nods]
(7) Doctor: what's it like? /tell me/.
```

The doctor introduces the topic of "depression (in the past)" in a tentative way. The pace is slow, with emphatic stress on the Portuguese address term *a senho::ra:* "you::," "sa:d," "for no rea:son;" she hedges "let's see;" and uses an if-clause followed by the past tense. The use of indirectness (slow-paced questioning and hedging) reduces the amount of coercion of the patient vis-à-vis a topic that may present a "face-threatening act" (Brown and Levinson [1978] 1979). Dona Jurema answers promptly (turn 2)—so promptly that her answer latches onto and overlaps with the doctor's incomplete question. She then restates her answer (4). However, both times she uses the present tense ("I have, yes, doctor" *tenho sim, doutora*). The form *tenho* is the simple present tense in Portuguese and should not be confused with the English present perfect form "have (had)."

While a time switch can signal the participant's interest in the topic (Brown and Levinson [1978] 1979:126), in this segment it signals something more: In using the present form, Dona Jurema indicates that she is talking about "depression in the present" (and, in doing so, excludes from her answer "depression in the past"). Her answer is emphatic: She uses a yes-form (which is a marked form in Portuguese), and she gives the same response twice.[11] The doctor then requests clarification using the present tense (turn 5):

Doctor: **you have?** =

Dona Jurema repeats for the second time, "I have, yes," and in doing so successfully engages the doctor within this time shift to reframe the talk as talk about "depression in the present."

In the interaction that follows, the doctor asks how Dona Jurema feels when she is depressed, if she cries a lot, and whether she stops eating. Then she asks about her grooming habits:

[Because of important prosodic and lexical information that occurs in this segment, the Portuguese text is displayed]

(22)

		[dec]
(1)	Doctor:	and let's see:, ...
(2)		you <u>take ca::re</u> of yourself, ..
(3)		/you ba:the/,
		[acc]
(4)		you do everything as usual?
(5)	Patient:	oh, yes:,
(6)		e:verything just right,
(7)		e:verything ju:st right .
(8)	Doctor:	⌐weren't there periods of time=
		=that you did not take care of=
		=yourself?=
(9)	Patient:	=no:, absolutely not,
(10)		when I am myself,
(11)		absolutely not.=
(12)	Doctor:	⌐even during these periods-
(13)	Patient:	⌐I am an extremely neat person, you=
		=know.=
(14)	Doctor:	=mmm ...
(15)		even during these periods when you're sad,
(16)		feel sad,
(17)		an:guished,
(18)		you go on taking care of yourself, right?
(19)	Patient:	⌐oh: yes:,
(20)		yes:,
(21)		of course,
(22)		I go on taking care of myself,
(23)		naturally.=

		[dec]
(1)	Doctor:	e assim:, ...
(2)		cuida de si::, ..
(3)		/toma ba:nho,/
		[acc]
(4)		faz tudo normalmente?
(5)	Patient:	ah, cui:do,
(6)		tu:do direitinho,
(7)		tu:do
		⌐direi:tinho.
(8)	Doctor:	⌐num houve fases da senhora se descuidá=
		=disso?=
(9)	Patient:	=não:, absolutamente,

(10)   eu estando normal,
(11)   abisolutamente. =
(12) Doctor: ⌐-mesmo nessas fase-
(13) Patient: └-sou uma criatura limpíssima, sabe =.
(14) Doctor: = mmm, ...
(15)   mesmo nessas fases em que a senhora tá =
                  = triste,
(16)   sente tristc,
(17)   angustia:da,
(18)   a senhora: permanece tomando conta =
                  = não é?⌐
(19) Patient: └ ah: cui:do,
(20)   cui:do,
(21)   lógico,
(22)   da minha pessoa,
(23)   naturalmente. =

The doctor's questions about Dona Jurema's personal cleanliness habits ("do you take care of yourself?"; "do you bathe?") raise a touchy issue for the patient, who prides herself on being a neat, orderly person. Dona Jurema's sister wrote a letter to Doctor Edna entitled "my small contribution," in which she describes Dona Jurema's behavior at home during her four-day leave from the hospital (the discharge interview took place just after this leave). During the patient's stay at home, her sister said she had to help her with her eating and grooming routines (because of her arms). However, Dona Jurema was very concerned and unhappy about this (as stated in the sister's letter).

The doctor is well aware of how touchy the situation is; before stating her full question, she slows the pace of her talk, hedges "and let's see:," pauses, and formulates her request with a change in pace:

```
          [dec]
Doctor:  and let's see:, ....
          you take ca::re of yourself, ..
          /you ba:the/,
          [acc]
          you do everything as usual?
```

Dona Jurema's answer to the doctor's request is prefaced by the marker "oh":

```
Patient:  oh, yes:,
          e:verything just right,
          e:verything ju:st right.
```

As Schiffrin points out, "*oh* occurs as speakers shift their orientation to information" (1987a:74). In this instance it seems that the Portuguese marker *ah*, just like the English marker "oh," indicates two things: first, a shift in Dona Jurema's "subjective orientation" (1987a:95) regarding the information requested by the doctor. Schiffrin states that "orientation involves the evaluation of information: speakers respond affectively and subjectively to what is said, what they are thinking of, and what happens around them. . . . One such subjective orientation is **intensity**: a speaker is so committed to the truth of a proposition that future estimates of his or her character hinge on that truth" (1987a:95). Second, "oh" is used as "recognition display" (1987a:91); that is, "oh" marks the correctness of the doctor's prompt

Doctor: **and let's see:, ...**
         you take ca::re of yourself, ..
Patient: **oh, yes:, (I take care)**

The intensity of the patient's response can be observed in the use of "oh" and other features: vowel elongation in the forms "ca:re" *cui:do,* "e:verything" *tu:do,* "ju:st right" *direi:tinho;* emphatic voice stress in "e:verything ju:st right" *tu:do direi:tinho;* the use of the Portuguese diminutive morpheme for signaling intensity *(-inho* in *direitinho),* and repetition of forms

   e:very thing just right, e:very thing ju:st right.
   tu:do direitinho, tu:do direi:tinho.

This shift of orientation seems to signal two things: that the patient views the doctor's request as a face-threatening act (Brown and Levinson [1978] 1979); and that the patient holds a strong position regarding this information, which is that today (indicated by the present form of "care") everything is under control. Doctor Edna, however, does not seem to take the potential face-threatening act into consideration. In line (8) she interrupts Dona Jurema to ask if there weren't times that she did not care for herself ("weren't there periods of time that you did not care for yourself?"). The doctor has in mind the depressive periods in the past, during Dona Jurema's crises, when the patient consistently demonstrated total disregard for her body and herself.[12] She attempts to accomplish this reframing in the following way: She rephrases her previous question from an affirmative stance in the present ("and, let's see, you take care of yourself, you bathe, you behave as usual?") to a negative stance in the past ("weren't there periods of time that you did not care for yourself?"). The patient's immediate answer is an emphatic "no:, absolutely not" (line 9), to which she adds in a different time coordinate (line 10) "when I am myself, absolutely not." Dona Jurema is generalizing about a time of "normality" that includes her present state of mind *(eu estando normal* = "when I am myself"). Besides, she is keeping her alignment to the initial time frame (the present tense); that is, she is making a contribution to the frame that had been established in the beginning of this segment. Both participants overlap in the next two turns (lines 12 and 13), which latch unto the previous one (line 11):

(9) Patient: =no:, **absolutely not,**
(10)   **when I am myself,**
(11)   **absolutely not.** =
(12) Doctor: ┌**even during these periods-** =
(13) Patient: └**I am an <u>extremely</u> neat person, you know.** =

The doctor tries unsuccessfully to reintroduce her question; the patient asserts, "when I am myself, absolutely not," and emphatically challenges the doctor, "I am an *extremely* neat person, you know."

The patient and the doctor seem to be operating within two different temporal indices. The doctor is asking about feelings of depression in the past, feelings that may precede or co-occur with the psychotic crisis, not about normal sadness during periods of mental health. The patient, on the other hand, is talking about her behavior during the time that she is "herself" again, when she is in control. Hence, there is a discrepancy between how the speakers view this frame of talk.

This misunderstanding, which could be interpreted as an apparent lack of coherence, occurs because the patient maintains the same subjective orientation assumed at the beginning; that is, that today everything is under control. The metamessage is "I am fine." Again (in lines 9–11 and 13), she uses markers of intensity to indicate this position: the adverb *absolutamente* "absolutely," the Portuguese morpheme of intensity *-íssima* in *limpíssima* "extremely neat," the emphatic stress in *abisolutamente,* and the repetition of the form *absolutamente:*

Patient: =**não:, absolutamente,**
          eu estando normal,
          abisolutamente. =
Patient: **sou uma criatura <u>limpíssima</u>, sabe=** .

Patient: =no:, **absolutely not,**
          when I am myself,
          absolutely not. =
Patient: =**<u>I am an extremely</u> neat person, you know.** =

The difference is not resolved. However, the doctor acknowledges the information with a back-channel and a pause. She rephrases her question as an affirmative statement in the present tense with a postposed tag, seeking agreement and proposing a settlement, "even during these periods when you're sad, feel sad, anguished, you go on taking care of yourself, right?" The patient promptly agrees, "oh yes:, of course, I go on taking care of myself, naturally."

In this segment Dona Jurema risks a confrontation by taking a stand. Her position is that she is subject to depression and she is in control of herself during times of depression; that is, she takes care of herself, she does everything as usual. This stand differs from what might have been the doctor's expectation; that is, during times of depression—which may be a preliminary phase for a psychotic crisis or occur during the crisis— Dona Jurema is out of control. Here Dona Jurema's metamessage seems to be: I am in command of the situation (and of my senses), I know what I am doing, I can take care of myself. In doing so she risks lacking coherence, as indicated in the analysis. She puts her presentation of self at risk, which could be a threat to what she has invested in this interview. Nevertheless, she consistently maintains her initial position.

The fact that Dona Jurema is a sixty-one-year-old patient addressing a much younger doctor makes a shift of power possible, for although the doctor has a high professional status, the patient has the advantage of years. This sequence ends, therefore, with the doctor renegotiating the frame within the patient's perspective so as to cooperate in the interaction and redress the participant's face.

Reframing: "I used to be very active, doctor. I was a saleswoman, y'know."

There are a few moments in the interview in which the doctor and the patient share a strong sense of involvement. Tannen (1989) discusses how involvement is created in discourse. This feeling of being "connected" produces a more conversational discourse. Here, rapport seems to blur the considerable difference that otherwise prevails in the institutional framings.

[This text follows example (22); the camera focuses exclusively on Dona Jurema, who frequently nods and sometimes smiles at the doctor; since we have no information about the doctor's nonverbal behavior, I have altogether omitted nonverbal information in the transcript. Once again, I transcribe in verse: one intonational unit per line.]

(23)

(1) Doctor: = bu:t, do you stop doing what you =
              = usually do?
              [dec]
(2)   li:ke activities- ...
(3)   home out:side, ...
(4)   or you never- stopped let's see /being =
              = active?/
(5) Patient: └no,
              [acc]
(6)   I used to be very active, doctor. =
(7) Doctor: = //yeah?// =

(8) Patient: = I was a saleswoman, y'know, =
(9) Doctor: = //yeah?// =

In the preceding segment the two participants negotiate a topic transition from "depressive times" to "working activities." It is, indeed, Dona Jurema who establishes the topic and sets the pace for talk (lines 6 and 8). The doctor signals her acceptance of the topic by joining in. Twice her responses latch unto Dona Jurema's statements (lines 7 and 9), both times conveying an earnest request to go on talking.[13]

In addition to a change in topic, we also have a change in rhythm. Doctor Edna's slow-paced question (in lines 1–4) is interrupted and refuted by the patient (in lines 5 and 6), who then shifts to a rapid pacing. From then on, responses latch and overlap, a style that demonstrates the participants' degree of involvement in the topic (Tannen 1984):

```
                  [acc]
(6)               I used to be very active, doctor. =
(7)  Doctor:      = //yeah?// =
(8)  Patient:     = I was a saleswoman, y'know, =
(9)  Doctor:      = //yeah?// =
(10) Patient:     = for many years. ....
(11) Doctor:      /mmm./
(12) Patient:     I worked for a charity institution for =
                  = little old people ( )
(13) Doctor:      mmm: ...
(14) Patient:     see. ....
(15)              I used to sell for (it),
                  [acc]
(16)              I also used to sell for myself a little =
                  = bit, ..
(17) Doctor:      mmm: ,,,
(18) Patient:     I worked for many years as a saleswoman.
                  (1.5)
                  [acc]
(19) Doctor:      was that the only job /you had?/ ..
(20) Patient:     what? =
(21) Doctor:      = was that the only job?
(22) Patient:                      Lno.
(23)              I also worked for the Navy,
(24)              [as a] civil <ser- ser-> servant, =
(25) Doctor:      = civil servant, =
(26) Patient:     = in the Navy =
(27) Doctor:      = with a CON:tract, ..
(28) Patient:     e:verything just right. ..
(29) Doctor:      how many years did you work (there)? =
(30) Patient:     = twelve years. ..
(31) Doctor:      /yeah?/ ....
(32) Patient:     then I gave it up as-,
```

                           [acc]
(33)   I found myself a boyfriend,
(34)   you know sometimes these things make =
              = things worse, don't they.
(35) Doctor: /mmm,mmm./
(36) Patient: and this boyfriend made me quit the job,
                           [acc]
(37)   unfortunately.
(38)   I could be retired today ..
(39)   in the Navy, y'know.
(40) Doctor: /I see./ =
(41) Patient: = even earning a good <reti- reti-> =
              = retirement pension and all that,
              y'know. ...
(42) Doctor: ⌐before these twelve years,
(43)   you also didn't work?
(44) Patient: what? =
(45) Doctor: = before these twelve years in the Navy,
(46)   you didn't work either ...
(47) Patient: always as a saleswoman.
(48) Doctor: /saleswoman/. =
(49) Patient: = yeah,
(50)   I've always enjoyed selling. ....
(51)   I'm goo:d at that,
(52)   I've always enjoyed selling, Doctor Edna. ...

The turn structure, topic introduction and development, and a certain rhythmic synchrony all contribute to make this segment more balanced, more conversational than previous excerpts. Topics are brought up either by the patient ("the saleswoman," "the boyfriend," "retirement") or by the doctor ("the other job"). Hence, both speakers participate equally in topic change.

Dona Jurema takes an active role in conversing by volunteering more information (lines 10, 12, 15, 16, 24, 26, 32, 33, 36, 38, 39), providing evaluations (lines 28, 37, 38, 41, 50–52), complaining about a personal matter (lines 36–39), and inviting the doctor's opinion on an old affair (how boyfriends may endanger one's professional life (line 34). Turns are sometimes taken at the instigation of the doctor, as in:

(29) Doctor: **how many years did you work (there)?** =
(30) Patient: **= twelve years. ..**

For the most part, however, Dona Jurema holds the floor. She offers new information when she reports on previous activities:

(24)

(6) Patient: **I used to be very active, doctor.** =
(8)   **= I was a saleswoman, y'know,** =

(10)   = for many years. ....
(12)   I worked for a charity institution for =
              = little old people (   ),
(14)   see. ....
(15)   I used to sell for (it),
(16)   I also used to sell for myself a little bit, ..
(18)   I worked for many years as a saleswoman.

Or embeds a short narrative:

(25)

(32) Patient: then I gave it up as-,
(33)   I found myself a boyfriend,
(34)   you know sometimes these things make =
              = things worse, don't they.
(36)   and this boyfriend made me quit the job,
(37)   unfortunately.
(38)   I could be retired today ..
(39)   in the Navy, y'know.
(41)   = even earning a good <reti- reti->
              retirement pension and all that, y'know. ...

Or even just restates a few evaluative remarks:

(26)

(47) Patient: [I worked] always as a saleswoman.
(49)   yeah,
(50)   I've always enjoyed selling. ....
(51)   I'm goo:d at that,
(52)   I've always enjoyed selling, Doctor Edna. ...

These examples (24–26) portray a different type of interaction from the standard medical model: question/answer/comment. Instead, Dona Jurema holds the floor, and the doctor provides a series of "continuers" (Schegloff 1982:81), while her turns latch unto Dona Jurema's. The doctor's metamessage to the patient is "I'm with you, go on." She signals rapport by keeping up with the pace of talk (latching turns) as well as by encouraging the patient to talk more:

(6) Patient: I used to be very active, doctor. =
(7) Doctor: = //yeah?// =
(8) Patient: = I was a saleswoman, y'know, =
(9) Doctor: = //yeah?// =

And also:

(29) Doctor: **how many years did you work (there)?=**
(30) Patient: **=twelve years. ..**
(31) Doctor: **/yeah?/ ....**

As a response, in both instances, more talk follows (examples 25 and 26).

Dueting

Tannen (1984:77) says that "rapid rate of speech, overlap and latching of utterances are devices by which some speakers show solidarity, enthusiasm, and interest in others' talk." Rapport is also signaled here by other involvement strategies (Tannen 1989): repetition of forms (or reiteration) and collocation, as in the following fragment:

(23)   **I also worked for the Navy,**
(24)   **[as a] civil <ser- ser-> servant,=**
(25) Doctor: **=civil servant,=**
(26) Patient: **=in the Navy=**
(27) Doctor: **=with a CON:tract, ..**
(28) Patient: **e:verything just right. ..**

This text could have been uttered by a single speaker (the patient). Instead, we have the doctor as a cospeaker, participating in a duet with the patient (before the video audience). Falk (1979) discusses the degree of synchronicity needed for speakers to execute a duet, where the two participants become partners in a "dual-speaker role" (1979:108). This interaction frames a symmetrical relationship, where participants share the floor and turns display a rhythmic ensemble (Tannen 1989). Again, talk tends to be more conversational and less like interview talk. What triggers this partnership may be the participants' awareness of Dona Jurema's articulatory problem. She stutters as she says:

(23)   **I also worked for the Navy,**
(24)   **[as a] civil <ser- ser-> servant,=**

The doctor echoes the patient's words, signaling, "I'm with you":

(25) Doctor: **=civil servant,=**

Still in the speaker's role, Dona Jurema provides additional information:

(26) Patient: **=in the Navy=**

The doctor emphatically complements:

(27) Doctor: **=with a CON:tract, ..**

After a short pause, Dona Jurema agrees, evaluates, and concludes by saying, **"e:verything just right."**

Interruptions to the Personal Framing

Since this entire excerpt is marked by a high degree of synchronicity in pace through latching (lines 6–9, 20/21, 24–27, 40/41, 44/45, 48/49) and overlap (lines 4/5, 21/22), it is intriguing to see the patient's frequent interruptions.[14] Twice Dona Jurema introduces a "rerun signal" (Goffman 1981b:34):

(19) Doctor: **was that the only job /you had?/ ..**
(20) Patient: **what?=**
(21) Doctor: **=was that the only job?**

And also in:

(42) Doctor: ⌐**before these twelve years,**
(43)   **you also didn't work?**
(44) Patient: **what?=**
(45) Doctor: **=before these twelve years in the Navy,**
(46)   **you didn't work either ...**

Sometime later, while still discussing work activities, Dona Jurema introduces a third rerun signal:

(65) Doctor: **and why did you stop selling eight=**
               =months- eight months ago? ...
(66) Patient: **what?**
(67) Doctor: **why did you stop (selling eight months**
               ago?)

The communication problem that takes place here has to do with reframings. By introducing a question (lines 19, 42, and 65), Doctor Edna interrupts the patient's personal talk. She signals a return to the Q/A/Q/A format and, therefore, to the interview frame. Dona Jurema responds with a rerun signal that demonstrates at least two things: a reaction to a change in the turn structure and a reluctance to reenter the official frame.

It is her resistance that makes these rerun signals particularly interesting. Reentering the institutional frame of the interview entails several losses for Dona Jurema. She loses a more symmetrical relationship, the right to hold the floor, to introduce personal topics and evaluative remarks. Most of all, she loses a personal role (the active woman, the saleswoman), for role dispossession is bound to occur in the institutional framing, as Goffman (1961:14) points out. A rerun signal is, therefore, a way of resisting the official framing.

Reframing: "I am a mother. I've been in labor. How about you?"

In the second part of the interview, Dona Jurema gradually interacts with the doctor in a more symmetrical way: She offers more information, she challenges the doctor, she uses the doctor's first name when addressing an answer to her, and she shifts topics, with the doctor ratifying the shifts. Every reframing that takes place from an institutional to a personal context increases her level of rapport. This may be clearly perceived toward the close of the interview.

Before I illustrate this point, however, some background information is needed. A few moments before the excerpt I will be focusing on, the doctor had performed a physical examination and had asked the patient about her plans for the future. The doctor then recycles a topic that had been introduced at the beginning of the interview: the amount of contact that Dona Jurema has with her son. This topic triggers a series of other topics: the son and the marriage; the separation and her husband's betrayal; bearing children. While addressing these difficult topics, Dona Jurema shows discomfort, as conveyed by both her verbal and nonverbal communication. However, in the discussion of each of the topics, Dona Jurema conveys a higher level of control over the interaction: She provides more information than requested, makes evaluations about past events and actions concerning her husband, and introduces complaints about her situation, as in the following:

(27)

Patient: ⌐no, 'cause I found out,
there was a huge betrayal, y'know doctor.
· ·
so much so I separated from him.
I was the one who wanted the separation,
y'know.
· ·
but oh: ... It was a very serious situation, doctor.
there really had to be a separation, y'know.

Dona Jurema takes this topic to heart; in most of her statements she takes the responsibility for being the agent: "I found out," "I separated," "I was the one who wanted the separation." In these assertions she conveys the metamessage "I am in charge." This message is important for understanding the next interaction, in which Doctor Edna changes the topic again and asks Dona Jurema about childbirth.

[The doctor shifts her posture: she folds both hands together, bends slightly forward, turns her head to the right, bends further forward, getting closer to the patient.]

(28)

           [acc]
(1) Doctor: =and why did you only have one child?....
(2) Patient: ⌐because (it didn't),
       [moves torso backward, raises head and right hand, turns it outward]

Patient: I didn-, I suffered a lot,
          [hand gesture, head gesture toward the left, facing the doctor]
          I thought childbirth was terrible=
                              [shakes head]
          =the pain, ... y'know,
Doctor: [nod and slight movement backward]
          [acc]
Patient: so that afterwards then I had a=
          =procedure so that I wouldn't have any=
          =more (children),
                    [smile, lowers head slightly]
          [dec]
          I avoi:ded it.
          [nod]
(3) Doctor: /you were afraid to have children./=
          [short nods]
(4) Patient: =yes. (1.7)
          [nods]
          because the pain is terrible,
          isn't it, doctor. (1.3)
Doctor: //mmm mmm//
          [nod]
Patient: /I don't know/ do you have children?
          [nods, bends forward, and smiles]
          (2.0)
(5) Doctor: /mmm./
          [short nod]
(6) Patient: do you have children?=
          [bends further forward and to the right and smiles]
(7) Doctor: =/yes, I do./=
          [nods]   [bends more, elbows touch thighs, hands folded tighter]
(8) Patient: =yes, then you know that it is a=
          =terrible pain, right.
          ⌐the pain of childbirth is-
(9) Doctor:└then, because of that, you did not want=
          =any-=
          [raises torso, shoulder up against the chair, raises head, and bends
          slightly forward]
(10) Patient: =/yes, it was, it was/ because of that=
          =that I did not want any more. (1.8)
          [series of nods, looks away to the right and down, long nod]
          because of the pain. (2.7)
          [looks away]
(11) Doctor: //mmm, mmm.//
          [acc]
          ⌐and your son,
          [gesture of arms, opening up]
          do you- well::, go out often with him or=
          =does he come to visit you? ...

Although it is an uncomfortable topic, Dona Jurema provides more information, gives evaluations, and seeks ratification (this is conveyed
through verbal and nonverbal communication) in the first two turns.
Dona Jurema's wordiness stands out from the start.

The doctor asks the patient why she had only one child. Whatever
the answer is, she is expected to provide an explanation. The why-
question + the adverb "only" establish that there is an "expectation"
regarding the number of children in a family.[15] This question marks a
confrontation. The shift in posture of the doctor (bending forward) signals the doctor's involvement regarding the topic.

In answering, Dona Jurema presents a series of false starts and neg-
atives in a higher-pitched voice "because (it didn't [work-]), I didn't
[ha-]"; she shifts to a clause with no subject in Brazilian Portuguese and
attempts to answer: *porque (num deu)* "because (it didn't [work-])"; then
she adds "I didn't [ha-]." She moves backward and raises her head, in a
countermovement to that of the doctor. However, in her next contribution, she changes to a positive stand, faces the doctor, and emphatically
tells her: "I suffered a lot." She regains her agent status in this statement
and in her subsequent ones: "I thought childbirth was terrible," "so that
afterwards then I had a procedure so that I wouldn't have any more
(children)," "I avoided it."

Talking about childbirth accomplishes a new reframing: a woman-
to-woman conversation. In Dona Jurema's response she seeks agreement
with the woman she is talking to, who happens also to be a doctor:
"because the pain is terrible, isn't it, doctor." The doctor answers with a
short nod. Dona Jurema then introduces a question and in doing so
accomplishes a reversal of roles:

Patient: /I don't know/ do you have children? (2.0)
          [nods and bends forward and smiles]
Doctor: /mmm./
          [short nod]
Patient: do you have children?=
          [bends further forward and to the right and smiles]
Doctor: =/yes, I do./=
          [nods, bends more, elbows touch thighs, hands folded tighter]
Patient: =yes, then you know that it is a terrible=
          =pain, right.

For the first time in the interview, we have a reversal of the turn structure. It is the patient who bends forward toward the doctor, takes the
floor, and asks a question. The turn structure is:

Patient: Question
  Doctor: Answer (?)
  Patient: Question repeated

Doctor: Answer
Patient: Acknowledgment

When Dona Jurema asks the doctor whether she has children, the doctor responds in an ambiguous way: Her answer is barely audible or visible to the patient. This accounts for Dona Jurema's restating her question in such a way that the doctor must address it: She repeats the question in a clearer voice and with no hedging. Still the doctor satisfies only minimally this conversational requirement: She answers yes and provides no further information, and again her answer is hardly audible. The segment ends with Dona Jurema addressing the doctor's answer.

This reframing illustrates the gradual symmetry that is achieved by the end of the interview. Here, Dona Jurema subverts the prescribed roles of the institution. She talks to the doctor in a woman-to-woman relationship and, as a result, establishes a more symmetrical interaction. Doctor Edna, however, does not feel comfortable. As she watched this segment during the playback session she commented: "I tried to interrupt her. I showed distance in my answer; otherwise this would look like a chat". Hence, her first answer is barely audible, accompanied by a barely visible nod. After her second answer, she makes sure she gets the floor and overlaps with Dona Jurema in turns (8) and (9):

(8) Patient.   − yes, then you know that it is a =
               = terrible pain, right.
               ┌the pain of labor is-
(9) Doctor:└then, because of that,
               you did not want any- =

In (8) Dona Jurema attempts to provide another evaluation ("the pain of labor is-"), but the doctor makes a conclusive statement ("then, because of that, you did not want any-"), which Dona Jurema ratifies ("yes, it was, it was because of that that I did not want any more, because of the pain"). Doctor Edna, then, changes the topic and in doing so regains control of the turn structure. She also shifts back to the institutional frame.

Conclusion

In the discharge interview, participants engage in two major frames of talk—institutional and noninstitutional. I have argued that, while the doctor controls what happens in the former frames, it is the patient who controls the reframings that take place in the latter contexts. In the institutional frames, both the doctor and the patient perform official roles. However, Dona Jurema also performs her social identities: As a grandmother, she conveys rapport and camaraderie in her relationship with a very young doctor who reminds her of her granddaughter; as an elderly woman, she challenges the young doctor and takes a stand regarding the information that she chooses to convey; in a woman-to-woman relationship, she tries to establish rapport with the doctor over her feelings regarding two personal matters ("an old affair"; "childbirth"). In each reframing Dona Jurema changes her communicative strategies from providing less information to providing more information; her communicative style changes from less involvement to more involvement (signaled by paralinguistic and linguistic cues); and a topic change or a change in focus on the ongoing topic occurs.

Dona Jurema's performance of her social roles represents *a gradual transition from patient to person*, a necessary process to reenter the wider world, lest she remain subdued in a passive and disidentifying role: the role of patient. Each personal reframing stages what I have called "an expansion of self." We have, therefore, an inverse movement from the one described by Goffman (1961), in which a prepatient becomes an inpatient and curtailment of self occurs (1961:14). The discharge interview represents Dona Jurema's transition from an inpatient to an expatient stance. Proposing and accomplishing social reframings is, therefore, a way of regaining control over her social identities. It is also a way of displaying a feeling of communion with the outside world.

It is important to emphasize that throughout these reframings the interaction between the doctor and the patient remains coherent. In the institutional contexts the doctor frames the situation as a medical encounter, whether a psychiatric evaluation or a clinical, neurological examination. Dona Jurema correctly assesses the situation and then acts accordingly. That is, she mostly stays in the frame created by the doctor. In the social reframings, Dona Jurema proposes a transformation of the situation she is in. She shifts social contexts and reframes the talk as a personal encounter. When the doctor ratifies these shifts, the patient is successful at inserting the personal frame into the official frame, and talk follows until a new reframing occurs. During all this interactional work, Dona Jurema remains coherent.

A major frame tension, worthy of note, is the doctor's resistance to staying in the frame created by the patient. While Doctor Edna does ratify Dona Jurema's shifts (from the medical encounter to the social encounter), she does not stay for long in this frame of talk. Instead, she closes that segment of talk, changes topic, and shifts back to the medical encounter, as we saw in the frame shifts discussed in this chapter.

These shifts also have implications for a progressive symmetry that is sought by the patient. The reframings proposed by Dona Jurema and related to a personal agenda have implications for the major frame—the interview, which is an evaluation based on the doctor's agenda. These reframings do not alter the larger frame, with its norms and roles; they do not redefine the interview as a different type of encounter—between an older woman and a young woman, or between two women, for example. However, this interactional work introduces some change in the initial distancing assumed by the two participants in the interview.

This chapter has examined the official and unofficial frames of talk created by the two participants during the discharge interview. It has looked at the structure of social participation and analyzed how doctor and patient signal and ratify a frame of talk. The next chapter addresses topics and the structure of the discourse. We will see that a large part of what creates the institutional frame is related to the topic agenda that the doctor brings to the encounter. Within this frame I will address the issue of coherence in the discharge interview and relate it to topic shift and topic maintenance. I will also relate topic introduction to the reframings that the patient engenders in her efforts to establish a progressive symmetry.

Notes

1. It is important to characterize and differentiate between a *turn* and a *move*. According to Goffman (1981b), a turn at talk refers to holding the floor, not to "what is said while holding it" (1981b:23), while a move refers to the speech action taken during one's turn at talk.

2. Between the video presentation of the admitting and the discharge interviews, there is a five-minute report in which the doctor gives a summary assessment of what happened to the patient during the eighteen days she has been hospitalized (the kind of medication she was given, when and why it was suspended). In this context the doctor uses the "reporting register" described by Tannen and Wallat (1987), using "a markedly flat intonation" and giving "a running account" of the patient's health conditions and improvements. It is also "addressed to no present party, but designed for the benefit of [psychiatric] residents who might later view the videotape in the teaching facility" (1987:209).

3. In the analysis of this interview there are instances where both nonverbal and verbal behavior are complementary (as in the referred segment). There are also instances in which they are contrastive (as when the patient is providing information about her son, with whom she has a difficult relationship). I will refer to the nonverbal communication whenever it complements or provides new (contrastive) information to a change in frames.

4. Frankel (1984) distinguishes between two types of comments present in doctor-patient interviews: "value statements," which agree or contrast with the patient's previous response, and "neutral statements," which indicate that the speaker has heard and/or understood a previous statement. In the former, the doctor performs "evaluations" and "assessments"; in the latter, she just acknowledges the information provided by the patient. In this analysis I do not make this distinction. Virtually all comment responses from Doctor Edna are "neutral statements"; a few can be considered as agreeing assessments.

5. The other possibility would have been to address each other with title + last name. However, this form of address does not occur in the interviews.

6. In Brazilian Portuguese, the use of subject pronoun "you" (colloquial forms: *você/tu;* formal term: *a senhora/o senhor*) is optional as long as the antecedent is recoverable from the preceding context; hence, in many instances during

this interview we have zero pronoun subject, most instances being when the talk flows from a topic to a subtopic.

7. In a personal communication, Doctor Edna stated that Dona Jurema had a very difficult relationship with her son. In the discharge interview, however, the patient does not assert that. Quite to the contrary, she emphatically states that she sees him frequently and is very fond of him. Nonetheless, her nonverbal behavior (shaking her head, looking down) does not match her statements; in fact, in the three instances that Dona Jurema talks about her son, her nonverbal communication directly contradicts her verbal communication. In the admitting interview, as we will see in chapters 6 and 7, Dona Jurema indicates strong resentment toward her son.

8. The term *medical examination frame* comes from Tannen and Wallat (1987)—an analysis of conflicting frames and schemas in a medical encounter.

9. In this segment, the Portuguese markers *ah* ("oh"), *bom* ("well"), and *não é* ("y'know") seem to work in much the same way as their English equivalents, as described in Schiffrin (1987a).

10. Dona Jurema lived with two of her sisters. One of them, Dona Teresa, was also a sick woman. The other, Dona Idete, was in fact the caretaker of both and the housekeeper.

11. In Brazilian Portuguese, speakers signal agreement by restating the verb (for example, to answer positively the following request for information "do you have a car?" *você tem um carro?*—where *tem* is the conjugated form of the verb *ter* ("to have")—the speaker would say *tenho* "(I) have"). The "yes-form" may be added for emphasis: *tenho, sim* "(I) have, yes".

12. This lack of interest in herself and in others was documented during Dona Jurema's stay at the hospital. It was also registered in her sister's letters to Doctor Edna.

13. The doctor's contributions are requests for confirmation in form; however, they work as enthusiastic back-channels signaling the patient to "go on talking."

14. The doctor had initially suspected a slight memory impairment, which would account for the frequent repair signals used by the patient. However, neurological tests were inconclusive in this respect.

15. Important cultural and interactional presuppositions underlie this question. On one hand, in a Catholic country such as Brazil, it is still very common to have a family with more than two children. This sort of question is often addressed to a family with a single child—from relatives, friends, and even acquaintances. The question frequently has at least three functional meanings: a request for information, a complaint, and a request for action (have more children). The presupposition is that "there is something wrong with you" (something at odds with the culture). On the other hand, in this specific interaction the doctor had some previous knowledge about the difficult relationship that Dona Jurema has with her only son. She also knew that the patient had avoided subsequent pregnancies.

5

Topic Coherence in
the Discharge Interview

Topicality . . . is a matter not only of content, but is partly constituted in the procedures *conversationalists utilize to display understanding and to achieve one turn's proper fit with a prior.*
  Douglas Maynard, "Placement of Topic Changes in Conversation," p. 263.

The discourse of physicians and patients is controlled by physicians who, in asking questions, "request" that patients respond on specific topics. And the development of discourse topics is also controlled by physicians, who, with each successive question or request, shape the meaning of what is said.
  Marianne A. Paget, "On the Work of Talk:
  Studies in Misunderstandings," p. 73.

My discussion so far has dealt with the different frames that emerged in the discharge interview. We have seen that the doctor controls the institutional frames of the interview by introducing questions which the patient must address. We will see that all of these questions follow an official topic agenda that Doctor Edna brings to the interview.

In answering the doctor's questions, Dona Jurema sometimes shifts out of the institutional frame and reframes the talk as a personal encounter. Doctor Edna may ratify this shift. When she does, she goes along during a short segment of talk until she finally steers the patient back to the interview frame by introducing or reintroducing a topic on her agenda. Topics, therefore, play a crucial role in reframings as well as in the shaping of frames.

In this chapter I turn from a focus on frames to a focus on topic shift and topic maintenance as a way of assessing the patient's discourse coherence. One way of addressing the question "Is Dona Jurema coherent in the discharge interview?" is to look at what is talked about and the patterning of topics. Is talk restricted to the topic agenda that Doctor Edna brings to the interview? How does the patient respond to the doctor's requests for information? Do these responses sometime propose reframings?. This discussion of topic and coherence provides a standard against which the admitting interview will be compared.

The first part of the chapter discusses theoretical and methodological issues related to topic analysis and the relevance of these issues to the data. There are two sections to this part. In "On Establishing Referential Meaning," I present the concept of topic that I have used in the analysis. An excerpt from the interview illustrates how semantic and interactional shifts indicate topic boundaries. In "On Classifying Topics and Subtopics," I discuss the need for a two-level analysis and the resulting problems of this type of analysis.

The second part of this chapter describes the types of topic contributions that each participant makes in the encounter and how these contributions produce coherent on-topic discourse. "The Components of a Medical Interview" discusses the doctor's official topic agenda, which constitutes a major part of the institutional frames. The next section relates the concepts of *discontinuity* and *continuity* discussed by Keenan and Schieffelin (1976) to the preestablished doctor-patient roles in the institutional frames of the psychiatric interview. Since these framings are marked by role differentiation (namely interviewer versus interviewee, doctor versus patient), the types of topic contributions accomplished by each participant may be clearly contrasted. "Topic Shifts within the Institutional Frame" examines ways in which topic transitions are successfully accomplished in the interview. I discuss the participants' interactive moves related to topic introduction and development, which successively result in topic transition and eventual topic change.

In the third part, "Topics and Frames," I relate the topics and subtopics of this interview to the components of a standard medical interview and to interactional frames. We see that successive topic development may favor changes in frames. Thus, in addressing a topic, Dona Jurema sometimes introduces subtopics and, in so doing, may trigger a change in the context of talk. Finally, I argue that, if one looks at topics and subtopics, there is a slight progressive symmetry taking place, since in the second half of the interview the patient not only collaborates on a topic but also introduces subtopics. We see how the patient is again trying to decrease the asymmetry between herself and the doctor, which would mitigate doctor-patient alignment and contribute to the metamessage "I'm fine."

A Topic Analysis of the Interview

On Establishing Referential Meaning

One way of assessing regularities in discourse structure is to look at what speakers talk about, that is, topics. Speakers introduce and maintain topics; they talk about something. Hence, the process of establishing referents is necessary for a successful conversation.

In the analysis of the discharge interview, I look at what the speakers do in building ongoing talk and at how the message encodes new information. These two aspects of the analysis follow from Schiffrin's (1987b) discussion of topic "as a process which is both social and linguistic." In order to identify topics, the following signals were considered:

1. A sharp semantic change, and a subsequent change in information status of a referent, from new information to old;
2. Contextualization cues that indicate a topic transition. These cues may be prosodic or kinesic;
3. Interactional patterns in doctor-patient interviews;
4. The use of discourse markers.

Each of these signals is discussed below in one topical excerpt. The Portuguese text is also included because it encodes semantic information that would not surface in English.

The following short topical segment takes place at the beginning of the interview. The doctor has asked Dona Jurema her birthdate. Then she asks about her son:

(1)

                                         [acc]
(1) Doctor: =**you have a son, don't you?**
(2) Patient: ⌊**I have a son,**
                             [nods] [short smile]
            [acc]
(3) Doctor: **what's his name?** =
(4) Patient: =**Francisco Ferreira de Souza.** ...
            [dec]
(5) Doctor: **and he is how old now?** ..
(6) Patient: **he's- about forty-two.**
            [looks away, looks at doctor and smiles]
(7) Doctor: /mmm/ ...

                                      [acc]
(1) Doctor: =**a senhora tem um filho, não é isso?**
(2) Patient: ⌊**tenho um filho.**
                             [nods] [smile]
            [acc]
(3) Doctor: **como é o nome** ⌈**dele?** =
(4) Patient: =**Francisco Ferreira de Souza.** ...
            [dec]
(5) Doctor: **e ele tá com quantos anos** ⌊**agora?** ..
(6) Patient: **tá- cuns quarenta e dois.**
            [looks away, looks at doctor and smiles]
(7) Doctor: /mmm/ ...

a) A Sharp Semantic Change (and a subsequent change of status from new information to old information)

A change in reference is first encoded by a noun phrase in a final position. The doctor introduces the new referent "son" with the indefinite article, in a clause-final position, following a semantically weak predicate "have." This is a position associated with new information (Vachek 1966; Firbas 1974; Chafe 1976). Once the referent has been introduced, the doctor proceeds by asking two questions related to the referent (3) "what's his name?" *como é o nome dele?* and (5) "and he is how old now?" *e ele tá com quantos anos agora?* Two changes take place here. First, there is a change from an indefinite noun to a pronoun ("a son" in line 1 becomes "he" in line 5). Second, there is a change in the position of this referent from clause-final position (the position associated with new information) to clause-initial position (associated with old information and topics). In line (6) Dona Jurema answers the doctor's last question using zero pronoun anaphora:

Doctor: **and he has how many years now**
　　　　e ele tá com quantos anos agora?
　　　　(and he is how old now?)
Patient: **has- about forty-two.**
　　　　tá- cuns quarenta e dois.
　　　　(he's about forty-two.)

If we look at the message, this segment illustrates two aspects of topic development: (1) a process of topicalizing the new information (which is introduced in a final position, frequently following a semantically weak predicate, and which changes to initial position during the ongoing talk); and (2) the degree of topic accessibility discussed by Givón (1983), of the person referred to (from an indefinite noun (a son), less accessible, to zero anaphora, most accessible.[1]

b) Contextualization Cues

If we look at the interaction, contrastive intonational patterns are important contextualization cues (Gumperz 1982). Among other things, these cues indicate that a topic unit is being developed. In line (1) the doctor introduces the topic at a fast pace:

　　　　　　　　　　[acc]
(1) Doctor: **=you have a son, don't you?**
　　　　　　　　　　[acc]
(1) Doctor: **=a senhora tem um filho, não é isso?**

In line (3) the doctor keeps up a fast pace as she develops the topic, using a high pitch and a rising intonation (the English translation does not capture this rising intonation):

　　　　　　　[acc]
(3) Doctor: **what's his name?**
　　　　　　　[acc]
(3) Doctor: **como é o nome ⌐dele?**

This accelerated pace may signal more involvement of the speaker with the topic (Tannen 1984). However, in the doctor's next turn (line 5), she changes pace again and uses a lower pitch and falling intonation:

[dec]
(5) Doctor: **and he is how old now? ..**

[dec]
(5) Doctor: **e ele tá com quantos anos ˌagora? ..**

Doctor Edna's slower pace and low pitch signal a final question on the topic and the end of that talk.

This example portrays a frequent pattern in the interview. That is, new topics are often introduced by Doctor Edna in a faster pace and a higher key, thus marking the beginning of a topic sequence, and she uses a slower pace and a lower key to signal the ending or completion of that unit of talk.

Coulthard discusses differences in pitch in successive tone groups in doctor-patient communication: "A doctor, having exhausted one line of inquiry will sometimes begin a new sequence of questions in high key" ([1977] 1981:129). In the discharge interview, pitch variations from the doctor constitute cues for topic management and turn allocation.

c) Interactional Patterns

Still looking at the interaction and at the exchange structure, the pattern of this stretch of talk is a short expansion on the three-turn question/answer/acknowledgment, which is the basic unit of coherent on-topic discourse in doctor-patient interviews (Frankel 1984; West 1984). That is, the doctor requests information, the patient provides the information requested, and the sequence ends with an acknowledgment from the doctor. In the discharge interview this basic unit is often expanded with embedded turns, where the three-part turn structure represents a closing to most topics.

d) Discourse Markers

We have seen that in the preceding segment the doctor asks the patient three questions:

(1) Doctor: **=you have a son, don't you?**
(3) Doctor: **what's his name?=**
(5) Doctor: **and he is how old now? ..**

While the first two questions are introduced with no connector, Doctor Edna uses "and" to preface her last question. As a discourse marker, "and" can relate "questions in a question agenda, i.e. a pre-arranged set of questions through which speakers plan to proceed in a fixed order" (Schiffrin 1987a:146). Here, it seems that "and" marks the speaker's continuation on the topic. It also signals a closing to the ongoing topic unit (together with the intonational cues discussed previously).

This example illustrates a short on-topic segment. Not all topic units are as short or have as clear-cut boundaries as this one.

Of the indicators noted, I want to emphasize the occurrence of topic-comment structures, which, in the discharge interview occur in short as well as longer segments of discourse and constitute a major criterion for identifying units of on-topic talk. The doctor introduces a new referent in the following way:

[In the following sentence, the topic is "you" and the comment is "other hospitalizations." I am using underlining to indicate the comment.]

(2)

Doctor: you   already had <u>other</u> hospitalizations,
         a senhora   já   teve <u>outras</u> <u>internações</u>,

         haven't you?
         não é?

         (you have already had other hospitalizations, haven't you?)

"Other hospitalizations" contrasts with the "present hospitalization" (a previous referent), and it is introduced in final position in a clause. During the next sixteen turns it is established as a topic for talk. Then Doctor Edna closes the segment by saying:

(3)

<u>of these</u> hospitalizations <u>all</u>,   never you remember?
<u>dessas</u>   <u>internações</u>   <u>todas</u>, nunca se lembra?
(of all these hospitalizations, do you ever remember anything?)

The referent "these [past] hospitalizations" is reintroduced in initial position in the clause, rather than final position (as was the case when the information was first mentioned). This shift in position reflects the change in information status through this discourse.

The interview format also has changes in information status. For example, characters that are introduced in the first part of the interview (such as the patient's son and granddaughter) are coded as new information, occupying a final position in a clause. This can be seen in example (1), repeated here, as well as in example (4):

(1)

Doctor: you   have <u>a son</u>,   not is this?
         a senhora tem <u>um filho</u>, não é isso?
         (you have a son, don't you?)

(4)

Doctor: have granddaughter also,   not is this?
        tem <u>neta</u>   também, não é isso?
        (you also have a granddaughter, don't you?)

These referents are recycled at the end of the interview in a topicalized position, occupying an initial position in a clause. They constitute one of the cues that indicate the closing of the interview.

(5)

Doctor: and <u>the</u> your <u>son</u>,
        e   <u>o</u>   <u>seu</u>   <u>filho</u>,
        (and your son,)

        you-   uhm: go out always with him?
        a senhora- é::   sai   sempre com ele?
        (do you- uhm: do you always see him?)

(6)

Doctor: and <u>the</u> your <u>granddaughter</u>.
        e   <u>a</u>   <u>sua</u>   <u>neta</u>.
        (and your granddaughter,)

        you   have contacts   a lot   with her
        a senhora tem contato   bastante com ela?
        (do you see her a lot?)

These cues helped me identify on-topic discourse. Of the different linguistic indicators, I emphasized the occurrence of change in information status (from clause-final to clause-initial position). Schiffrin (1987b) discusses processes of topicalization and topic continuity in narratives. A psychiatric interview also presents a bounded unit, where topics are introduced, developed, and closed. Hence, for this type of data, changes in information status constitute important markers for referential change.

On Classifying Topics and Subtopics

The following discussion presents arguments for doing a topic analysis that involves a level of subordination (topic and subtopic). It also discusses the problems involved in topic and subtopic categorization and the fact that any topic taxonomy has to be regarded with caution (Tannen 1984:42).

Arguments for a Two-Level Analysis

Throughout the discharge interview the participants introduce topics that present different levels of generality. The relationship that exists between a topic and a subtopic is set on a general-to-specific dimension (van Dijk 1977). I have used only two of these levels to indicate a subordination of semantic information: *topic,* which introduces a referent with a relative degree of generality, and *subtopic,* which introduces a referent with a relative degree of specificity.

As mentioned previously, in the interview, topics are signaled through a sharp semantic change, that is, a change in reference, as well as changes in the turn structure. In this way topics present boundaries that tend to be marked semantically and interactionally. In this analysis, topics are also a generalization on a set of subtopics. Subtopics have finer referential boundaries: Each subtopic is related to the other by "co-referential chains" (Brown and Yule 1983:190), for example, by lexical cohesion, clausal substitutions, comparison, syntactic repetition, or consistency of tense.

Subtopics present a greater level of complexity to the discourse analyst, but they are worth exploring in this analysis for four reasons: The first and most important one is that if I were to map only the topics, I would be indicating only the referential information introduced by the doctor, with very few contributions from the patient. As we will see, Dona Jurema assures "topic continuity" (Keenan and Schieffelin 1976) by collaborating on a topic and introducing subtopics. The subtopics represent the new information provided spontaneously by the patient. On the other hand, Dona Jurema never introduces new topics.

Second, the doctor's official agenda contains items that surface in the interview as both topics and subtopics. She is following Sullivan's list of items (1954:147) that should be discussed during a psychiatric interview: "toilet and grooming habits," "eating habits," "sleep and sleep functions," "parenthood," among others. These items are, therefore "mentionables" for this interview and for these participants; they fit what Sacks, Schegloff, and Jefferson (1974:727) call the "recipient design."

Third, specific information requested by the doctor is also portrayed through subtopic categorization. Several of Dona Jurema's contributions (with small variations) fall into the following pattern:

> Doctor: introduces and requests information on topic X
> Patient: provides information on topic X
> Doctor: closes topic X—acknowledges

Expansion on this pattern is sought by the doctor as she requests specific information on a given topic. The expansion looks like this:

> Doctor: introduces and requests information on topic X
> Patient: provides information on topic X
>   Doctor: requests information on topic Xa
>   Patient: provides information on topic Xa

> Doctor: requests information on topic Xb
> Patient: provides information on topic Xb
>   and so on
>   Doctor: closes topic X—acknowledges

Another reason for a detailed topic analysis (one that notes boundaries between subtopics as well as topics) has to do with cross-referencing information. We will see later that some referents brought up for discussion in the discharge interview have a different topic status in the admitting interview—what Schiffrin (1987b:8) calls a "thematic status." For example, in the admitting interview, while in a psychotic crisis, Dona Jurema refers to her husband and curses him. She also refers to a "secret." This referent assumes a thematic topic status in the text. In the discharge interview, as a detailed topic analysis indicates, the participants talk about "Dona Jurema's marriage," a topic introduced by the doctor. However, they also talk about "separation and betrayal," an embedded topic. This subtopic is introduced by Dona Jurema. This information about the "separation and betrayal" helps in understanding "the curse" and "the secret" themes in the admitting interview. Hence, subtopics are indicated because they contain information meaningful for the patient and introduce referents that appeared in the admitting interview.

Problems Involved in Subtopic Categorization

Since subtopics contain important information, the question is not whether one should do a finer-level analysis but, rather, what type of contribution qualifies for subtopic categorization and how specific the branching of information should be. The difficulty arises in consistently segmenting these "embedded topics." This analysis takes into consideration two criteria: first, whether the participants develop the subtopic; second, whether it is on the doctor's official agenda. Thus, certain referents are classified as subtopics because they are part of the doctor's agenda, whether or not they are expanded.

The next example indicates the types of contributions that were counted as subtopics. We will see that the participants' strategies alternate: In the first part, we see the use of repetition as a cohesive tie, with no new referents being introduced and therefore no subtopics. As a contrast, in the second part the participants introduce contributions that may qualify for subtopic categorization.

(7)

                        [dec]
(1) Doctor: ⌐do you:: remem:ber, let's see,
(2)   if you (had already) had periods of=
(3)   =being very sa:d, for no rea:son,=
(4) Patient: =I have, yes, doctor.
(5) Doctor: └of being depressed,=

(6) Patient: =I have, yes.
(7) Doctor: you have?=
(8) Patient: = I have, yes. ....
(9) Doctor: what is it like? /tell me/.
(10) Patient: I become sa:d, for nothing, for no=
            =reason, you know. =
(11) Doctor: =I know:.
(12)   and what else happens?
(13)   do you cry a lot?=
(14) Patient: =no, I don't cry. ...
(15) Doctor: what do you feel? (when-)? (1.1)
(16) Patient: what? =
(17) Doctor: =what do you feel when you get like=
            =that?..
(18) Patient: ⌐I feel such a sadness, such an anguish. ...
(19) Doctor: //I know.// ....
(20)   do you stop eating?=
(21) Patient: =no, I even eat very well, doctor.=
(22) Doctor: =yeah? =
(23) Patient: =thank God, I eat very well.
            [dec]
(24) Doctor: and let's see: .... you take ca::re of=
(25)   =yourself, .. /you ba:the/,
            [acc]
(26)   you do everything as usual?
(27) Patient: oh, yes:, e:verything just right,
(28)   e:verything ju:st right.
(29) Doctor: ⌊weren't there periods of time=
            =that you did not care for yourself?=
(30) Patient: =no:, absolutely not,
(31)   when I am myself, absolutely not.=
(32) Doctor:⌐even during these periods-
(33) Patient:⌊I am an extremely neat person, you=
            =know?=
(34) Doctor: =mmm ...
(35)   even during these periods when you're=
(36)   =sad, feel sad, an:guished,
(37)   you go on taking care of yourself,
            right? │
(38) Patient: ⌊oh: yes: yes:, of course,
(39)   I go on taking care of myself,
            naturally. =

First Doctor Edna introduces the topic "depressive times" in lines (1) and (2). After this topic has been negotiated and ratified by both participants (lines 1–8), the doctor makes a general request for information (line 9):

Doctor: what is it like? /tell me/.

Dona Jurema responds to this request by repeating (with variation) entire lexical units of the doctor's original question.

[Here underlining indicates repetition. The Portuguese text is also included.]

Doctor: you   yourself remember let's see
      a senhora se   lembra   assim,

        if already had periods of becoming very <u>sad,</u>
        se já   teve fases de <u>ficar</u>   muito <u>triste,</u>

        <u>without motive,</u>
        <u>sem motivo,</u> =

Patient: I <u>become</u> <u>sad,</u>   <u>without having</u> cause,
       eu <u>fico</u>   <u>triste,</u> <u>sem haver</u> causa,

       <u>without having</u> <u>reason,</u> not is.

       <u>sem</u>   <u>haver</u>   <u>razão,</u> não é.

The following structures are repeated (with variation) by the patient:

Doctor	Patient
. becoming . sad	... become sad
without motive	without having cause
	without having reason

What seems to be happening here is that Dona Jurema continues to participate in the interaction: She addresses the question in an affirmative way, but she has nothing new to say. The doctor's next strategy is to ask the patient a series of specific questions concerning her behavior under depression so as to elicit more information (lines 11–17):

Doctor: = I know:.
       → **and what else happens?**
       → **do you cry a lot?** =
Patient: = no, I don't cry. ...
Doctor: → **what do you feel? (when-)? (1.1)**
Patient: what? =
Doctor: = **what do you feel when you get like**
       that?..

First, Doctor Edna acknowledges the patient's answer, "I know," and then she requests more information "and what else happens?" However, she does not wait for the patient's answer and immediately inserts a new question "do you cry a lot?" "Crying a lot" could, therefore, be a candidate for subtopic categorization, but the patient does not pick it up. Thus, not every referent that is mentioned becomes a subtopic (or topic), only those comments that are developed by the participants (Tannen 1984:41).

In pursuing the same line of inquiry, the doctor asks Dona Jurema about her feelings under depression. Here again, Dona Jurema states her answer for the second time (line 18):

> I feel such a <u>sadness</u>, such an <u>anguish</u>.
> sinto aquela <u>tristeza</u>, aquela <u>angústia</u>. ...

Repetition binds this stretch of talk, making the discourse highly cohesive.[2] In fact, the patient not only paraphrases the doctor's utterance twice but also in each occurrence repeats a paradigm:

First occurrence: I become sad, for nothing,
                                  for no reason,

                            eu fico triste, sem haver causa,
                                  sem haver razão,

Second occurrence   I feel such a sadness,
                                  such an anguish.

                            sinto aquela tristeza,
                                  aquela angústia.

This paradigm repeats linguistic forms *(sem haver* and *aquela)* and rhythm. Johnstone (1984:251) points out that the two parts of the paraphrase function together as a semantic, cohesive, and rhetorical unit. The rephrasing is an expansion that works "to create greater, not different, understanding." Additionally, the repetition binds the text together.

On the interactional level, repetition helps the patient get and keep the floor. It also signals listenership; that is, it shows that Dona Jurema is attending to the interaction (Tannen 1987a:583).

However, by using repetition as a strategy, Dona Jurema does not expand on the referent. On the contrary, both forms convey very general information: "such a sadness" *(aquela tristeza),* "such an anguish" *(aquela angústia).* The doctor, on the other hand, wants to pursue more specific information. Thus, in line (20) she goes on asking:

(20) Doctor: → **do you stop eating?** =
(21) Patient: = no, I even eat very well, doctor. =
(22) Doctor: = yeah? =
(23) Patient: = thank God, I eat very well.
(24) Doctor: → **and let's see, ... you take ca::re** =
(25)   → **= of yourself, .. /you ba:the/,**

(26)   **you do everything as usual?**
(27) Patient: **oh, yes:, e:verything just right,**
                    <u>**e:verything ju:st right.**</u>

Two questions in this excerpt present candidates for subtopic categorization: eating habits under depression (line 20), and personal cleanliness under depression (line 24). Both were counted as subtopics—eating habits because it is part of the official topic agenda and personal cleanliness because it is developed in the interaction (lines 29–34):

(29) Doctor: **weren't there periods of time that you=**
                =did not care for yourself?=
(30) Patient: **=no:, absolutely not,**
(31)   **when I am myself, <u>absolutely not.</u>=**
(32) Doctor:⌐**even during these periods-**
(33) Patient:⌐**I am an extremely neat person, you=**
                =know?=
(34) Doctor: **=mmm ...**

This segment closes with the doctor recycling the topic "periods of depression" in sentence-initial position (the slot for the given information):

Doctor: **even during these periods when you're sad,**
        feel sad, an:guished,
        you go on taking care of yourself, right?
Patient: ⌐**oh: yes:, yes:, of course, I go=**
        =on taking care of myself, naturally.=

It is important to stress that subtopic categorization and the distinction between topic and subtopic are not always clear-cut. The analysis is complex because subtopics present a higher degree of lexical cohesion and anaphoric reference. Thus, there is no such thing as a sharp semantic shift, and fewer interactional cues occur within these subsets to indicate any change.

The second part of this chapter focuses on the type of work that each participant accomplishes to produce coherent on-topic discourse. The doctor's topic agenda orients topic selection and topic introduction. We see the patient consistently responding to the doctor's topic agenda, and thereby signaling discourse understanding. We also see the patient providing an answer to every question raised by the doctor. In responding to all questions as legitimate, Dona Jurema displays an appropriate patient's schema. That is, she matches the set of expectations for patient responses in doctor-patient interaction (Mishler 1984:120; West 1983:99).

Topic and Coherence

In everyday talk, people are continuously trying to make sense out of a given piece of discourse. That is, when listeners are presented with chunks of language, they "will make every effort to impose a coherent interpretation" (Brown and Yule 1983:199). They assume coherence; they assume that the linguistic message makes sense and is appropriate to the context of the interaction. Listeners expect, therefore, that the speaker is abiding by the co-operative principle: "You must make your conversational contribution such as is required, at the stage at which it occurs, by the accepted purpose or direction of the talk exchange in which you are engaged" (Grice 1975:45). Participants in a talk exchange refer both to the linguistic message and to extralinguistic information that should provide the necessary clues to the interpretation of the discourse.

In a medical interview, primary attention is given to the pursuit of referential information: The doctor introduces a topic for discussion, and the patient addresses the doctor's topic.[3] This habitual exchange of information imposes on the doctor and the patient certain preestablished patterns for topic management. Thus, there is a specific type of work involved in the joint development of topics. The doctor orchestrates topics since she is the one who establishes what talk will be about. The patient achieves coherence by providing on-topic responses. If these patterns are followed and knowledge schemas are shared, then discourse coheres.

The Doctor's Topics: The Components of the Medical Interview

The topics that are introduced during the interview are the doctor's topics. Doctor Edna comes to the encounter with a "topic agenda" that has been determined as a format for recording medical research data. She thus directs talk by closely following a prescribed set of points, introducing every topic by asking the patient a question.[4]

The topics introduced by Doctor Edna belong to specific domains of talk that are expected parts of a medical interview. The following format has become a standard for medical interviews (Reiser and Schroder [1980] 1984:167):

1. Identifying data (the patient's name, age, race, marital status, and occupation);
2. Informant (assessing the patient's reliability as a historian);
3. Chief complaint;
4. Present illness;
5. Past history;
6. Family history;
7. Review of systems (final historical cross-check);
8. Social history and patient profile.

This schema proves to be useful since it underlies the doctor's agenda for this interview. I will comment briefly on each component.

1. *Identifying data:* Doctors generally begin an interview with a patient profile before focusing on the present illness, as "this prepares the patient for the medical portion of the interview both emotionally and cognitively. . . . The outcomes will usually be increased rapport, communicativeness, and trust" (Reiser and Schroder [1980] 1984:206). Thus, at the beginning of the discharge interview, Doctor Edna asks Dona Jurema: "When were you born?"; "You have a son, don't you?"; "What's his name?"; "How old is he now?"

2. *Informant:* Doctors sometimes request information so as to evaluate the patient's reliability as a historian. Doctor Edna already knows the history of the patient from interviews with the patient's sister. She needs, however, to evaluate how much the patient knows and remembers about this factual information. This relationship mirrors a classroom interaction, where the teacher asks known-answer questions (requests for display) that have the sole purpose of verifying the student's knowledge. So questions of the type "Were you married?" and "How long were you married?" assess Dona Jurema's memory of her personal life story, while questions of the type "Do you remember the day you came to the hospital? to this hospital?" and "Do you have any idea how long you have been here?" assess the patient's knowledge of her psychiatric history.

3. *The chief complaint* is the major problem that concerns the patient: What is disturbing the patient (as the patient sees it). In the discharge interview the doctor assesses the patient's present psychiatric health state by asking, "Are you having some problems now?"; "Do you feel that something still isn't quite right?" At this point in her treatment, Dona Jurema has been worried about some specific physical problems related to arthritis in her hand and difficulties in eating, getting dressed, and keeping herself tidy. The following questions aim at this specific problem: "You complained about a weakness in your arms, remember?" "What sort of weakness is it?"; "Are you unable to move (your arms)?"; "What do you feel when you move (your arms)?"

4. *The history of the present illness* contains the most important information for an adequate evaluation; it is also the most difficult part of the medical interview. Patients present their symptoms "in bits and pieces, fits and starts, as they interpret their distress through a prism of fear, pain, life experiences, and personal priorities" (Reiser and Schroder [1980] 1984:171). Doctors use several guidelines to request further information on the present illness. Of all of these guidelines, the dimension of time is considered by far the most important element (Reiser and Schroder [1980] 1984:173). In this interview the doctor asks questions

about chronological information in an attempt to establish certain dates and time when symptoms first began: "Dona Jurema, do you remember the day that you came to the hospital, to this hospital?"; "Do you have any idea how long you have been here?"; "Do you remember what has happened since then?"; "What is the last event that you can recall?"

5. *The past history,* among other things, reviews past hospitalizations and previous crises. Since her first crisis in 1975, Dona Jurema has already been hospitalized five times, and the historical information about her previous hospitalizations is relevant to her present illness: "You have had other hospitalizations, haven't you?"; "How many hospitalizations have you had?"; "Do you remember the places that you were admitted to?"; "And how often were you at Doctor Eiras Hospital?"

6. *The family history* is another important component of the patient's medical interview. "A minimum family history consists of knowing the state of health of the parents and siblings" (Reiser and Schroder [1980] 1984:177). In the discharge interview the doctor already has this information. However, she needs to gather it from the patient herself, to see what facts stand out from the patient's perspective: "Is there any one in your family with a similar problem?"; "What did your brother have?"; "Do you remember him?"; "Do you remember what would happen to him?"

7. *Review of systems* is a final scanning, a "historical cross-check," which may "vary in depth and detail" (Reiser and Schroder [1980] 1984:177). At the end of the interview the doctor makes an overall evaluation: "Do you feel better now than a few days ago?"; "What makes you feel better?"; "How did you use to feel before? How do you feel now?" She then proceeds to check on specific problems concerning sight ("Can you see well?"), swallowing ("Can you swallow again?"), and walking ("And with walking, you're not having any problems?").

8. *The social history* involves a wide selection of issues: (a) housing and living arrangements: "Dona Jurema, where do you live?"; "You live with your two sisters, don't you?"; (b) daily activities: "What do you usually do at home?"; "What do you intend to do when you go home?"; (c) occupation: "But, [during your crisis] do you stop doing what you usually do?"; "Was that the only job you had?"; (d) financial status: "Did you live off that wage?"; (e) availability of family: "And your son, do you see him a lot?"; "Do you go out with him or does he usually come to see you?"; (f) religious activities: "Are you religious?"; "Do you go to church often?"

The schema presented by Reiser and Schroder outlines the flow of topics. It creates an underlying format for the interview as a medical encounter, and thus establishes "what officially constitutes this talk."

In the topic analysis I use topics as titles to summarize a stretch of talk. I make use of a notion of "topic = title," bearing in mind that "for any text, there are a number of different ways of expressing the topic" (Brown and Yule 1983:73). Each way of expressing the topic represents, therefore, a judgment of what is being talked about. (Appendix C presents the list of topics introduced during this interview and relates them to the different components of the medical interview.)

In the discharge interview Dona Jurema addresses the doctor's topics and stays on topic. She does not introduce topics from her own personal agenda. For the most part she simply provides an answer to the doctor's questions, assuring topic continuity and discourse coherence.

Continuous and Discontinuous Discourse

Continuity and *discontinuity* (Keenan and Schieffelin 1976) in discourse concern distinctions about the way discourse topics emerge. Each time a speaker introduces a new topic, she brings about discontinuity in the discourse; on the other hand, when the speaker addresses and expands an ongoing topic, she provides for continuity.

Continuous and discontinuous discourse relate to the preestablished doctor-patient roles in the psychiatric interview. Dona Jurema as the interviewee must work to provide discourse continuity, while Doctor Edna as the interviewer has the complementary role of promoting discontinuity in the discourse.

Continuity in Discourse

There are two processes to achieve continuity in discourse (Keenan and Schieffelin 1976)—by *collaborating on a topic* and by *incorporating a topic*. Question-answer pairs constitute the most commonly used type of collaboration in the interview. We have seen this process taking place repeatedly in several excerpts. Dona Jurema, as the patient, addresses the questions raised by the doctor and, in doing so, collaborates on the topic.

The other way of showing collaboration on a topic is by repetition. In addition to the cohesive function of repetitions, they indicate that the speakers are sharing the same topic (or subtopic) and thus producing continuous discourse. In this domain there are a variety of ways in which the doctor and the patient recycle information, among which the following are the most common.

First, there are question-answer pairs (in yes-no questions), where Dona Jurema provides a positive answer by echoing the doctor's question:

(8)

Doctor: **when you- ... were able to remember**
            anything, or recognize things

$\rightarrow$ you were already in here? =

Patient: $\rightarrow$ = I was already in here. (1.9)

Doctor: quando a senhora- ... conseguiu se =
           = lembrá de alguma coisa, ou reconhecê =
           = as coisas,
       $\rightarrow$ a senhora já estava aqui dentro? =

Patient: $\rightarrow$ = <u>já estava aqui dentro</u> (1.9).

In Portuguese, as the underlined forms indicate, the doctor and patient repeat the same verb paradigm without any change for the first and third persons. Additionally, no subject pronouns are used (the fact that the first- and third-persons singular have the same form in Portuguese cannot be captured in the English version).[5] Hence, Dona Jurema's answer echoes the doctor's question.

Second, a question-answer pair is frequently repeated, as when the doctor asks Dona Jurema if she remembers what happened since she was taken to the hospital:

(9)

Doctor: **and do you remember what happened from then =**
        = (to now)?
Patient: **no, I remember nothing, nothing, nothing, =**
        = nothing.   [shakes head]
Doctor: **=/you don't remember?/**
Patient: **nothing, nothing, nothing, nothing.**
         [shakes head]

Doctor: **e a senhora lembra o que aconteceu (de lá) =**
        = pra cá? =
Patient: **não, num lembro nada, nada, nada, nada. =**
            [shakes head]
Doctor: **=/não se lembra?/**
Patient: **nada, nada, nada, nada.**
         [shakes head]

Another instance of continuous discourse occurs in the three-part turn structure (question/answer/acknowledgment), which provides a natural slot for repetition to take place:

(10)

Doctor: **do you have any idea of how long it's been?**
Patient: **about twenty days or so, hasn't it been =**
              = doctor?
Doctor: $\rightarrow$ **/about twenty days or so./**

In echoing the patient's words, the doctor signals continuity and encourages Dona Jurema to go on talking (Reiser and Schroder [1980]

1984:128). A three-part sequence can be further expanded, with Dona Jurema taking another turn, as in the following example:

(11)

Doctor:	**do you see well?** =
Patient:	= **I see-, no, I use glasses.** =
Doctor:	= **/you use glasses./** =
Patient: →	= **I use glasses. ...**

In these segments the same topic is sustained from speaker to speaker. Both participants work to collaborate on a topic.

The second process for producing continuous discourse is by incorporating a topic. In this analysis this means introducing or recycling subtopics in the discourse. In the discharge interview, both the doctor and the patient introduce or recycle subtopics successfully. It is still the doctor who introduces most subtopics (80%), seven of which are recycled. The patient, however, also provides expansions, most of which take place in the second half of the interview (see Appendix C for the flow of topics). The subtopics represent the information provided spontaneously by Dona Jurema.

Discontinuity in Discourse

There are two ways of producing discontinuity in the discourse: by *introducing topics,* that is, by presenting new referents into the talk, and by *recycling topics,* that is, by reintroducing topics. In both cases it is Doctor Edna who produces discontinuous discourse, through topic disjuncts or through gradual disengagement from the previous topic.

In the discharge interview, topic continuity and topic discontinuity are important distinctions that characterize each participant's contribution to the interaction. These contributions, in turn, reflect the participants' roles. A patient's role is to provide topic continuity in the discourse, which Dona Jurema does by collaborating on a topic and by introducing subtopics. Although the doctor also provides for topic continuity, her major work is to introduce new referents and therefore promote the discontinuity of the discourse. Doctor Edna does so by introducing and recycling topics. (Table 5.1 mirrors the types of contributions from Dona Jurema and Doctor Edna.)

The patterning for topic introduction and topic maintenance reflects the commonly observed division of labor present in the medical interview situation (Byrne and Long 1976; Shuy 1983; West 1983; Fisher 1983; Mishler 1984, among others). Specifically, Erickson and Rittenberg (1987) observe that the asymmetrical format of medical interviews (the difference in rank between physician and patient) does not favor equality. By being allocated the "answerer" slot, and indeed by accepting it, the patient displays understanding about the general schema that underlies topic structure in interviews. To be topically coherent, Dona Ju-

Table 5.1 Types of Contributions in the Discharge Interview

Patient	Doctor/Patient	Doctor	Doctor
Collaborating on a topic	Introducing subtopics	Introducing topics	Reintroducing topics

Topic Continuity		Topic Discontinuity

D i s c o u r s e

rema must successively contribute with the second pair part of the question-answer unit.

Thus, were Dona Jurema to initiate topics, she would change her role. She would also disrupt the general schema in which the doctor is generally the agent for topic change (and for promoting discontinuity) in the discourse. Above all, she would risk her presentation of self by not displaying the expected behavior for the official frame.

Topic Shifts within the Institutional Frame

The institutional frame molds the prevailing contexts of talk in the interview. It is where and when participants distinctly display their official identities as doctor and patient. The doctor's topic agenda contributes to the continuity of these framings. Thus, topic shifts are ways of maintaining or reintroducing the institutional frame. Most of the time, Dona Jurema's on-topic responses provide for topic and frame continuity.

Though the frame may remain the same, topic transitions occur. They represent moments where new referential information is introduced and a new understanding must be established. When agreement is reached, then the discourse coheres.

In the discharge interview, there are two processes of topic transitions—by "topic disjunct" and by a gradual shift in a "stepwise transition" (Sacks 1971; Jefferson 1984). In each process the participants work together to negotiate and establish "what talk is about."

A Topic Disjunct Transition

Prior to the following segment, the participants have been discussing the patient's past hospitalizations. The doctor has inquired about the number of admittances, places of hospitalization, and what used to happen. Turn taking follows the Q/A/Q/A structure as well as the three-part structure question/answer/comment. The topic sequence closes with the doctor restating her question:

(12)

Doctor: **of all these hospitalizations, /you never**
remember?/

Patient: | no, ... I ne:ver remembered.
          (1.5).
Doctor: **mmm.**

The presentation of the referent "all these [past] hospitalizations" in initial position in the sentence signals a closing to the topic. The doctor then asks:

(13)

Doctor: **and you: ... uhm .. who takes care of you,**
          who looks after you, /who is your caretaker?/

Prosodic, semantic, and interactional cues indicate that new information is being introduced. The pace is slow, with word lengthening (you:), a filler "uhm," and pauses. After introducing her question ("who takes care of you?"), the doctor repeats it twice by paraphrasing:

   who looks after you,
   who is your caretaker?

By restating her question the doctor secures successful topic ratification, as the patient correctly identifies the referent and responds on-topic:

Patient: **my sister, y'know, Idete.**
Doctor: | **/your sister./ =**
Patient: **=yes, my sister. =**

Topic shifts place an extra burden on the respondent—the patient and interviewee. During these moments a prior understanding of what talk is about must be renegotiated. Transitions by topic disjunct are particularly difficult since referential change does not occur gradually.

A Topic Closing

Once a topic has been successfully introduced and ratified by both participants as the ongoing topic of conversation, the speakers expand on it, adding new and relevant information. This successively results in topic transition and eventual topic change.

The talk that follows is a closing to a segment on the topic "times of depression." The doctor's first question on this topic had been: "do you remember, let's see, if you had periods of being very sad, for no reason?" Once the "conversational topic" (Brown and Yule 1983) has been accepted, Doctor Edna and Dona Jurema discuss the patient's eating habits and personal cleanliness under depression. Not quite satisfied with the patient's responses, the doctor pursues her inquiry and asks:

(14)

(1) Doctor: =weren't there periods of time that you
             did not take care of yourself?=
(2) Patient: =no:, absolutely not,
(3)   when I am myself, absolutely not.=
(4) Doctor ⌐even during these periods-
(5) Patient.└ I am an <u>extremely</u> neat person, you know?=
(6) Doctor: =mmm ...

This closing segment presents a change in the information status of the referent. In line (1) the doctor restates her opening question, "weren't there periods of time that you did not take care of yourself?" Then she makes another attempt to recycle the question in line (4). Finally, in line (7), she reintroduces "times of sadness," which is now presented as background information:

(7) **even during these periods when you're sad,**
(8) **feel sad, an:guished,**
(9) **you go on taking care of yourself, right?**

The presentation of the referent in initial position in the sentence, rather than in final position as when it was first introduced, portrays the change in information status that took place during this stretch of talk (Schiffrin 1987b). This is another example of the process of topicalization. Here, the doctor reintroduces the referent in initial position. In doing so, she signals a preclosing to the topic. Hence, this sequence ends with the doctor accepting the patient's position and requesting confirmation on her previous statements (line 9).

A Stepwise Transition

The next contributions (lines 10–21) present a topic change in a "stepwise transition" (Sacks 1971; Jefferson 1984). In this segment Dona Jurema and Doctor Edna gradually disengage from the topic "times of sadness":

(15)

(7) Doctor: **even during these periods when you're=**
(8)   **=sad, feel sad, an:guished,**
(9)   **you go on taking care of yourself,**
              right? |
(10) Patient: └ **oh: yes:, yes:, of course, I go on=**
             =taking care of myself, naturally.=
(11) Doctor: **=bu:t, do you stop doing what you=**
                                    [dec]
(12)   **=usually do? li:ke activities- home=**
              =ou:tside, ...
(13)   **or you never- stopped let's see, /being=**
              =active?/ |

|[acc]
(14) Patient: | no, I used to =
= be very active outside (the home), doctor. =
(15) Doctor: = //yeah?// =
(16) Patient: = I was a saleswoman, y'know, =
(17) Doctor: = //yeah?// =
(18) Patient: = for many years. ....
(19) Doctor: /mmm/.
(20) Patient: I worked for a charity institution for =
= little old people (   )
(21) Doctor: mmm: ...
(22) Patient: see. .... I used to sell for (it),
                                        [acc]
(23)   I also used to sell for myself a little =
= bit, ..
(24) Doctor: mmm: ...
(25) Patient: I worked for many years as a saleswoman.
               (1.5)
               [acc]
(26) Doctor: was that the only job /you had?/ ..

During this segment of talk the patient and the doctor seem to be sticking to the old topic "times of depression" and shifting to a new topic "work activities" at the same time, with Dona Jurema's responses contributing to a topic switch. In line (11) the doctor's question initiates a transition to the new topic "work activities." She uses the adversative conjunction *but* to signal two things. On one hand, she indicates that the ongoing topic has not yet been resolved. She needs to pursue more information about the patient's behavior when depressed. So, she returns to her prior concern:

(11) Doctor: = but, do you stop doing what you usually do?

The underlying question is still the same: "when you are depressed, do you stop doing what you typically do?" On the other hand, *but* prefaces a question that contrasts with the previous concluding statement, which had been:

(9) you go on taking care of yourself, right?

The doctor's question in line (11) presents a referential contrast to the concluding statement in line (9). It introduces a verb of action in "what you usually do" and expands on it by proposing specific referents:

like activities at home, outside (the home),

What seems to occur in this instance is a potential for topic shift. In a stepwise transition, speakers must at the same time stick to the topic and introduce potential new topics. The doctor's next utterance, an "or-clause," restates the new topic candidate, shifts to the past, and offers an option to the patient:

(13) **or you never stopped, let's see, being active?**

In the following interaction a topic transition is negotiated from "depressive times" (in the present) to "activities" (in the past):

(14) Patient: **no, I used to be very active outside =**
                  = (the home), doctor.
(15) Doctor: **//yeah?// =**
(16) Patient: **= I was a saleswoman, y'know,**
(17) Doctor: **//yeah?// =**
(18) Patient: **= for many years. ....**
(19) Doctor: **mmm.**
(20) Patient: **I worked for a charity institution for =**
                  = little old people ( )
(21) Doctor: **mmm: ...**
(22) Patient: **see. .... I used to sell for (it),**
                         [acc]
(23)   **I also used to sell for myself a little =**
                  = bit, ..
(24) Doctor: **mmm: ...**
(25) Patient: **I worked for many years as a saleswoman.**
                (1.5)
                [acc]
(26) Doctor: **was that the only job /you had?/ ..**

In response to the doctor's question, Dona Jurema addresses the referent "activities" (in the past) in line (14), and expands on it (in lines 16, 18, 20, 22, 23, and 25). This stretch of talk is punctuated by the doctor's back-channel responses "yeah?" (lines 15, 17, 19, 21, and 24). Then the doctor asks:

            [acc]
(26) Doctor: **was that the only job you had? ..**

A new topic has been introduced in a stepwise transition and ratified; it opens a twenty-eight-turn sequence where different types of jobs and job-related activities are discussed.

    This fragment illustrates a standard role relationship in doctor-patient communication: The doctor is the one who either proposes a topic or introduces the possibility of topic change (lines 11–13); the patient addresses the topic or negotiates for a topic transition (lines 14, 16, 18, 20, 22, 23, 25); the doctor then ratifies the new topic (line 26).

We have seen that the doctor uses different strategies to introduce a referent into the discourse. The first part of this section (excerpt 13) presents a "topic disjunct" situation (Sacks 1971; Jefferson 1984), where the doctor shifts from the referent "past hospitalizations" and requests information on a new topic, "the caretaker." Dona Jurema's response ratifies the doctor's topic. The last part of this section (excerpt 15, lines 11–13) shows a "stepwise transition" (Sacks 1971; Jefferson 1984), where Dona Jurema's contributions gradually shift the topic.

Topic transitions represent moments in talk where a prior understanding of what talk is about may break down. New referents are introduced by the doctor. Dona Jurema's responses and her degree of participation signal the access she has to these referents and to the context of communication. By attending to the interaction and responding to abrupt shifts of topic as well as participating in gradual transition from one topic to another, Dona Jurema remains coherent and maintains a certain amount of control.

Frames and Topics

The Frames Where Topics Emerge

The analysis reveals that the discharge interview contains twenty-four topics, introduced by Doctor Edna as part of her topic agenda. Of these, twelve are expanded by Dona Jurema and Doctor Edna. The expansion of each topic can be quantified by the number of subtopics introduced and recycled, which ranges from one to eleven.[6] For example, a topic introduced by the doctor on "[Dona Jurema's] sleeping problems" has five subtopics: "taking drugs," "waking up early," "length of time," "behavior before the illness," and "behavior after the illness." The subtopics indicate topic development and are introduced by either one of the participants.

Doctor Edna views any one of the topics brought up for discussion as merely talk within the institutional frames. Dona Jurema, however, seems to operate with a different set of expectations. For Dona Jurema, requests for information about her social history may trigger a personal framing and a change in the participation structure. Thus, there is one component of the medical interview—the social history component— that specifically favors changes in the context of talk. In these instances a more symmetrical interaction is more likely to follow.[7]

The contributions introduced by the patient are of three types: They are expansions on the ongoing topic but do not constitute a subtopic; they qualify for subtopic categorization; or they recycle a previous topic or subtopic. Any of these three could trigger a reframing in the context of communication.

This point will be illustrated by two situations. In the first, the patient reframes the talk while still addressing the doctor's topic. Thus, no topic shift occurs. In the second, Dona Jurema shifts the topic and in doing so accomplishes a reframing.

A Frame Shift with No Topic Shift

The following segment takes place in the first half of the interview. The doctor had previously introduced the topic "the caretaker," and then she asks:

[The Portuguese text is also presented due to relevant lexical information.]

(16)

  (1) Doctor: = **you're the youngest, aren't you?** =
                  [slight movement to the right, toward
                  the patient]
  (2) Patient: = **I'm the youngest of them.**
                  [nods]   [nods]
  (3) Doctor: **mmm ...**
                  [turns head slightly to the left]
  (4) Patient: **though I'm already a grandma,**
                              [smiles]
  (5)   **a little old lady,**
                  [smiles]
  (6)   **I am the youngest. ..**
                      [large smile; doctor smiles back]
  (7) Doctor: **mmm. ..** [smiles]
  (8) Patient: **I am sixty-one years old.**
                  [nods and smiles]
  (9) Doctor: **/I see./ ...**
                  [smiles]
(10) Patient: ⌐**Idete is ( )**
(11) Doctor:⌐**and how long have you been living there** =
                = **with her?**
                [torso movement to the left, bends to the left, presses both hands
                together]

---

  (1) Doctor: = **a senhora é a mais nova, não é?** =
                  [slight movement to the right, toward
                  the patient]
  (2) Patient: = **eu sou a mais nova delas.**
                    [nods]   [nods]
  (3) Doctor: **mmm ...**
                  [turns head slightly to the left]
  (4) Patient: **apesar de ser já vovó,**
                      [smiles]
  (5)   **tá velhinha,**
                  [smiles]
  (6)   **eu sou a mais nova. ..**
                  [large smile; doctor smiles back]

(7) Doctor: **mmm. ..** [smiles]
(8) Patient: **tou com sessenta e um anos.**
        [nods and smiles]
(9) Doctor: **/sei./ ...**
        [smiles]
(10) Patient:⌐**Idete tá cum ( )**
(11) Doctor:└**e a senhora mora lá com ela há quanto =**
        = tempo?
        [torso movement to the left, bends to the left, presses both hands together]

This segment falls into three parts. In the first part (lines 1–3) we have the standard three-turn pattern (Q/A/C) where the nonverbal communication is complementary to the talk: The doctor initially turns toward Dona Jurema (line 1) and requests information on "the patient as the younger sister"; Dona Jurema responds to the request (line 2); the doctor then turns slightly away from the patient and acknowledges her answer (line 3).

In the second part (lines 4–10) the turn structure changes, from the Q/A/C structure to a stretch of talk in which Dona Jurema introduces contributions and the doctor provides back-channels. The context of communication also changes. In line (4) Dona Jurema reframes the talk as "talk as grandma." She uses an adversative conjunction (*apesar de* "though"/"in spite of") to preface information that might seem to be at odds with her previous statement:

(2) eu sou a mais nova delas.
    I am the most young of them.
    (I am the youngest)

(4) apesar de ser já vovó,
    though to be already grandma
    (though I'm already a grandma)

(5) tá velhinha,
    be rather old
    (a little old lady)

Dona Jurema provides more information than is strictly necessary and introduces a series of evaluative remarks. She speaks of herself but impersonalizes the speaker (the use of the conjunction *apesar de* requires a postposed noun phrase; thus, the verb form that follows the conjunction must be in the infinitive). She uses the form "grandma" (*vovó*), an address term that grandchildren use in talking to their grandparents. And she adds that she is quite old (*tá velhinha*), making use of the Portuguese diminutive morpheme for signaling affection *-inho* in *velhinha* (equivalent to "old" and meaning "little old lady").[8] The doctor provides a series of back-channels "mmm" in lines (3) and (7). Both participants exchange smiles during this talk. Then Dona Jurema restates the information concerning her age (line 8), nods, and smiles. Doctor Edna provides another back-channel (line 9) and smiles. Dona Jurema now holds the floor and, in her next turn, begins to talk about Idete's age (line 10); however, at that point the doctor overlaps with her.

In the last part of this segment the doctor changes her verbal and nonverbal behavior: She moves and bends to the left, away from the patient, while pressing both hands together; she asks another question and, in so doing, changes the topic:

(10) Patient: ┌ **Idete is (   )**
(11) Doctor: └ **and how long have you been living=**
                    =there with her?
                    [torso movement to the left, bends to the left, presses both hands
                    together]

Doctor Edna's overlap with Dona Jurema interrupts the patient's talk and prevents her from going on to mention the age of Idete, and then, perhaps, the age of her other sister, Tereza. As pointed out by Erickson (1982) and also Tannen (1987a), these contributions tend to occur in a list. In introducing a subtopic, the doctor also proposes to shift the frame from a personal talk to talk within the institutional context.

A Topic Shift and a Frame Shift

There are also two instances in which Dona Jurema accomplishes a reframing in shifting and recycling a previous topic. The first takes place when Dona Jurema shifts from the medical examination frame back to the evaluative frame, as she introduces an assessment of her present state of health (discussed in chapter 4). In the second, Dona Jurema interrupts a sequence of topics that the doctor had been raising related to her present illness and past history. After inquiring for the second time about past hospitalizations, the doctor asks a broad question about the patient's medical history and then more specifically about her physical conditions:

[Again the Portuguese text is also presented due to relevant lexical information.]

(17)

(1) Doctor: ┌ **not e:ven .. physical problems?**
                    [acc]
                    /you never had any physical problem/?
(2) Patient: └ **ne:ver, I never had an=**
                    =operation, doctor.=
(3) Doctor: **=/no/?=**
(4) Patient: **=never had an operation till today.**
(5) Doctor: └ **(never) had=**
                    =any difficulty in wa::lking, in mo:ving=
                    =around /in talking?/

(6) Patient: | no. nothing, nothing, nothing,
                    nothing.... on the contrary,
                    really a saleswoman has to talk a lot=
                    =right Doctor Edna. (1.2)
(7) Doctor: mmm.
(8) Patient: I'd really talk a lo:t, =
(9) Doctor: =//you'd talk a lot//
(10) Patient: ⌊to the customers. //yeah.//
(11) Doctor: did you live on that money? ...

---

(1) Doctor: ⌈nem: .. problemas <u>físicos</u>?
                    [acc]
                    /a senhora sentia alguma coisa <u>física</u>/?
(2) Patient: ⌊nun:ca, nunca fui=
                    =operada, doutora. =
(3) Doctor: =/não/? =
(4) Patient: =nunca fiz uma operação até agora.
(5) Doctor: ⌊(nunca) sentiu=
                    =dificuldade em andá::, em se movê:,
                 ⌐/em <u>falá</u>:/?
(6) Patient⌊ não. nada, nada, nada, nada. ....
                    pelo contrário,
                    até vendedora tem que falá muito=
                    ▪né doutora Edna. (1.2)
(7) Doctor: mmm.
(8) Patient: falava até bas:tante, =
(9) Doctor: =//falava bastante,//
(10) Patient: ⌊com as freguesas. //é.//
(11) Doctor: a senhora vivia desse dinheiro? ...

The doctor first introduces a broad question about Dona Jurema's past physical condition:

(1) Doctor: ⌈not e:ven .. <u>physical</u> problems?
                    [acc]
                    /you never had any physical problem/?

Dona Jurema responds in the negative by denying any previous medical difficulties, and she also adds some specific information about a medical operation. In turn (5) the doctor becomes more specific and asks about problems related to walking, moving around, and talking (these were difficulties that the patient had had when she entered the hospital). This time Dona Jurema provides a strong negative answer ("no. nothing, nothing, nothing, nothing"), pauses, and then expands by saying:

> on the contrary,
> really a saleswoman has to talk a lot,
> right Doctor Edna.
> I'd really talk a lo:t,
> to the customers, yeah.

There is a change of topic as Dona Jurema reintroduces "the sales-woman" ("I was a saleswoman"), a topic that had been talked about some time before. In shifting the topic, Dona Jurema also reframes the situation, signaling that she is a more powerful participant.

Several forms indicate this change in frame. First, she prefaces what she will say by the conjunction "on the contrary" *pelo contrário,* which explicitly signals that information contrary to expectation will follow. In her next utterance she makes a strong statement: She uses the marker "really" *até* to single out the referent "saleswoman"; she uses the modal "must" *tem* to modify the verb "speak" *falar* as well as the adverb of intensity "a lot" *muito.* She repeats this statement again using the em-phatic forms "really" *até* and "a lot" *bastante.* In calling the doctor by title + first name, she indicates that she is positioning herself in a more symmetrical relationship to the doctor. The marker "right" *né,* which prefaces the address form, underlines the strong stand that Dona Jurema takes in shifting the topic.

As a response to Dona Jurema's shift—in topic and in frame—the doctor echoes, in a low voice, the patient's last statement, "you'd talk a lot" (again a repetition of the verb paradigm with no changes for the first and third persons, which cannot be captured in English):

(8) Patient: **I'd really talk a lo:t, =**
(9) Doctor: **= //you'd talk a lot//**

with the repeating forms (in Portuguese):

Patient: **falava até bastante**
Doctor: **falava   bastante**

And then the doctor introduces a subtopic (embedded in the topic rein-troduced by Dona Jurema):

did you live on that money?

In this way the doctor ratifies Dona Jurema's shift of topic.

This segment illustrates a situation in which the patient exercises a function that typically belongs to the interviewer: shifting a topic. Dona Jurema shifts from the topic "[past] physical conditions" to the topic "being a saleswoman." In doing so, she also shifts the component of the medical interview: from "past [medical] history" to "social history," and the doctor follows suit. That is, Doctor Edna introduces a subtopic to that topic and thereby ratifies the patient's shift in topic and frame.

The Progressive Symmetry

Whenever the doctor introduces topics that refer to Dona Jurema's social history, there is more talk from the patient; for instance, she provides information, gives evaluations, illustrates her point with a short narrative, or requests the doctor's opinion. These contributions relate to what Mishler has called "the voice of the lifeworld" in doctor-patient communication: "the patient's contextually-grounded experiences of events and problems in her life" (1984:104).

Mishler differentiates two types of discourse that commonly unfold in a medical interview. The "voice of medicine" conveys the doctor's voice; it reflects a "technical interest" and expresses a "scientific attitude." The "voice of the lifeworld" is the patient's voice referring to the personal and social contexts of her problems (1984:95). Each discourse has its own norms for turn taking and for establishing what kind of talk is appropriate. Mishler tells us that when doctors and patients meet, there are conflicting expectations of what talk should be about and how it should be structured.

Mishler's voices correspond to what Goffman (1974, 1981a) and Tannen (1984, 1986) have discussed as frames. In describing the dialectics between these two voices, Mishler describes the structuring of conflicting voices and how they operate in discourse: "Both physician and patient may speak in either voice and each may switch voices within or between utterances or turns" (1984:103). Mishler adds, however, that shifts from the voice of medicine to the voice of the lifeworld are done mostly by the patient (1984:108). He describes how doctors use the voice of medicine to interrupt the discourse of patients (who frequently talk using the voice of the lifeworld). While the doctor brings up topics for discussion under the voice of medicine, the patient expands them under the voice of the lifeworld by bringing detailed personal information to the foreground.

To a certain extent, therefore, Mishler's discussion relates to the institutional and non-institutional frames described in chapter 4, where the institutional frames correspond to the voice of medicine and the noninstitutional frames correspond to the voice of the lifeworld. Frequently, "what talk is about" in the noninstitutional frames refers to Dona Jurema's personal and social contexts. Three of the examples given in chapter 4 describe this situation ("I am a nurturing grandmother," "I enjoyed being a saleswoman," and "I am a mother. I have given birth"). So do both example (16) (about a frame shift within an ongoing topic) and example (17) (about a frame and topic shift) in this chapter.

The frames discussed previously describe a slightly more complex interactional situation than the dichotomy "voice of medicine" versus "voice of the lifeworld" might suggest. Subtle social changes are brought about by reframings. That is, each reframing—each metamessage—that takes place during an interview can bring about changes in the overall structure of social participation. That is what is meant by the dynamic nature of frames: "The framing that is going on at any moment is part of what establishes the frame for what goes on next, and is partly created by the framing that went before" (Tannen 1986:99).

In the discharge interview, both the doctor and the patient accomplish reframings. The speaker who sets the frame exercises control over the context of communication (Tannen 1986). While Doctor Edna continuously proposes and builds talk within the institutional contexts, each time Dona Jurema reframes the situation, she signals more control over the context of talk. These reframings provoke microchanges regarding the social symmetry of the participants during the development of the interview.

Consequently, subtle changes in frame and shifts in topic seem to mitigate the initial distancing between Dona Jurema and Doctor Edna. If one looks at interactive frames, one notices changes in the metamessages conveyed by Dona Jurema in the interview. She initially frames talk as a nurturing grandmother, where she stresses the asymmetrical axis of age differences between her and Doctor Edna (with Dona Jurema in the superior position (as we have seen in example (16) in this chapter and example (20) in chapter 4); she then goes on to framing talk as a woman who today is in control, and therein stresses a more symmetrical relationship with the doctor, as we have seen in example (17) in this section and examples (22), (23), and (28) in chapter 4.

If one looks at who introduces topics and subtopics, there is also a slight progressive symmetry taking place in the interview. In the second half of the interview Dona Jurema not only collaborates on a topic but also introduces subtopics. She also recycles two topics and, in doing so, triggers a reframing of the situation. Again Dona Jurema is trying to decrease the asymmetry between herself and Doctor Edna.

Conclusion

The analysis performed here describes how the doctor and the patient establish and negotiate referential meaning in discourse. On one hand, Doctor Edna's contributions provide for discontinuity in the discourse: New referents are introduced exclusively by the doctor, following a medical topic agenda. On the other hand, Dona Jurema must assure topic continuity by collaborating in an ongoing topic or incorporating a topic (i.e., introducing subtopics). Thus, participants have complementary roles in the interview.

Among the different domains of talk that organize medical interviews (MacKinnon and Michels 1971; Reiser and Schroder [1980] 1984), the patient's social history stands out as a favorable environment for generating talk. It is the patient's "personal agenda," which corresponds to Mishler's "voice of the lifeworld." In this domain of talk Dona Jurema expands her contributions and accomplishes microinteractional shifts that reframe the context of talk. Each reframing accomplished by Dona Jurema attempts to mitigate the asymmetrical relationship initially assumed by the participants. These subtle shifts have implications for topic management, as in the second part of the interview Dona Jurema

introduces more contributions: She expands on the ongoing topic, introduces subtopics, or recycles previous topics.

We have seen thus far how Dona Jurema manages topics and frames
in the discharge interview. This interview represents a measure against
which the admitting interview will be discussed. In the institutional
frames the patient follows the prescribed interactional norms for medical
interviews. She assesses the situation correctly: She provides the second
part of an adjacency pair, expands on the doctor's comments, and stays
on topic. In the noninstitutional frames Dona Jurema establishes talk as
a social encounter and behaves accordingly by presenting her nonofficial
social identities. In either frame of talk the patient's discourse coheres.

The next two chapters examine the admitting interview. The interview represents the deviation, where Dona Jurema displays unexpected
verbal and nonverbal behavior and where coherence breaks down. In
chapter 6 a topic analysis reveals incoherence. It shows the patient's refusal to participate in talk; that is, she does not attend to the doctor's
topics. Furthermore, both doctor and patient bring two unrelated topic
agendas to the encounter. Topics remain inconclusive and are hardly developed. Coherence breaks down in the turn structure as well as in the
action structure.

In chapter 7, however, a frame-analytic perspective provides a natural criterion for establishing "chunks" of coherent discourse in the patient's talk. I will discuss how frames operate differently in this situation,
and how Dona Jurema's official and nonofficial identities surface in this
interaction.

Notes

1. In this excerpt the discourse topic is a referring term ("the son," "Francisco Ferreira de Souza," "he"). There are few references to different people in
the interview, which has to do with the type of discourse: A psychiatric interview
is intrinsically concerned with a single individual—the psychiatric patient. Thus,
this interview can be reported as being "about" Dona Jurema. The other characters brought up during the talk (son, granddaughter, sister, and brother) are
mentioned in reference to her. Except for the brother, the other characters are
referred to only in the beginning of the interview, and then recycled at the end.

2. This is one of the many possible functions of repetition in talk, as
pointed by Tannen (1987a:581).

3. This is an oversimplification where psychiatric (therapeutic) interviews
are concerned. According to MacKinnon and Michels, "the 'content' of a (psychiatric) interview refers both to the factual information provided by the patient
and to the specific interventions of the interviewer." However, the authors add
that the content constitutes only one part of the interview data, and they alert
the young psychiatrist to the relevance of implicit meaning in discourse: "Very
often verbal content may be unrelated to the real message of the interview"
(1971:8).

4. In a personal communication, Doctor Edna stated that medical students

receive a broad outline of "topics" that serve as guidelines for medical and psychiatric interviews. In the playback session she mentioned how she would go from the patient profile to the patient family history and so on. In doing a topic analysis I am partially recovering from the data the doctor's original topic agenda.

5. In Brazilian Portuguese the second-person pronoun has been substituted by the third-person pronoun in most dialects.

6. It is not my intention here to discuss the number of topics and subtopics of the discharge interview since, as far as figures are concerned, Dona Jurema introduces only 20 percent of the subtopics. Numbers, therefore, do not express the type of social work that takes place during this interaction. According to Mishler (1984), this low percentage of entry talk from patients is expected in the discourse of medicine, where doctors are trained to select information and discard contributions that are considered marginal. He states that frequently, in the transcripts he analyzed, "patients' efforts to provide accounts of their problems within the contexts of their lifeworld situations were disrupted and fragmented" (1984:190).

7. Dona Jurema's social history concerns various issues in the patient's life, such as: housing: "I lived for two years by myself"; "I lived with my sister"; occupation: "I was a saleswoman, y'know"; and relationships: "I had a boyfriend"; "I was separated after twelve years." Whenever the doctor requests information that relates to this component of the medical interview, Dona Jurema provides more contributions to the ongoing topic.

8. In Portuguese the morpheme *-inho* is marked for gender; thus, the form *-inha* stands for the feminine form.

6

Topicality in
the Admitting Interview:
Where Coherence
Breaks Down

Very often the misconduct of the patient is a public fact, in that anyone in the same room with him would feel he was behaving improperly, and, if not quite anyone, then at least anyone in the same conversation.
Erving Goffman, *Interaction Ritual,* p 139

The question of language impairment in schizophrenia allows us to study the course of schizophrenic episodes in minute detail, and may consequently allow us to understand what distinguishes schizophrenic patients who show no signs of incoherent speech . . . from those whose discourse is disrupted.
Sherry Rochester and J. R. Martin, *Crazy Talk,* p. 189

Most of the time Dona Jurema displays a childish behavior. She uses child language and talks to me as if I were her "mama." Her speech is unintelligible. She does not use any formal code to communicate or to relate . . . refusing any talk on more objective grounds . . . [and] ignoring what we tell her. Her responses are not relevant or coherent.
Excerpt from the doctor's report, as cited in Dona Jurema's records

We have seen thus far that a large part of what constitutes the institutional frame of the medical encounter is related to the topic agenda that the doctor brings to the interview. To be successful in the interview situation (and hence assess the official frame correctly), the patient must address the doctor's topics. That is, she must be able to identify "what talk is about" and provide some sort of satisfying response, which either addresses the doctor's request for information or establishes a process of negotiation. Furthermore, the patient does not introduce topics from a personal agenda but instead may recycle a previous topic that the doctor has introduced or expand on an ongoing topic by introducing subtopics. That is, she must provide for topic continuity rather than topic introduction.

This chapter analyzes topical coherence in the patient's and doctor's discourse in the admitting interview. This interview took place when Dona Jurema was brought to the hospital in an acute psychotic crisis, twenty days before the discharge interview. Here the patient's discourse seems largely incoherent. It does not follow the social and linguistic constraints of standard medical interviews that were described in chapters 4 and 5.

Throughout this interview Dona Jurema takes on different roles. Most often, she shifts from speaking as the patient addressing the doctor to speaking as a child addressing her mother. This is a common regressive behavior in psychosis (Cameron [1944] 1964; Sullivan [1944] 1964; Kasanin [1944] 1964). She also speaks as other family members: her sister Idete, her grandmother Lena, and her own mother addressing the child Jurema. In addition, she talks *to* these family members (who are not present).

To complicate matters further, more subtle shifts in footing (Goffman 1981a) also take place. Dona Jurema shifts from being a dependent, regressed patient to acting as an irreverent and challenging woman. At other times she talks as a tired elderly lady addressing a young woman. Each one of these intermittent shifts produces major breakdowns in Dona Jurema's discourse.[1]

The following sections discuss topics and the lack of any apparent patterning of topical content. My previous discussion on topic introduction and topic maintenance will serve as a background for the analysis. Here we will see how topic coherence is not achieved in the admitting interview. Now that we have an understanding of how coherence is jointly produced in a "normal" (or "unremarkable") interview, we can use it as a measure against which to compare the admitting interview.

In this encounter the participants bring competing topic agendas. Dona Jurema's agenda consists of personal topics, several of which are vague and indefinite. She does not follow up on any of them. Doctor Edna introduces as topics referents that are part of her official agenda. These are the same referents discussed in the discharge interview (in chapter 5). As we will see, the patient partially addresses only a few of these topics. Furthermore, both doctor and patient fail to identify each other's topics. As a result, the process of topic negotiation breaks down, few topics are expanded, and others are recycled in competition with new topics.

When Doctor Edna faces inconsistencies in the patient's discourse, she uses a number of strategies to keep the communicative channel open: She constantly summons the patient to the frame of the interview, she acknowledges the patient's statements, and she responds to some of her questions. In doing so, Doctor Edna is constantly reassessing her assumptions about Dona Jurema's topic of talk and whether Dona Jurema is in fact engaged in a state of talk (Goffman [1967] 1982); she reconstructs her own discourse so as to maintain the interaction with the patient.

On Establishing a Referent

In the analysis of the discharge interview, topic was defined as "what the talk is about." It was also stated that in medical interviews topics are signaled most often in one of two ways: either through a sharp semantic change, that is, a change in reference, or through changes in the turn structure. In this way, topic boundaries are marked either semantically or interactionally. In the admitting interview, however, both types of boundaries break down. I will first discuss how the interactional patterns in doctor-patient interviews break down.

I use parallel columns for transcribing this interview (as discussed in chapter 2). This format portrays more adequately than a vertical, sequential transcript the type of interaction that takes place here, where Dona Jurema holds the floor for longer turns than the doctor and, at various times, does not conform to conversational norms. The lines in the transcript are numbered. When participants overlap, their utterances occupy the same line(s) and a // (double slash) indicates where the overlap starts.

The Doctor's Difficulty in Introducing Topics

The first problem that the doctor encounters in the admitting interview is catching the patient's attention and maintaining listenership. This is a prerequisite to introducing a topic. Hence, we see Doctor Edna continuously summoning Dona Jurema to participate in the interview. Most of the time, however, the patient answers neither the doctor's summons nor her questions, as in the following two examples.

[Here Dona Jurema is engaged in a speech play activity of her own—she starts chanting and tapping rhythmically with both hands.]
(1)

Doctor:	Patient:
	[chanting and baby talk]
	you yourself know very well,
	[gestures of left and right hands, tapping on the armchair]
	better than I do,
	better than anyone,
[camera focus on	**when I get,**
the patient]	**to my ward,**
	I'm gonna tell,
	[looks further away to the right, bends forward]
	I'm gonna tell,

Doctor:	Patient:
	[baby talk]
//DONA JURE:MA!	//this was,
	[looks down]
	this was,
	this was,
	my secret,
	this was, ..
	this was,
	and this was, =
= Dona Jurema! =	
	= my secret. ..

Here Doctor Edna tries unsuccessfully to interrupt the patient's stream of talk and to take a turn. She emphatically summons her to respond. Dona Jurema, however, proceeds with her chanting and does not provide any answer.

In the next example Dona Jurema again fails to produce a response and, thus, to address the doctor's topic:

[This excerpt takes place at the beginning of the interview. The patient has been calling her mother. She chants about a secret, and then refers to her husband.]:

(2)

Doctor:	Patient:
	[singing and baby talk]
	my dear husband,
	[looks down, face turns sightly to the left]
	knew very well,
	he did not come to help,
	his dear dear wife,
	but it does not matter, ..
	his good luck will not last, ..
	that is all =
	= I can wish on him with all my heart:::. (1.5)
	[face turns to the right to the doctor, looks up, looks at the doctor]
DONA JUREMA!	
⌐how long have you =	
= been in the hospital?	
	[new tune: church hymn]
	[dec]
	/⌐dressed in white/
	[looks down, hand gestures not visible]
	[creaky voice, baby talk]
	she appeared,
	bearing ˙round her waist,
	the colors of the sky,

        [whining]
        ⌈**Hail:, hail:, hail Ma:ry.**
        Hail:, hail:, ⌊hail ⌊Ma:ry.

Three unrelated topics are introduced in this segment. First Dona Jurema sings a song about her husband. She provides some information about him, complains, and ends her song by putting a curse on him. Then, Doctor Edna takes the floor and requests information about the patient's stay at the hospital (proposing a topic from the medical agenda). In her next turn, Dona Jurema ignores the doctor's request and starts a new song about the Virgin Mary. This example illustrates another breakdown in "what talk is about." On one hand, the patient's personal topic—the husband—does not trigger any questions from the doctor, who ignores the patient's topic. On the other hand, the doctor's next topic—the patient's length of stay in the hospital—does not elicit an answer from the patient but yet another personal topic, the Virgin Mary.

The first problem to arise in Dona Jurema's discourse is the non-occurrence of the second pair part in a sequentially constrained pair of turns. That is, the patient fails to produce a response to the doctor's request, thus failing to address the doctor's topic. We also see two competing topic agendas. Each speaker introduces different topics of talk, and none of them are interactionally picked up and developed.

There are a few instances, however, where the patient responds to the doctor's summonses. When this happens, Doctor Edna gets the floor and introduces a topic, as in the following:

(3)

Doctor:	Patient:
Dona Jure:ma!	
	[looks up to the doctor]
	hi!
how old are you?	
	[looks to the left]
	⌈**HI! IVE::TE!! DE:TE!...**
	Deti::nha! ....

The doctor summons the patient by her name, "Dona Jurema!" Dona Jurema takes her turn and provides the second part of the adjacency pair: She responds to the summon with a greeting ("hi!"). Turns alternate rather than overlap. Dona Jurema's nonverbal behaviors match her verbal response. As she greets the doctor, she also looks up and makes eye contact. Hence, both verbal and nonverbal communication signal "I'm here." In her next turn Doctor Edna introduces a topic from her agenda—the patient's age. This topic, however, is never addressed by the patient. Dona Jurema shifts frames and uses the same cue ("hi!") to greet her sister (who is not present).

The lack of adequate answers from the patient results in the absence of the three-part structure question/answer/comment in the admitting interview. As discussed previously this is the basic unit of coherent on-topic discourse in doctor-patient interviews, where the doctor requests information, the patient provides the information requested, and the sequence ends with an acknowledgment from the doctor. The comment slot indicates the place where the doctor regains control of the turn structure and often introduces a new topic.

In the admitting interview, the lack of a comment from the doctor often indicates the lack of a satisfying response from the patient. Furthermore, the absence of a three-part turn structure results in the doctor's inability to "step in" and get control of the floor.

Two Unrelated Topic Agendas

The interaction that takes place in the admitting interview is, on first hearing, incoherent. The talk sounds in some ways like a monologue, with the patient occupying longer turns than the doctor and, in most instances, not responding to the doctor's requests or summonses. However, the interview has different types of dialogue structuring, as the patient converses both with people who are not present and with the doctor.

The doctor, as we have seen, makes a series of unsuccessful attempts to propose a topic agenda to the encounter, as in examples (2) and (3). When Doctor Edna asks a question, Dona Jurema provides one of three types of responses, all of which will be discussed: (1) She may ignore the doctor's request and continue to be engaged in an activity of her own; (2) she may address the doctor's request and in doing so provide some sort of answer; or (3) she may introduce another topic from her personal agenda, which is ratified by the doctor. In the last two cases, an on-topic interaction takes place.

The Patient Ignores the Doctor's Request

First, topic coherence breaks down when the doctor introduces a topic that the patient does not address, as we have seen in examples (2) and (3). In example (2) she sings a little song to the Virgin Mary, and in example (3) she turns to her (absent) sister instead of answering the doctor's question. In both instances the patient proceeds with another type of activity (verbal or nonverbal) and does not attend to the institutional frame of the interview.

In these excerpts the topics that the doctor proposes are not addressed by the patient and, therefore, are never developed. This accounts for the doctor's introducing, or attempting to introduce, a much smaller number of topics in this interview than in the discharge interview. Whereas in the discharge interview twenty-four topics were introduced by the doctor (and these generated a large number of subtopics), in the admitting interview the doctor introduces only thirteen topics. These topics evidence the doctor's effort to get referential information from the patient on her "name," "age," "place of residence," "length of stay at hospital," and so on.

The Patient Addresses the Doctor's Request

Second, Dona Jurema may actually respond to the doctor's question. When she does respond, her answers vary in degrees of acceptability and coherence, as the following excerpts illustrate:

(4)

Doctor: Patient:

[acc]

(1) ⌐WHERE DO YOU LIVE? ...

                                        [coarse voice, baby talk]
                                        (2) I live over there with =
                                              = the pope,
                                        (3) over there in the Lome.

(4) you live with the pope?

                                        (5) yes, over there in the Lome.

Here Doctor Edna requests information about the patient's place of residence. Dona Jurema addresses the doctor's request but gives an untrue answer: She says that she lives with the pope, in Rome. She uses child language when answering the question, substituting the phoneme /l/ for /r/ in the words "live" *(molo)* and "Rome" *(Loma)*. Doctor Edna then requests confirmation (in line 4), which the patient provides as she repeats her previous answer (in line 5).

We know from the discharge interview that Dona Jurema lives with her sister Idete. I will not discuss here the underlying inferences that psychiatrists and psychoanalysts could make from the patient's statement (e.g., equating the patient's relationship with her sister to her relationship with an extremely powerful person, as powerful as the head of the Catholic church). The discussion here focuses on the literal meaning, the referential information that the doctor seeks. Thus, in this excerpt, Dona Jurema does address the doctor's topic "place of residence," although she provides an inadequate referent.

The next segment, which takes place at the beginning of the interview, conveys the doctor's first question to the patient. During this segment Doctor Edna is sitting very close to the patient. She speaks emphatically as she asks the patient to state her full name:

(5)

Doctor: Patient:

(1) ⌐tell me your FULL=
      =name.=

                          [baby talk]
                          (2) =there is no need

Doctor: Patient:
                                    (3) 'cause the doc,
                                    (4) doc,
                                    (5) doc,
                                    (6) the doc-
                                    (7) papapapapapapapapa = ['hhh]
                                    (8) papapapa-<u>Pau-lo-de-</u>
                                        [starts moving her face to the right]
                                    (9) <u>A-ze-ve-do-Mur-ti-nho.</u>
                                        [looks up, looks down]
                                        [chanting and baby talk]
                                    (10) **you yourself know quite** =
                                         = **well,**
                                    (11) **better than I,**
                                    (12) **better than anyone,**
                                         [baby talk]
                                    (13) **when I get,**
                                    (14) **to my ward,**
                                    (15) **I'm gonna tell,**
                                    (16) **I'm gonna tell,**
                                         [baby talk]
// **DONA JURE:MA!**   (17) //**this was,**
                                    (18) **this was,**
                                    (19) **this was my secret.** ...

Dona Jurema addresses the doctor's question (in line 2) in two ways. First she says that "there is no need" (for her to tell her full name), and then she starts to explain why. In lines (3) through (6) she refers repeatedly to a doctor (using an informal register "the doc," in Portuguese *o doutô*); finally, in lines (8) and (9) she gives the full name of a doctor at another hospital. Referential substitution takes place: Instead of providing her own full name, she gives the doctor's full name.

During the playback session, Doctor Edna mentioned that Doctor Paulo Murtinho had probably taken care of the patient in previous crises, when she had been taken to another hospital. The underlying assumption in what Dona Jurema is trying to say seems to be that Doctor Paulo already knows her name (which implies that the institution already has this information in its records). One must bear in mind that this is Dona Jurema's fifth hospitalization; therefore, she has had repeated experiences in psychiatric interviews with different doctors. Thus, the patient's first answer seems to be an indirect response to the doctor's question: There is no need for me to tell you my name; the other doctor already knows my name (and has already asked me all these questions).

The second answer she provides is in line (10) ("you yourself know quite well"), which could refer to "you know my name well; therefore, there is no need for me to tell you." A known-answer question on the doctor's part (a test question) frequently triggers indirect or negative answers from the patient. In chapter 7 we will see how Dona Jurema often responds with challenges to this type of question.

The next excerpt takes place at the end of a section where Dona Jurema has been engaged in different types of activities. She closes this segment by telling the doctor that she cannot talk to her. At this point Doctor Edna asks:

(6)

Doctor: Patient:

(1) =⌐you can't=
      // talk to me?

                                    (2) //tototototototo:. ['hhh]
                                        [moves hand back to armchair; looks be-
                                        yond the doctor]
                                    (3) ⌐the tototô::::!
                                        [gesture with right hand pointing straight
                                        ahead]

(4) what's totô?

                                    (5) the totô totô::!
                                        [series of pointing gestures]

(6) what's totô?

                                    (7) that totô::::! (1.5)
                                        [pointing gestures]

(8) what is it you're saying?

                                        [acc]
                                    (9) totododododododododododo
                                   (10) /dodododododdodo/ ...
                                        [gesture with hands indicating "who
                                        knows"; looks down]

(11) you don't know, do you.

Dona Jurema responds to the doctor's request (in line 2) with nonsensical language as she continuously repeats the alveolar stops /d/ and /t/, then inhales and says "the tototo," a nonsensical word (line 3). In her next turn Doctor Edna requests information on this word (in line 4). As she answers the doctor's request (in lines 5 and 7), Dona Jurema seems to be engaged in a speech play that involves the use of deixis (the definite article "the" *(o)* and "that" *(aquele)* in the expressions "the totô-totô" and "that totô," indicating specific referential information), while at the same time pointing in front of her. When the doctor again requests information on the referent that Dona Jurema has introduced, the patient engages in a continuous nonsensical muttering, which ends with a nonverbal gesture that indicates "who knows!" (the gesture consists of raising both hands together and opening them to the sides, with changes in facial expression that indicate doubt). The doctor concludes this segment (line 11) by saying out loud what Dona Jurema had communicated nonverbally ("you don't know, do you?") and thereby acknowledging the patient's answer.[2]

Examples (4) through (6) illustrate different types of incoherent response from the patient. On one hand, we see that Dona Jurema addresses the doctor's questions. On the other hand, coherence breaks down regarding the types of referents that the patient provides. Her answers vary in degrees of acceptability and truthfulness.

The Patient Introduces Topics from Her Personal Agenda

The third type of incoherence occurs when Dona Jurema introduces a topic from her own agenda. In this situation the topics that are introduced are the *patient's topics,* and Dona Jurema is the one who produces topic discontinuity, as described by Keenan and Schieffelin (1976). This contrasts with the discharge interview, where the doctor is the one who introduces discontinuous topics and the patient provides for topic continuity. The following excerpt shows the patient switching topics abruptly.

The doctor is summoning the patient to the interview, but Dona Jurema is engaged in another activity: She is pointing to one side of the room and indicating that the doctor should be quiet. Then there is a shift:

(7)

Doctor: Patient:
  (1) **Dona Jure:ma!**

                         (2) **popopodedededdddd**
                         (3) **shshshshshshshshshshsh**
                         [raises head, looks up, raises left hand, brings right finger to mouth to indicate silence; looks beyond the doctor, points and nods, looks straightahead, wide-open eyes]

  (4) **what is happening over there?**
                         (5) **sssssshhhhhhhhhhhhhhhhhh**
                         (6) ['hhh] **sssshhhhhhhhhhhh**
                         (7) ['hhh] **sssshhhhhhhhhhhh**
                         [points and nods, turns sideways to the right, moves left arm to the right, bends down, looks down to the right]

  (8) **Dona JuRE:MA!**
                         [dec] [baby talk]
                         (9) ⌐**thank God! ....**
                         [raises head, looks up, turns to doctor, and smiles]

     [dec]
(10) **thank God, for what?** =
                        (11) = **it's all over! ....**
                        [holds the position and smiles]

     [acc]
(12) **what is over?**

Halfway through this segment Dona Jurema introduces a new topic ("it is over"). In the first part (lines 1–8) Dona Jurema is engaged in an activity (pointing and indicating that one should be quiet), while Doctor Edna is summoning the patient's attention (lines 1 and 8) and requesting information on what's going on (line 4). When Dona Jurema signals "to be quiet," she turns halfway around to the right (away from the doctor). Then, in line (9) there is a shift. She turns back to the doctor, looks at her, smiles, and expresses relief (by saying "thank God!"). In line (10) Doctor Edna asks the patient what she is relieved about. That is, the doctor continues (by asking for clarification) the topic that the patient has introduced. Dona Jurema states that "it's all over." Again Doctor Edna requests information on the referent (line 12). In both instances Doctor Edna requests more information to retrieve the implicit referent the patient has alluded to (lines 10 and 12).

While Dona Jurema is the one who provides for topic discontinuity (by introducing a new topic), Doctor Edna provides for continuity in discourse (i.e., she is the one who collaborates on a discourse topic by introducing more questions related to that new referent). This type of exchange takes place in several segments of the interview, as the following discussion illustrates.

The Doctor Responds to the Patient's Topics

The following examples present a reversal of the traditional roles for doctor-patient interviews. We see the doctor's attempts to provide for discourse continuity (and thereby contribute to topic coherence). In each instance Doctor Edna picks up the referents introduced by Dona Jurema and requests further information:

(8)

Doctor:	Patient:
	[baby talk]
	that's why:,
	that's why:,
	[dec]
	⌈**oh, tha:t's why:,**
	⌈**OH:, THA::T'S WHY:!**
	that's why I̲v̲e̲-
	i̲-, i̲-, i̲-. ..
	[coarse voice]
	⌊**can you send for** =
→ **=Iveti (for me)?**	
	[looks up at doctor]
→ **who is Iveti?**	
	[coarse voice, baby talk]
	=she's the maid (who works) at my house,
	[looks down and sideways to the left]
→ **at my sister's,**	
not at my house,	

Doctor: Patient:
                                → at my sister's house.
                                  you give the orders (there)?

→ what's the name=
  =of your sister?

                                  I- if I speak=
                                  =<proproproperly>,
                                  would you let me say,
                                → that it is Idetinha?....
                                  [slowly turns head to the right]
→ who's Idetinha,
  your sister?=

                                  =my sister.=

(9)
                                → grandma Lena is the one that knows,
                                  I am going to ask grandma Lena, O.K.?
→ who is grandma Lena?
                                  my grandma who is in heaven.

(10)
  =⌈**look**, ...
  get up and stretch
  for a little while
                                → /only <if Francisco allows>/
                                  [looks down, looks up at the doctor]
→ **who is Francisco?**
                                  FRAN-CIS-QUI-NHO!
                                  (little Francisco)
  who's that?
                                → my LI:TTLE BOY.
                                  [looks down and up, looks at the doctor]
→ **your son?**
  //how old is he?   //yeah.
                                  'round forty-two more or less.

In each of these excerpts, Dona Jurema introduces new referents; the
doctor provides topic continuity by requesting further information.
Dona Jurema first responds by addressing the doctor's question; she then
shifts the topic and discontinues that talk, as in segment (10), here repeated:

Doctor: Patient:
your son?
//how old is he?   //yeah.
                                  'round forty-two more or less.
                                  [looks away and to the right]

Patient:
**he is the one that knows more
or less I know nothing** =
[turns to the right]
[coarse voice]
nothingnothingnothingnothing
[looks to the far right and smiles]

These segments portray a different type of interaction from the discharge interview. Here Dona Jurema's personal topics give talk a direction. Frequently, an assertion from the patient triggers a question from the doctor (which the patient may or may not address). This type of exchange differs from standard doctor-patient interviews. The doctor has little choice but to collaborate with the patient's topics. Since Doctor Edna is left stranded whenever she keeps exclusively to her official topic agenda, she often shifts strategies by pursuing talk on Dona Jurema's personal topics.[3]

In the analysis of the discharge interview, we saw that topic continuity and topic discontinuity depict the types of contributions the doctor and the patient make in the interaction and these contributions, in turn, reflect their roles. Typically, the role of the patient is to provide topic continuity in the discourse; Dona Jurema follows this convention by collaborating on a topic and introducing subtopics. Although the doctor also provides for topic continuity, her major work is to introduce new referents and therefore promote the discontinuity of the discourse. Doctor Edna does that by introducing and recycling topics.

In the admitting interview, however, we see that both participants provide for topic discontinuity. That is, both introduce topics from different agendas (as each has her own agenda).[4] In addition, Doctor Edna also makes an effort to provide for topic continuity. Dona Jurema may or may not follow suit. Table 6.1 illustrates the types of contribution that Dona Jurema and Doctor Edna make in the admitting interview, where two agendas are in conflict.

Table 6.1   Types of Contributions in the Admitting
Interview

Patient	Doctor	Doctor/Patient
Introduces personal topics	Introduces official topics	Collaborates on a topic
Topic Discontinuity	Topic Discontinuity and Continuity	

D i s c o u r s e

The Lack of Subtopics

Topic analysis of the discharge interview involved a level of subordination: topic and subtopic. The first argument for classifying subtopics was that if one were to map exclusively topics, only the referents introduced by the doctor would be singled out, with no contributions from the patient. Although Dona Jurema did not introduce topics, she did contribute to talk by introducing subtopics. Hence, a topic introduced by the doctor (e.g., "family history") might have as many as eight subtopics, with both doctor and patient contributing to entry talk. The second major argument for a subtopic categorization has to do with the doctor's topic agenda, where both topics and subtopics matched the doctor's standard psychiatric agenda (Sullivan 1954).

The admitting interview presents a different situation. First, new referents are introduced by both participants and are frequently in competition. This is what we saw in examples (2) through (7), where both Doctor Edna and Dona Jurema introduce topics as they shift turns.[5] The doctor proposes several topics in an unsuccessful attempt to give talk some direction—topics such as the patient's name ("tell me your full name"); length of stay at the hospital ("how long have you been in the hospital?"); place of residence ("where do you live?"); time orientation ("is it day or is it night?"); space orientation ("where are you?"); general orientation ("how did you get here?"), among others. Only a few of these topics are ever addressed by the patient. When she does address them, no entry talk follows (excerpts 4 and 5).

The patient introduces a different set of topics from the doctor's. These are personal topics. Most are referring terms, that is, people about whom some message is formed (the most common topics are the patient herself, the doctor/the mother, the sister Idete, the maid Ivete, the son Francisco, the husband [unnamed], and Grandma Lena). As we will see, all of these characters people Dona Jurema's discourse, but little or no further information is provided about any of them.

The second major difference between the two interviews concerns the status of these topics (either the doctor's or the patient's). These referents cannot be arrayed on a general-to-specific dimension, which the topic-subtopic embedding implies (excerpts 4–9). Here every referent that is introduced by either participant has a "topic" status, and that referent is not developed in the interaction.

The discussion thus far has focused on how topic development breaks down in the doctor-patient interaction. Next we will see how Dona Jurema continuously brings in indefinite referents that are never made explicit during the interview.

What Is the Topic?

In the discharge interview, participants introduce and develop topics, referents that are signaled through a sharp semantic change. In the admitting interview, however, there is an absence of explicit referents in Dona Jurema's discourse, as the patient continuously makes use of expressions such as "something," "everything," and "nothing." For instance, she says that "mother wants to know something" or that "mother knows everything" and "I know nothing." She makes constant use of the expression "that's why" (Portuguese: *polisso/por isso*), the repetition of which makes the expression formulaic in her discourse, as in the following example.

[A translation would not indicate the rhythm pattern, so I am also presenting the original Portuguese text and keeping the Portuguese form *polisso* "that's why" in the English version.]

(11)

Patient:
[singing and baby talk]
⌐poli:sso!
⌐poli:sso!
⌐polisso, lisso, lisso!! ...
[acc]
['hhh] ⌐polisso!
polisso!
polisso!
[whimpering]
polisso, ma:ma::! ma:ma::!
ma:ma::! ma:ma::!
[crying]
it's polisso, ma:ma::!

Patient:
[singing and baby talk]
⌐poli:sso!
⌐poli:sso!
⌐polisso, lisso, lisso!! ...
[acc]
['hhh] ⌐polisso!
polisso!
polisso!
[whimpering]
polisso, mãe:! mãe:!
mãe:! mãe:!
[crying]
é polisso, mãe:!

Dona Jurema frequently repeats certain formulas pointing to an un-known referent, as in the following:

(12)

> Patient:
> [chanting and baby talk]
> **that's what I wanted!**
> **that's what I wanted!**
> **that's what I wanted!**
> **that's what I wanted!**

> Patient:
> [chanting and baby talk]
> **ela isso o que eu quelia!**
> **ela isso o que eu quelia!**
> **ela isso o que eu quelia!**
> **ela isso o que eu quelia!**

Examples (11) and (12) are typical of much of Dona Jurema's speech where the referent is never made explicit.[6] As a result, Doctor Edna often requests information and uses specific question forms. She asks: "you wanted what?"; "you have what?"; "what's happening?"; "thank God for what?"; "what is over?" These questions may or may not be addressed by Dona Jurema. When she does address them, she introduces vague referents, as in example (13):

(13)

Doctor:	Patient:
	[dec]
	(1) ⌐**Thank God! ....**
	[raises head, looks up, turns to doctor, and smiles]
[dec]	
(2) **thank God, for <u>what</u>?** =	
	(3) **=it's all over! ....**
	[holds the position and smiles]
[acc]	
(4) **<u>what is over</u>?**	

Again we see the doctor requesting specific referential information (lines 2 and 4), while the patient provides indefinite references (lines 1 and 3).

The other way that Dona Jurema responds to the doctor's request for information is by shifting the topic as in example (14), which follows example (13):

(14)

Doctor:	Patient:
[acc]	
(4) what is over?	

                              (5) ⌐**Jurema is a little dizzy, y'know.**
                              [turns torso and head to face doctor, moves left hand down
                              and grabs armchair]

(6) mmm.

In line (5) the patient introduces a new referent, "Jurema." She further develops it, with no contribution from the doctor:

(15)

        Patient:
           (7) **could you give ⌐my little =**
           (8) **= sister a glass of water,**
           (9) **she didn't even know that =**
          (10) **= this would happen to her.**

What we see (lines 5–10) is the patient introducing and developing a topic. First there is a sharp semantic change encoded by a noun phrase ("Jurema"). Topic continuity is assured by the maintenance of the same referent ("Jurema" = "my little sister") and then by a change from a noun phrase to a pronominal reference ("she"), which indicates topic progression and a higher degree of topic accessibility (Givón 1983).

    Referring terms are the most identifiable topics in Dona Jurema's discourse. They are important cues to the signaling of frames. However, the patient skips from one referring term to another without an apparent link between them:

(16)

        Patient:
           (5) ⌐**Jurema is a little dizzy,**
           (6) **y'know.**
           (7) **could you give ⌐my little =**
           (8) **= sister a glass of water,**
           (9) **she didn't even know that =**
          (10) **= this would happen to her.**
          (11) **you are very polite. ..**
                 [acc]
          (12) **/⌐then I only (knew), ...**
          (13) **/⌐then I only (knew),**
        [moves forward, leans forward and down, then repeats a movement to
        get up]

[coarse voice]
(14) **see, mother!** [**'hhh**]
(15) **see, mother!**
(16) **she even forgot the** =
(17) **= glass of water,**

Above the patient proposes four topics, three of which are referring terms: (1) "Jurema" (also "my little sister" and "she"); (2) "I" (the speaker); and (3) "she" (a previous addressee, i.e., the doctor). The fourth is "this" (line 10), a referent used to indicate something already familiar in Dona Jurema's discourse (though the antecedent of "this" was never named). Dona Jurema also introduces two addressing terms: "you" (the real addressee, i.e., the doctor); and "mother" (the imaginary addressee, who is not really present).

What makes this excerpt semantically and pragmatically loaded is the co-occurrence of several referring terms (with topic status) together with two addressing terms. The speaker talks about someone (Jurema, my little sister, she, I) while she explicitly addresses "you" (the doctor) or the mother. The doctor (listener) is left with a discourse peopled by far too many characters and references.[7]

Concerning topic, the preceding discussion points to two recurrent traits in Dona Jurema's discourse. The first is the use of referents—mostly encoded by pronouns—that presuppose a high degree of topic accessibility (Givón 1983), as in examples (11) through (13). That is, for the patient's discourse to make any sense to the listener, the doctor must be familiar with the pronoun reference. In the admitting interview, however, these antecedents were never made explicit by the patient. Also, the doctor's repetitive efforts to uncover these topics were mostly unsuccessful.

The second common trait is the use of referring terms —encoded by a noun phrase or a pronoun—which tend to cluster in a single speaker's turn. These topics often co-occur with changes of addressee. Hence, Dona Jurema's discourse either unfolds a profusion of referents (showing excess in topic introduction) or lacks referential specificity (displaying deficiency in topic accessibility).

Inconclusive Topics

The topics that Doctor Edna introduces are only partially addressed by the patient, if at all. This is what we saw in the previous discussion. Every topic that Dona Jurema brings up (as she talks to the doctor or to other absent addressees) is also only partially developed. Sometimes topics are interrupted abruptly, as in example (5), here repeated:

(5)

Doctor:
(1) ⌐**tell me your FULL** =
    = name. =

Doctor: Patient:
                           [baby talk]
                      (2) = there is no need =
                      (3) = 'cause the doc,
                      (4) doc,
                      (5) doc,
                      (6) the doc-
                      (7) papapapapapapapapa- ['hhh]
                      (8) papapapa-Pau-lo-de-
                           [starts moving her face to the right]
                      (9) A-ze-ve-do-Mur-ti-nho.
                           [looks up, looks down]
                           [chanting and baby talk]
                     (10) you yourself know quite =
                           = well,
                           [tapping on the armchair]
                     (11) better than I,
                     (12) better than anyone,
                     (13) when I get,
                     (14) to my ward,
                     (15) I'm gonna tell,
                     (16) I'm gonna tell,
//DONA JURE:MA!   (17) //this was,
                     (18) this was,
                     (19) this was my secret. ...

Here Dona Jurema answers by saying that she need not (tell her full name), and then she starts to explain why. However, she never completes her "explanation." As discussed previously, part of Dona Jurema's answer refers to Doctor Paulo Murtinho. Once again, she does not complete her statement. She shifts from the referent "Doctor Paulo" to "you," Doctor Edna (line 10), and then to "I," Jurema (lines 13–16). She also shifts activities and starts chanting and using child's language. By the end of this segment she shifts topic again to the deictic term "this," which lacks specificity in the patient's discourse (lines 17–19).

In another instance, Dona Jurema seems to be taking the role of a former elderly maid or servant, addressing someone in a higher social position. The address form *mecê* is used in the rural areas of Brazil, mostly by older people:

[The Portuguese text is also displayed for the rhythmic information.]

(17)

            Patient:
            [staccato and baby talk]
            so-you-ma'am-will-do-like-
            this-later-so-over-there-at-
            home-it-will-be-bad-oh-very-
            bad-for-you-it-will-be. ..

but I won't allow (it),
I won't allow (it),

Patient:
[staccato and baby talk]
então-você-mecê-vai-fazê-
assim-logo-mais-então-lá-em-
casa-vai-ficá-feio-oh-muito-
feio-pá-sinola-vai-ficá. ..
mas eu não vou deisá,
eu não vou deisá,

In this entire segment Dona Jurema does not indicate what she is referring to. She seems to be giving a series of instructions to *você-mecê* "you-
ma'am." However, the information is incomplete: The hearer does not
know "what you-ma'am will do (at home and later)," "what will be bad,"
nor "what won't be allowed." A series of indexical expressions are pack-
aged together ("you-ma'am," a person deixis; "later," a time deixis; "over
there," "at home," space deixis). What the hearer lacks, however, is the
referential information that substantiates each one of these contextual
anchor points.

Lexical Cohesion and Incoherent Discourse

It has been assumed that cohesive ties account for one level of coherence
in texts. Halliday and Hassan (1976) demonstrate that cohesion establishes continuity in a text and that continuity is a primary factor in the
"intelligibility" of discourse. And, as Tannen (1987:583) also indicates,
repetition has a referential and tying function. In the admitting interview, Dona Jurema relies heavily on repetition as lexical cohesion. We
see that her talk is cohesive but not coherent. She repeats single lexical
items or certain structures, as in the following:

the doc,
doc,
doc.
the doc-

this was,
this was,
this was,
my secret

I've told,
I've told,
I've told,
told, told.

It's a (little) caress
It's a (little) caress
it's a (little) caress

I'm not going to tell,
I'm not going to tell,
I'm not going to tell,
I'm not going to tell,

Repetition occurs in songs and jingles, which are frequently used by Dona Jurema throughout the development of this interview. It does not, however, help in establishing "what talk is about." The simple repetition of an indefinite referent does not extend its meaning, nor does it make it more specific.

Repetition also occurs across the doctor and patient turns, as in the following exchange:

(18)

Doctor:	Patient:
let's talk for a =	
= little bit more,	
//O.K.	//no. it's time. ...
it's time for what? =	
	= it's time for me to go. ...
to go where? =	
	= to go where? ...
yeah:.	
	and what do you know?
	what do you know? ...

The repetition of lexical forms makes this text highly cohesive. So do the regular rhythmic patterns of pause intervals (between the patient's and doctor's turns) and latched turns (between the doctor's and patient's turns). A series of references, however, are missing. Speakers do not establish time or place referents despite the doctor's repetitive effort ("time for what?"; "go where?").

Another example takes place a bit further on, as Dona Jurema complains:

(19)

Doctor:	Patient:
	[baby talk; slow pace]
	(1) **you already saw me!** ...
	[smiles, looks at doctor]
(2) **I already saw =**	
= you today? =	
	[baby talk; slow pace]
	(3) **= you already <forgot =**
	= (me)!>
	[nods]

Doctor: Patient:
(4) <u>what?</u> what time did =
    = I see you? =

                                 [baby talk; slow pace]
                             (5) = it was I that saw you! =
                                 [smiles; short nod]

(6) = when was that? =

                                 [baby talk; slow pace]
                             (7) = you did not see me.
                                 [looks down] (2.3)

(8) when was it that =
    = you saw me? =

Again, repetition binds this stretch of talk together, making the discourse highly cohesive. In fact, the patient repeats (with small variations) the same paradigm:

```
you already    saw     me
you already    forgot  me
you (did not)  see     me
I              saw     you
```

As Dona Jurema repeats linguistic forms, she keeps the same rhythm throughout her utterances. The pace is slow; it contrasts, however, with the fast pace of the interaction with the doctor (four latching turns in lines 2–3; 4–5; 5–6; 6–7).

When Doctor Edna requests further information, she does so by also restating the same linguistic forms:

```
I      already  saw   you   today
I      (did)    see   you
you             saw   me
```

```
when was that
when was it
```

In addition to word repetition, several other forms of repetition are noticeable in this talk exchange. Statements are transformed into questions and questions transformed into statements lines 1–2, 3–4, 5–6, and 7–8 (Tannen 1989:54); also, a patterned rhythm—slow and chanted—occurs in every assertion by Dona Jurema (lines 1, 3, 5, and 7). This sense of unity contrasts, nevertheless, with the participants' responses to one another.

Each assertion from Dona Jurema raises a question from the doctor, which is addressed only indirectly by the patient. The first ("I have already seen you today?") is a yes-no question; from the patient's response (line 3), one infers a "yes" ("(yes, you saw me but) you have already forgotten (me)"). This is what the doctor inferred, as evidenced by her following question ("(if it is true that I saw you) what time did I see you?" in line 4). Now, Dona Jurema does not address the doctor's question. She shifts the topic from "you saw me" to "I saw you" (line 5). To establish coherence in this segment one must understand Dona Jurema's contribution as a repair ("(it wasn't really you who saw me, but rather) it was I who saw you!"). The doctor accepts this repair (line 6); she probes to request further information ("when was that?" and then "when was it that you saw me?" in line 8). In her next statement (line 7), once more Dona Jurema shifts the personal referent from "I" to "you" ("I saw you" to "you did not see me"). The doctor's last question is left unanswered as the patient shifts topic again.[8]

Shifts between subject and object pronouns ("I"/"me" and "you") take place throughout the segment. Both doctor and patient alternate between mirror statements ("you saw me" and "I saw you") in inverted propositions. They never catch up with one another's referent in spite of the doctor's efforts. Hence, at the end it is still left in doubt who exactly saw whom, according to the patient's perspective.

In the admitting interview, participants jointly, as well as individually, build a tightly knit discourse. However, this does not assure topic coherence. On one hand, we see Dona Jurema providing a series of lexical and prosodic ties. Even in a talk exchange, both doctor and patient show heavy reliance on lexical cohesion and patterned rhythm. On the other hand, we see Dona Jurema using limited lexical bonds. That is, she repeats continuously the same linguistic forms. Only seldom does she use a conjunctive link that would help establish (or clarify) the connection among different referents.[9]

Topic Transitions

Topic transitions presuppose a jointly built discourse. A standard role relationship in doctor-patient communication establishes that the doctor is the one who either proposes a topic or introduces the possibility of topic change; the patient addresses the topic or negotiates for a topic transition; the doctor then ratifies the new topic. No such process of negotiation takes place in the admitting interview. Most of the time the patient introduces different disjunct referents, as in the following:

[This excerpt follows example (13); it was also used to illustrate a different point in example (8).]

(20)

Doctor: Patient:
                                   [coarse voice]
                           (1) **see, mother,** ['hhh]
                           (2) **see, mother,**
                           (3)   **she even forgot the** =
                                 = **glass of water,**
                           (4) **y'see, oh mother.**
                                 [acc] [baby talk]
                           (5) **that's why:,**
                           (6) **that's why:,**

Doctor: Patient:
                                     [dec]
                               (7) ⌜oh, tha:t's why:,
                               (8) ⌜OH:, THA::T'S WHY:!
                               (9) that's why I<u>ve-</u>
                              (10) i-, i-, i-. ..
                                     [coarse voice]
                              (11) ⌊can you send for=
                                     =Iveti (for me)?

(12) who is Iveti?

                                     [coarse voice, baby talk]
                              (13) =she's the maid (who=
                                     =works) at my house,
                                     [looks down and sideways to the left]
                              (14) at my sister's,
                              (15) not at my house,
                              (16) at my sister's house.
                              (17) you give the orders=
                                     =(there)?

(18) what's the name=
       =of your sister?

                              (19) I- if I speak=
                                     =<proproproperly>,
                              (20) would you let me say,
                                     that it is Idetinha?....
                                     [slowly turns head to the right]

(21) who's Idetinha,
(22) your sister?=
                              (23) =my sister.=
(24) =yeah::?
                                     [baby talk]
                              (25) do you believe me? ....
                              (26) really believe me? ...
                              (27) can I go then? ...
(28) //no, we'll still=   //can I?
       =talk for a little=
       =while, O.K.?=

First Dona Jurema addresses her mother and conveys a complaint as she refers to the doctor ("she") and to a glass of water (line 3).[10] Next she shifts topic in line 5 as she repeats "that's why!" and finally (lines 9 and 10) introduces "Ivete," her sister's maid. In this next segment (lines 11–16) both doctor and patient talk about Ivete. The doctor asks who Ivete is (line 12), and the patient provides an answer that consists of two parts: She states that Ivete works at her house (line 13) and then she introduces a repair (lines 14–16) and states that she works not at her house but at her sister's house. In line (17) the patient introduces another topic disjunct. Dona Jurema asks the doctor an apparently unrelated question. She addresses Doctor Edna and says:

(17) **you give the orders (there)?**
(17) **a senhola <u>manda</u> (lá)?**

The Portuguese verb *mandar* is ambiguous. One sense of it is "to send"; the other sense is "to command," "to order," "to direct." In line (11) Dona Jurema had asked:

(11) **can you send for Iveti for me?**
(11) **a senhora <u>manda</u> a Iveti pa mim?**

Here *mandar* means to "send for." However, in line (17) she repeats the same form (a touch-off of the sort discussed in chapter 2) but with a different meaning:

(11) **you send for Ivete**
(17) **you command there**

(11) **a senhora <u>manda</u> a Ivete**
(17) **a senhora <u>manda</u> lá**

A lexical touch-off (where one lexical form provokes a further occurrence of the same form) triggers a change in topic. This is particularly interesting as it suggests that topic disjuncts in Dona Jurema's discourse can be the result of lexical or sound touch-offs (see also "Translating Spoken Discourse" in chapter 2). The patient's odd sort of topic shifts would then not be completely at random.[11]

The doctor does not pick up on this new proposition ("the doctor giving orders at Idete's").[12] Instead, she shifts back to Dona Jurema's sister and asks her name (line 18). In the following segment (lines 19–23) the patient answers the doctor's question by providing the name of her sister. She ends this segment by challenging the doctor (in lines 25 and 26) and requesting permission to leave (line 27), which the doctor denies (line 28).

In this segment a series of referents are brought up by the patient, and few are developed in the interaction. Dona Jurema addresses her mother and refers to *she* (the doctor) who has failed to bring her a glass of water; then she mentions *Ivete* (the maid) who works for her sister. Next the doctor requests her sister's name. "The sister's name" becomes a topic of talk for the next two turns, with the patient closing that topic with a challenge (and a topic shift to "you," the doctor) and a request to leave (and a topic shift to "I," the patient).

Again we see new referents being introduced in a disjunct manner, and there is little understanding of what the topic of talk is. Any attempt from the doctor to further develop "what talk is about" ends with the patient either shifting topics or challenging the doctor.

Themes versus Topics

In the analysis of both the admitting and the discharge interviews, I have used the notion of topic to indicate whether and how the participants jointly build a coherent discourse. Topic coherence breaks down in the admitting interview, as noted previously. There seems to be, however, one propositional level—a thematic level—on which Dona Jurema's discourse makes sense. In discussing different levels for topics, Schiffrin (1987b:8) states that "topics have also been seen as general frameworks or macro-propositions which underlie an entire text, something like the 'title' of a story, or maybe the topic sentence of a paragraph, might capture its underlying message." This is the level at which psychiatrists and psychoanalysts operate (Almeida 1987), and where inferences are made about the underlying messages in psychotic discourse.

At a macrolevel, certain recurrent references (e.g., "the child's secret" or "the mother's knowledge") do indicate to the doctor that specific themes are being constantly recycled throughout this interview, and therefore represent important information for the patient. Substantial inferencing by the listener is necessary to achieve this understanding, as Schiffrin, also referring to Grice (1975), points out: "Responses which do not draw from the conventional range of coherence options . . . may require hearers to undertake substantial inferencing if they are to construct for them a coherent interpretation" (1987a:23). The following section will briefly illustrate this point.

Thematic Units

Several recurrent references, representing major themes, are brought up by the patient during the interview. At the very beginning, Dona Jurema introduces a series of key references that she will allude to throughout the development of the interview: (1) She addresses her mother, referring to the knowledge the mother has and to the secret the child Jurema has, which she will (or will not) tell; (2) she refers to her husband and complains about him having deceived her; and (3) she refers to the Virgin Mary (portrayed through a religious hymn). After bringing up these referents, Dona Jurema turns to the doctor and asks "what more do you need to know?" as if she had summarized her topics right there. As the interview develops, these referents gain a thematic status: They are recycled at different points, often with little textual cohesiveness.

The Mother's Knowledge

The main theme seems to address the doctor's underlying question: "Dona Jurema, what's the problem? what's wrong with you?" The patient answers this question indirectly by marking deference and restating over and over again the asymmetrical relationship that underlies the doctor-patient relation as well as the mother-child relation. On one hand, she emphasizes the mother-doctor knowledge:

you know very well
you know better than I
you know better than anyone

On the other hand, she states her own ignorance:

I know nothing,
nothing,
nothing.

"To know," in all its grammatical forms (indicating person and tense), constitutes the most frequent verb used by Dona Jurema (apart from the auxiliaries "to be"/"to have"). The theme of knowledge and motherhood is recycled throughout the interview and constitutes a major reference for the psychotic frame (discussed in chapter 7).

The Child's Credibility

There are two correlates to the knowledge theme—the credibility theme and the secrecy theme. While Dona Jurema asserts the mother's knowledge ("the mother is the one who knows"), she questions the child's credibility. Over and over again, Dona Jurema asks the doctor/mother whether she believes her report to be truthful:

[baby talk]
do you believe (me)?
you really believe (me)?
can I go then?

In different segments of the interview she interrupts her talk and says:

[baby talk]
are you going to believe me if I say it right?

As a jingle she states:

[baby talk]
if you want to believe (me)
you can believe (me).
those who don't want to
they may do this.
[makes playful gestures with right hand]

And the interview ends with the patient making eye contact with the doctor and asking:

do you believe (me)?

The Child's Secrecy

As an expansion of the credibility theme, Dona Jurema refers continuously to a secret:

> [baby talk]
> **this was,**
> **this was,**
> **my secret,**
> **this was, ..**
> **this was,**
> **and this was my secret. ..**

She also refers to whether she will (or will not) tell this secret:

> **I'll never tell!**
> **I'll never tell!**
> **I'll never tell!**
> **I'll never tell!**

MacKinnon and Michels (1971:249), in discussing the schizophrenic's need for secrecy, indicate that "the patient's need to have a secret is often more important than the content of the secret" (1971:250). It shows a concern over privacy and the patient's fear that she may be hurt if the interviewer gets to know her too well (1971:250). Regarding communicative strategies, Sullivan refers to the attitude of the patient toward secrecy, assuming "secret understandings" between him and the therapist. The language used by the patient is described as "stereo-typical," with recurrent "tags of expression" (1954:193).[13]

The Husband and the Marriage

Intertwined with the secrecy/credibility/knowledge themes is Dona Jurema's reference to the betrayal of her husband. This topic is also referred to in the discharge interview. In the opening of the admitting interview, Dona Jurema first brings up the topic "husband" when she puts a curse on him:

> [singing as in a nursery rhyme]
> **my dear husband,**
> **knew very well,**
> **he did not come to help,**
> **his dear dear wife,**
> **but it does not matter,**
> **his good luck will not last,**
> **that is all I can wish on him with all my heart.**

It is interesting to note that Dona Jurema packages a complaint about her husband's behavior (and then a curse) within a nursery rhyme. Actually, she mixes two well-known Brazilian nursery rhymes: She uses partially the lyrics of one song ("but it does not matter, his good luck will not last") and the beat of another.[14] The use of speech play reduces the force of the complaint and the curse. It is also an indirect way of mentioning a threatening topic.

Again, halfway through the interview Dona Jurema complains:

Doctor:	Patient:
	a house with a home,
	another house without a home,
//mmm::.	//a house with a home,
	another house without without=
	=without a home.
	isn't it, isn't it funny. ...
	so isn't it my son-
	look how they are.
	[raises head up high, raises neck, looks to the extreme right]
	look how they are. ...
	look how they look.
	[moves sideways, still staring at the same corner]
	look how they look. ...

Doctor:	Patient:
	uma casa com casa,
	outra casa sem casa,
//mmm::.	//uma casa com casa,
	uma casa sem sem sem casa.
	não é, não é engraçado. ... não é meu fio-
	olha como eles é.
	[raises head up high, raises neck, looks to the extreme right]
	olha como eles é. ...
	olha como eles ó.
	[moves sideways, still staring at the same corner]
	olha como eles ó. ...

In Portuguese the word *casa* refers to both "home" and "house." The "house" and "home" distinction is therefore a personal interpretation. This segment might refer back to the patient's separation from her husband and to having "a house without a home" since then. This is another instance of a lexical touch-off and wordplay (much subtler since here the patient uses a homonym, a word with the same sound and same spelling but different meanings).

The second part of the excerpt proposes an indefinite topic "they" as the patient requests the addressee to "look": "look how they are"; "look how they look." Again the noun phrase antecedent was never introduced by the patient. The listener (as the doctor) must infer from the patient's discourse what the most likely topic could be.[15]

As a conclusive remark, she repeats throughout the interview the statement of "discovery" *por isso!* "that's why" (with the phonological variant /l/ for /r/, resulting in the form *polisso*). It is mostly repeated in short, fragmented jingles, as in the following:

Patient:
[singing]
tha:t's why,
tha:t's why,
that's why,
why, why.
['hhh]
that's why,
that's why,
that's why,
[whining]
that's why <u>ma:ma</u>::!
<u>ma:ma</u>::! <u>ma:ma</u>::!
<u>ma:ma</u>::!
[crying]
that's why, <u>ma:ma</u>::!

Patient:
[singing]
poli:sso,
poli:sso,
polisso,
lisso,
lisso.
['hhh]
polisso,
polisso,
polisso,
[whining]
polisso, mã<u>e</u>:! mã<u>e</u>:!
mã<u>e</u>:! mã<u>e</u>:!
[crying]
é polisso, mã<u>e</u>:!

The Religious Themes

The religious themes are evoked through church hymns and in jingles where religious references are made. At the beginning of the interview we see Dona Jurema singing a church hymn addressing the Virgin Mary. At another point the patient refers to her granddaughter and sings as if in church:

Maliene
Sacred Liene
To me she is
Sanctified

Maliene is the patient's granddaughter. Dona Jurema uses a current formulaic expression in Portuguese for "the most dear one" (*a coisa mais sagrada deste mundo* "the most sacred thing in all the world"). The formula could have a religious connotation activated by the word *sacred*, but in colloquial everyday usage, it means simply "dearest." Dona Jurema transforms this expression into a "church script" by packaging the formula within a religious chant, thus alluding to a church ceremony. It is as though one way of expanding a formulaic expression (which, in this case, is achieved by providing a literal meaning that the original expression does not contain) could be through creating a proper script to fit the formula.

Other religious references are interspersed throughout the interview: Dona Jurema states at one point that she lives in Lome (= Rome with the pope); she seems to say that her name is *Nossa Senhora de Aparecida* (the manifestation of the Virgin Mary, who is the patron saint of Brazil), but is interrupted by the doctor; she expresses thanks to God and kneels down, obeying her sister's suggestion.[16]

These themes constitute important information that the patient recycles in the admitting interview. They are part of the different frames of talk referred to in the next chapter. Thus, themes, rather than topics, seem to capture meaningful messages in the patient's discourse. One has the feeling that some sort of coherence is achieved at a more general level. There are a few reasons why this assumption may be true.

The first and most salient one has to do with the difference between topic structure and thematic structure. Topics are normally interactively built and presuppose a joint effort by the participants. As Goffman ([1967] 1982) says, participation in a topic reveals involvement in a joint conversation. Thus, it is not enough for a speaker to propose a referent. At best, this referent would constitute one topic candidate among many (see, e.g., Button and Casey 1984). To assure topic continuity, a dialogic structure seems to be a major requisite. Themes, however, need not be interactionally built. They can be individually sustained and are subjectively referred to (i.e., in reference to a speaker or a writer, one often talks about "the theme of a speech," "the theme of a short story," "the theme of a poem"). The author (speaker or writer) selects a thematic thread, receiving no contribution from the audience (listener or reader). Themes are usually discussed in discourse genres that tend to be monologic (such as narratives, descriptions, reports, and the like).

A second and closely related point has to do with the level of specificity of topics (the one undertaken in this study) versus the level of generality of themes. Topics were defined as "what talk is about." Here this notion implies that the topic is explicitly mentioned. The analyst must work with the referential, denotative semantic information. Also, a microanalysis is required, the sort of analysis that looks at every speaker's contributions, pursues local coherence, and considers listening and speaking to be inextricably intertwined. Themes, on the other hand, derive from general propositions (Schiffrin 1987b). They are overall statements that capture the implicit message that has been conveyed in an entire text (a story, a report, an account, etc.). As a consequence, themes need not require the level of specificity of topic units, nor must they be constrained by rules of local coherence. Rather, they dwell on general leitmotifs.

A third point has to do with the recurrent nature of themes. Their repetition throughout a discourse makes themes dominant semantic units: They seem to motivate and generate talk. Thematic recurrence also works to integrate what otherwise may be a fragmented piece of talk. This unifying function helps establish a sense of content coherence.

Conclusion

Major problems in Dona Jurema's discourse can be identified by topic analysis. As one listens to Dona Jurema's talk, one hears a series of indefinite referents that are never made explicit. Most of these referents are never developed or brought to conclusion. They represent fragmentary information, and they are part of a personal (nonofficial) topic agenda that the patient keeps recycling throughout the interview.

Doctor Edna has few opportunities to intervene in Dona Jurema's talk. When she gets the floor, she often summons the patient's attention and makes a series of attempts to introduce a topic of talk. As we have seen, Dona Jurema rarely addresses the doctor's topics. When she does, her answers vary in degrees of acceptability and coherence.

Two aspects of topic development that were important to the analysis of the discharge interview—subtopic categorization and topic transitions—posed problems in the analysis of the admitting interview. Both types of analysis presuppose a jointly built discourse, which does not occur in the admitting interview. Subtopic categorization is useful to indicate specific information that each participant brings to the development of a topic. However, there are no subtopics in this interview, implying that topics are not developed. Topic transitions represent moments where participants jointly negotiate referential meaning and an understanding of what the next topic is about. No such process of negotiation takes place in the admitting interview.

This is also the case with the absence of the three-part structure question/answer/comment, where the comment slot provides for a transition between a topic unit that is ending and another that is about to begin. The lack of a comment from the doctor signals the absence of a satisfying, coherent response from the patient.

The topic structure that prevails in this interview is of a different nature. It can be captured by a three-part structure where the patient has the leading role: assertion/question/answer(?). Several excerpts show Dona Jurema making some sort of assertion; the doctor then requests information on the referent proposed by the patient; lastly, the patient may or may not address the doctor's question. Thus, in this three-part structure (assertion/question/answer) the doctor's questions are requests for clarification and the patient's responses, when they come, are provisions of clarification. The clarification requests and responses constitute the bulk of the interaction in this interview.[17]

The last part of the chapter discussed a general and macrolevel of interpretation—a thematic level—where Dona Jurema's references may be meaningful and coherent. Throughout the development of this interview, there are recurrent references in her discourse that point to the relevance of certain themes. In chapter 7 we will see how some of these themes relate to various frames that emerge in this interview.

Topic analysis indicates where coherence breaks down in the admitting interview. This analysis works, therefore, to point out failures in the patient's discourse regarding topic continuity and topic shift. Topic analysis can be used as an evaluation tool for the patient's social and linguistic performances. It can detect the amount of interactional work the patient is willing or able to undertake. It can also be used to describe the range of specificity of topic content.

The analysis of topic structure and topic content also captures some language and cognitive behaviors usually used by psychiatrists to classify psychotic talk (see Appendix A for a checklist and description). Specifically, disorders such as tangentiality, distractible speech, pressure of speech, derailment, clanging, loss of goal, and preservation are covered under the topic discussion presented in this chapter. There is, therefore, a strong linguistic component to the diagnosis of these disorders.

Notes

1. While shifts in footing per se do not cause breakdown in everyday interactions (in themselves they signal and constitute new alignments participants take up to themselves and others in interaction), in the admitting interview these subtle shifts compete with other framings, those that pertain to the psychotic crisis. The multitude of frame embeddings and frame laminations attest to the complexity of this encounter.

2. Rochester and Martin present interesting results on the performance of thought-disordered speakers in task-based contexts: They say that these speakers "rarely describe but often 'point' with their words, using pronouns and demonstratives and omitting the thing which would clarify their reference" (1979:167). In order to recover the referents for definite nominal groups in a conversation,

Rochester and Martin add, "the listener should search both the nonverbal and the verbal context" (1979:167).

3. During the playback session Doctor Edna said that she had tried to conduct a standard interview. When she felt that the interview was not proceeding as expected, she decided to go along with talk as it came up.

4. Ribeiro (1991b) examines how *both* participants—the doctor and the patient—are indeed dissociated from one another throughout this interview. The patient aligns herself with a series of characters that are not really present; the doctor aligns herself with her official role and with the official topic agenda that she keeps proposing in the interview. The result is mutual detachment and alienation: No spontaneous involvement in a topic of conversation takes place *from either end*.

5. A similar conflict of interests is demonstrated by Mehan in the analysis of a psychiatric interview, where the participants fail "to reach a mutually agreed-upon definition of the situation" (1990:166). Mehan indicates how both doctors and patients engage in "oracular reasoning," a practice where "both cling to their basic assertions, denying the information presented which has the potential of undermining those basic beliefs" (1990:170).

6. Rochester and Martin observe that "thought-disordered speakers use high proportions of unclear reference, relative to other speakers, and often fail to initiate chains of reference in their texts" (1979:201). Durbin and Marshall investigate speech in manic patients and also conclude that under a crisis "it is not possible for the listener to supply the processes which would recover enough old information for the discourse to be meaningful" (1977:217).

7. Rochester and Martin (1979) point to several factors that affect talk in thought-disordered speakers. Among them they mention the packaging of "too much information, coupled with a miscalculation of referential ties" (1979:181). Thought-disordered speakers also have a problem in initiating chains of reference and in "matching initial and subsequent references to a given participant," for instance, matching the participant "Francisco" to the anaphoric pronoun "he" (1979:180).

8. Each one of Jurema's statements carries an underlying complaint to the doctor as well as a request for attention. The various functions that these statements may have do not affect the analysis.

9. Studies focusing on cohesion in psychotic discourse have been developed by Martin and Rochester (1975), Rochester, Martin, and Thurston (1977), Durbin and Marshall (1977), Rochester and Martin (1979), and Wykes and Leff (1982). Most of these studies use linguistic variables to describe psychotic discourse and measure the extent to which spoken and written pathological discourse present deviations from normal speakers' production. Halliday and Hassan's (1976) cohesion analysis is used to describe the textual features that scholars find useful in identifying thought-disordered discourse.

Rochester, Martin, and Thurston investigated thought disorder as it occurs in acute schizophrenia, and the extent to which thought-disordered speech can be reliably distinguished from both non-thought-disordered schizophrenic speech and normal utterances. They conclude that thought-disordered speech makes the listener's task difficult in two ways: It makes the listener search for information that is never clearly given, and it provides few conjunctive links between clauses (i.e., the speaker has a tendency to use limited lexical bonds rather than extensive conjunctive bonds) (1977:111).

In a longer study, Rochester and Martin (1979) examine the discourse production of schizophrenic thought-disordered and non-thought-disordered speakers versus normal speakers. They present the following "tentative conclusions": (1) Thought-disordered speakers can use complex structural elements, but they avoid doing so whenever the situational context provides the information to be encoded; (2) thought-disordered speakers "rely heavily on lexical cohesion"; and (3) these same speakers "do not establish chains of reference through their texts to the same extent and in the same manner as other speakers" (1979:203). The authors conclude by suggesting that thought-disordered speakers may sometimes fail to use "elaborate verbal encoding strategies" (1979:203).

10. The discussion of frames in chapter 7 indicates that the patient is referring to the doctor. In the preceding discourse Dona Jurema had addressed the doctor, acknowledged the doctor's help, and requested a glass of water. She performs an entire script while taking the role of her sister Idete addressing Doctor Edna.

11. Salzinger, Portnoy, and Feldman (1978) used cloze tests to construct a method of quantitative measurement of communicability for studying schizophrenic communicative dysfunction. Success in these tests is based on a subject's use of implicit rules of grammar. Salzinger tested the immediacy hypothesis (1966), which states that "schizophrenic behavior is primarily controlled by stimuli that are immediate in the environment." This means that "when there are several stimuli acting simultaneously upon a schizophrenic, the one that controls behavior is the one that comes closest to the occasion for the response" (1978:37). In terms of language it means that a specific word in a schizophrenic utterance is more likely to be a response to some immediate word in the preceding utterance than to words that had occurred much earlier in the discourse. This would explain why a speaker under a psychotic crisis is particularly prone to use sound or lexical "touch-offs."

The authors state that schizophrenic speech is more predictable than normal speech in "low context," while normal speech is more predictable in "high context." That is, given a short text, judges could predict the word omitted from schizophrenic utterances, a longer text made it increasingly possible for judges to predict which word had been omitted by a normal speaker but was less helpful when dealing with schizophrenic discourse. This fact seems to provide evidence for schizophrenic speech failures regarding topic continuity in discourse; that is, they fail "to adhere to a topic while having inter-relationships among words over short spans" (1978:47).

12. "The doctor giving orders" is a proposition. In Schiffrin's terms (1987b) it is an open proposition because it is a question. A proposition— whether asserted or questioned—can be a topic, just as much as a referent can.

13. On a different note, Goffman comments on the environment of secrecy that surrounds mental patients in psychiatric institutions. Staff, more often than not, conceal patients' records from them. However, all staff levels have access to the daily course of each patient's disease (1961:159). These records are available, and patients have no control over who gets to see them. Goffman comments on the formal (e.g., staff meetings) and informal (e.g., gossip, small talk) patterns of communication on the patient's case or on the patient's behavior. In chapter 7 we will see that a secret understanding may be one type of alignment the child has toward the mother; however, it is also a fleeting enactment of a behavior indigenous to the environment of total institutions, as Goffman points out (1961:161).

14. The Portuguese excerpt is the following:

Dona Jurema	(translation)
(I)	
meu malidinho,	my dear husband
ja sabia de cor,	knew it by heart
não veio acudir,	he did not come to help
a mulherzinha dele dele,	his dear dear wife
(II)	
mas não faz mal,	but it does not matter
a lagoa há de secar,	the lake will dry up
eu só posso,	I can only
a ele desejar!	wish that on him!

The original lyrics in Portuguese match partially the second stanza:

(II)	
Jacaré está na lagoa	alligator is by the lake
Com preguiça de nadar;	too lazy to swim;
Deixa estar, "seu" Jacaré,	O.K., "Mr." alligator,
Que a lagoa há de secar!	this lake will dry up!

Chacon Jurado Filho (1986) describes the functions that these nursery rhymes have among Brazilian children. Usually, these rhymes are used by children to convey some specific understanding of a given situation (1986:39). Their semantic import lies in the implicit message.

15. Background information suggests that "they" could refer to neighbors and their behavior. Dona Jurema might, therefore, be alluding to a moment in the past when the neighbors demonstrated a reaction to or curiosity about her separation (and her life as a single woman). Referring to neighbors could also activate Dona Jurema's perception of her own reaction to her neighbors' curiosity about her present crisis: "look how they look!"; "look how they are!"

16. Dona Jurema's sister Idete was not present at the interview. The actions were a result of a set of commands Jurema kept telling herself to follow (commands from Idete to Jurema).

17. This is one of the structural reasons that the discourse does not proceed. Normally, a request for clarification and its response are embedded within an ongoing discourse. They do not change the direction of the talk; they are what Schegloff ([1972b] 1988) calls an *insertion sequence*. The general pattern is:

    A1: what's your name?
      B2: my name?
      A2: yes.
    B1: Mary Jones.
    A3: Oh, are you Sally Jones's sister?
    B3: No, she's my cousin.
      etc.

The clarification request (B2–A2) does not disrupt the ongoing conversation; instead, the participants keep the conversation going after the problem (e.g., mishearing) is resolved. This is not the case in the admitting interview. I thank Susan Hoyle for pointing this out to me.

7

Frame Analysis in the Admitting Interview: Where Coherence Emerges

In many psychiatric settings, one can witness what seems to be the same central encounter between a patient and a psychiatrist: the psychiatrist begins the exchange by proffering the patient the civil regard that is owed a client, receives a response that cannot be integrated into a continuation of the conventional service interaction, and then, even while attempting to sustain some of the outward forms of server-client relations, must twist and squirm his way out of the predicament.
Erving Goffman, *Asylums*, p. 368

[The patient] sees the psychiatrist as the person in power. In contact with the psychiatrist the patient is likely to make those kinds of demands and requests and take those stands that pull the relationship out of the service schema to, for example, that of a charge pleading with his master for more privileges, a prisoner remonstrating with an unlawful jailor, or a prideful man declining to exchange communications with someone who thinks he is crazy.
Erving Goffman, *Asylums*, p. 367

As one listens to Dona Jurema's talk in the admitting interview, one has at first the impression of a totally fragmented and incoherent text. Chunks of language are connected in a seemingly illogical way, and new references are presented without any link to the previous talk. Doctor Edna, as a listener, feels that she cannot follow what the patient says, although she may be familiar with the vocabulary and the sentence structure patterns. The patient, as a speaker, seems uninterested in participating in the encounter proposed by the doctor.

As seen in chapter 6, topic coherence is not achieved in the admitting interview. Instead, competing topic agendas are at work: The doctor

Note: An earlier, abridged version of this chapter is found in Ribeiro, "Framing in Psychotic Discourse," in 1993.

proposes official topics, while the patient brings a personal agenda to the encounter. The doctor seldom picks up a referent introduced by the patient, and rarely does Dona Jurema address any of the doctor's topics. Cameron describes this communicative process when both the doctor and the patient "are repeatedly missing each other's points" (1947:50). Often the patient's discourse is elliptical, lacking the proper reference needed for making sense. Nor do her contributions assure topic development, and throughout the interview entry talk is sparse. A topic analysis, therefore, works to indicate the different levels on which the patient's discourse lacks coherence, though the discourse may be cohesive, as demonstrated by Rochester and Martin (1979).

There are ways, however, in which Dona Jurema, as a thought-disordered patient, achieves coherence within successive frames of talk. Despite the incoherent responses she provides throughout the development of this interview, several consistent chunks of discourse can be identified. In each, the patient accomplishes communicative action of some sort. She uses language as an instrument for getting things done. She also responds coherently to the doctor's requests. The end result—that is, the communicative import that follows—can be quite impressive. The frames that are proposed and sustained in the admitting interview point to a different level of discourse coherence—where Dona Jurema's talk is consistent within a frame. As we will see, the patient's discourse is shown to obey some linguistic and social constraints that underlie her "projected" contexts.

Dona Jurema performs different roles in this interview. She seldom takes on the patient's role and addresses the doctor. Most often she speaks as a child and addresses her mother—a common behavior in psychosis (Cameron [1944]1964; Sullivan [1944] 1964; Kasanin [1944] 1964). Still as a child, she talks to other family members as, for example, her sister Idete and her grandmother Lena. Furthermore, she shifts role and speaks as any one of these figures who might be addressing the child Jurema. These frames carry different communicative intent. In each of them, Dona Jurema remains coherent.

Changes in footing (Goffman 1981a) also take place within the institutional frame of the psychiatric interview. These are shifts in Dona Jurema's alignment, stance, posture, or projected self (Goffman 1981a:128) as a patient. For example, she shifts from being a tired old patient to acting as an irreverent and challenging woman. As she takes on different footings, consistent texts emerge, each presenting a coherence of its own.

I distinguish between *roles* and *footings* in the analysis of this interview. *Role* is used to refer to major changes in persona, that is, when the patient literally takes the role of the mother, the sister, the grandmother, and so on. *Footing* refers to microchanges in traits or attributes of the speaker that change her alignment vis-à-vis the hearer and thus reframe talk.[1] This distinction captures the difference in degree of contextual transformation. There is less transformation when the speaker's traits or attributes shift the frame of talk (here, a change in footing); there is more transformation (to the point of psychosis) when the persona shifts completely and assumes a new role (for a discussion on roles and footings see also S. Hoyle and B. T. Ribeiro, "Roles and Footings: Frame Analysis of Two Genres of Spoken Discourse," in preparation).

The contextual transformations that take place in the admitting interview follow the patterns for reframings described by Goffman (1974:45): A systematic transformation is involved, and cues will be available for establishing when the transformation is to begin and when it is to end.

A number of signals, indicating when transformations take place, help identify the frames of the admitting interview. Though some of these cues were mentioned previously (in chapter 3), they are described fully here, as some cues are exaggerated, while others are altogether new:

1. Contextualization cues (Gumperz 1977, 1982), which may be prosodic or kinesic. In this interview there is an exaggeration in the use of the prosodic and kinesic features, and in certain frames, text cohesion is often accomplished through the rhythmic organization of talk as described by Erickson (1982:64–66). Speech play (singing, chanting, and rhymes) also indicates a change of activity.

2. Role switching and persona cues (the participant's projected self) indicated by noun and pronoun reference.

3. Role switching and audience cues (the participant's projected audience) indicated by noun and pronoun reference. Address forms are used to label the addressee that Dona Jurema is referring to and which in turn characterizes her role (tokens such as "mother," "daughter," "grandma," "sis," etc.). These lexical items behave as "particles" having a specific functional meaning in her discourse.

4. Language function cues: different moves are assigned to the various participants and are adequate to each frame of talk.

5. Discourse markers that often occur attached to the name of the addressed person (e.g., "see mother" *viu mãe*, "y'see mother" *tá vendo mãe*, "y'know mother" *sabe mãe*, "oh Grandma Lena" *ai vó Lena*, "right daughter" *né fi'a*).

In the analysis of the discharge interview, two major frames were identified: the institutional frame, where the medical and psychiatric interview takes place, and the noninstitutional frame, where talk emerges as a personal encounter. We saw that while the doctor framed the context of talk as a medical encounter, the patient often reframed it as a personal encounter.

In the admitting interview, the same frames are at play in Dona Jurema's discourse: the institutional frame, which operates in the background with a "pale" participant (on only a very few occasions does Dona Jurema bring forth her role as a patient), and the frame of the psychotic crisis, which operates in the foreground. In both frames there are shifts in the structure of participation: In one situation, the speaker and listener alternate turns; in the other, the speaker (Dona Jurema) projects an addressee (the mother, the grandmother, the sister) and the doctor stands as an unratified participant (Goffman [1967] 1982:34), "held at bay" by the patient as someone who is not requested to partici- pate in the occasion. There is also the video-camera operator as a third participant. In the last part of this interview, Dona Jurema refers and talks to the camera. When she addresses the camera, however, she talks as if she were addressing her grandmother Lena. This indicates that she acknowledges the presence of another audience, but she inserts it into her own family frames.

Several schemas (Tannen 1985; Tannen and Wallat 1987) emerge in Dona Jurema's disconnected discourse at different times during this in- terview. These may be social routine scripts as described by Schank and Abelson (1977), associated with conventional situations such as "leave- taking," "waking up and talking to people," "praying," and so on. Schank and Abelson distinguish between different types of scripts, of which the "personal script" is particularly interesting as: "[It] exists solely in the mind of its main actor. It consists of a sequence of possible actions that will lead to a desired goal. . . . [The actor] is participating in a sequence of events much like other sequences he has used many times before. . . . There is very little planning involved because he has done this personal script repeatedly" (1977:62). The personal scripts intro- duced by Dona Jurema share most of these features. These schemas are not performed in their entire sequence, but even as fragments they pre- sent some of the expected social and linguistic features: the proper role- playing and the use of formulaic expressions.

Fillmore's discussion of formulaic expressions seems appropriate here, since Dona Jurema's language is mostly rehearsed and automatic. Fillmore (1976), says there are many formulas, routines, or clichés that are learned with specific topics, specific social roles, and specific social occasions. While some of these expressions are idioms, others are not, and their meanings are quite predictable from the meanings of their con- stituent parts. In order to analyze such expressions, one must understand the kinds of social contexts in which they occur (1976:25).

This discussion is useful when analyzing different "bits" or "chunks" of language used by the patient in this interview. They are often inter- related with the various roles assumed by the patient for herself or for her audience. Together with other linguistic features, these expressions evidence the frame in which the discourse takes place.

The following analysis describes how Dona Jurema can be coherent within a frame and how frames and schemas interact in the admitting interview. Again I transcribe the data in a parallel-column format to more adequately capture the type of interaction that occurs in this interview. Whenever participants overlap, their utterances occupy the same line(s) and a // (double slash) indicates the place the overlap starts.

The Institutional Frame of the Psychiatric Interview: "Dona Jurema, let's talk for a little while."

In the institutional context the doctor is the one who frames the event as a psychiatric interview. She invites Dona Jurema to talk to her; that is, in Goffman's ([1967] 1982) terms she invites the patient to "engage in a state of talk" and "reciprocal ratification." Dona Jurema sometimes engages in talk. When she does, she alternates between participating as a patient, and thereby answering the doctor, or responding as a child addressing a mother. When the patient does not engage in talk, Doctor Edna keeps summoning her to the institutional frame. She uses the address form *Dona Jurema* to continuously call the patient, as in the following:

(1)

Doctor:	Patient:
	[chanting and baby talk]
	I'm gonna tell,
//DONA JURE:MA!	**//this was,**
	[looks down]
	this was,
	this was,
	my secret,
	this was, ..
	this was,
	and this was,=
=Dona Jurema!=	
	=my secret. ..
[acc]	
DONA JUREMA!	
	[singing and baby talk]
	my dear husband,
	[looks down, face turns sightly to the left]

Doctor Edna tries unsuccessfully to interrupt the patient's stream of talk. She emphatically summons Dona Jurema to the institutional frame. Dona Jurema, however, is engaged in a speech-play activity of her own. She chants and sings, and does not provide any answer.

The address form *Dona Jurema* occurs twenty-four times in this interview (out of 104 attempted or actual doctor turns). In 85 percent of the cases it occurs as a summons. In the other 15 percent it introduces a topic of talk. These figures contrast with the discharge interview, where the doctor uses this address form only three times, twice at the opening and once at the closing of the interview. Rather than calling the patient by her name in the discharge interview, the doctor prefers to use the neutral V-form *a senhora,* formal "you." Hence, in the admitting interview the form *Dona Jurema* is indeed a "call" word to summon the patient's attention to the frame of the psychiatric interview.

During this interview the doctor has to attend to three types of activities: First, she requests factual information from the patient and evaluates Dona Jurema's responses to her official topic agenda. Second, Doctor Edna is concerned with the patient's physical needs. She asks her: "do you want to walk a little?"; "can you get up by yourself?"; "do you want to hold my hand?"; "get up and walk a bit"; "are you tired?" Most of the time, however, Doctor Edna's questions reveal a concern for the management of the interview. Frequently, she requests that the patient talk: "let's talk a little bit"; "we'll still talk for a little while"; "let's talk a little bit more"; "answer something for me." She requests information on the patient's inability to communicate: "you can't talk to me?"; "what is 'totô'?"; "what are you saying?"; "tell me what's happening?" She monitors the communicative channel: "can't you hear me?" All of these are requests or directives that Doctor Edna presents to the patient.

There are a few moments during this interview in which Dona Jurema, as a patient and interviewee, does engage in a state of talk. During the playback session, Doctor Edna stated that Dona Jurema was aware of the interview situation and that at several points the patient engaged in a conversation with her. She said that "the patient knew I was there, she knew that it was an interview, she expected me to say that it [the interview] was over, and to take her back to her ward." The excerpts that I will discuss in this section represent some of the instances in which the institutional frame emerges.

In contrast to the discharge interview, here the patient never uses the address forms *doctor* or *Doctor Edna*. She addresses the doctor as *a senhora* (formal "you"), which is an ambiguous form, since it could be used to address either the doctor or the mother. Hence, the use of *a senhora* (with the variant forms *a senhola, a senola, a sinola*) and the absence of the address form "mother" *mãe* frequently leave the frame of talk undefined.

Reframings from the Psychotic Crisis
into the Institutional Frame

In the institutional frame Doctor Edna keeps inviting the patient to talk. She repeats the request "let's talk for a little while," which often receives more emphasis ("we'll still talk for a little while"). Dona Jurema responds to this request with a series of indirect negative answers. Although indirect, these answers do show her attention to the interview. Her refusal to cooperate can be captured in three ways: (1) she turns to the doctor and expresses a complaint; (2) she shifts to nonverbal communication; and (3) she requests permission to leave and thereby close the interview. The following discussion illustrates each situation.

The Patient Expresses a Complaint

In the first situation Dona Jurema shifts out of the psychotic frame into the institutional frame to tell Doctor Edna that she cannot talk and to complain about the doctor's initial request to "talk for a little while."

The example is the closing to a segment that takes place at the opening of the interview. Prior to this segment the doctor had requested:

Doctor: **Dona Jurema, let's talk a little bit. ..**

This request opens the interview. As a response, Dona Jurema chants and sings. She holds the floor, while the doctor keeps on summoning her unsuccessfully. As she chants, she addresses her mother ("ma:ma::, ma:ma::, what-is-it-that-you-wish-to-know, madam-my-mother"). She sings a little song about her husband who let her down ("my dear husband, did not come to help, his dear, dear wife"), and also sings a religious hymn ("all dressed in white, she appeared"). Dona Jurema ends this segment by raising her pitch increasingly higher while raising both hands toward the doctor. She then makes a supplicating gesture toward the doctor:

(2)

Doctor:	Patient:
	(1) [whining and singing; baby talk]
	⌐**Hail:, Hail:, Hail Ma:ry,**
	(2) **Hail:, Hail:, ⌐Hail ⌐Ma:ry.**
	[raises both hands together, raises head, raises her eyes]
	[creaky voice]
	[acc]
→(3)	**what more do you want,**
	[looks at the doctor]
→(4)	**umh::? ....**
	[freezes position, right hand shaking and pointing]
[dec]	
(5) **Dona Jure::ma!**	
[half smiling]	
	[creaky voice]
→(6)	**umh:?**
→(7)	**you know that I can't::.**
	(1.3)
	[freezes position, right hand shaking and pointing]

Prior to this segment, there had been no eye contact with the doctor. Dona Jurema had been singing and chanting. Toward the end of the hymn (lines 1–2), Dona Jurema turns to the left, toward the doctor, and raises both hands and arms in a very slow gesture. As she raises her head, she looks up at the doctor. This is the very first time in the interview that Dona Jurema turns to the doctor and makes eye contact. It is also the first time that she actually talks (instead of chanting or singing). As she speaks (lines 3–4 and 6–7), she gives a negative response ("what more do you want?") to the doctor's initial request, the underlying meaning being "I have already said everything there is to know" and "you should know better than to ask me questions." She looks at the doctor and says, pleadingly, that she cannot (talk anymore) (line 7). At this moment she has shifted to the interview context, and she relinquishes the floor to the doctor.

Another reframing of the same pattern also occurs in the following excerpt. Again Dona Jurema turns to the doctor and addresses her, thus yielding the floor to the doctor. This segment takes place after a long stretch of talk, at the end of which the patient starts to play with the doctor's feet while referring to her granddaughter, Mariene. She sings another religious hymn (substituting her granddaughter for the Virgin Mary). Then she raises her head, looks up at the doctor, and asks another question.

(3)

Doctor:

(7) = I'm going to ask,
     Dona Jure:ma.

[acc]
(9) **WHERE DO YOU LIVE?** ...

Patient:
[hymn; baby talk]
(1) **Malie:::ne:::,**
(2) **Sa:::cred Lie:ne,**
(3) **to me she is:::is:,**
(4) **sanctifi::ed,**
[gets halfway up in the chair, sits at the edge of the armchair, looks down, and holds posture; her verbal communication matches her nonverbal as she repeats six times in a crescendo the form "that's why!" *polisso*]

[creaky voice, baby talk]
→(5) **aren't you going to=**
(6) **=ask me questions now?=**
[raises her head, holds her body halfway up, hands pressing on the chair, looks at doctor]

[sighing]
→(8) **what are you going to ask?**
[stands and holds her body halfway up]

Again, as in example (2), Dona Jurema closes an entire stretch of talk by "touching base" with the doctor—that is, she makes eye contact and asks the doctor a question (lines 5–6). The question accomplishes two related moves: She introduces a complaint about the doctor not managing the process of communication, and she challenges the doctor to take action. She also relinquishes the floor to the doctor. Doctor Edna addresses the patient's request by stating that she will take some action (in line 7). In her next turn Dona Jurema challenges the doctor again and requests information about what will be asked. Doctor Edna's response (line 9) is a question on the topic "place of residence," which is part of her topic agenda. She therefore resumes the interviewer's role, which the patient had challenged.

These two segments (examples 2 and 3) illustrate how Dona Jurema may shift out of the frame of the psychotic crisis and into the frame of the interview. In both segments the patient establishes eye contact with the doctor and shifts from singing to speaking. As she speaks, she makes a request that has the force of a complaint. She also relinquishes the floor to the doctor. Once the shift takes place, the doctor regains control over the turn system and the action structure: She takes the floor and makes the next move as she requests referential information on a given topic.

The Patient Shifts to Nonverbal Communication

The second type of response that the patient provides to the doctor's requests is a change in the communicative channel: To address the doctor's question, Dona Jurema switches to nonverbal behavior.

I have discussed the following segment elsewhere to illustrate a situation in which Dona Jurema provides an inadequate answer to the doctor's request "let's talk," describing it as an example of a "nonsensical referent" (see chapter 6). Here, however, I want to examine the same excerpt and argue for its coherence.

This segment follows example (2). After the patient has stated that she is unable to talk, Doctor Edna takes her turn and asks if Dona Jurema cannot talk to her:

(4)

Doctor:	Patient:
(1) ⌐=**you can't talk to me?**	
	(2) **totototototototo:. ['hhh]** [moves hand back to armchair; looks beyond the doctor]
	(3) ⌐**the tototô:::!** [gesture with right hand pointing straight ahead]
(4) **what's totô?**	
	(5) **the totô totô::!** [series of pointing gestures]
(6) **what's totô?**	

Doctor: Patient:
                                     (7) **that totô:::!** (1.5)
                                         [pointing gestures]
   (8) **what is it you're saying?**

                                         [acc]
                                     (9) **totododododododododododo**
                                    (10) **/dododododododdodo/** ...
              →   [gesture with hands indicating "who
                                         knows"; looks down]
(11) **you don't know, do you.**

This entire excerpt could be viewed as a response to the doctor's initial request, "Dona Jurema, let's talk for a little while." Dona Jurema indicates that she does not want to engage in a state of talk with the doctor. She addresses the doctor's initial question ("you can't talk to me?") by engaging in nonsensical communication, thereby metacommunicating, "no, I cannot (or will not) talk to you" (in line 2). The segment that follows serves to illustrate her response: She cannot talk (or will not talk) because she is talking gibberish. She creates a form *tototô* to which she refers repeatedly (in lines 3, 5, and 7) until it becomes unintelligible (lines 9–10). Finally, she shifts to a nonverbal channel to address the doctor's question "what is it you're saying?" (line 8), and in doing so indicates that she is aware of the fact that she is talking gibberish. Doctor Edna picks up on this cue and responds to the patient's gesture by stating verbally what the patient had expressed nonverbally, "you don't know, do you" (line 11).[2]

The Patient Closes the Interview

The third type of response represents the patient's last move in the interview: She requests permission to leave and thereby closes the interview:

(5)

Patient: **can I stand upupupupupupupup?**
Doctor: **yes, you can.**
         can you get up by ⌐yourself?

This interview ends with Dona Jurema requesting permission to stand up. She has been signaling from the beginning that she wanted to get up and leave: She has been swinging herself back and forth in her chair, getting up halfway and sitting on the arm of the chair; she has been asking to *azular* (a colloquial term for "leave," translated as "split"), saying that "it's time to leave." In the following segment below she says:

(6)

Patient: **it's that time.**
Doctor: **it's that time for what?**
Patient: **it's time to go.**

This last request completes a coherent set of responses through which Dona Jurema signals that she does not want to engage in talk. She first addresses the doctor, conveying a complaint (examples 2 and 3); then she shifts to nonverbal communication to address Doctor Edna's question (example 4); finally, she asks to leave (examples 5 and 6). All of these constitute Dona Jurema's answer to the doctor's request for interaction within the psychiatric interview frame.

These conflicting interests between the doctor and the involuntary patient are a natural product of mental hospitalization (Goffman 1961:366–67). The type of relationship that develops in a service encounter of this sort is problematic, since "the psychiatrist must extend service civility from the stance of a server but can no more continue that stance than the patient can accept it. Each party to the relationship is destined to seek out the other to offer what the other cannot accept, and each is destined to reject what the other offers" (1961:368). Thus, it is not surprising to see the persistence with which Dona Jurema conveys her refusal to participate in the institutional framing. Indeed, she did not contract this service herself (as she was taken to the hospital involuntarily), nor did she agree to be institutionalized. Under these circumstances, Dona Jurema's responses to the doctor's requests for conversation could only signal a departure from the conventional service interaction.

Place, Time, and Persona Cues

Dona Jurema also has the appropriate contextual place, time, and even persona references of the institutional frame. Regarding place, for example, at the very opening of the interview Dona Jurema makes a reference to her "ward":

(7)

when I get, to my ward,

Halfway through the interview, Dona Jurema says emphatically that she is "here, at the hospital":

[The patient held the floor for a long stretch of talk, where she said that she had to get going, that she was very tired, that one could not make any noise "here." The doctor then asks the following.]

(8)

Doctor:	Patient:
(1) ⌐**HERE where,**	
Dona Jurema? =	
	[acc] [babytalk]
	(2) = **here, here, here**. =
	[bends over, looks down, speaks into microphone]

Doctor: Patient:

(3) =where are you? ..

                                           (4) HERE! ...

(5) mmm? ..

                                           (6) here! =

(7) =what place is this=
(8) ="here" you're at now? ..

                                           [dec]
                                           (9) I am in a hospital. =
                                           [moves torso and head backward, raises
                                           head slightly, both hands on armchair,
                                           looks down]
(10) =//which hospital?   //I thought I'd be going=
                                           =to another hospital,

(11) mmm.

                                           (12) and I ended up in a very=
                                           (13) =beautiful hospital. ...

While she provides adequate referential information (being at the hospital), Dona Jurema does not provide the specific information the doctor requests when she asks "which hospital?" Instead Dona Jurema introduces a generic evaluative remark—"I ended up in a very beautiful hospital." At the closing of the interview, however, she mentions "the hospital" and more specifically "Pinel Hospital," an adequate reference that corresponds to the hospital she was taken to:

(9)

that's why Chico, <last night-> ...
came home. .. to get: me, ...
to ta:ke (me), ... to the hos:pital. ....
to Pinel Hospital.

These place cues provided by the patient indicate that she knows where she is (the ward, the hospital, and the Pinel Hospital).[3]

    There is also one time cue, which occurs at the closing of the interview. Dona Jurema mentions that her son, Chico, had come to fetch her the night before to take her to the hospital (example 9). The admitting interview took place two days after she had been admitted to the hospital; thus, Dona Jurema has some time reference, but she misses a day.

    Finally, Dona Jurema also has a perception about her own disability, a persona cue, that she introduces halfway through the interview. Prior to this segment, the doctor had been asking questions in an attempt to establish some common referential ground with the patient. She asks Dona Jurema about what she had seen on her way from her ward to the office interview:

[The Portuguese text is also displayed.]

(10)

Doctor:	Patient:
(1) //⌐DID YOU SEE=	// (see how-)
(2) =SOME LITTLE ANIMAL=	
(3) OUT THERE,	
(4) // WHEN YOU CAME=	//see how you got it right?
(5) =ON YOUR WAY HERE?	
(6) Huh:, Dona Jure:ma?=	
	[singing]
	(7) =I saw a little ant:!
(8) a little ant?	
	[singing]
	(9) I saw a little ant:!
(10) what about the other=	
(11) =animal you showed=	
	[baby talk]
(12) //=me outside?=	//=the otherotherother animal?=
(13) =which was it?=	
	(14) =it's a ((grown-up)).
	(15) we cannot talk about=
	(16) =grown:-ups.=
(17) =mmm.	
	(18) we can only talk about=
	(19) =li:ttle people.
	→(20) and me, since I am a= =little midget-

Doctor:	Patient:
(1) //⌐A SENHORA VIU=	// (viu como-)
(2) =ALGUM BICHINHO=	
(3) =LÁ FORA,	
(4) // QUANDO PASSOU=	//viu como a senhora acertou?
(5) =POR AQUI?	
(6) Hein:, Dona Jure:ma?=	
	[singing]
	(7) =eu vi uma formigui:nha.
(8) formiguinha?	
	[singing]
	(9) eu vi uma formigui:nha.
(10) e o outro bicho,	
(11) que a senhora=	[baby talk]
(12) //=mostrou lá fora?=	// =o outooutooutoouto biso?=
(13) =qual foi?=	
	(14) =é gente grande.
	(15) a gente não pode falá=
	(16) =de gente gran::de.=

Doctor: Patient:
(17) =mmm.

                                                  (18) só pode falá de gente=
                                                  (19) =peque:na.
                                              →(20) e eu como sou anãozinho

When the doctor asks about "the other animal" (lines 10–11), she is trying to see whether Dona Jurema has some recollection of having walked across the hospital patio and pointed at some chickens and ducks that were there.[4] In her answer, however, Dona Jurema refers to the people (*gente grande,* which means "grown-up"—literally, "big people") that she saw, and she adds that one cannot talk about "big people," one can only talk about "little people" *gente pequena.* Then (in line 20) she states that she is a midget, that is, not a full-fledged adult.[5] When she calls herself a midget, Dona Jurema uses the diminutive form *anãozinho,* which can be interpreted as a "little midget" or a "nice-cute little midget," since the suffix *-inho* can indicate an affective dimension.

Here the asymmetry is exaggerated. We have the social asymmetry of the medical encounter, where Doctor Edna—the gatekeeper—interviews and evaluates the patient Dona Jurema, as in any medical encounter. Then, in an exaggerated dimension, we have Dona Jurema assuming the stance of "little midget" talking to a "grown-up." In this respect Dona Jurema is probably not much different than any other psychiatric patient. Goffman tells us that all patients experience some downgrading:

> "In the mental hospital, the setting and the house rules press home to the patient that he is, after all, a mental case who has suffered some kind of social collapse on the outside, having failed in some over-all way, and that here he is of little social weight, being hardly capable of acting like a full-fledged person at all. (1961:151–52)

Thus, in the institutional frame of the psychiatric interview, Dona Jurema presents herself as neither a full-fledged adult nor a child, but rather something in between. On one hand, she has grown beyond childhood; on the other hand, she does not feel like an adult who has gained the grown-up *gente grande* identity. What Dona Jurema signals here is the perception she has of the institutional framings: In a mental establishment inpatients are defined as "not-fully-adults" (Goffman 1961:115).

Attempts to Mitigate the Asymmetry

At different moments during this interview, Dona Jurema challenges the position that Doctor Edna holds as a doctor and a grown-up. As a result, the two participants exchange reciprocal challenges. This type of interaction (challenges versus challenges) contributes momentarily to diminishing the distance that exists between the doctor and the patient, the "grown-up" and the "midget":

[This segment follows example (8).]

(11)

Doctor:	Patient:
(1) ⌐do you know this hospital HERE? =	
	(2) = no one knows it. ..
(3) <u>no: one</u> knows it? =	
	(4) = no one in this world. ...
(5) rea:lly?	
//and you already =	// only me!
	[smiles]

Doctor Edna introduces a request for referential information (line 1) about the hospital the patient has been taken to. This known-answer question is part of the doctor's agenda, and psychiatric patients often challenge this type of question, since it represents a face-threatening act (Brown and Levinson [1978] 1979).[6] In line (2) Dona Jurema provides a strong negative answer, which has the force of a challenge. This response generates a series of challenges from both participants, where the turn structure can be represented as:

Doctor: Requests information on X
        Challenges (?) the patient
Patient: Provides information
         Challenges the doctor
    Doctor: Requests confirmation
            Challenges the patient
    Patient: Provides information
             Challenges the doctor
        Doctor: Requests confirmation
                Challenges the patient
        Patient: Provides information
                 Challenges the doctor

This reciprocal exchange of challenges reduces the asymmetry that exists in the doctor-patient relationship and the "grown-up" versus "midget" relationship. The following is another instance of the same type of interaction, in which the doctor tries to follow a standard interview format. She requests referential information from the patient—the type of information Dona Jurema knows the doctor already has.

(12)

Doctor:	Patient:
(1) ⌐what's your full name?	
	(2) will you believe me =

Doctor: Patient:
                                   (3) = if I say it right? ...

(4) ⌐I'll believe you. =

                                   (5) = you know why? =

(6) = mmm? ...

                                   (7) you don't know why. (1.2)

(9) what is it =
(10) = I don't know?

                                   (11) let me speak because, ..
                                   (12) because I know my full =
                                   (13) na::::me =
                                   (14) = Holy Mother =
                                   (15) = of God. (see)

Again we have the same situation. The doctor's request can be seen as a challenge to Dona Jurema, since it is a request for a known answer. As a result, a series of challenges are introduced on both sides, where the turn structure can be represented as the following:

Doctor:	Request information on X
	Challenges (?) the patient
Patient:	Reformulates the request
	Challenges the doctor
Doctor:	Provides an answer
Patient:	Requests information
	Challenges the doctor
Doctor:	Introduces a rerun
Patient:	Provides an answer
	Challenges the doctor
Doctor:	Requests clarification
	Challenges the patient
Patient:	Introduces a directive
	Provides an answer
	Challenges the doctor

Both examples (11) and (12) illustrate a situation in which the doctor asks a question, seeking referential information from the patient. As a response, Dona Jurema challenges the position that Doctor Edna holds as a doctor and a grown-up (i.e., the one who has the right to ask questions). A series of reciprocal challenges occurs, indicating that during these segments a more symmetrical relationship emerges, in which Dona Jurema challenges the doctor's authority as well as her knowledge.[7]

The discussion so far has indicated that in spite of Dona Jurema's bizarre and in many ways inappropriate conversational behavior, there are instances in which both the doctor and the patient talk and interact within the institutional frame of the psychiatric interview. Quite frequently Doctor Edna attempts to interact with the patient, repeatedly summoning her to the frame of the interview. Dona Jurema attends to very few of these requests. There are instances, however, when Dona Jurema shifts from the frame of the psychotic crisis into the frame of the interview. When she does so, she relinquishes the floor to the doctor and asks for the doctor's help. Her requests have the force of a complaint or a challenge to the doctor's authority. She also provides references for where she is, when she arrived at the hospital, and who she is now. In the interview frame, Doctor Edna asks the patient to talk. She also challenges the patient by asking known-answer questions. Dona Jurema coherently answers the doctor by telling her, "you know everything," "I've shown you everything," and "you know I cannot talk."

When discussing the complex relation between the institutional psychiatrist and a patient, Goffman reminds us that often the psychiatrist (by training, orientation, and status) approaches the patient "in the guise of offering an expert service to a client who has voluntarily sought it" (1961:366). In most cases, however (as in the case of Dona Jurema), the patient is not a voluntary client and has many reasons for "being disgruntled at [her] condition. [She] sees the psychiatrist as the person in power" (1961:367).

Subtle Reframings within the Interview Frame

Within the institutional frame of the interview, certain subtle shifts in footing occur between Dona Jurema and Doctor Edna, indicating a change in how Dona Jurema, as a speaker, positions herself regarding the doctor, as a listener. I will describe two types of footing, both of which are part of the way the patient presents herself in this frame of talk. In the first, Dona Jurema positions herself as an old woman and introduces a series of complaints. In the second, she takes a confrontational stand and introduces a series of challenges.

The Elderly Woman to the Young Woman: "I don't know where I've been, my child."

We saw that there are certain moments in the discharge interview when the asymmetrical doctor-patient relationship is reversed. This occurs when Dona Jurema, as an older woman, addresses Doctor Edna as a very young woman. In power semantics (Brown and Gilman [1972] 1979) age replaces profession as the variable that confers status. This is what we saw when the patient reframes talk as "I am in control" and "I can take care of myself" (see chapter 4).

In the admitting interview Dona Jurema also behaves as if she feels that seniority entitles her to complain to the doctor about the stressful situation she has been dealing with, as the following exchange indicates:

[Prior to this segment, Dona Jurema has been talking about leaving and returning to her ward. Doctor Edna asks her to stay a bit longer and then asks her how she got to the office for the interview.]

(13)

Doctor: Patient:
  (1) ⌜WHAT PATH DID YOU
  (2) = TAKE TO GET HERE? =   [dec]
                                      (3) = a ve::ry long <u>jour:ney</u>. =
  (4) ⌜= from your WARD?
                                      (5) = yeah:.
  (6) //WHAT PLACES DID   // ⌞but at my a:ge.
  (7) = YOU GO BY?
                                      (8) I have no idea =
                                      (9) = where I've been,
                                         my child, =
(10) = no? =
                                   (11) = only God knows and =
                                   (12) = my Guardian Angel.

In line (3) Dona Jurema responds at a very slow pace to Doctor Edna's question (indicated by the vowel lengthening in "jour:ney" and "ve:ry"), as if she is taking time to weigh what she says. She tells the doctor that she has undertaken a "very long journey." The slow pace of her utterance mirrors the length of her "journey" (at the time of this interview, Dona Jurema was having difficulty in walking by herself; to get to the doctor's office she had to walk across a small patio and go upstairs to the second floor). The doctor's next question ("from your ward?") has the force of a challenge. In line (6) the patient answers with a counterargument "but at my age." This is one of the few times that the marker "but" *mas* (Schiffrin 1987a) is used in this interview, introducing information that contrasts with what was implicit in the doctor's previous point. This answer also overlaps with the doctor's next turn (lines 6 and 7), when she requests specific information about where the patient had been. Dona Jurema answers the doctor's request with a general statement, saying that she has no idea where she has been (lines 8 and 9), that only God and her Guardian Angel know (lines 11 and 12). Here Dona Jurema addresses Doctor Edna as "my child" (line 9), thus signaling the age difference between them. She reinforces this position as she makes explicit references to her age (line 6) and to "the long journey" she has undertaken (line 3), perhaps an indirect reference to her own life.

The Irreverent Patient to the Doctor: "Can I 'split'?"

In the asymmetrical doctor-patient relationship, Dona Jurema often challenges the doctor's authority and knowledge, as in the following excerpt, where Dona Jurema shifts to a colloquial register while assuming a confrontational stand. Prior to this exchange, Dona Jurema had been touching and playing with the doctor's hair. She has established a close relationship with the doctor (i.e., caressing); there is physical closeness, too

(Dona Jurema is sitting forward on the edge of her chair). Suddenly, Dona Jurema moves back and says:

(14)

Doctor:

Patient:

(1) **I got it!**
[as if holding a strand of hair, moves hand and torso backward]
[baby talk]

(2) **I got a little hair.** =
[nods; lowers right hand]

(3) = **you got a little hair?**

[baby talk]

(4) **a little hair.**
[looks at doctor]

(5) **and what will you** =
= **do with it?**

[acc]

(6) **can I split?**

[acc]

(7) **can you what?**

(8) **split.**

(9) **what is this?**

(10) **split from here.** =

(11) = **oh:, split from here?** =

[acc]

(12) = **yeah:, can I?**

(13) **you want to leave?** =

[dec]

(14) = **I know. ...**
[looks down]

[dec]

(15) **no:, let's talk** =

(16) = **a little bit more, O.K.?** =

[acc]

(17) = **no. it's time. ...**
[shakes head, sits backward]

(18) **it's time for what?** =

(19) = **it's time for me** =

(20) = **to go...**
[raises head and eyes, lowers head and eyes]

(21) **to go where?** =

(22) = **to go where? ...**
[raises head higher and tosses it backwards]

(23) **yeah:.**

Doctor: Patient:
                                            (24) **and what do you know?**
                                            [raises left hand, pointing gesture, head
                                            tossed slightly backward]
                                            (25) **what do you know? ....**
                                            [lowers head, bends chest forward, both
                                            hands hold armchair, in a position to get
                                            up; looks down]
                                            (26) **(I said so,) y'see.**
                                            [looks down, moves feet]

In lines (1) and (2) Dona Jurema tells the doctor that she has got a
"hair."[8] Doctor Edna first asks Dona Jurema what she will do with this
"hair." In response, Dona Jurema requests to leave by introducing the
Portuguese dated colloquial expression *zulá*, which can be translated as
"split." This is a strong request from the patient. The meaning of *zulá*
derives from street youngsters who needed to "split" or "get away."[9] In
using this form Dona Jurema fleetingly takes on the identity of a rebel-
lious youngster, which contrasts with her previous footing of closeness
to the doctor. With this sudden shift she issues a challenge and assumes
an irreverent alignment (as a street youngster) vis-à-vis the doctor. Doctor Edna does not understand the meaning of this term. This triggers an
interaction where the doctor requests information on the meaning of
"split" *(zulá)* (lines 7 and 9) and the patient emphatically repeats the
form (lines 8 and 10). Dona Jurema's responses are cut-and-dried. She
introduces short answers, which latch onto the doctor's questions (lines
11 and 12, 13 and 14). She keeps repeating her request to "split" and
does not accept the doctor's negative answer (line 15). In line (17) she
turns down Doctor Edna's request and adds "it's time." In saying so, she
commits an "on-record" face-threatening act (Brown and Levinson [1978]
1979), as she decides to take leave and close the encounter with no common agreement from the doctor. Doctor Edna picks up on this cue and
requests further information by asking, "it's time for what?" (line 18);
Dona Jurema answers, "it's time for me to go" (lines 19–20). During
this exchange the patient maintains her initial position: that she wants to
leave immediately. In line (21) Doctor Edna responds to Dona Jurema
with another challenge ("to go where?"), which generates a strong series
of complaints from the patient (lines 22–27). Again the pace of talk
accelerates as Dona Jurema's answers latch onto the doctor's questions
(lines 16 and 17; lines 18 and 19; and lines 21 and 22).

   This exchange portrays a different type of footing from that of the
tired, elderly woman discussed previously. Here a defiant, fast-talking
patient takes a strong position and challenges the doctor's authority in
two ways. First, Dona Jurema challenges the interviewer by initiating a
closing of the interview. She explicitly takes a stand, stating that "it's
time for me to go." In doing so, Dona Jurema takes upon herself the
authority to declare an end to the medical encounter. Second, Dona Ju-

rema challenges the doctor and gatekeeper by questioning her level of knowledge and information ("and what do you know?"), with the underlying implication "you do not know any more than I do about where I am going."

What Are These Institutional Framings?

Both the doctor and the patient reframe talk from the context of the psychotic crisis to the institutional frame of the psychiatric interview. Doctor Edna interacts with the patient, summoning her repeatedly to the interview context. The patient engages in a series of requests (for help), which have the force of a complaint or a challenge (to defy the doctor's authority). Doctor Edna asks the patient to talk. Dona Jurema provides different answers to the doctor's request. In each of these instances Dona Jurema is communicatively on target, since these moves conform to frame expectations.

These reframings introduce changes in the participation structure. That is, in the interview frame, turns alternate and both participants, doctor and patient, contribute to the development of the interview. Each response ratifies a previous contribution, and talk goes on. The doctor controls the turn structure (gets the floor and introduces questions), while the patient provides information, requests help, and asks to leave.

Subtle changes in footing also take place within the institutional frame of the psychiatric interview. These are microreframings in which Dona Jurema shifts her alignment as she addresses the doctor. In the first one the patient aligns herself as an elderly woman. She complains to a very young woman about the "long journey" she has undertaken. In the second, Dona Jurema challenges the doctor's authority and questions the doctor's knowledge about her illness.

In the asymmetrical doctor-patient encounter, Dona Jurema states that the doctor already knows everything ("I've shown you everything") and that, as the doctor knows (or should know), Dona Jurema is unable to say more ("you know I cannot talk"). In the asymmetrical elderly woman-young woman encounter, Dona Jurema complains that it's been "a long journey" and that "only God and my Guardian Angel know where I've been." And finally, in the asymmetrical youngster-doctor exchange, she defies the authority of the doctor ("and what do you know?") and initiates a closing to the interview ("it's time for me to go"). Dona Jurema, therefore, responds coherently to the doctor's requests. She also assesses correctly the adequacy of her answers for that frame of talk. Since Doctor Edna already knows the answer to each one of the questions she officially introduces in the interview (which are known-answer questions), there is indeed no need for the patient to say anything more.

The Noninstitutional Frame of the Psychotic Crisis:
"*Mother, you know everything.*"

The frame of the psychotic crisis is embedded within the interview frame. The predominant characteristic of this frame is that the patient speaks as if she were a child addressing her mother. At times she addresses the doctor as if the doctor were her mother. At other times she addresses her absent mother, treating the doctor as a third party. This frame is a psychotic fabrication (Goffman 1974:115)—a transformation of ordinary behavior, where the doctor is treated literally (and not metaphorically) as Dona Jurema's mother. Hence, to the patient there is a transformation from "the doctor who 'is' my mother" (a metaphor and, in psychoanalytic terms, a transference) to "the doctor who *is* my mother." Goffman states that "one of the upsetting things 'psychotics' do is to treat literally what ordinarily is treated as metaphor, or at least to seem to do so" (1974:115).

The most striking aspect of Dona Jurema's behavior is her assumption of the role of a child: She establishes with her real audience (Doctor Edna), and with an imaginary audience (her absent mother), a mother-daughter relationship.[10] Dona Jurema addresses the listener (the doctor in the mother's role) or the addressee (Dona Jurema's absent mother) as *a senhora* (formal "you"), using the child's variants *a senhola, a senola,* and *a sinola.* She also uses the address form *mãe* "mother," with emphatic stress on the last syllable *mãe:,* transcribed as "ma:ma::,," a form generally used by young children when soliciting attention from the mother. The following excerpt takes place at the opening of the interview and illustrates two different frames of talk.

[The Portuguese text is also displayed to illustrate the use of the forms just discussed.]

(15)

Doctor:	Patient:
	[whining]
	(1) **ma:ma::!** =
(2) **= Dona Jurema!**	
	[whining]
	(3) **ma:ma::!** ..
	(4) **/what is it, my child?/**
(5) **Dona Jurema,**	
(6) **let's talk a little bit.** ..	
	[staccato and baby talk]
	(7) **what-is-it-you-wish-to** =
(8) **//O.K.?**	**// = know-madam-my-mother,**
	(9) **don't you already know** =
	(10) **= everything?**
// **/mmm./**	(11) **// /has she not shown you (everything?)/**

Doctor:	Patient:
	[whining]
	(1) **mãe:!** =
(2) = **Dona Jurema!**	
	(3) **mãe:!** ..
	(4) /**que é, (filhinha)**?/
(5) **Dona Jurema,**	
(6) **vamo conversá um pouquinho. ..**	
	[staccato and baby talk]
	(7) **que-qua-senhora -qué-**
(8) //**viu?**	//-**sabê-madame-minha-mãe,**
	(9) **a-senhora-não-soube-** =
	(10) = **já-de-tudo?**
// /**mmm./**	(11) // /**ela já não mostrou (tudo)**-/

At the opening of the interview two frames conflict. While Doctor Edna summons the patient to the institutional frame of the interview, Dona Jurema creates another context of talk where, as a child, she calls her mother twice (lines 1 and 3) and also provides the child with the mother's answer *from the mother* (line 4). In lines (5) and (6) the doctor requests the patient to participate in a conversation. In Dona Jurema's next turn (lines 7–11) she addresses the doctor's request as if it had been her mother's request. She thus shifts from her own projected context of talk to engage in talk with the doctor/mother.

Sullivan ([1944] 1964) points out that, in any communicative context, speakers depend on a "consensual validation" to get their messages across. That is, there must be an agreement between the speaker and listener that the message has been understood, and "it is in this consensual validation that the schizophrenic fails" ([1944] 1964:14). When one looks at the patient conversing within a frame, however, we sometimes see her effort to provide for a response to her queries. This seems to be the situation in line (4), when the mother addresses the child's summons.

The schema of a very powerful mother underlies the psychotic frame. Dona Jurema addresses her mother as "madam-my-mother"—the one who knows everything (lines 8–11). The Portuguese address form *madame* is used in asymmetrical relationships. The predominant action in the child's discourse vis-à-vis her mother is establishing and marking deference.[11] As example (15) illustrates, this interview opens with the child addressing her mother and asking, "what do you want to know, madam-my-mother?" and "don't you already know everything?" The core statement "mother knows" is repeated throughout the interview, and is often transformed to:

> **my mother knows**
> **you (the mother/the doctor) know**
> **grandmother Lena knows**
> **my son knows**

> my husband knows
> my sister knows
> only God knows

or expanded to:

> mother is the one who knows
> you know very well
> you know better than I
> you know better than anyone

In some moments of the interview, it is part of a speech play presented as a chant reminiscent of a nursery rhyme:

(16)

> you know that you knew. ....
> all all that I wanted. ....
> you are the one who knows. ....
> it's the mother,
> it's the mother
> it's the mother,
> it's the mother,
> it's the mother,
> it's the mother
> it's the mother,
> it's the mother,
> huh:::::::!
> it's the mother of her so:::nny!

Knowledge and power come together when Dona Jurema says:

> you know better than I
> you know better than anyone

This position contrasts with the child's lack of knowledge, as she states several times:

> I know nothing, nothing, nothing
> I didn't know.

Or as she represents herself (addressing the camera as her mother):

(17)

> then it's with you. ...
> then it's been since that time, ma:ma::? ...
> then only now that I know, ma:ma::.....

I was a little silly girl,
I didn't know anything. ..
I knew only how to suck my thumb. (6.1)

[Lifts right hand and puts thumb in the mouth, closes eyes, turns to the doctor, opens eyes, takes thumb out of the mouth.]

This discussion refers back to the description in chapter 6 of the different themes that the patient recycles during this interview. Within this frame of talk, the mother holds the position of authority, expressed through Dona Jurema's repetitive statement "the mother is the one who knows" or addressed to the doctor/mother: "you are the one who knows." Thus, the schema of an asymmetrical mother-daughter relationship dictates certain constraints in the child's role while addressing her mother. This schema is signaled through the types of moves the child performs, through speech-play activities she introduces, and through her use of child language.

Types of Moves Performed

In the frame of the psychotic crisis, the child, Jurema, keeps calling her mother. This is what we saw in example (15), here repeated:

(15)

Doctor:	Patient:
	[whining]
	(1) ma:ma::! =
(2) = Dona Jurema!	
	[whining]
	(3) ma:ma::! ..

This summons from the child is particularly interesting since it mirrors (and echoes in an inverted form) the doctor's summons to the patient, as in example (1), here repeated:

(1)

Doctor:	Patient:
	[chanting and baby talk]
	I'm gonna tell,
//DONA JURE:MA!	//this was,
	[looks down]
	this was,
	this was,
	my secret,
	this was, ..
	this was,
	and this was, =

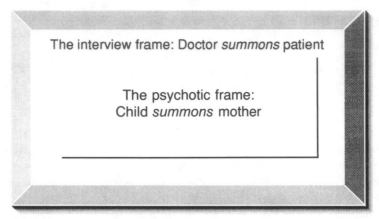

Figure 7.1. The two major conflicting frames.

Doctor:	Patient:
=**Dona Jurema!**=	
	=my secret. ..
[acc]	
DONA JUREMA!	[singing and baby talk]
	my dear husband,
	[looks down, face turns sightly to the left]

The doctor summons the patient to the interview frame with the intention of engaging her in a speech activity appropriate to the institutional framing. In Goffman's terms, Doctor Edna wants to get her patient closer to the "rim" of the frame, to the least transformed activity, the one closer to the real-world situation (1974:82). The patient, however, often responds with a reframing. She speaks as the child Jurema summoning her mother, repeatedly calling for her mother's attention and in so doing redirecting the doctor to participate as a bystander in some other type of activity. This reframing corresponds to what Goffman calls a "dramatic activity," which takes place in an innermost frame layering (1974:82). These two equivalent and conflicting moves are represented in Figure 7.1.

Summonses, therefore, constitute a major bracketing device in framing. They signal a shift from a previous activity to a new one. The speaker (either the child Jurema or the doctor) makes an urgent request for attention (a strong invitation to attend on some occasion). This call redirects the activity and thus proposes a new framing.

What sort of actions take place within the frame of the psychotic crisis? First, we see that Jurema, the child, marks deference when she addresses her mother. In example (15) Jurema uses the address form "madam my mother," and in example (16) she stresses that the mother is the one who knows everything. Through deference she establishes an asymmetrical relationship. In addition, Jurema keeps trying to appease the authority figure of the mother:

[In the following discussion the Portuguese and English texts are displayed. Prior to this segment, Dona Jurema had been complaining about the heavy rain.]

(18)

> Patient:
> (1) **I'm afraid of the rain...**
>   [bends more forward]
> (2) **Francisco has warned us,**
>   [moves slightly backward]
> (3) **ma:ma. ...**
> (4) **right, ma:ma? ... ['hhh]**
>   [looking down]
> (5) **is everything fine? ...**
> (6) **everything all right? ..**
> (7) **is this really how he =**
>   **= wanted things? (1.2)**
>   [looks up to the right and tightens lips]

> Patient:
> (1) **eu tou com medo da chuva.**
>   [bends more forward]
> (2) **bem que Francisco falou,**
>   [moves slightly backward]
> (3) **mãe:. ...**
> (4) **tá certo, mãe:? ... ['hhh]**
>   [looking down]
> (5) **tá tudo bonzinho? ...**
> (6) **tudo certinho? ..**
> (7) **ela assim que ele quelia? (1.2)**
>   [looks up to the right and tightens lips]

The child Jurema introduces a series of questions through which she requests the mother's approval (lines 4–6). She repeats (with variation) three times the same request, making use of the Portuguese morpheme *-inho* to signal affection:

> **right, mother? ...**
> **is everything fine? ..**
> **is everything all right? ...**
>
> **tá certo, mãe? ...**
> → **tá tudo bonzinho? ...**
> → **tá tudo certinho? ..**

This type of request places the mother as an evaluator and judge: The mother is the one who knows. As a consequence, she is also the one who defines right and wrong, and who determines when things go right or not.

In some instances, as Jurema addresses her mother, she keeps trying to call her mother's attention. Here the marker "see" *viu* is used repeatedly to stress the child's effort in calling the mother's attention to some point she wants to make (examples 19–21 illustrate three instances of this type of occurrence):

(19)

Doctor:	Patient:
	[baby talk]
	it was so sim:ple, see!
	see ma:ma::!
	[moves legs, rearranges sitting position, gets up]
// can you stand up=	**// see ma:ma::!**
=on your own?	**see ma:ma::!**

Doctor:	Patient:
	[baby talk]
	ela tão sim:pes, viu!
	viu mãe:!
	[moves legs, rearranges sitting position, gets up]
//a senhora consegue=	**// viu mãe:!**
=levantá sozinha?	**viu mãe:.**

(20)

Doctor:	Patient:
[doctor leans forward to the left, with mic on the left hand]	**you-**
	dodododododododdod-
	you- see,
	see-see-see, see-see.
	[whining]
	y'see, ma:ma::. (3.1)

Doctor:	Patient:
[doctor leans forward to the left, with mic on the left hand]	**a senhora-**
	dodododododododdod-
	a senhora- viu,
	viu-viu-viu, viu-viu.
	[whining]
	tá vendo, mãe:. (3.1)

(21)

Doctor:	Patient:
	see. ...
	see so much idle curiosity,

	y'see, mother. ... see mother. ... [puts sandals on,
[doctor brings mic closer to patient]	takes sandals off] why (one) couldn't, mother?

Doctor:	Patient: viu. ... viu tanta curiosidade à-toa, tá vendo, mãe. ... viu mãe. ... [puts sandals on,
[doctor brings mic closer to patient]	takes sandals off] porque que não podia, mãe?

In these segments Dona Jurema calls on her mother and points emphatically (with the marker *viu*) to certain events whose referents are never clearly indicated. As a small child, Jurema does not introduce topics or provide the antecedent(s) for her reference. Instead, she uses pronominal forms or impersonal verbs.

To the mother, the child Jurema introduces complaints, saying, for example, that she is "veryveryveryvery tired"; she brings forth challenges ("do you believe?"; "do you really believe?"); she asserts apologetically that she wants "nothingnothing mother, nothing"; she reports general facts ("y'know mother, 'cause here you can't make any noise"); she requests approval ("is everything fine?"; "is everything alright?"); she requests permission to leave ("can I go then?"), permission to get up ("can I get up?"), and permission to take something ("can I take this?"). Most of these contributions help establish an asymmetrical mother-daughter relationship.

Speech Play Activities

In this interview, many instances of speech play recall the rhythm of children's lore and jingles. Often speech play provides a way for the patient to refer indirectly to difficult matters. Citing Bernstein's (1960) and Wolfenstein's (1954) work on children's traditional speech play, Kirshenblatt-Gimblett says that "the ready-made character of rhymes, jokes, taunts or insults makes the utterances impersonal and therefore helps to insulate or protect the child from full responsibility for what he says" (1976:73). Thus, it is not surprising that the patient makes use of jingles, chants, and rhymes when she refers to or addresses her mother. We have seen how Dona Jurema marks deference. In the following example she uses speech play to defy her mother indirectly, as she refers to a "secret":

(22)

Doctor:	Patient:
	[singing and baby talk]
	I'm gonna tell,
	I'm gonna tell,
//DONA JURE:MA!	//this was,
	this was,
	my secret,
	this was, ..
	this was,
	and this was=
=Dona Jurema!=	
	=my secret. ..

Here Dona Jurema ignores the doctor's (or mother's) summonses. She goes on with her own activity. To confront the doctor's/mother's power and knowledge, the patient/child needs secrecy and concealment (MacKinnon and Michels 1971:250).

In this frame of talk, the lack of topic candidates as well as the use of indefinite referents are particularly significant. Dona Jurema plays with the theme of secrecy. She chants about having said something:

> I've already said it!
> I've already said it!
> I've already said it!
> said it, said it, said it!

She also challenges her addressee by saying that she will not provide the information, which will be kept secret:

> I'll never tell!
> I'll never tell!
> I'll never tell!
> I'll never tell!

Goffman alludes to the smalltalk that takes place among staff members in hospitals: "Mental hospitals systematically provide for circulation about each patient the kind of information that the patient is likely to try to hide" (1961:161). Thus, Dona Jurema's needs for concealment may be a reaction to hospital gossip (since hospital employees firmly believe that "everything about [the patient] is in some way [their] proper business" [Goffman 1961:161]). Once the patient's psychotic frame is subsumed under institutional framings, it is not surprising that certain institutional contents would surface in Jurema's talk as a child.

Dona Jurema, when addressing her mother, intersperses her talk with chanting and singing in a childish register. The setting is the family, and within this setting the child may play rhythmic and rhyming games "independent of any external needs" and present a series of activities that may be subject "to starting and stopping, to redoing, to discontinuation . . . and to mixing with sequences from other routines" (Goffman 1974:41–42).

The Use of Child Language

A third way to express the asymmetrical relationship between mother and child is through child language. In the admitting interview, Dona Jurema introduces certain phonetic changes variants that are typical of young children. The most common is the substitution of the alveolar lateral [l] for the r-sound, as when Dona Jurema substitutes the form "Lome" for "Rome." The most recurrent forms are the third person singular of the imperfect of *ser* "to be" *(era/ela)*; the formal "you" *(senhora/senhola)*; and the form "that's why" *(por isso/pol isso)* that has been transcribed at times as *polisso*. In each of these instances the [r] as an alveolar flap changes to [l]. The velar fricative [x] (in Rio) or the alveolar trill [r] (in São Paulo) changes to [l] in words such as *Terra/Tela* "Earth"; *morrê/molê* "die." Another common consonant change is fronting: the palatal fricative [š] is replaced by the dental fricative [s] in words like *chega/sega* "arrive"; the velar stop [k] is sometimes replaced by the alveolar stop [t] in words such as *casa/tasa* "house"; the palatal lateral [ʎ] becomes the alveolar lateral [l] as in *melhor/melor* "better"; the palatal nasal [ñ] becomes the alveolar nasal [n] as in *senhola/senola* "madam."

There is also a simplification of consonant clusters in initial positions in the following groups: /pr/ *primeiro/pimeiro* "first"; /gr/ *graças/gaças* "grace"; /tr/ *trazendo/tazendo* "bringing"; in medial position in the following groups: /pr/ *empregada/empegada* "maid"; /pl/ *simples/simpes* "simple"; /gr/ *segredo/segedo* "secret"; /kr/ *acredita/aquedita* "believe." Some words drop the initial vowel, as in: *acredita/quedita* "believe" (together with the loss of a consonant cluster) and *aparece/palece* "show up" (together with a change of /r/ to /l/).

All of these variants, among others, occur asystematically throughout this interview. They never occur in the discharge interview. As such, they constitute another cue of Jurema's stance as a child.

To sum up, I have described the frame of the psychotic crisis. Here the patient creates two figures: a child and a mother. Within this frame the child's statements or requests frequently end with the address form *mãe* "mother," which has a whining, demanding tone (transcribed as mãe: "ma:ma::"). Besides the address term *(mãe)*, the patient uses the marker *viu* "see" to call the mother attention. Within this frame Dona Jurema, the child, marks deference vis-à-vis her mother, seeks approval from her mother, or teasingly defies her mother's authority.

Throughout this interview the patient most often speaks as if she were talking to her mother, treating the doctor as if she were the mother. In the next sections, however, we will see that at times the patient also speaks as a child addressing her grandmother or her sister. In addition, she also shifts roles with these figures. She becomes the mother or grand-mother addressing the child Jurema.

The Emergence of Consistent Texts in the Psychotic Fabrication

In the frame of the psychotic crisis, Dona Jurema shifts roles and estab-lishes new contexts of communication. The different characters that Dona Jurema introduces in her discourse perform different actions and accomplish different things. Here major reframings take place, where the patient takes on a new role, that is, she presents herself as a different figure. However, it is important to bear in mind that by changing an alignment, Dona Jurema is "not so much terminating the prior align-ment as holding it in abeyance with the understanding that it will almost immediately be reengaged" (Goffman 1981a:155).

Thus, throughout the psychotic frame, the alignment between the child and the mother may be temporarily suspended and then suddenly reenacted. Furthermore, there are various frame shifts within the frame of the psychotic fabrication (see Table 7.1). These reframings present, more often than not, an embedded reflexive nature. That is, the child addresses the mother and in another instance the mother addresses the child—thereby indicating that the subject (child) embraces the object (mother), since the child can shift roles with the mother. The same is true for the child Jurema and the grandmother Lena.

The Mother to the Child: "Ask to be excused, my child."

Embedded within the mother-child frame, Dona Jurema shifts roles with her own mother. This frame seems to be the mother's response to the child's anxious requests:

Table 7.1 Major Role Shifts in the Psychotic Frame

Speaker	Addressee
Child	⟶ Mother
Child	⟶ Grandma Lena
Child	⟶ Sis Dete (as child)
Mother	⟶ Child
Grandma Lena	⟶ Child
Grandma Jurema	⟶ Grandchild Maliene
Sister (as older woman)	⟶ Doctor

[Prior to this segment, the patient and the doctor exchanged challenges concerning the patient's name. The patient then pauses, catches her breath, and accelerates her pace as she calls upon her mother.]

(23)

Doctor:	Patient:
	(1) = no, only if you have, (1.3)
	(2) do you have?
	[acc]
	(3) / oh, ma:ma!/
	[bends over to gets the slipper]
(4) have what?	
	[acc]
	(5) ma:ma:: ! ...
(6) mmm?	
	(7) ma:ma::! ma:ma::! ...
	(8) she says she has, ma:ma:: ...
	(9) she says we can leave,
	ma:ma:: ...
	[picks up slipper, pushes it away to the right, moves torso and right leg to the right]
	▸(10) then ask to be excused,
	(11) my child. ..
	[looks at slippers; puts slipper on right foot]
	(12) it's like this that we ask ..
	[bending down and forward, bending right, slippers on]
	(13) so much curiosity, ['hhh] ..
	(14) they wanted to have,
	(15) didn't they child, ['hhh] ...
	[acc]
	(16) to: know about you,
	(17) right child,
	(18) just because- ['hhh]
	(19) they saw you barefooted (out =
	(20) = of doors), right child,['hhh]
	(21) they thought that you had-
(22) Dona Jure:ma!	
	(23) popopodedededddddd
	(24) sssssshhhhhhhhhhhhhhhhhhhh
	[raises head, looks up, raises left hand, brings right finger to mouth to indicate silence, looks beyond the doctor, points and nods, looks straight ahead, wide open eyes]
(25) what's happening over there?	
	(26) ssssshhhhhhhhhhhhhhhhhhh

Doctor: Patient:
                            give in,
                            give in,
                            give in,
                            give in,
                            give in for your own good.
                            for your own good.
                            the young lady is also=
                            =telling you, ..
                            it's for your own good, ..
                            then listen,
                            listen,
                            listen,
                            listen,
                            listen,
                            listen,
                            listen,
                            listen.
// Dona Jurema!   //so I listen.=
                            [turns head and torso slightly to the left]
 =⌐look, ...
// get up and walk=   // (it was because of this.)
a **little bit.**
                            [turns head and torso to the left]

Here the patient uses *Jurema* as the address form, evidence that she is
speaking not as Jurema but as someone else. Talk begins by introducing
a response to the grandchild's prior request "Can I speak, Grandma
Lena?" In an adjacency position, Grandma Lena gives directives to
young Jurema. She tells her to "give in" for "her own good," repeating
this formula nine times, with small variations, thereby stressing her request to Jurema. She also refers to "the young lady" (*a mocinha*) as a
bystander and reports on what the doctor has said ("the young lady is
also telling you that it's for your own good"). In paraphrasing the doctor, Grandma Lena endorses the doctor's position. She signals that she
sides with the doctor. Then Grandma Lena tells Jurema to "listen." At
the end of this segment there is another shift, prefaced by the marker
"so" and a change in persona. Dona Jurema—as the patient/child—concludes by accepting her grandmother's advice.

The second segment of talk within this frame takes place further on,
after an exchange in which Dona Jurema shows restlessness and anxiety.
She has been referring to her son, and she has mentioned that he did not
want to call the police (a reference to her crisis and to the family's response). Dona Jurema then addresses Grandma Lena:

(26)

Doctor: Patient:
                            [breathing hard]
                            (1) ⌐oh!!! [hhh]

Doctor:	Patient:
	(2) ⌐oh how ⌐exhausting,
	(3) Grandma Lena! ...
(4) you're <u>tired</u>,	
(5) /Dona Jurema?/	
	(6) oh, Grandma Lena!
	(7) oh, Grandma Lena,
	(8) here on Earth only if=
	(9) =one does-
	[looks down, leans forward, moves legs]
	[acc]
	(10) you wanted to know?
	(11) I I don't know anything..
	(12) y'see, Grandma Lena?

Dona Jurema introduces a series of strong complaints. She uses the marker "oh" to express her anxiety and tiredness. She continuously uses this marker (in lines 1–2 and 6–7), followed by the address form *Grandma Lena*. In line (8) she refers to the Earth, indicating that she is aware that Lena is in another place (not "here on Earth"). She repeats a formula (in lines 10–11) that she also uses with her mother, which reveals the child's deference toward a more powerful figure. Again she presents herself as a child who knows nothing (line 11) and reenacts the schema discussed previously in the asymmetrical mother-daughter relationship.

The third instance of this frame takes place further on, at the end of the interview. Here, Dona Jurema closes the interview by acknowledging Grandma Lena and stating that she will say "good-bye" only to her:

(27)

[nonverbal behavior from Dona Jurema]	
	Patient:
	[baby talk]
	(1) I'm leaving 'cause it's=
	(2) =already very late. ...
[looks up and addresses the camera]	
	(3) ['hhh] "excuse me." ..
→	(4) only by Grandma Lena=
	(5) =will I ask to be=
	(6) =excused. ...
[looks down, moves right hand down]	(7) ['hhh] "excuse me,
	(8) Grandma Lena, excuse me."
[moves backward, bends down]	(9) ... that's it. y'see.
	(10) this is it.

[keeps looking down, moves backward, as if putting on her slippers]

Dona Jurema singles out Grandma Lena as the one she addresses at the
end of the interview (lines 4–6), the only one she takes leave of (lines
7–8). Grandma Lena is also the one to whom Jurema complains (as in
example 26). Finally, she is the one who gives directives to Jurema,
which Jurema accepts (as in example 25). Within this frame of talk, the
patient never challenges her addressee. Rather, in Dona Jurema's schema
for grandmothers, they are to be "listened to" and, therefore, in her own
words, Jurema "listens."

Dona Jurema to Her Grandchild, Mariene: "It's only a caress."

A different grandmother is enacted when Dona Jurema addresses the
doctor as her own grandchild, Mariene (here called "Maliene"). The age
difference between Dona Jurema, who is sixty-one, and Doctor Edna,
who is twenty-five, may trigger this frame. The metaphor "the doctor
who 'is' like my granddaughter" is treated literally as "the doctor who *is*
my granddaughter."[13] The patient uses a speech-play activity to package
this talk.

[Prior to this segment, Dona Jurema had been addressing her mother.
She then swings herself forward on her chair and gets up halfway; then
she sits back, only this time she sits on the arm of the armchair; she now
faces the doctor and starts chanting. The doctor keeps her baseline posture. At this point the camera moves the focus away from the patient.]

(28)

Patient:
[chanting and baby talk]
(1) **I've already said it,**
(2) **I've already said it,**
(3) **I've already said it,**
(4) **said, said,**

→   [camera focus on patient;
her right foot plays with
the doctor's feet; patient
looks down to their feet]
[chanting and baby talk]

(5) **that now,**
(6) **that now,**

→ (7) **it is the foot of (Tuxa).**
[moves feet away; takes
slipper off right foot;
points with foot at
doctor's left foot]

[doctor looks down]

(8) **['hhh] I've already said,**
(9) **I've already said,**
[caresses doctor's foot
with her foot]

(10) I've already said,
(11) it's a little caress,
[looks up at doctor]

(12) ['hhh] a little caress,
(13) a little caress,
(14) a little caress,
→(15) ['hhh] to the little tip=
(16) =of the little toe of my=
(17) =li::ttle grand:daughter.

[hymn and baby talk]
→(18) ⌐Malie::ne::::,
(19) ⌐Sa:cred Lie:ne,
[moves feet away, searches
for slippers, makes
movement up and forward,
looking down]

(20) to me she is::is:,
(21) sanctifi::ed,

[looking straight at | [gets halfway up in the
the patient; turned | chair, sits at the edge
her torso further to | of the armchair, looks
the right, leaning | down and holds position]
forward closer to |
the patient] |

[chanting and baby talk]
(22) ['hhh] that's why,
(23) that's why::! y:::. ...
(24) ['hhh] that's why
(25) that's why::! y:::. ...
(26) ['hhh] THAT'S WHY,
(27) THAT'S WHY::! y:::. ...

Two types of activities take place here, and the doctor has two different roles. First, Dona Jurema addresses the doctor as her granddaughter, Maliele (lines 1–17) and provides Maliene/doctor with an explanation for her nonverbal behavior: She says that it (touching the doctor's feet) is "a little caress" and should be understood as such (lines 10–11 and 15–17). Hence, within this frame, Dona Jurema performs a physical action (touching and pointing with her feet) and also instructs Maliene/doctor on how to interpret her action. She uses a series of diminutive and expressive forms (lines 11–17): a "little caress" (the Portuguese form *festinha* instead of *festa*), the "little tip of foot" (the Portuguese form *pontinha* instead of *ponta*), the "little toe" (the form *dedinho* instead of *dedo*, and "little granddaughter" (the form *netinha* instead of *neta*). Second, Dona Jurema sings a church hymn in which she uses her granddaughter's name as in an invocatory prayer. There is a worship intent signaled by the address form ("Sacred Liene") as well as by the granddaughter's appraisal (lines 20–21). Here, Doctor Edna ceases to be the granddaughter and she stands instead as a bystander.

Examples (25) and (28) indicate that Dona Jurema has at least two roles for the grandmother: Grandma Lena (her own grandmother) and Grandma Jurema (herself as a grandmother). She performs both. She also role-plays the granddaughter (Jurema as a child) as well as addresses the doctor as her granddaughter, Maliene. In each frame Dona Jurema coherently assesses their contextual restrictions. That is, she never mixes her persona figures (Grandma Lena or Grandma Jurema) and addressees (child Jurema or child Maliene). While Grandma Lena has something to say to the child Jurema, Grandma Jurema speaks to the child Maliene. These reframings present different degrees of transformation and frame embedding. Grandma Jurema is clearly closer to the rim of the frame, to the outermost lamination (Goffman 1974:82). It is only natural that Dona Jurema sees in Doctor Edna someone who resembles her granddaughter and treats her as such ("it's only a little caress," she says). Grandma Lena (Jurema's late grandmother), however, would be closer to the innermost layerings, further removed from real-world activity.

The Child to Her Sister Idete: "Didn't I tell you, Deta?"

As a child, Dona Jurema also addresses her sister Idete (with variant forms *Deta* or *Detinha*). In the interview there are four short segments within this context of talk, of which I will describe two. The first consists of only two utterances, where Dona Jurema seems to be proving a point as she addresses her sister:

(29)

    (1) oh, ohohohohohohohoh.
         [acc]
    (2) slowly,
    (3) slowly,
    (4) slowly,
    (5) 'cause it was, waswaswa-
→(6) didn't I say so, Deta.
→(7) didn't I say Deta=
    (8) =that it had- ['hhh]
    (9) popopopopopopopopopopopo=

Prior to this segment, Dona Jurema had been referring to her mother. Then, in line (1), as she bends over and looks down, she plays with her slippers and utters a continuous expressive remark. At first (in lines 2–4) she seems to be monitoring her gestures as she tries to put on her slippers. Then (in lines 6–7) she addresses her sister. She repeats her statement twice; the second time, she adds more incomplete information, interrupts herself (line 8), and engages in nonsensical talk (line 9).

At another time, after having talked to Grandma Lena, Dona Jurema addresses her sister again.

(30)

> **that's it, sis. ...**
> **(little) sis(ter). ...**

She uses two affective terms to refer to Idete, calling her "sis" (Portuguese *mana*) and "little sis(ter)" (Portuguese *maninha*). She then reports on what she used to call her sister (example 31). This report has no specific addressee, it could be addressed to Grandma Lena (the last addressee), to the doctor, or to the mother, who is Dona Jurema's most salient addressee.

(31)

Patient:
> [baby talk]
> (1) **I only know it was like this,**
> (2) **I only know I used to call=**
> (3) **=Idetinha as Detinha, ..**
> (4) **then later I started to call**
> (5) **=her sis:. ..**
> (6) **she was plea:::sed,**
>   [smiles, raises head and torso]
> (7) **plea:::sed,**
>   [smiles, bends forward, and speaks to the mic]
> (8) **but then:::,**
>   [looks down, raises head slowly, moves torso backward]
> (9) **she is ve:::ry,**
> (10) **she is ve:::ry,**

Dona Jurema introduces factual information about what she used to call her sister and the types of responses she would get from her. Idete is the patient's caretaker and her closest relative. Here Dona Jurema signals that she wants to leave the information "on record." Her nonverbal behavior indicates that she is aware of presenting a report statement that will be recorded (as in an interview). In line (8) she introduces contrastive information prefaced by the marker "but" about Idete (now referred to by the pronoun "she"). She makes an evaluative remark, which she leaves incomplete (in lines 9–10).

When Dona Jurema "talks to" her sister Idete, affection is revealed by the various address forms. In the beginning of the interview, for example, there is a frame break (from the child/mother frame to the sister/sister frame), when the patient looks to the far-left corner, as if someone were there, and cries out loud, "Dete! Deti::nha!" Throughout the interview, within this frame of talk, Dona Jurema addresses her sister by the short form *Dete* or *Deta;* by the expressive diminutive *Idetinha* or *De-tinha;* and by indicating her status as sibling in the forms "sis" *(mana)* and "little sis(ter)" *(maninha)*.

The Sister Idete to the Doctor: "Thank God! It's all over!"

Of all the family members evoked in Jurema's talk, the only one who interacts with the doctor is the sister Idete. She is Dona Jurema's care-taker and the only person who has maintained constant contact with the doctor. There are various statements from Idete to the doctor on the patient's hospital records. As we know from the discharge interview, Dona Jurema lives with Idete.

In the first part of the admitting interview there is a reframing in which Dona Jurema shifts and assumes Idete's role. She addresses the doctor, states that Dona Jurema has been a bit sick but is now recovered, and closes by praising the doctor.

[Prior to this segment, Dona Jurema had been signaling "to be quiet" as she says, "sssshhhhhhh" and points forward.]

(32)

Doctor:	Patient:
(1) **Dona Jure:ma**	
	(2) **popopodedededddddd**
	(3) **sssssshhhhhhhhhhhhhhhhhh**
	[raises head, looks up, raises left hand, brings right finger to mouth, indicates silence; looks beyond the doctor, points and nods, looks straight ahead, wide-open eyes]
(4) **what's happening over there?**	
	(5) [ʼhhh] **sssssshhhhhhhhhhhhhh**
	(6) [ʼhhh] **sssssshhhhhhhhhhhhhh**
	(7) [ʼhhh] **sssssshhhhhhhhhhhhhh**
	[points and nods, turns sideways to the right moves left arm to the right, bends down, looks down to the right]
(8) **Dona JuRE:MA!**	
	[dec] [baby talk]
→ (9) ⌜**thank God! ....**	
	[interrupts movement, raises head, looks up, turns to doctor and smiles]

Doctor: Patient:

    [dec]
(10) **thank God, for <u>what</u>?**

                            (11) **= it's all over. ....**
                                 [holds the position and
                                 smiles]

    [acc]
(12) **what is over?**

                                 [dec]
            →(13) **⌐Jurema is a little dizzy**
               (14) **y'know.**
                                 [turns torso and head to
                                 face doctor, moves left
                                 hand down and grabs
                                 armchair]
(15) **mmm.**

                            (16) **could you give ⌐my little =**
                            (17) **= sister a glass of water,**
                            (18) **she didn't even know =**
                            (19) **= that this would happen =**
                            (20) **= to her. ..**
                            (21) **you are very polite. ..**

In the first part of this segment, Dona Jurema signals the doctor to be quiet. She also points to the right corner of the room. Then she turns to the right and leans on the armchair, away from the doctor. She also looks down. This movement takes place between lines (3) and (7). Then, in a different move, she raises her head, turns to the left, and looks at the doctor. As she shifts movements, she also changes her role, and in a higher pitch and slower pace she speaks as Idete, her sister. She expresses relief and gives "thanks to God" (in line 9). Doctor Edna then requests information about what is taking place or has taken place. In line (11) Dona Jurema, in the role of her sister Idete, smiles at the doctor as she states that "it's all over." Doctor Edna again requests information about what is over (line 12). In her next turn the patient refers to herself in the third person and provides information on Dona Jurema's general well-being. She states that Jurema is a bit dizzy (lines 13–14). Then she requests a glass of water for her sister Jurema. In lines (18) and (19) she informs the doctor that Dona Jurema did not really know that "this"—which seems to refer to Dona Jurema's psychotic crisis—was going to happen. She concludes by praising the doctor (line 21).

When the patient as Idete addresses the doctor, she accomplishes a set of sequential moves: She expresses relief because Jurema now feels better; she explains to the doctor what has happened; she requests an action of the doctor; she apologizes for what happened and provides an explanation; finally, she concludes by praising the doctor. All of these moves integrate Dona Jurema's schema regarding her sister's behavior with Doctor Edna or doctors in general. As Tannen and Wallat state, a knowledge schema "refer[s] to participants' expectations about people, objects, events and settings in the world" (1987:207). It seems that, in Dona Jurema's prior experiences with her own crisis, she recalls her sister performing a series of sequential moves like the ones described.

Conclusion

As one listens to Dona Jurema's talk, one hears a multitude of speakers addressing distinct listeners. In the midst of several discourses, there are two major frames at play: the frame of the psychiatric interview and the frame of the psychotic crisis. The first encompasses the second. Goffman argues that the rim of the frame defines the activities regarding its status in the real world, and the core of the frame defines what the dramatic "transformed" activity is (1974:82). It seems that in the psychotic fabrications, the core of the frame is further removed from the rim.

In these different performances, two things seem to occur. First, Dona Jurema changes her role by shifting from being the patient to being the child. As a child she addresses her mother, her grandmother, her sister Idete. She also changes roles so as to speak as her own mother, or her own grandmother, or her own sister. This is one type of transformation. These reframings take place in the innermost layerings of the psychotic frame. Second, Dona Jurema, as a patient, also shifts her footing regarding her audience (Doctor Edna): For example, she may address the doctor either from an asymmetrical position in the social scale (where patients are less powerful than doctors) or from the asymmetrical position in the age scale (where an elder woman is more powerful than a younger woman). These are some of the patient's social attributes that surface in the interview. These transformations are closer to the rim of the frame—they are closer to the outermost layerings of the interview frame.

Thus, in the institutional frame of the psychiatric interview, Dona Jurema's responses often convey complaints about her well-being, or about the doctor's unreasonable demands (bringing her to an interview); she also introduces requests that challenge the doctor's authority as the gatekeeper and interviewer. In each of these instances, Dona Jurema's discourse coheres.

In the noninstitutional frames of the psychotic crisis, Dona Jurema makes use of family figures (the mother, the grandmother, the sister) to create different contexts of talk. In each of these she coherently performs a series of moves that reveal the frame of talk she has created.

Within each frame of talk, Dona Jurema also reveals schemas that are associated with certain referents. As a patient, Dona Jurema states that one cannot make any noise at the hospital and one must, therefore, go elsewhere to be noisy. To her mother, the child Jurema marks deference. When Dona Jurema speaks as the mother, she is the mother as the instructor and also the sympathetic mother who sides with her child Jurema. Speaking as her sister Idete, she also performs a role according to an entire schema: She thanks God because Jurema feels better; she explains to the doctor what has happened; she requests a glass of water for Jurema; and she apologizes and praises the doctor.

Dona Jurema as child addresses her mother and her grandmother in different ways. Grandma Lena is the one singled out by the child when leaving. Jurema may report opinions or complain to Grandma Lena, but she seldom marks deference to her. When addressing her mother, on the other hand, she repeatedly marks deference as she reasserts the knowledge (power) the mother has.

What emerges is the fact that Dona Jurema uses language to mirror the social functions that each participant has in her discourse. She uses different personas to convey different actions and to accomplish different things interactively. On this level of analysis, she never "misfires" (Austin [1962] 1975), which is rather unexpected from a "thought-disordered patient."

Notes

1 Ribeiro (1991b) discusses knowledge schemas and interactive frames. These structuring principles are related to the sociological concept of "role" and the interactional notion of "footing." Differentiating between these two concepts (role and footing) in a psychotic episode captures the degree of transformation involved in reframings.

2. The nonsensical form *tototô* could be interpreted as a variation of the Portuguese form *doutô* ("doc" for "doctor"). In this case a nonsensical muttering "totototototô" would have triggered (by means of a sound touch-off) the new form *tô* in *tô tô tô*, an aphaeresis (deletion of initial sounds) of the form *doutô*, derived from *dout- + -or*.

3. Dona Jurema's statement refers to "Pinel" as the hospital in which she was institutionalized. However, she was actually hospitalized in the Psychiatric Institute of the Federal University of Rio de Janeiro, which is next to Pinel. Most Rio dwellers refer to the two institutions collectively as Pinel.

4. There have been chickens, ducks, and birds on the hospital grounds for many years. The presence of chickens is actually a topic for jokes among psychiatric students. After all, Rio de Janeiro is a developed and sophisticated urban center, and the Psychiatric Institute is considered a major mental institution in the country. Hence, one does not "expect" to see chickens or ducks there.

5. I thank Lucia Quental Almeida for calling my attention to the relevance of this cue early in the analysis.

6. There is a common joke among psychiatric students concerning the degree of comprehension of psychotic patients in interviews. Given certain types of questions (most of which are known-answer questions), a patient is said to reply, "Doctor, I may be crazy, but I'm not stupid."

7. By not responding and also by challenging the doctor's queries, Dona Jurema contradicts a well-known schema in doctor-patient interaction: the cultural assumption that says that doctors always have "reasons" for their questions,

no matter how unreasonable these questions may seem to the patients (or to outsiders). Patients, therefore, are known not to reject doctors' queries as inappropriate. On the contrary, they assume that these questions are relevant (otherwise the doctor would not be asking them), and they address the issues with their best efforts (Mishler 1984:120).

8. In the Portuguese text, the patient uses the word *belinho,* a word she has just created. The doctor understands it as *pelinho* (a change from voiced [b] to voiceless [p]). *Pelinho* is the diminutive form for *pelo,* which, in Portuguese, refers to "body hair." Using a child register, Dona Jurema probably derives the form *belinho* from *cabelinho* (little hair), deleting the initial syllable.

9. The form "split" is used here as a translation for *azular.* It is not a reference to "split hairs."

10. Most psychiatrists (Cameron, Sullivan, Kasanin) agree that schizophrenic behavior often mirrors the behavior of very young children. As such, schizophrenics engage in "asocial thinking," believed to be natural in youngsters. The two groups (youngsters and schizophrenics) stand at opposite ends; one is in the process of developing the pragmatics of social interaction and thought organization, while the other is in the process of losing them. However, Cameron points out that the processes are not the reverse of each other; to analyze it in this way would lead to an oversimplification and to inadequate inferences, as the process of the schizophrenic "is new and unique in his life history" (Cameron [1944] 1964:60).

11. Brazilian children often use the V-form to address their parents (the *senhor* or *senhora* form discussed previously). They receive the T-form from their parents (and elder relatives). This pattern may prevail into adulthood. However, the address form *madame* (from the French "ma" + "dame") is never used in the family context. Originally a title of courtesy for a married woman, today it remains mostly as a class marker (generally, a middle-class woman over twenty would receive the *madame* treatment from cabdrivers, vendors on the street, or housemaids). In this respect, Dona Jurema's use of the form *madame* to address her mother alludes to a servant-housewife relationship. In a daugher-mother interaction, this allusion conveys defiance and detachment.

12. The patient's medical records indicate that during a crisis Dona Jurema would address living as well as dead relatives. One should bear in mind that, in the Brazilian culture, there are religious rituals in which people engage in "speaking to the dead" as well as "listening to the dead." These rituals (called *umbanda* and *quimbanda*), of African origin, are practiced on a regular basis among Brazilians, with no class or ethnic distinctions. Dona Jurema's medical records indicate that, at an earlier time, she had been "introduced" to the rituals of *umbanda* by a previous boyfriend, causing the boyfriend (one of the topics discussed in the discharge interview) to be looked down on by Dona Jurema's family. Hence, for Dona Jurema, communicating with a dead relative is part of a "prior text" (Becker 1979). This can also be viewed as another schema (Tannen and Wallat 1987) that she has in this frame.

13. During the playback session, Doctor Edna stated that she had always felt very close to the patient. She said that the patient saw her as "a very young doctor, who reminded Dona Jurema of her own granddaughter".

8

Toward Listening

I do crazy things when I am sick, and then I don't know why when I'm well.
Susan Sheehan, *Is There No Place on Earth for Me?*, p. 8

—*What was it like your insanity at Nevers?*
—*Madness is like intelligence, you know. One cannot explain it. Just like*
intelligence. It comes to you, it fills you up, and then you grasp it. But when it
leaves you, you no longer understand it at all.
Marguerite Duras (from the film *Hiroshima Mon Amour,* 1959)

Laing says that people experience madness as a major breakdown, "an
exile from the scene of being as we know it": a breakdown in communication, in interaction, in relationships. One stops relating to the other,
to the world, and even to oneself. One becomes a stranger by losing
one's sense of self, one's feelings, one's place in the world as we know it
([1967] 1974:110).

It is not surprising, therefore, that a person remembers so little after
a psychotic episode. In Dona Jurema's discharge interview, for instance,
the queries by the doctor about the patient's earlier experiences remain
mostly unanswered:

Doctor: ⌐=well, what was the last thing that you=
=remember? ... from- from- from- the=
=beginning of- of- your illness,
what is it that you remember?
/what did you have-/
Patient: └I didn't have anything, doctor=
Doctor: =/you weren't feeling anything./
Patient: it was all of a sudden.
I wasn't feeling anything, anything,
anything.=
Doctor: =what was it that happened all of a sudden?
explain it to us.=
Patient: =all of a sudden I lost ah .. my mind,
my senses, y'know, ...
I didn't see anything anymore,

Patient: **when I could see again I was here in the=**
=hospital, y'know. (1.7)
but I did not see anything that happened to=
=me (y'know)
Doctor: **you don't remember what you used to fee::l,**
what you used to do::, /you don't remember./
Patient: **no. nothing, nothing, nothing. ..**
Doctor: **//mmm, mmm. // ...**
when you- ... were able to remember anything,
or to recognize things, you were already in
here?=
Patient: **=I was already in here. (1.9)**
Doctor: **//mmm.//**
Patient: **I had already been hospitalized.=**
Doctor: **=//mmm, mmm.//**

Laing tells us, however, that a psychotic episode does not need to be experienced as a breakdown ([1967] 1974:110). A visit to the inner world need not lead to great estrangement. One way of bridging the gap may be by listening to those that have traveled beyond. In listening, a different kind of understanding may come into being.

This study has proposed two ways of listening and interpreting discourse. One may listen to the *message*, the exchange of referential information in talk and interaction. Or one may listen to the *metamessage*, the implicit sociolinguistic information on how the message is to be understood. In both cases, one listens and attends to the interaction: to the ways the hearer and the speaker jointly build discourse. Each way of listening sheds a different light on conversational coherence. Both ways of listening bring an understanding of how language can be used to convey linguistic and social meaning in different types of discourse.

A Brief Discussion

This book analyzes two psychiatric interviews, which took place twenty days apart and involved the same participants, a doctor and a patient. The first interview (the admitting interview) took place two days after the patient was taken to the hospital. She was diagnosed to be in an acute manic-psychotic crisis but had not yet been medicated. The second interview (the discharge interview) took place when the patient was considered fully recovered and ready to go home. At the time of this interview, she had been taken off medication.

The patient's discourse in the discharge interview could be used as the reference point for what is "expected" or considered "normal" talk from an interviewee. The patient followed the expected interactional rules for medical interviews. For example, she provided the second pair part of an adjacency pair, expanded on the doctor's comments, and stayed on topic, addressing the agenda that the doctor brought to the interview.

The admitting interview, in contrast, represents the deviation, where the patient displayed unexpected verbal and nonverbal behavior. She lacked coherence in attending to the sequencing of the turn structure or topic development. If, however, one takes a frame-analytic perspective, the patient's discourse coheres.

In listening to the discourse that emerges in these two events, one is struck by both their differences and their similarities. *Topic analysis* highlights the differences between the two interviews. For the discharge interview, a topic analysis indicates how participants achieve a jointly built discourse. The doctor requests information on a set of topics that she brings to the interview. The patient stays on topic and addresses the doctor's topic agenda; she may also negotiate for a topic shift. In the admitting interview, on the other hand, a topic analysis shows how coherence breaks down: Participants bring competitive agendas to the encounter; topics are seldom jointly developed, nor are they concluded; no process of topic negotiation takes place. Hence, a topic analysis performed for both interviews indicates contrastive sets of data.

On the other hand, *frame analysis* points to similarities in the two interviews. For both interviews the same two major frames emerged: the institutional frame of the psychiatric interview and the noninstitutional frame of the personal encounter. The doctor establishes and controls what goes on in the institutional frame, while the patient shifts frames and establishes what takes place in the personal frame. In assessing each frame of talk correctly, the patient's discourse coheres in *both* interviews.

Different Interviews, Similar Frames

How do the frames described in the discharge interview compare with those described in the admitting interview? What sort of metamessages surface in both events? Are there similarities in the relationships and alignments that are established between the two participants?

In both interviews it is *the doctor* who creates and manages the institutional framings. Within these contexts she controls the turn structure, introduces and shifts the topics, and opens and closes the interview. She is the institutional gatekeeper. In both interviews the patient correctly assesses the situation she is in and acts accordingly. In the discharge interview Dona Jurema answers the doctor's questions, addresses the topics, and thus provides for sequencing in talk. In the admitting interview she tells the doctor in indirect ways that she does not want to engage in talk. Thus, she refuses to participate and collaborate in the interview.

In the two interviews, *the patient* creates and controls the unofficial framings. That is, she proposes a transformation of the situation she finds herself in (i.e., the institutional context). In doing so, she shifts and reframes talk as a personal encounter. In the discharge interview the doctor sometimes ratifies these shifts. A new alignment then takes place, where Dona Jurema performs her unofficial identities. However, in the admitting interview, when the patient is in a psychotic crisis, the doctor never ratifies the patient's personal framings. Doctor Edna remains in her official role, summoning the patient to the frame of the psychiatric interview.

The differences in frames in the two interviews have to do with the degree of transformation. There is less transformation when the speakers' traits or attributes shift the frame of talk; there is more transformation— to the point of psychosis—when the persona shifts completely and assumes a new role. Thus, role shifts were distinguished from changes in footings. *Role* was used to refer to major changes in persona, that is, when the patient would literally take the role of the mother, the sister, the grandmother, and so on. *Footing* was used to refer to microchanges in traits or attributes of the speaker that would change her alignment vis-à-vis the hearer and thus reframe talk.

In the discharge interview, reframings take place as microinteractional shifts of footing occur. Within talk framed as a personal encounter, Dona Jurema performs her unofficial identities: As a grandmother, she conveys rapport and camaraderie in her relationship with a very young doctor who reminds her of her granddaughter; as an older woman, she challenges the young doctor and takes a stand regarding the information that she chooses to convey; in a woman-to-woman relationship, she questions Doctor Edna regarding a woman's matter (childbirth). In each reframing Dona Jurema changes her communicative strategies from providing less information to providing more information; her communicative style changes from less involvement to more involvement; and a topic change or a change in focus on the ongoing topic occurs. During all this interactional work Dona Jurema remains coherent.

In the admitting interview, however, we see major shifts (role shifts) as well as microshifts (shifts of footing). Within the frame of the psychotic crisis, Dona Jurema makes use of family figures (the mother, the grandmother, the sister) to create different contexts of talk. She shifts from *addressing* one of these figures (i.e., performing the role of a child addressing her mother) to *speaking as* one of them (i.e., performing the mother addressing the child Jurema). In each of these situations, Dona Jurema coherently performs a series of moves that reveal the frame of talk she has created. That is, there is a set of specific moves performed by the mother, another set performed by the grandmother, and so on. The few discourse markers used in this interview are also distributed according to each frame of talk.

Hence, in the admitting interview, frames occur within the contexts projected by the patient as well as in the context of the psychiatric interview. The nature of reframings and frame embeddings makes the interaction complex. For example, a change in footing within a frame of talk constitutes an embedded frame. That is, when Dona Jurema assumes the footing of an elderly patient, she is operating within the frame of the psychiatric interview. In each frame, and each footing within a given frame, the patient is coherent. She correctly assesses the frame she creates and does not mix frames.

Goffman (1974) says that the "rim" of the frame defines the activities regarding its status in the real world, and the "core" of the frame defines what the meaning of the dramatic (transformed) activity is. It seems that in psychotic fabrications, the "core" of the frame is further removed from the "rim" of the frame.

Different Interviews, Similar Footings

Similar microshifts also take place in the interviews, with the same social attributes of the patient and the doctor frequently surfacing in both events. Furthermore, the same sort of relationship is conveyed, in different ways but through similar metamessages. For example, as a patient, Dona Jurema assumes similar footings in both interviews. Once in each interview we see her as a willful woman challenging the doctor and taking a stand. The metamessage that underlies this reframing is "I can take care of myself."

In the discharge interview Dona Jurema aligns herself as "the nurturing grandmother." While holding this footing she offers more contributions, shows more involvement with the topic of talk (the granddaughter), and conveys a higher degree of cooperation. In the admitting interview, however, these features are exaggerated as the patient actually acts out the role of the grandmother by caressing the doctor as if she were her own granddaughter.

Another example can be seen in the patient's responses to the doctor in both interviews, where little referential information is conveyed. Within the official interview framing, the doctor explicitly requests the patient to engage in a "state of talk." In the admitting interview Dona Jurema responds to this request with an implicit negative answer. Her refusal is described in three ways: She expresses a complaint; she shifts to nonverbal communication; and she requests permission to leave and close the interview. In the discharge interview Dona Jurema engages in talk with the doctor. In her schema for doctor-patient communication, she knows she must do so if she is to be "released" from the hospital. However, she consistently keeps her answers short, causing the doctor to comment afterward that the patient answered "minimally." In both circumstances the patient's metamessage seems to be the same: "I do not have much to tell you [since you already know everything]."

Apparently, the differences in framing do not lie in the metamessages themselves but rather in the way the patient communicates these messages. In the psychotic crisis Dona Jurema performs entire scripts while changing personas and addressees. Her discourse is peopled by various characters that function to channel Jurema's social attributes (Jurema, the

mother; Jurema, the child; Jurema, the grandmother, and so on). There
are no metaphors. In the discharge interview Dona Jurema coherently
performs her social attributes (which come up in her personal alignments
to Doctor Edna) yet always stays in contact with the foremost context of
the psychiatric interview.

The Direction of Reframings

While both participants reframe talk, the direction in which reframings
are proposed is more or less fixed for both interviews. The doctor frames
the situation as a "medical encounter," the patient reframes it as a "personal encounter," and talk follows until the doctor reframes it again. If
this direction were reversed, the discourse of the doctor would be considered "incoherent," that is, not attending to the "main frame," the interview situation. Commenting on a frame break, Doctor Edna said: "If
I had let her talk, this [the interview] would look like a chat" (personal
communication).

Topic Structure: Focused versus Unfocused Discourse

A topic analysis of the admitting and discharge interviews yields differences in the ways participants structure discourse. Such an analysis also
reveals a substantial contrast in the doctor's and patient's schemas regarding the encounter at hand. Part of the doctor's role as an interviewer is
to introduce topics from her topic agenda. Hence, the questions that the
doctor asks the patient follow a standard medical interview format; this
is an important part of the institutional frame. To obtain relevant data
from the patient, the doctor asks about such things as her sleeping habits, hygiene, and vocational history.

In the discharge interview Dona Jurema mostly stays in the frame
created by the doctor. She addresses the doctor's topics by providing the
requested information or by negotiating what talk is about. She never
risks introducing a topic from her personal agenda. If she did so, she
could jeopardize what she has invested in this interview: to display discourse coherence while attending to the requirements of the interview.

Since Doctor Edna is the one who introduces new referents, she
provides for "discontinuity" in the discourse. Topics shift from the patient's social history to her present illness, to her past history, and so on,
often in a disjunctive manner. The patient, on the other hand, assures
"topic continuity." She does so by collaborating on the topics introduced
by the doctor or by introducing subtopics. Here Dona Jurema sustains a
state of talk, or *focused interaction,* with the doctor (Goffman [1967]
1982:145).

In the admitting interview the patient is undergoing a severe psychotic crisis. Most of her contributions do not make sense. A topic analysis indicates where coherence breaks down. The patient rarely addresses
the doctor's questions; she shifts idiosyncratically from one topic to an-

other; and she engages in activities that are noninteractional (such as singing and chanting). Regarding topic, an *unfocused interaction* often results.

In this interview Doctor Edna makes only a few successful attempts to intervene in Dona Jurema's talk. Whenever she gets the floor, she repeatedly summons the patient's attention. This is a preliminary move to introducing a topic. Dona Jurema rarely addresses the doctor's summonses, which implies that she is not available for talk. However, when she does answer a summons (and consequently agrees to enter a "state of talk"), her answers vary in degrees of acceptability and coherence.

Topic Content: Competing Agendas in the Admitting Interview

In Dona Jurema's talk, one hears a series of referents from a personal agenda. These referents are seldom made explicit and, when stated, they are neither developed nor concluded. They represent fragmentary referential information and are part of a personal topic agenda that the patient recycles throughout the interview. Doctor Edna's talk contains questions that propose referents from an official topic agenda. The questions recycle information known to both the doctor and the patient: the patient's full name, age, place of residence, and so on. These topics are rarely picked up or developed in the interaction.

Instead, Doctor Edna and Dona Jurema often compete for topic control. Most of the time, in both discourses, topics are brought up as topic disjuncts. No "stepwise topic transitions" are negotiated between the doctor and the patient. Nor is "subtopic categorization" important, as participants do not introduce new referents with different levels of embedding. The lack of these processes tells us that both participants have failed to build a topically coherent and joint discourse.

Different knowledge schemas on the part of the doctor and the patient orient topic selection and impose obligations on topic development. For Dona Jurema a family encounter brings up personal topics, which are old shared information among family members. For Doctor Edna a medical encounter binds one to official topics, which are often introduced through known-answer questions. This difference is not resolved and progressively isolates the participants from one another: As Doctor Edna aligns herself with her official interviewer role, Dona Jurema distances herself from a shared interaction with the doctor. In listening to the admitting interview, one has the impression of listening to *two* dissociated (or unfocused) discourses: the patient's and the doctor's.

Summary

Frame and topic analysis have proved to be powerful tools in interpreting two very different types of discourse: a standard interview and a crisis interview. For both interviews the participants continuously conveyed two types of information: referential information on "what the message is" and information on how the message is to be understood (i.e., the metamessage).

A topic analysis of both interviews indicates that topic is a good predictor for assessing coherence in the structure of the discourse. This type of analysis presents *discourse-based*, rather than *thought-based*, descriptions. It assesses coherence from the patient's discourse rather than from thought variables. Frame analysis indicates that the patient's discourse in the admitting interview, though seemingly incoherent on one level, is coherent on another. The patient consistently created different frames of talk and assessed correctly the frame she was in. As Goffman says, "A frame perspective . . . allows us to generate crazy behavior and to see that it is not all that crazy" (1974:246).

For those concerned with medical interaction, this study points to differences in how a doctor and a patient frame talk. While the doctor operates in the official medical frame, the patient seems to be more comfortable while operating within the frame of the personal encounter. Within this frame she provides more information and offers a series of evaluative remarks. This results in an inherent frame tension between the doctor and the patient. As pointed out by Mishler (1984), in the process of gathering information, doctors constantly interrupt their patients (i.e., steering the patient back to the medical frame) and thus curtail the opportunity of getting the very information they seek.

For those concerned specifically with psychiatric interviews, a comparative frame analysis of the two interviews—with the patient in a psychotic crisis and again with the patient out of the crisis—indicates that frames are pervasive in both events, and that similar metamessages may be established for both interviews.

This study also points to the importance of accessing thought disorders from the patient's discourse, as Lakoff (1981) has urged. Looking at the discourse of a patient in a psychotic crisis uncovers ways in which human communication works more generally. Frame and topic analyses indicate that while coherence may break down on one discourse level, it may still be achieved on another. In analyzing discourse coherence, one must attend to these two levels.

Appendix A

Definitions of Language and Cognitive Behaviors

The following definitions derive from clinical experience (Andreasen 1979a). They represent a clinical assessment of thought, language, and communication disorders. In defining terms, Andreasen avoids making inferences about underlying processes of thought (1979a:1315). This is but an abridged version of the original text, in the same order of presentation.

1. *Poverty of Speech:* Also referred to as "poverty of thought" or "laconic speech," a pathology that signals a restriction in the *amount* of spontaneous speech, resulting in short, concrete, monosyllabic, unelaborated replies to questions. Unprompted additional information is seldom given. Unanswered questions are common.

2. *Poverty of Content of Speech:* Also known as "poverty of thought," "empty speech," "alogia," "verbigeration," "negative formal thought disorder," where long replies convey little information; language tends to be vague (overabstract or overconcrete, repetitive, and stereotyped); tendency to lengthy replies with great amount of redundancy.

3. *Pressure of Speech:* There is an increase in the amount of spontaneous speech; the patient talks fast and is difficult to interrupt; speech tends to be loud and emphatic. The eagerness to "go on with a new idea" may force the speaker to leave sentences uncompleted; even when interrupted, he often continues to talk. Derailment, tangentiality, or incoherence may accompany this disorder.

4. *Distractible Speech:* Sudden changes in discourse topic in response to a nearby stimulus.

5. *Tangentiality:* In reply to a question, the speaker adopts an evasive attitude; the answer may be related to the question in an indirect way or not related at all. Andreasen states that the concept of tangentiality used to be roughly equivalent to that of "loose associations" or "derailment"; it has now been redefined so as to refer exclusively "to questions and not to transitions in spontaneous speech" (1979a:1319). As such, this disorder occurs as the immediate response to a question.

6. *Derailment:* Also known as "loose associations" and "flight of ideas," it refers to instances of behavior where the patient may shift idiosyncratically from one topic to another and where things may be said "in juxtaposition that lack a meaningful relationship" (1979a:1319). The most common manifestation of this pathology is "a slow, steady slippage" with no apparent severe derailment to the point that "the speaker gets farther and farther off the track" and his reply has no relation to the question asked (1979a:1319). This disorder often occurs in the context of pressured speech.

7. *Incoherence*: Also known as "word salad," "jargon aphasia," "schizophasia," "paragrammatism," this phenomenon includes several different mechanisms that may co-occur at the level of the sentence. On the syntactic level, linguistic forms are juxtaposed arbitrarily, rules of grammar are ignored, and "portions of coherent sentences may be observed in the midst of a sentence that is incoherent as a whole" (1979a:1319). On the semantic level, "word choice may seem totally random or may appear to have some oblique connection with the context." Andreasen states that "this type of disorder is relatively rare [and] when it occurs, it tends to be severe or extreme" (1979a:1319). It may resemble Wernicke's aphasia or jargon aphasia. Often, incoherence is followed by derailment.

8. *Illogicality*: This disorder is described as a pattern of speech in which the speaker does not make the proper inferences from the communicative context. It may take the form of "faulty inductive inferences" or of "conclusions based on faulty premises" (1979a:1320). In either case, actual delusional thinking does not take place. Andreasen adds that illogicality may also occur with nonpatients (1979a:1320).

9. *Clanging:* This speech pattern implies rhythmic relationships, where sound play rather than pragmatic and semantic meaning governs word choice. Lexical redundancy and punning associations are also common.

10. *Neologisms:* When referring to new word formations, Andreasen defines a neologism as "a completely new word or phrase whose derivation cannot be understood" (1979a:1320). Thus, neologisms differ from word approximations because of their anomalous morphological processes.

11. *Word Approximations:* Also known as "paraphasia" or "metonyms," this disorder implies using words in a new and unconventional way, or in developing new words according to the morphological rules of a given language. Most of the time, meaning can be understood from word analogy, though "[its] usage seems peculiar or bizarre" (1979a:1320).

12. *Circumstantiality:* This process refers to a rhetorical style that is also quite common among nonpatients. In answering a question, the speaker chooses to be indirect and brings in numerous details or parenthetical remarks. Interviewers must often interrupt a patient in order to bring her back "to the point" and therefore complete the anamnesis (history-taking process).

13. *Loss of Goal:* This disorder frequently occurs together with derailment. It implies a failure to follow a "chain of thought to its natural conclusion" (1979a:1320). Hence, it results in poor topic continuity processes.

14. *Perseveration:* The speaker continuously repeats words and expressions, bringing up the same topic over and over again. The speaker also persists in reusing the same linguistic forms throughout his discourse although, as Andreasen states, these forms are used "in ways appropriate to their usual meaning" (1979a:1320). Hence, though they may be repetitive, their use seems to be adequate. She also adds that "pause-fillers" (such as "you know," "like") should not be considered perseverations.

15. *Echolalia:* A type of repetition in which the speaker keeps repeating the interviewer's words or phrases by echoing them in "a mocking, mumbling, or staccato intonation" (1979a:1321). This pattern is more common in children's speech.

16. *Blocking:* This process refers to an interruption before the discourse has been completed. This interruption is followed by a moment of silence (that may last from a few seconds to minutes) and an indication from the patient that he cannot recall what "he had been saying or meant to say" (1979a:1321). There must be an acknowledgment from the speaker in order for this pathology to be diagnosed.

17. *Stilted Speech:* The use of speech styles that appear to be pompous, distant, or overpolite, or may be rather outdated or quaint. Speakers use "particular word choices (multisyllabic when monosyllabic alternatives are available and equally appropriate)," extremely polite request forms, or stiff and formal syntactic patterns (1979a:1321).

18. *Self-reference:* The patient continuously refers the topic under discussion "back to himself when someone else is talking"; he also refers neutral topics "to himself when he himself is talking" (1979a:1321).

19. *Paraphasia, Phonemic:* These are "recognizable mispronunciation of a word because sounds or syllables have slipped out of sequence" (1979a:1321). In everyday speech, one faces milder forms of this disorder, which occur as "slips of the tongue"; however, severe forms occur in aphasia.

20. *Paraphasia, Semantic:* The speaker substitutes an inappropriate word in her effort to be specific. She may or may not acknowledge her error and try to correct it. This disorder is typical of Broca's aphasia and Wernicke's aphasia. Testing must be done so as to distinguish it from incoherence.

Appendix B

Summary of the Patient's Stay in the Hospital

The following is a brief summary of the patient's stay in the hospital. It lists the dates, a description of the patient's behavior, and the medication given to her (drugs are listed according to the terminology used in the hospital forms).

Date	Description	Medication
12/14	Admitted to hospital (temporary medication)	Stelazine Fenergan
12/15	Examined in clinical meeting (behavior evaluated as "bizarre"; symptoms of dementia (?); florid and childish behavior; an organic pathology (?); physical exam; restrained in bed)	
12/16	Admitting interview (videotaped) (patient refuses to eat; she refuses to groom herself and presents unstable mood; patient is indifferent to environment; refuses to cooperate in clinical examination) Performs EEG (electroencephalogram)	Nitrazepan Fenergan
12/17	Patient is medicated (neuroleptic medication) (the doses: 10 milligrams of Haldol twice a day, 25 milligrams of Prometazina three times a day, 15 milligrams of Nitrazepan at night) Neurological exam requested	Haldol Prometazina Nitrazepan

Date	Description	Medication
12/18–20	Patient's symptoms deteriorate: she shows withdrawal and immobility; keeps silent and indifferent to environment; she refuses to be fed, maintains stereotyped postures, and displays catatonic behavior	
12/21	All neuroleptic medication is suspended, except for the night medication	Nitrazepan
12/23	Unaltered state; apathy, childish behavior; crying; patient refuses to eat (eats only with help and when coerced)	
12/24	First recovery from the initial psychiatric state; patient identifies place/time; walks without help; still labile and childish; easier to converse with; small mnemonic deficit observed; difficulty with certain movements (like getting dressed, also related to a slight reduction of strength); patient demonstrates cooperative behavior while undergoing complementary examinations	
12/26	Patient cries, eats very little, and says that she needs to get better	
12/29	Patient improves and displays "global orientation," awareness, and cooperative behavior; she complains about a hand paralysis (she says she is unable to hold spoon to eat); patient walks without support from nurse but bends forward and drags feet	
12/30	Patient's overall behavior improves; she still presents muscular hand and leg problems; patient is allowed to leave the hospital on short-term leave	
1/3	Patient returns to the hospital Patient sleeps with no medication	All drugs suspended
1/4	Discharge interview (videotaped)	
1/5	Patient goes to the neurology center for a diagnosis; performs a new EEG	

Date	Description	Medication
1/6	Patient leaves the hospital on a "short-term" basis Patient is cooperative and aware of environment; shows happiness when someone comes closer and even smiles; she still has difficulty in holding small objects or performing movements such as dressing and undressing, putting on shoes, going up or down stairs; tends to remain mostly in the same posture	
1/8	Patient comes back for a checkup; new EEG; another short-term leave	
1/11	Patient is discharged from the hospital	

When she left the hospital, Dona Jurema was considered to have recovered. She was advised to receive outpatient follow-up treatment, which she did for a few months.

Appendix C

The Discharge Interview: Topics, Subtopics, and Components

Topic/subtopic	Speaker	Component	Activity	How It Came About
Birthdate	Doctor	Identifying data	Introducing topic	You were born on what *date*?
Parental status (1): the son	Doctor	Identifying data	Introducing topic	you have a son, don't you?
Parental status (2): the grand-daughter	Doctor	Identifying data	Introducing topic	you also have a granddaughter, don't you?
• Family contacts	Doctor	Identifying data	Introducing subtopic	do you always keep in touch with them?
Place of residence	Doctor	Social history	Introducing topic	where do you live, Dona Jurema?
Present hospitalization	Doctor	Present illness	Introducing topic	Dona Jurema, .. do you remember the day when you came to the hospital? to this hospital?
• Time elapsed	Doctor	Present illness	Introducing subtopic	do you have an idea more or less of how long it's been?
• What happened	Doctor	Present illness	Introducing subtopic	and do you remember what has happened (from then) till now?
• The last event (recalled)	Doctor	Present illness	Introducing subtopic	what was the last thing, let's see, that you recall?
• It happened all of a sudden	Patient	Present illness	Introducing subtopic	it happened all of a sudden.

Topic/subtopic	Speaker	Component	Activity	How It Came About
• The last event (recalled)	Doctor	Present illness	Recycling subtopic	you don't recall what you felt, what you did,
• The first event recalled	Doctor	Present illness	Introducing subtopic	when you- ... were able to recall anything, or *recognize* things, you were already here?
Past hospitalizations	Doctor	Past history	Introducing topic	you have already had other hospitalizations, haven't you?
• Number of admittances	Doctor	Past history	Introducing subtopic	how many hospitalizations have you already had?
• Places	Doctor	Past history	Introd. subtopic	do you remember the *places* where you were hospit*alized?*
• Number of admittances to Dr. Eiras	Doctor	Past history	Introducing subtopic	and how many times were you *there?*
• What used to happen	Doctor	Past history	Introducing subtopic	and do you remember *why* you were hospital*ized* there / what was happening?/
• Feeling different	Doctor	Past history	Introducing subtopic	do you remember, let's see, if you start feeling diff:erent,
• It happens all of a sudden	Patient	Past history	Recycling subtopic	it happens all of a sudden, doctor
The caretaker	Doctor	Social history	Introducing topic	and *who* ... takes care of you?
The youngest sister	Doctor	Social history	Introducing topic	you are the youngest, aren't you?
• Living with Idete	Doctor	Social history	Recycling subtopic	and how long have you been living with her?
• Living by herself	Patient	Social history	Introducing subtopic	I lived two years by myself,
• Living with Idete	Patient	Social history	Recycling subtopic	since then, .. almost always with my sister,
Depressive times	Doctor	Present illness	Introducing topic	do you:: remember, let's see, if you (had already) had periods of being very *sa:d, for no rea:son,*

Topic/subtopic	Speaker	Component	Activity	How It Came About
• Eating habits	Doctor	Present illness	Introducing subtopic	do you stop eating or not?
• Personal cleanliness	Doctor	Present illness	Introducing subtopic	and let's see:, .. you take care of yourself .. /you ba:the,/ you do everything as usual?
Working activities	Doctor	Social history	Introducing topic	but:, do you stop doing what you usually do, like activities, ... home, outside, ... or you ne:ver- stopped, let's see, being active?
• The saleswoman	Patient	Social history	Introducing subtopic	I was a saleswoman, y'know,
• The other job	Doctor	Social history	Introducing subtopic	was that the only job you had?
• Length of time at this job	Doctor	Social history	Introducing subtopic	how many years did you work (there)?
• Quitting this job: the boyfriend	Patient	Social history	Introducing subtopic	then I gave it up becau- I found a boyfriend,
• The saleswoman	Doctor	Social history	Recycling subtopic	before these twelve years, you also didn't work?
• Stopping work altogether	Doctor	Social history	Introducing subtopic	since then, you never worked again?
• The saleswoman	Doctor	Social history	Recycling subtopic	even when you left the Navy, you went on selling?
Depressive times	Doctor	Present illness	Recycling topic	those periods that you spoke to me of: .. sadness, of anguish, do you feel less *enthusiasm* to do things, to work or:
Sleeping problems	Doctor	Present illness	Introducing topic	and sleep, .. do you have any problems sleeping?
• Taking drugs	Patient	Present illness	Introducing subtopic	actually, ⟨after my illness⟩, I started taking medicine,
• Waking up early	Doctor	Present illness	Introducing subtopic	do you remem:ber not sleeping at ni:ght, waking up very ear:ly?

Topic/subtopic	Speaker	Component	Activity	How It Came About
• Length of time	Doctor	Present illness	Introducing subtopic	for how *long* has this been happening?
• Behavior before the illness	Doctor	Present illness	Introducing subtopic	before this wouldn't happen?
• Behavior after the illness	Doctor	Present illness	Introducing subtopic	and now at the hospital ... you wa-, you fall asleep quickly, you sleep well?
Eating problems	Doctor	Present illness	Introducing topic	why wouldn't you eat well here at the hospital?
• Eating at home	Doctor	Present illness	Introducing subtopic	and at home did you eat well?
Mania	Doctor	Past history	Introducing topic	and did you have:: .... *ups and downs,* when you felt ve:ry *happy, ve:ry ... exci:ted, talking a lot, sin:ging,*
Past hospitalizations	Doctor	Past history	Recycling topic	so until: . . six years ago you d- didn- didn't have any problems?
Antecedents	Doctor	Past history	Introducing topic	you did not feel *any::thing* before?
• Physical conditions	Doctor	Past history	Introducing subtopic	not e:ven .. *physical* problems?
The saleswoman	Patient	Social history	Recycling topic	on the contrary, really a saleswoman has to talk a lot,
• The income	Doctor	Social history	Introducing subtopic	did you live on that money?
Psychiatric treatment	Doctor	Past history	Introducing topic	you had never had a psychiatric treatment before?
Family history	Doctor	Family history	Introducing topic	is there anyone in your fa:mily that has: a problem similar to yours?
• The elder brother's illness	Doctor	Family history	Introducing subtopic	what was it that //he had?//
The patient's illness	Patient	Present illness	Recycling topic	it was more or less what I had-, what I have,
• The elder brother's illness	Doctor	Family history	Recycling subtopic	what do you remember let's see, would happen to him?

Topic/subtopic	Speaker	Component	Activity	How It Came About
The patient's illness	Patient	Present illness	Recycling topic	well, my sister is the one who explains, y'know doctor, 'cau:se I lose my::: mind,
• The elder brother's illness	Doctor	Family history	Recycling subtopic	(with) your brother that *also* used to happen?
• The hospitalizations	Doctor	Family history	Introducing subtopic	did he also go to the hospital?
• The brother's illness: duration	Doctor	Family history	Introducing subtopic	was he ill for many years?
• The brother's death	Doctor	Family history	Introducing subtopic	and is he already dead?
• The brother's age	Doctor	Family history	Introducing subtopic	how old was he?
• The brother's health	Doctor	Family history	Introducing subtopic	and he would walk: normally/, he would talk:,
• The brother's living arrangements	Doctor	Family history	Introducing subtopic	but he was li:ving by himself or he was always in the hospital
• The brother's caretaker	Doctor	Family history	Introducing subtopic	and was there someone ta- caring for him?
• The brother's health condition	Doctor	Family history	Recycling subtopic	but did one need: ... to bathe him?
Religious attitudes	Doctor	Social history	Introducing topic	are you religious?
Assessing present health state	Doctor	Chief complaint	Introducing topic	are you having some pro:blems now?
• Complaint: weakness in the arms	Doctor	Chief complaint	Introducing subtopic	you had complained, .. of a weakness in your arms /remember?
• Inability to move hands: getting help in eating	Doctor	Chief complaint	Introducing subtopic	do you eat by yourself?
• Testing the patient's movements	Doctor	Chief complaint	Introducing subtopic	/make this movement/.
• Inability to move hands: bathroom routines	Doctor	Chief complaint	Introducing subtopic	and to go to the bathroom, you also need somebody's help?
• Assessing present health state	Patient	Chief complaint	Recycling subtopic	but I think that now I'm getting much better,
• Specific improvements	Doctor	Chief complaint	Introducing subtopic	what do you think is better?

Topic/subtopic	Speaker	Component	Activity	How It Came About
Physical evaluation: swallowing	Doctor	Review of systems	Introducing topic	have you been able to *swallow* normally again?
Physical evaluation: sight	Doctor	Review of systems	Introducing topic	do you see well?
Physical evaluation: walking	Doctor	Review of systems	Introducing topic	and with *walking*, you're not having any problems?
Plans for the future	Doctor	Social history	Introducing topic	what do you intend to do, ... when you leave (here)?
• Daily routines	Doctor	Social history	Introducing subtopic	what do you normally do, ... /well when you're at home?/
Family contacts: the son	Doctor	Social history	Recycling topic	and your *son*, do you have a lot of contact with him:?
The marriage	Doctor	Social history	Introducing topic	your son is from your marriage, isn't he?
• Length of time	Doctor	Social history	Introducing subtopic	how long (were you married)?
• The separation	Patient	Social history	Introducing subtopic	I separated after twelve years.
• Bearing children	Doctor	Social history	Introducing subtopic	and why did you only have one child?
Family contacts: the son	Doctor	Social history	Recycling topic	and your son:, you-uhm:: often go out with him or he comes to see you::?
Family contacts: the granddaughter	Doctor	Social history	Recycling topic	and your granddaughter, do you *see* her frequently?
Assessing present health state	Doctor	Review of systems	Recycling topic	so now- you ... are feeling well?
• Going home	Doctor	Social history	Introducing subtopic	do you think you can go home and: take care of your things?
Closing talk	Doctor		Introducing topic	so, O.K., Dona Jurema, ... we'll still talk (before you go).

Appendix D

Transcripts

The Admitting Interview

Doctor:
Dona Jurema!

=**Dona Jurema!**

Dona Jurema,
let's talk a little bit. ..

//**O.K.?**

// /**mmm**/

⌐**tell me your FULL name.** =

Patient:

[whining]
ma:ma::! =

[whining]
ma:ma::! ..
/**what is it, (my child)?**/

[staccato and baby talk]
what-is-it-you-wish-to-know =
// = **madam-my-mother,**
don't you already know =
= **everything**
// /**has she not shown you** =
= (**everything?**)

[baby talk]
= **there is no need 'cause the** =
= **doc, doc, doc, the doc-**
papapapapapapapapapapapapa-
[moves face to the right]
Pau-lo-de-A-ze-ve-do-Mur-ti-nho
[looks up, looks down]

[chanting and baby talk]
you yourself know quite well,

258

Doctor:	Patient:
	[gestures with left and right hand, taps on armchair]
	better than I,
[camera focus exclusively on the patient]	**better than anyone,**
	[baby talk]
	when I get,
	to my ward,
	I'm gonna tell,
	[looks further away to the right, bends forward]
	I'm gonna tell,
	[baby talk]
//DONA JURE:MA!	**//this was,**
	[looks down]
	this was,
	this was,
	my secret,
	[looks down]
	this was, ..
	this was,
	and this was,=
=Dona Jurema!=	
	=my secret. ..
[acc]	
DONA JUREMA!	
	[singing; baby talk]
	my dear husband,
	[looks down, turns face slightly to the left]
	knew very well
	he did not come to help,
	his dear dear wife,
	but it does not matter, ..
	his good luck will not last, ..
	that is all I can wish on him=
	=with all my heart:::. (1.5)
	[turns face to the right, looks up at doctor]
[dec]	
DONA JUREMA!	
how long have you been=	
=in the hospital?	
	[sings new tune: church hymn]
	/⌐dressed in white,/
	[looks down]
	[creaky voice; baby talk]
	she appeared,

Doctor:

Patient:
bearing 'round her waist,
the colors of the sky,
[whining and baby talk]
⌐**Hail:, hail:, hail Ma:ry,**
Hail:, hail:, ⌐hail ⌐Ma:ry,
[raises both hands together, raises
head, raises eyes]
[creaky voice]
what more do you want,
[looks at doctor]
umh? ....
[freezes position, shakes and points
right hand]

[dec]
Dona Jure::ma!

[creaky voice]
umh:?
you know that I can't:: = (1.3)
[freezes position, shakes and points
right hand]

[dec]
=⌐you can't =
// = talk to me?

//totototototototo:. ['hhh]
[moves hand back to armchair; looks
beyond doctor]
⌐**the tototô:::!**
[gestures with right hand pointing
straight ahead]

what's totô?

the totô totô::!
[series of pointing gestures]

what's totô?

that totô:::! (1.5)
[pointing gestures]

what is it =
= you're saying?

[acc]
totododododododododododo
/dododododododdodo/ ...
[gestures with hands indicating "who
knows"; looks down]

you don't know, do you. ...
[hhh'] Dona Jure:ma! ..

hi!
[looks up to doctor]

[acc]
how old are you?

Doctor:

[bends torso forward, with microphone in
right hand pointing toward patient; left
arm resting on chair]

Patient:
⌐HI! IVE::TE!! DE:TE!...
[looks to the left, then looks further
away, smiles, and turns to the left,
moving body backward, with back
pressing against the right arm of arm-
chair]

Deti::nha! ....
[looks to the far-left corner of the
room, as if someone were there]

[staccato and baby talk]
so-you-ma'am-will-do-like=
=this-later-so-over-there-at-
home-it-will-be-bad-oh-very-
bad-for-you-it-will-be. ..
[moves closer to doctor;
bends and leans forward]
[acc] [baby talk]
['hhh] but I won't allow=
=((it)),
I won't allow ((it)),
[slowly turns to the right; moves torso
backward and then forward, looks
down; moves both hands backward
and holds chair in a movement to get
up]

[baby talk]
oh, so that's what you wanted to
know ...

[keeps position]

[swings body forward; gets up halfway,
sits back down halfway in armchair;
faces doctor; holds body slightly up,
pressing both hands on armchair]

[camera focus moves away from patient]

[chanting]
I've already said it,
I've already said it,

[camera focus on patient]

I've already said it,
said, said,
[right foot plays with doctor's feet;
looks down at their feet]

['hhh] that now,
that now,

[looks down]

it is the foot of (Tuxa).
[moves feet away; takes slipper off
right foot; points with foot at doctor's
left foot]

Doctor: Patient:
                                               ['hhh] I've already said,
                                               I've already said,
                                               [caresses doctor's foot with her foot]
                                               I've already said,
                                               it's a caress,
                                               [looks up at doctor]
                                               ['hhh] a caress,
                                               a caress,
                                               a caress,
                                               ['hhh] to the little tip of =
                                               = the little toe of my li:ttle =
                                               = granddaughter.

                                               [hymn; baby talk]
                                               ⌐Malie::ne:::,
                                               ⌐Sa:cred Lie::ne:,
                                               [moves feet away, searches for slip-
                                               pers, makes movement up and for-
                                               ward, looking down]

                                               to me she is:: is::,
                                               sanctifi::ed,
[looks straight at patient, leans forward   [gets halfway up from armchair, sits at
and to the right toward patient]   the edge of armchair, looks down and
                                               holds posture]

                                               [chanting, baby talk]
                                               ['hhh] that's why,
                                               that's why::: y:::. ...
                                               ['hhh] that's why,
                                               that's why::: y:::. ...
                                               ['hhh] THAT'S WHY,
                                               THAT'S WHY::: Y:::. ...

                                               [whimpering, baby talk]
                                               ['hhh] ⌐aren't you going to =
                                               = ask me questions now? =

                                               [raises head, holds body halfway up,
                                               hands pressing on chair, looks at
                                               doctor]

= I'm going to ask,
Dona Jure:ma. =

                                               [sighing]
                                               = what are you going to ask?
                                               [stands and holds body halfway up]

    [acc]
⌐WHERE DO YOU LIVE? ...

Doctor:	Patient:
	[coarse voice, baby talk]
	I live over there with the=
	=pope,
	over there in the Lome. ...
[dec]	
you live with the pope.=	
	=yes,
//you do?	//over there in the Lome.
WHAT'S YOUR FULL NAME?	
	will you believe me if I=
	=say it right? ...
⌐I'll believe you.=	
	=you know why?=
=mmm? ...	
	you don't know why.= (1.2)
what is it=	[acc]
=I don't know?	//let me speak because, ..
	because I know my full=
	na:::::me=
	[baby talk]
	=Holy Mother of God. (see)
⌐so tell me your=	
=full name.=	
	=no, only if you have, (1.3)
	do you have?
	[acc]
	⌐oh, ma:ma!/
	[bends over to get slipper]
have what?	
	[acc]
	ma:ma::! ...
mmm?	
	[acc]
	ma:ma::! ma:ma::! ...
	she says she has, ma:ma::...
	she says we can leave,
	ma:ma:: ...
	[picks slipper up, pushes it away to the right, moves torso and right leg to the right]
	then ask to be excused,
	my child. ..
	[looks at slippers; puts slipper on right foot]
	it's like this that we ask ..
	[bends down and forward, bends right]
	so much curiosity, ['hhh] ..

Doctor:

Patient:
they wanted to have,
didn't they child, ['hhh] ...
          [acc]
to: know about you,
right child,
just because- ['hhh]
they saw you barefooted (out=
=of doors), right child, ['hhh]
they thought that you had-

Dona Jure:ma!

popopodedededddddd
Shsssssssssssssssssssssss
[raises head, looks up, brings
right finger to mouth to
indicate silence, looks beyond
the doctor, points and nods,
looks straight ahead with eyes wide-
open]

what's happening over there?

Shsssssssssssssssssssss
['hhh] shssssssssssss
['hhh] shssssssssssss
[points and nods, turns
sideways to the right, moves
left arm to the right, bends
down, looks down to the right]

Dona JuRE:MA!

[dec]
⌐thank God! ....
[interrupts movement, raises head,
looks up, turns to doctor and smiles]

[dec]
thank God, for what?

it's all over. ....
[holds position and smiles]

     [acc]
what is over?

          [dec]
⌐Jurema is a little dizzy
y'know.
[turns torso and head to face doctor,
moves left hand down and grabs arm-
chair]

/mmm/ .

['hhh] could you give ⌐my=
=dear sister a glass of=
=water,
['hhh] she didn't even know=

Doctor:	Patient:
	=that this would happen to=
	=her. ..
	you are very polite. ....
	[acc]
	/then, I only (knew), ...
	/then, I only (knew),
[following the	[moves forward, leans forward and
patient's gestures]	down, looks down, then repeats
	movement to get up]
	[coarse voice] [acc]
	see, mother!
	['hhh] see, mother!
	she even forgot the glass of=
	=water,
	y'see, oh mother.
	[baby talk]
	['hhh] that's why:,
	that's why:,
	[dec]
	⌜oh, tha:t's why:,
	⌜OII., TIIA.;T'S WIIY.!
	that's why Ive-
	i-, i-, i-. ..
	[coarse voice]
	∟can you send for=
	=Iveti (for me)?
	[looks up at doctor]
who's Iveti?	
	[coarse voice, baby talk]
	=she's the maid ((who works))=
	=at my house,
	[looks down and sideways to the left]
	at my sister's,
	not at my house,
	['hhh] at my sister's house.
[acc]	you // give the orders
//what's the name=	(there)?=
of your sister?	=I- if I speak=
	=⟨propiproperly⟩,
	would you let me say,
	['hhh] that it is=
	=Idetinha?....
	[turns head to the right]
[dec]	
who's Idetinha,	
your sister?=	
	=my sister.=
=yeah::?	

Doctor:

Patient:
[baby talk]
do you believe ((me))? ....
really believe ((me))? ...

[acc]   can I go then? ...
//no, we'll still =   //can I?
= talk for a little =
= while, O.K.? =

                                         = no, mother,
                                         [acc]
                                         /I'm veryveryveryvery tired./
                                         ['hhh] excuse me,
                                         [series of nods] [baby talk]
                                         but let's leave it for another
                                         day, ..
                                         [series of nods]
[comes closer]   ['hhh] 'cause one can't make
                                         any noise here y'know mother
                                         'cause-,
                                         ['hhh] 'cause
                                         herehereherehereherehere.
                                         ['hhh] I'll never tell!
                                         I'll never tell!
                                         I'll never tell!
                                         I'll never tell!
                                         ['hhh] so much so that he
                                         asked me, ⟨that he will ⟨⟨ha-
                                         ha-⟩⟩havehavehavehavehave-

⌐HERE where,
Dona Jurema? =   [acc] [baby talk]
                                         = here! here! here! =
                                         [bends over, looks down, speaks into
                                         microphone]

= where are you? ..
                                         [dec]
                                         HERE! ...

mmm? ..
                                         here! =
= what place is this =
= "here" you're at now? ..

                                              [dec]
                                         I am in a hospital. =
                                         [moves torso and head backward,
                                         raises head slightly, puts both hands on
                                         armchair, looks down]

  [acc]
= //which hospital?   //I thought I'd be going to =
                                         = another hospital, =

= mmm. =

Doctor:

Patient:
[baby talk]
= and I ended up in a very=
= beautiful hospital. ...

⌜do you know this=
=hospital HERE?=

=no one knows it. ..

no: one knows it?=

=no one in this world....

rea:lly?
//and you've been=
= in this hospital=
=for how long?=

// only me!

=oh::::::
[smiles]
in this vastness of this ...
Rio de Janeiro,
[looks to the right]
see didn't I say that we'd=
[coarse voice] [baby talk]
=have pou::ring rain,
[looks to the far right,
slightly raises head and eyes]

[baby talk]
pou::ring rain,
[leans to the right, away from
doctor]
[baby talk]
pou:ring rain.
see how even the glass chair
of .. the President ((of this
place)) got wet.
[moves backward, turns left,
looks down]
[baby talk]
is it the President ((of this
place)), mother? ...
I don't know,
you are the one who knows,
can I get ((it))? ...

[acc]
//what do you want=
to get?=

// (no, my child.)

[acc] [shaky voice]
=nothing, nothing, mother,
nothing.
[bends forward and down, looks
down]

mmm.

Doctor:

Patient:
I'm afraid of the rain...
[bends forward]
Francisco has warned us,
[moves slightly backward]
ma:ma. ...
right, ma:ma? ... ['hhh]
[looks down]
is everything fine? ...
everything all right? ..
is this really how he =
=wanted things? (1.2)
[looks up to the right and
tightens lips]

⌐oh:::::.
[series of nods]
⌐oh:::::.
[looks down and straight ahead, past
the doctor]
['hhh] if I only knew:!
['hhh] Dona JuRE:MA, ...   [turns to the doctor
is it daytime or   with puzzled look;
nighttime right now? ....   smiles; tightens lips]
HUH? (2.5)
⌐is it day or night? (23.5)

[turns head and eyes past doctor, to
the far left; raises eyebrows, raises left
hand in a very slow movement, then
opens her hand; eyes follow hand
movement; rests right hand on the lap;
lowers left hand and makes eye contact with the doctor; moves left hand
toward the doctor's microphone;
touches microphone with fingertips,
then points to door on the left; lowers left hand and presses both hands
against the arms of the armchair in a
gesture to get up: she holds the armchair, looks down, swinging herself
forward; gets up halfway and rearranges sitting position to face the doctor.]

        [acc]
⌐tell me what's =   [touches doctor's right
=happening. ..   hand; points at doctor and
speak to me! ....   at herself: points back and
what is this? (3.5)   forth as in a child's game]
what is this? ...
mmm? (2.5)

Doctor:

explain to me =
<u>=what it is.</u> (5.5)

Patient:

[points back and forth;
series of nods]

[singing]
⌜"tonação" and "tonação,"
[turns to the right; looks
down, holds the armchair,
rearranges herself on the
armchair]

[singing]
⌜"tonação" and "tonação,"

[coarse voice]
⌜it's mother,
it's my dear mother,
[bends down, bends over, as if to get
something on the floor]
[baby talk]
['hhh] ⌊(she) didn't know =
=that it was her good friend,
['hhh] that's why she spoke,
['hhh] of someone named Dona =
=Consuelo.
oh, ohohohohohohoh.
slowly, slowly, slowly,
'cause it was, waswaswa-
[acc]
['hhh] didn't I say so, Deta.
didn't I say Deta =
=that it had- ['hhh]
popopopopopopopopopopo =
[raises herself up, both hands
on the armchair, looks down]
=popopopopopopo.
[raises head and torso, looks
at the doctor, puts both hands on
the armchair; shakes head,
turns and looks to the left]
popopo:!
[looks at the doctor] [nods]
popopopopopopopopopopopo-
popo.
[gestures with left hand: points at
herself and at the doctor]
((you)) didn't popo? Then!
(5.5)
[raises both hands; gestures
with hands indicating "who
knows"; looks straight ahead,
nods and tightens lips]

Doctor:

Patient:
[dec] [coarse voice]
⌊then, ..
[turns right, looks down]
until my husband divorced
((me)). ...
[bends down]

see! ...
[turns left, toward the doctor]
[acc]
see, mother, see,
why one can't look! =
[faces the doctor]

[acc]
= **what can't one look at?**

⌊**one can't look, mother.**
[moves forward, raises right
hand toward the doctor]

[acc] [baby talk]
where I come from, y'know,
[smiles; right hand playing
with the doctor's hair]
['hhh] **where I come from,**
mother,
[smiles and plays with doctor's hair]
⌊**excuse my bad breath I** =
= **haven't got up yet, y'know**
mother, =
[smiles and plays with doctor's hair]

= **mmm.** =

[baby talk]
= ⌊**but where I come from,**
mother, ['hhh] **everything one** =
= **says must be true,**
isn't that true?
[plays as if caressing the doctor]

[baby talk]
⌈**tha:t's why!**

Dona JuRE:ma!

⌈**tha:t's why,**
that's why I saw:: ((it)). ...
[series of smiles]
and you told me that I =
= **shouldn't even say a::nything ...**
[smiles, still holding the doctor's hair]
['hhh] **and I sai::d ...**
and ((it)) stayed-

Doctor:

=you got a little hair?=

and what will you do=
=with this little hair?=

[acc]
can you what?=

=what is this?

=oh:, split from here?=

you want to leave?=

no:, let's talk=
=a little bit more,
//O.K.?

it's time for what?=

to go where?=

yeah:.

Patient:
[acc] [baby talk]
now ⟨(it's the prettiest thing
on Earth)⟩,
[acc]
⌐you will see.
you will see.
['hhh] I got it!
[as if holding a strand of hair, moves
hand and torso backward]

[baby talk]
I got a little hair.=
[nods; lowers right hand]

[baby talk]
=a little hair.
[looks at doctor]

=can I split? . . .

=split.=

split from here.=

=yeah:, can I?

=(I know.) ...
[looks down]

//no. it's time. ...
[shakes head, sits back]

=it's time for me to go. ..
[raises head and eyes, lowers head
and eyes]

=to go where? ...
[raises head higher and tosses it back]

[acc]
and what do you know?
[raises left hand, with pointing gesture, tosses head back slightly]

what do you know? ....
[lowers head, bends torso forward,

Doctor:

⌜WHAT PATH DID YOU
=TAKE TO GET HERE?=

⌜=from your WARD?=

//WHAT PLACES DID=
=YOU GO BY?

//=no?=

//⌜DID YOU SEE=
=SOME LITTLE ANIMAL=
OUT THERE,
//‾WHEN YOU WERE=
=ON YOUR WAY HERE?
  [acc]
Huh:, Dona Jure:ma?=

a little ant?

what about the other=
=animal you showed=
//=me outside?=

=which was it?=

=mmm.

Patient:

holds armchair with both hands, in a
position to get up; looks down]

⌞(I said so,) y'see.
[looks down, moves feet]

= a ve::ry long jour:ney.=

=yeah:.
//⌞but at my a:ge.

I have no idea where I've
//been, my child,
only God knows and my guardian
angel.
['hhh] oh: that's what I=
=wanted to know,
OH::: mother.
[slowly raises chest and head]

[acc]
so that was it.
[looks up]
see how he (saw). ...
[looks down]
see how he knew that was it.
// see how-

//see how you got it right?

[singing]
=I saw a little ant:!
[singing]
I saw a little ant:!

[baby talk]
//=the otherotherother
animal?=

=it's a ((grown-up)).
we cannot talk about=
=grown:-ups.=

we can only talk about=
=li:ttle people.

Doctor:

Patient:
and me, since I am a =
= little midget-
[singing and baby talk]
⌐that's why:!
⌐that's why:!
⌐that's why:, why:. ...
            [acc]
['hhh]⌐that's why!
that's why!
that's why!
[creaky voice]
that's why, <u>ma:ma::</u>! <u>ma:ma::</u>!
<u>ma:ma::! ma:ma::</u>!
[crying]
that's why <u>ma:ma::</u>!

⌐DO YOU REMEMBER PASSING =
= BY A GARDEN ...
SEEING SOME CHICKENS =
= OUT THERE?

[whining]
⌐I saw a little chick –
[gets up and sits on the arm of the
armchair; looks down]
= as I was getting here,

//REA:LLY? ....

//ma:ma.
[moves closer to the doctor]

AND ONCE YOU GOT HERE,
.. YOU WALKED FURTHER ..
YOU WENT   <u>UPSTAIRS?</u>

I went up a lon:::g stairway,
mother! =
[slowly raises her head]

= LARGE OR SMALL? =

= ⟨but ((that)) was the
stairway of ((my)) life⟩.
[raises eyes, turns to the right]

= oh, that was the stair- =
= way of ((your)) life? =

= yeah:. a house with a home,
another house without a home,
//a house with a home,

//mmm::.

another house without without =
= without a home.
isn't it, isn't it funny. ...
so isn't it my son-
look how they are.
[raises her head up high,
looks to the extreme right]
look how they are. ...

Doctor:

DONA JURE:MA!

   [acc]
tell me something.

I already saw=
=you today?=

what? what time did=
=I see you?=

=when was that?=

[dec]
when was it that=
=you saw me?

[looks at patient's
right foot]

Patient:
look how they look.
[moves sideways, still staring
at the same corner]
look how they look. ...
look- dadadadadadadadada-
eeeeeeeeeeeeeeeeededede
bebebebebebebebebebebe
[turns left, wide-open eyes]

bebebebebebebebebe
[turns right; faces the doctor]

[baby talk; chanting]
you already saw me! ...
[smiles, looks at the doctor]

[baby talk, chanting]
=you already ⟨forgot ((me))!⟩
[nods]

[baby talk; chanting]
=it was I that saw you!=
[smiles; short nod]

[baby talk; chanting]
=you did not see me.
[looks down] (2.3)

[looks up at the doctor]

[acc] [baby talk]
you know yourself quite well,
[looks up and away; looks
down, moves legs and feet]
better than I,
that everything one does here=
=in this world,
is done in a hurry,
[baby talk]
['hhh] in a hurry,

[acc] [baby talk]
now ⟨that mother,⟩
[touches slippers with right
foot]

now mother will like ((it)).
...

Doctor:	Patient:
	[baby talk]
	'cause she would often ask
	(yesterday) my sonny,
	my sonny,
	"oh my sonny,"
	that was a lie, see. ..
	that was a lie. ..
	'cause everybody lies,
[looks at patient]	why can't my dear mother lie=
	=too, poor thing she only
	wanted a little thing,
	[rearranges herself on the seat, facing the doctor again; looking down]
	and I didn't know anything,
	[baby talk]
	that's why I hurt her. ...
	that's why. ...
	[touches doctor's left foot with her left foot, then touches doctor's right foot]
	[baby talk]
	that's why she-
	that's why I tested her.
	and she ((knows))
//⌐Dona Jure:ma!	//now she found out. ...
Dona Jurema!	[gets up and sits on the arm of the armchair]
do you want to walk=	
=a little bit? (1.2)	WHAT? ...
	[bends over; answers directly into the microphone; sits facing the micro-phone]
do you want to walk=	
=a bit around here? ..	[dec] [in Spanish]
	['hhh] WALK WHERE? ....
walk around here=	[in Spanish]
=// (in this place).	//ON THE FLOOR? ...
yeah.=	[acc] [in Spanish]
	=ON THE FLOOR?=
=yeah, /on the floor./=	[in Spanish]
	=ON THE FLOOR? ..
	[in Portuguese]
	oh! on the floor?=

Doctor:
= you want to walk? =

= yeah. =

Patient:

= on the floor? =

[baby talk]
= my sonny allows it? ...
but-, my so::nny,
[turns to the right: moves
torso, head, and eye gaze]
[baby talk]
it was so sim:ple, see!
see ma:ma::!
[moves legs, rearranges
sitting position, gets up]

[acc]
// can you stand up =
= on your own?

// see ma:ma::!
// see ma:ma::!
only if sonny helps me. ....
['hhh] my sonny will help me?
...
[looks at doctor]

you want me to help =
= you to walk a little bit? =

= no, I want my sonny. ....

where's your son? =

[acc]
= you send him to hell. ...

where's your son? =

= you know that you knew. ....
everythingeverything that I
wanted. ....
[dec]
you are the one who knows.
....
[acc]
it's the mother,
[raises her head and neck,
raises chest and shoulders]
it's the mother,
it's the mother,
it's the mother,
it's the mother,
it's the mother,
it's the mother,
it's the mother, UHM:::::::!
[dec]
it's the mother of her =
= /so:::nny!/
[relaxes posture and lowers shoulders,
neck, and chest; bends slightly for-
ward]

Doctor:

what have I =
// = (asked you?)

mmm:.

= who is Grandma Lena?

mmm:.

Dona JuRE:MA! ..

Patient:
/and her mother ... thought/
.. that- ⟨it was very-⟩
cololololololololololo.
[comes closer and closer to
the microphone and to the doctor]
lalalalalalalalalalala.
[raises left hand, touches the doctor's
head and face]
côcôcôcôcôcôcôcôcôcô.
ngungungugungungungung.
dedededededededededede.
[moves left hand away, follows right
hand movement to the right, turns to
the right]
dedededededede ⌜DEDEDEDE-
DEDE.
[dec] [sighs]
⌜the dédédé! ...
[points to the right; turns to the doctor on the left]

[looks down; turns to the right, rubs
her left ear]

[breathing hard]
did I answer your question?
(1.2)
            [dec]
//it may be in those days- ..
[looking down while still
rubbing her left ear]

Grandma Lena is the one =
= who knows, ..
[baby talk]
I'm gonna ask Grandma =
= Lena, O.K? =

my grandma who is up in =
= heaven.

can I speak Grandma Lena? ....
gi:ve in. ..
⌊then give in. ...
give in, Jurema give in,
[lowers left hand, touches face, turns
slightly to the left, looks down]
give in, give in,
give in, give in,
['hhh] give in for your own =

Doctor:	Patient:
	=good. for your own good. the young lady is also= =telling you, .. it's for your own good, ... then listen, listen, listen, listen, listen, listen, listen, listen, listen.
//Dona Jurema!	//so I listen.= [turns head and torso slightly to the left]
=look, ... get up and walk= =//a little bit.	// (it was because of this.) [turns head and torso to the left]
	[baby talk] /only ⟨if Francisco allows⟩/ [looks down, looks up at the doctor]
who is Francisco?	FRAN-CIS-QUI-NHO! (little Francisco)
who's that? ...	my LI:TTLE BOY. [looks down and up, looks at the doctor]
your son? //how old is he?	//yeah. 'round forty-two more or less. [looks away and to the right]
	[acc] he's the one that knows more or less I know nothing= [turns to the right]
[dec] =//I see.	[coarse voice] //nothingnothingnothing= =(nothing.) [looks to the far right and smiles]
[acc] //what other children= =do you have?	// /( ) who is right./
	[whimpering] =I don't have any other children.= [looks away to the right]
=no?=	=how sad, you know why?=

Doctor:
=mmm?=

Patient:

=I didn't know:::. ...
[acc] [baby talk]
that's why my sister Idete=
=said: "y'see Jurema,"
[lowers her head]
"you have only one child. ..
thank the good Lord."
[beats on chest with right hand,
looks at the camera; hand beat follows
the pace of her statements]
    [acc]
"thank the good Lord.
thank the good Lord."
and I thanked the good Lord.
[baby talk]
['hhh] do you believe ((it)),
do you believe ((it)),
['hhh] if you want to kneel,
[moves forward; gets up]
you may kneel.
['hhh] she may kneel down=
[holds herself onto the table
and kneels down]

[dcc]
='cause no one will do anything
to her:. ...

[moves backward on the chair with   [bows down, kneels down, rests
microphone in the left hand]   head on left arm, which is touching
    the table]

I know. ..
'cause my son is here close to
me. ..

[moves slightly   [raises her head]
forward]

I know very well what to do,
[gets up and sits down; looks
down]
    [acc]

[leans forward to the left, with   ['hhh] you-
microphone on the left hand]   dodododododododo-
you- see,
see-see-see, see-see.
[whining]
['hhh] y'see, ma:ma::. (3.1)
[turns to the doctor]

Doctor:
['hhh] **Dona Jure:ma!**

=⌈**is it daytime or is**
it nighttime?=

[acc]
you can't hear me? ...

[brings microphone closer
to the patient]

Patient:

[dec]
⌊**what?**=
[looks at the doctor]

=⌊**what?** ...

[dec]
ma'am let me see first. ....
[turns to the camera, to the
right, looks at the camera]
if the tree is green,
[baby talk]
it signals rain,
if the tree is yellow, ..
[acc]
it signals-
[chanting] [baby talk]
['hhh] **I'm going to die::!**
[raises herself up on the
armchair, looks at the camera]
['hhh] **I'm going to die:::!**

[dec] [baby talk]
that's why, ..
[moves head slightly to the
left]
that's why, ..
[moves head to the right,
toward the camera]

[baby talk]
that's why Chico didn't want=
=**to call the police.** ..
that's why, ..
that's why, ..
that's why, ..
['hhh] ⌊**that's why!** ...

[acc] [breathing hard]
['hhh] ⌊**oh!!!**
oh how ⌊**exhausting,**
Grandma Lena! ...

[camera focus moves to the
extreme right and stops on an
air conditioner]

    [acc]
you're tired,
/**Dona Jurema?**/

//⌊**oh, Grandma Lena!**
⌊**oh, Grandma Lena,**
here on Earth only if one-

Doctor:

Patient:
[looks down, leans forward, moves legs]
[acc]
you wanted to know?
I I don't know anything. ..
y'see, Grandma Lena?
that's it, sis. ...
((dear)) sis(ter). ...
[baby talk]
I only know it was like this,
I only know I used to call=
=Idetinha Detinha, ..
then later I started to call=
=her sis:. ..
[smiles]
she was plea:::sed,
[smiles, raises head and torso]
plea:::sed,
[smiles, bends forward and speaks to the microphone]
but then:::,
[looks down, raises head slowly, moves torso backward]
she is ve:::ry,
she is ve:::ry,
[chanting and baby talk]
that's what I wanted!
that's what I wanted!
that's what I wanted!
that's what I wanted!

//Dona Jure:ma!

//['hhh] then the doc-
[turns to the doctor, looks at the microphone, speaks to the microphone]
my mymymymymymymymymymy
['hhh] my mymymymymymymy
mymymymymymymy-
mymmmmmmmm
[gets closer to the microphone; faces the doctor; speaks to the microphone]
dododo doc doc ooooo-ofofof
ofofofofofofofofofofofofofofof-
[turns face and torso to the right, looks up, looks at the camera and smiles]
of te::levision, ma:ma!. ....
ma:ma!=.

=where's the television?

uhm:? ..

ma:ma::!. ....
[looks at the camera and addresses it]

Doctor:

is there a television =
= over there?
[faces the camera and turns
back to the patient]

Patient:
ma:ma::!. (1.8)

then it's with you. ...
[faces the camera]

[acc]
then it's been since that =
= time, ma:ma::? ...
then only now that I know,
ma:ma:: ....
I was a little silly girl,
I didn't know anything. ..
I only knew how to suck my
thumb. (6.1)
[lifts right hand and puts
thumb in mouth, closes
eyes, turns to the doctor,
opens eyes, takes thumb out of
mouth]

[baby talk] [dec]
if you want to believe ((me)) =
= you can believe ((me)).
those who don't want to =
= they may do this. ...
[makes a cross on the microphone
with right finger; looks down;
makes a movement to get up]

[baby talk] [acc]
I'm leaving 'cause it's =
= already very late. ...
[looks up at the camera]
['hhh] "excuse me." ..
only by Grandma Lena =
= will I ask to be excused. ...
[looks down, moves backward]
['hhh] "excuse me,
Grandma Lena, excuse me."
[bends down]
... that's it. y'see.
this is it.
[keeps looking down, moves farther
backward, as if putting on her slippers]
see. ...
see so much idle curiosity,

[moves microphone to right
hand; follows patient's
movements]

Doctor:

[doctor brings microphone
closer to patient]

[moves backward,
looks at patient]

//yes, you can.

Patient:
y'see, mother. ...
see mother. ...
[puts slippers on,
takes slippers off]
why ((one)) couldn't, mother?
.... only my son knows. ...
but ⟨today⟩ my son came to=
=see me. ... oh:: good! ...
I thought that he ⟨hadn't⟩=
=hadn't come ..
[baby talk]
then I will wait for a little=
=while, can I wait? ....
⌊the young lady ⟨says that=
[bends down to get slippers]
=(here)⟩ I am the boss. ..
I am not the boss. ..
(I) still need need to reach a
bit more. ..
the young lady says that I am=
=the one who knows. ..
I am the one who knows. ..
⌐"you are the one who knows."
.. OH::::,
[stops movements; raises torso, head
and eyes to the camera]
['hhh] ⌐OH::::,
['hhh] ⌐OH::::,

[baby talk]
⌐tha:::t's why:. ...
⌐that's why Chico,
[looks down]
⟨last night-⟩ ...
came home. .. to get: me, ...
to ta:ke ((me)), ...
to the hos:pital. ....
to Pener Hospital. ...
do you know what "pener" is?
... not "peneu." .. "peneu."
..do you know what "peneu" is?
['hhh] no, it's my son's car ..
do you know who my son is? ..
no:, ((he's)) the most sacred
thing in the world. ...
Can I stand upupupupupupup-
//upupupupup?
cancancancancancancancan.
cancancancancancancan?

Doctor: Patient:
can you get up=
// =by ⌐yourself?

                                           //can̲ca̲n? (1.6)
                                           do yo͟u believe ((me))?

The Discharge Interview

[nonverbal information: both participants are in baseline postures[1]]

                         [acc]
Doctor: ⌐**You were born on what date?** ..
Patient: **on January 11** ..
                         [nods]

                         [acc]
Doctor: ⌊**of what year?**
Patient: **of 1921. ... I am sixty-one.=**
                         [nods]   [smiles]   [acc]
Doctor: **=you have a son, don't you?**
           [nods]
Patient: ⌊**I have a son.**
                                        [nods]   [short smile]
Doctor: **what's his name?=**
Patient: **=Francisco Ferreira de Souza. ...**
                         [dec]
Doctor: **and how old is he now?** ..
Patient: **he's- about forty-two.**
           [looks away, looks at doctor and smiles]
Doctor: **/mmm/** ...
                                                   [acc]
           you also have a granddaughter, don't you?=
Patient: **I've got a ((little)) sixteen-year-old granddaughter.** (1.4)
           [raises head]   [smiles]
Doctor: **//mmm//**
Patient: **she's my li:fe.**
           [raises head, looks up, big smile]
Doctor: **do you- really?=**
Patient: **=really. I am crazy (about her). I like=**
           =(her) ve-   [smiling]
Doctor: ⌊**do you take care of her?=**
Patient: **=I don't take care of her because my=**
           =daughter-in-law takes very good care, y'know....
                         [short smile]
           I just see her, and all that. (I don't)
Doctor: **do you always k̲e̲e̲p̲ ̲i̲n̲ ̲t̲o̲u̲c̲h̲ with them?**
Patient: **oh, yes, a̲l̲w̲a̲y̲s̲.** ..
                         [nods]
           well as much as possible I do, y'know=
           =doctor. ...
           [nods and smiles, looks at doctor]

Doctor: ⌜where do you live, Dona Jurema?
Patient: what?=
[tightens lips and frowns]
Doctor: =//you-//
Patient: ⌞I live with my sister. (1.2)
[series of short nods]
Dona Ide:te, Dona Tere:za,
[series of short nods]
161 Alvorada Avenue apartment 1001.
[series of short nods, smile]
Doctor: you live with your two sisters, don't you?
Patient: yes, ... the three of us live together. ..
[nods]   [tightens lips and frowns]
Doctor: /mmm./
⌜Dona Jurema, .. do you remember the day=
=that you came to the hospital? to this=
=hospital?
Patient: =no, I don't remember doctor.
[looks down, to the right; shakes head]
Doctor: /you don't remember./
Patient: /I don't (remember)/
[looks at the doctor; tightens lips]
Doctor: do you have any idea of how long it's been?
Patient: about twenty days or so, hasn't it been=
=doctor?
Doctor: /about twenty days or so./
Patient: ⁻yeah, I think so, hasn't it.
Doctor: ⌞mmm.
and do you remember what happened from then=
=(to now)?=
Patient: ▪no, I remember nothing, nothing, nothing,=
=nothing.   [shakes head]
Doctor: =/you don't remember?/
Patient: nothing, nothing, nothing, nothing.
[looks down; looks up; shakes head]
Doctor: ⌜=well, what was the last thing that you=
=remember? ...
[raises head slightly]
Patient: [looks down; tightens lips]
Doctor: from- from- from- the beginning of- of-=
=your illness, what is it that you remember?
[gestures with right hand]
/what did you have-/
Patient: ⌞I didn't have anything, doctor=
[looks up; gestures with left hand]
Doctor: =/you weren't feeling anything./
Patient: it was all of a sudden. I wasn't feeling=
=anything, anything, anything.=
[series of head shakes]
Doctor: =what was it that happened all of a sudden?
[gestures with both hands]

Doctor: explain it to us. =
           [folds both hands]
Patient: = all of a sudden I lost ah .. my mind,
                         [turns both hands outward]
           my senses, y'know, ...
                         [begins to turn hands inward]
           I didn't see anything anymore,
           [brings hands back to baseline position]
           when I could see again I was here in the =
           = hospital, y'know. (1.7)
           [series of nods from doctor]
           but I did not see anything that happened to =
           = me (y'know)
Doctor: you don't remember what you fel::t, what you
           di:d, /you don't remember./
           [moves head down and to the side]
Patient: no. nothing, nothing, nothing. ..
           [shakes head; looks down]
Doctor: //mmm, mmm// ...
           [acc]
           when you- ... were able to recall anything,
           [series of gestures with right hand]
           or recognize things,
           [gestures with right hand]
           you were already in here? =
           [points down]
Patient: = I was already in here. (1.9)
           [nods]
Doctor: /mmm./
           [short nods]
Patient: I was already here. =
           [series of nods]
Doctor: = /mmm, mmm./ (2.1)
           [series of short nods]

           [acc]
           you have already had other hospitalizations,
           [raises head slightly; moves torso slightly forward and then back]
           haven't you?
Patient: yes doctor. unfortunately yes, y'see.
           [nods]   [nods]
Doctor: how many hospitalizations, have you had? =
           [holds still and looks at patient]
Patient: = well:, I think some six:, more or less.
           [looks away and down; looks up at doctor and
           smiles]
Doctor: do you remember the places, where you were =
           = hospitalized? = [moves face to the left;
           slight hand gesture; nods]

Patient: = I remember, Doutor-Eiras. ...
[nods]
I've been often to Doutor-Eiras, y'know. =
[nods]   [nods]

Doctor: = **and how often were you <u>there</u>?**
[stretches both hands; rests hands on right
knee; then left hand on left thigh, turns
head to the right]

Patient: **I think two or three times. ...**
[looks away to the right; looks at doctor]

Doctor: **and do you remember why you were hospitalized
there?**
[slight body movement toward the patient;
gestures with left hand]
/what was happening?/

Patient: **the same thing,**
[opens hands outward]
all of a sudden, I'm fine, fine,
all of a sudden, right away
I lose my mind, I lose my senses, doctor
y'know ....
and that's what happens to me. (1.3)
[hands resume baseline position]

Doctor: ⌐**do you remember, let's see:,**
[torso inclination toward the patient;
gestures with left arm and hands]
if you begin to feel diffe:rent,
[gestures with hands; looks at the patient]
                    [acc]
you begin to feel something different than =
= **usual?** =   [hand gestures]

Patient: = **no, nothing, nothing, nothing.**
[shakes head]   [looks down]
the thing is all of a sudden, doctor. =
[looks up]   [looks at doctor]

Doctor: = **what happens all of a sudden with you?** ..
[gestures with both hands]

Patient: ⌐**all of a sudden** ⌐**I .. lose my mind, ...**
[turns head to the left]
I don't see anything anymore,
[turns hands outward; turns head
to the left, toward the doctor]
by the time I can see I'm hospitalized.
[turns hands inward, nods]

Doctor: //mmm, mmm// ...
[series of nods]

Patient: **y'see ... I don't remember anything that
happens. ...** [shakes head]
[looks down]

Doctor: you <u>never</u> remember? =
Patient: = I <u>ne:ver</u> remember.
Doctor: ⌐<u>of all these hospitalizations</u>, /you
           never remember?/   [raises right hand;
                                 points to the left]
Patient: ⌐no, ... [looks down]
           I ne:ver remembered. (1.5)
           [shakes head; looks up; looks at doctor]
Doctor: mmm. and <u>you</u>:... uhm.. who takes care of you,
           [nods] [moves head slightly to the right]
           who looks after you, /who is your caretaker?/
           [nods; gestures with right hand; nods]
Patient: my sister, y'know, Idete.
           [nods]   ⌐[nods; smiles]
Doctor: └/your sister./ =
Patient: = yes, my sister. =
Doctor: = you're the youngest, aren't you? =
           [slight movement to the right, toward the patient]
Patient: = I'm the youngest of them.
              [nods]   [nods]
Doctor: mmm ...
           [turns head slightly to the left]
Patient: though I'm already a grandma,
                               [smiles]
           a little old lady, I am the youngest. ..
              [smiles]   [large smile]
Doctor: mmm. .. [smiles]
Patient: I am sixty-one years old.
           [nods and smiles]
Doctor: /I see./ ...
           [smiles]
Patient: ⌐Idete is (   )
Doctor: └and how long have you been living there =
           = with her?
           [moves torso to the left, bends to the left, presses both hands together]
Patient: it's ⟨been many years already⟩, right. ..
           [looks down to the right; looks at doctor]
Doctor: yeah. ..
Patient: always with her. ... I lived two years by myself, (1.5)
           [camera focus exclusively on the patient; patient
           looks up; looks at doctor]
           I had a room, quite good,
           [series of nods]
           I rented it from a la:dy, quite nice,
                               [series of nods]
Doctor: mmm.
Patient: I lived for two years. .... since then, ..
           [nods; looks up]   [shakes head]
           I've lived always with my sister, ..

Patient: [looks down to the right and away from the
           doctor]
           most of the time with my sister, really.
           [nods and tightens lips]
Doctor: mmm, mmm. ....
                  [dec]
           ⌐do you:: remember, let's see,
           if you had periods of being very <u>sa:d</u>,
           for no <u>rea:son</u>, =
Patient: = I have, yes, doctor.
                  [nods]|
Doctor: └of being depressed? =
Patient: = I have, yes.
                  [nods]
Doctor: you have? =
Patient: = I have, yes. ....
                  [nods]
Doctor: what's it like? /tell me/.
Patient: I become sa:d, for nothing, for no reason, =
           [looks slightly away, to the left, then back
           to doctor]
           = you know. =
           [nods]
Doctor: = I know:. and what else happens? do you <u>cry</u> =
           = a lot? =
Patient: = no, I don't cry. ...
           [shakes head]
Doctor: what do you feel? (when-)? (1.1)
Patient: what? =
Doctor: = what do you feel when you get like that?..
Patient: ⌐I feel such a sadness, such an anguish. ...
           [looks slightly to the right; looks at the
           doctor; then looks slightly down]
Doctor: //I know.// .... do you stop eating? =
Patient: = no, I even eat very well, doctor. =
           [shakes head; smiles and nods]
Doctor: = yeah? =
Patient: = thank God, I eat very well.
           [series of nods]
                  [dec]
Doctor: and let's see: .... you take ca::re of =
           = yourself, .. /you ba:the/,
           [acc]
           you do everything as usual?
Patient: Oh, yes:, e:verything just right, <u>e:verything</u>
           <u>ju:st right</u>.
           [looks down to the right, head turned to the
           right; looks at doctor]
Doctor: └weren't =

Doctor: =there periods of time that you did not care
           for yourself?=
Patient: =no:, absolutely not, when I am myself,=
           [series of head shakes]
           =absolutely not.=
           [shakes head; tightens lips]
Doctor: ┌ =even during these periods-
Patient: └ I am an extremely neat person, you know?=
           [raises head and nods]
Doctor: =mmm ... even during these periods when
           you're sad, feel sad, an:guished, you go on
         ┌ taking care of yourself, right?
Patient: └ oh: yes: yes:, of course,
           [long nod; series of short nods]
           I go on taking care of myself, naturally.=
Doctor: =bu:t, do you stop doing what you usually do?
           [dec]
           li:ke activities- ... at home out:side, ... or
           you never- stopped let's see /being active?/
Patient: ⌊no,
                                        [raises head]
           [acc]
           I used to be very active, doctor.=
           [series of nods]
Doctor: =//yeah?//=
Patient: =I was a saleswoman, y'know,=
           [camera focus exclusively on patient; looks at doctor]
Doctor: =//yeah?//=
Patient: =for many years.=
Doctor: =/mmm./
Patient: .... I worked for a charity institution for=
           =little old people ( ) [nods]
           [series of nods]
Doctor: mmm: ...
Patient: see. .... I used to sell for (it),
           [looks at doctor; looks to the right]
           [acc]
           I also used to sell for myself a little=
           =bit, ..
           [looks at the doctor]
Doctor: mmm: ...
Patient: I worked for many years as a saleswoman. (1.5)
           [series of nods]
           [acc]
Doctor: was that the only job /you had?/ ..
Patient: what?=
Doctor: =was that the only job?
Patient: ⌊no. I also worked for=
           [looks down to the right; looks up at doctor]
           =the Navy, [as a] civil ⟨ser- ser-⟩ servant,=

Doctor: = civil servant, =
Patient: = in the Navy =
           [nods]
Doctor: = with a CON:tract, ..
Patient: e:verything just right. ..
           [series of nods]
Doctor: how many years did you work (there)? =
Patient: = twelve years. ..
Doctor: /yeah?/ ....
Patient: then I gave it up as-,
           [looks to the right, straight ahead]
                [acc]
           I found myself a boyfriend, you know =
           [looks at doctor and smiles]
           = sometimes these things make things worse,
                               [nods]
           don't they. =
           [nods]
Doctor: = /mmm, mmm./ =
Patient: = and this boyfriend made me quit the job,
           [slightly raises head; lowers head]
           [acc]
           unfortunately, I could be retired today ..
                           [tightens lips]
           in the Navy, y'know.
                [nods]   [nods]
Doctor: /I see./ =
Patient: = even earning a good ⟨reti- reti-⟩ =
                [series of nods]
           = retirement pension and all that, y'know. ...
                [series of nods]
Doctor: ⌐before these twelve years, you also didn't
           work? ...
Patient: what? =
Doctor: = before these twelve years in the Navy,
           you didn't work either ...
Patient: always as a saleswoman. ..
           [looks briefly to the right; turns head to
           the left; smiles]
Doctor: /saleswoman/. =
Patient: = yeah, I've always enjoyed selling. ....
           [series of nods]
           I'm goo:d at that, I've always enjoyed =
           [nods]   [series of nods]
           = selling, Doctor Edna. ...
Doctor: since that you have never worked again? =
Patient: = no. ... now, since I quit [it's been] some
           [shakes head] [looks away, to the right]
           ... that I've quit working, selling,
           [looks slightly to the right; nods]

it's been around eight months. (1.3)
Patient: [looks at the doctor; lowers head]
   ⎡ until then-
   ⎢ [acc]
Doctor: ⎣ even when you left the Navy, you went on =
    = selling? =
Patient: = oh, I went on se:lling. =
    [long nod, looking at doctor]
    [acc]
Doctor: = with this boyfriend, you went on-
Patient: ⎣I went on, I went on =
                  [nods] [series of nods]
    = selling. ...
Doctor: and why did you stop selling eight months-
    eight months ago? ...
Patient: what? =
Doctor: = why did you stop (selling)? =
Patient: 'cause I was already ti:red,
    [moves head slightly to the left; looks to
    the right, away from the doctor]
    y'know doctor Edna. ....
    [nods, looks at doctor, smiles briefly]
    (I was) feeling a bit tired,
        [nods]   [nods and smiles]
    so I decided to stop. =
    [series of nods]

Doctor: = ⎡during these periods of time that you told
    me abou:t .. of sadness, of anguish,
    do you feel less <u>enthusiasm</u> to do things, to
    work or: ( )
Patient: ⎣ what? =
Doctor: = it's much the same?
Patient: no. I worked pretty much the same.
    [looks down; raises and lowers head; nods]
Doctor: ⎡and sleep, .. do you have any problem
    sleeping? =
Patient: = no.
    [shakes head]
Doctor: never had?
Patient: I sleep very well. =
Doctor: = not even during these times? =
Patient: I always slept very well, y'know.
       [short nod]
Doctor: ⎣ really?
Patient: yeah. =
Doctor: = you never had any-
Patient: ⎣ actually, after my illnesses,
    I started to take medicine, (1.1)
       [short nod]
Doctor: mmm, mmm.

Patient: to sleep, ...
        [short nod]
Doctor: mmm, mmm.
Patient: y'know ....
Doctor: which medicine, do you remember?
Patient: it's the::: ....
        [looks to the right; looks down]
        I don't remember now, /doctor./ (1.6)
        [looking down]
        /I don't remember now./ (3.8)
Doctor: so then:::, you always slept very well, =
Patient: ⌐ /I always slept very well./
       └ [slow and long nod]
Doctor: ⌐ do you remem:ber not sleeping at night,
       waking up very ear:ly? ...
Patient: I wake up very early, doctor.
       [raises head] | [lowers head]
Doctor: └ yeah? =
Patient: = yeah, I wake up very early.
             ⌐ [series of nods]
Doctor: └ always? ... around what time /do =
       ⌐ you wake up?/
Patient: └ //lately-// around four thirty more or less ▬
       ⌐ I'm already up
Doctor: └ yeah?
Patient: five o'clock- (1.5) ⌐ see.
Doctor: └ for how <u>long</u> has this =
       = been happening? ....
Patient: waking up early? =
Doctor: = yeah. ....
Patient: ⌐ it was here at the hospital, doctor. =
       [turns left; looks down; looks at doctor]
Doctor: = yeah? =
Patient: = yeah:. ...
       [series of short nods]
Doctor: before this wouldn't happen?
Patient: └ no:. ...
                     [shakes head]
       I would always wake up around .... six,
       [looks straight ahead, turns to the right]
       seven o'clock in the morning. ...
       [looks at doctor and nods]
Doctor: mmm. .... you'd go to sleep right away =
       = and you'd wake up at six, seven o'clock. =
Patient: = and I'd wake up at six, seven o'clock in =
       [raises and lowers head; series of nods]
       ⌐ the morning.
Doctor: └ and now at the hospital ... you wa-, you =
       = fall asleep quickly, you sleep well?
Patient: yeah:, now I have ( ) I have been =
       [turns head slightly to the right; nods]

Patient: =sleeping- I sleep well through the night,
             [nods]
         but I wake up very early. ....
         [nods]   [nods and smiles]
Doctor: mmm.
Patient: four-thirty, five o'clock I'm already up. ....
          [gestures with head]
         and then I can't sleep anymore, right. ...
     [shakes head]
       [acc]
Doctor: why wouldn't you eat well here at the=
         =hospital? ... you didn't like the food
       ⌐or you didn't feel hungry?
Patient: ⌐it's the food, right doctor.=
     [nods]
Doctor: =yeah:.
Patient: no, it's really the food-=
        [long nod]
Doctor: =and at home did you eat well?=
Patient: =⟨mmm food- fr home⟩ I eat qui:te well. (1.6)
     [raises head; series of nods]
Doctor: mmm.
Patient: you know, ⟨food-⟩ a little food from home
     tastes quite differently, right doctor. ....
     [series of nods]   [smiles]
       [dec]
Doctor: ⌐and did you ha::ve .... <u>ups and downs</u>, when
     you felt ve:ry <u>happy</u>, <u>ve:ry</u> ... <u>exci:ted</u>,
     talking a lot, <u>sin:ging</u>, ... ener- full of
     energy, (1.3) you felt a sharp contrast?
Patient: /(never)/ I never sang much, doctor. ....
     [looks downward; shakes head and smiles]
Doctor: of feeling <u>very</u> happy, VERY WELL::?
     [acc]
Patient: well: ( ) we all have our happy moments,
     [raises head; series of short nods]
     don't we doctor,=
Doctor: mmm.
Patient: =of happiness and all, I also had mine. (1.3)
     [series of nods]
Doctor: /I see./ (1.4)
       [dec]
Patient: they are over.
     [long nod; stares at doctor, then looks down;
     lowers head; tightens lips; slowly raises head and eyes]
       [acc]
Doctor: so until: .. six years ago you d- didn-
     didn't have any problems?
Patient: no, no problems.
     [looks down to the right; shakes head and
     looks up]

[acc]

Doctor: six years ago these hospitalizations began. =
Patient: = these hospitalizations began, ...
[series of nods]
it was in '76, '77,
[looks at doctor]
that the hospitalizations began. ...
[looks straight ahead; head to the right]
[dec]

Doctor: you never felt any:thing before?
Patient: nothing, nothing, nothing, nothing. =
[series of short head shakes]

Doctor: = there wasn't anything unusual (happening)?
Patient: ne:ver had, ne:ver doctor, /never/.
[looks down; shakes head, looks at doctor]

Doctor: ⌐not e:ven .. physical problems?
[acc]
/you never had any physical problem/?

Patient: ⌐ne:ver, I never had an =
[shakes head]
= operation, doctor. =
[raises head, looks at doctor]

Doctor: ▬/no/? ▬
Patient: = never had an operation till today.
Doctor: ⌐(never) had
any difficulty in wa::lking, in mo:ving =
= around /in talking?/

Patient: ⌐no. nothing, nothing, nothing, nothing ....
[head shakes]
on the contrary, really a saleswoman has to =
[camera focus now exclusively on the doctor]
= talk a lot right Doctor Edna. (1.2)

Doctor: mmm.
Patient: I'd really talk a lo:t, =
Doctor: = //you'd talk a lot//
Patient: ⌐ to the customers. //yeah.//
Doctor: did you live on that money? ...
[doctor in focus: hands on thights; torso
inclined forward, toward the patient;
shoulders lifted slightly upward]

Patient: what? =
Doctor: = did you live on that (   ) money?
[turns face to the right; moves torso
backward and forward]

Patient: no, my son helps (me), right. and I also
have my social security, not much money but
it always helps, and my son also gives me
some money when he can, y'know, each month.
(1.5)

Doctor: /mmm, mmm./

Patient: so I have this little bit of money, I have
Doctor: [moves backward, stretches back]
Patient: .... from my son, there is the pen:sion. ....
            and I had (money) as a saleswoman, but (I
            stopped selling-) .... I have only these two
            sources of income now, y'know. ...
            [acc]
Doctor: you had never gone through a psychiatric
            treatment before? =
Patient: = no. (1.5)
            [camera focus on the patient]
            this started in '76, doctor. (1.8)
            [long nod]
Doctor: is there anyone in your fa:mily that has: a
            problem similar to yours?
Patient: (no.) ... there was a brother.
            [shakes her head] [looks up and nods]
Doctor: yeah:. what was it that //he had?//
            [acc]   [dec]
Patient: there is a brother. ⌈there was, that also
            [short nod]   [turns slightly to the left]
            lost his mind, y'know.
            [series of nods]
            [dec]
Doctor: do you remember him?
Patient: I remember. (of) my eldest brother.
            [series of short nods]
Doctor: /remember what used to happen to him?/
Patient: what?
            [acc]
Doctor: remember what used to happen to him?
Patient: yeah.
            [looks away to the right and downward]
            ⌈it was more or less what I had-,
            [looks down]
            what I have, right doctor. ...
            [looks at the doctor; nods and smiles]
            [dec]
Doctor: what do you remember, let's see, would happen
            to him? (1.3)
            [dec]
Patient: well:, he comple:tely lost his mind. ....
            [turns slightly to the right and nods]
            /right./
Doctor: what did he used to do? (what did-)
            [acc]
Patient: no, I was still too young,
            [raises head]
            I don't quite remember, doctor. =
            [shakes and lowers head]

Doctor: =what do you mean when you say "to lose one's mind"? (1.2)

Patient: to lose one's senses,
[looks away, to the right and downward]
not knowing what one is doing, right. (1.2)
[series of nods]

Doctor: he'd do things that you considered- absur:d?
(1.2)

Patient: well, my sister is the one who explains,
[slight movement to the right]
y'know doctor, 'cause I lose my::: mind,
[short nod]   [shakes head]
I don't know what I'm doing, right. ...
[shakes head]   [nods]
she is the one who explains, that I sing
[raises head, turns to the right]
that I laugh, all: these things, right. ...
          [short nod]
          [acc]

Doctor: /mmm./ (with) your brother that also used to
happen? (1.3)
          [acc]

Patient: (no) with my brother,
[turns head to the right, looks straight ahead,
away from the doctor]
I don't quite remember,
[shakes head; looks at doctor]
          [dec]
'cause I was ve:ry young, y'know. ....
          [smiles]
          [dec]

Doctor: did he also go to the hospital? ...

Patient: he did. (1.7) /he did./
[series of nods] [long nod]
          [acc]

Doctor: was he ill for many years?

Patient: he was, doctor. (1.1) // he was, yes.// =
[looks away, to the right, looks at doctor
and nods]

Doctor: =and is he already dead?=

Patient: =yes he is. he died recently.=
[nods]   [series of nods]
          [acc]

Doctor: =yes:. what did //he die from?// =

Patient: =what?

Doctor: what did /he die from?/ (1.6)
          [dec]

Patient: ⌈I don't know, doctor. I don't know. ...
[looks away to the right and downward,
shakes her head]

                      [acc]
Doctor: how old was he? ....
Patient: he was the oldest .... of all, y'know. (1.5)
          [raises her head]   [lowers her head]
                      [dec]
Doctor: but he: (still-)
Patient: he was around seventy years old.
          [raises head slightly and lowers it]
Doctor: really? =
Patient: = really. ...
          [series of short nods]
Doctor: and he would walk: /nor:mally/, he would
          talk:, let's see, or you- or he was already,
          let's see, ...
Patient: no, he suffered a lot:, doctor,
          [looks slightly away to the right; looks at
          the doctor]
          'cause he had this ne- neuralgic pain, see.
          [looks down]   [looks at the doctor]
Doctor: mmm.
Patient: it's not a neuralgic pain,
          [turns away completely to the right, looks
          straight ahead]
          it has another name, I don't remember now.
          [looks down; raises and lowers head]
          he suffered a lot: with this illness, y'know,
          [looks at doctor; raises head; nods]
          it was terrible. ....
          [series of nods]
Doctor: but he was li:ving by himself or he was
        ┌ always in the hospital?
Patient: └ no, married. =
          [raises head and nods]
Doctor: = /married./ =
Patient: = married. ....
          [nods]
Doctor: and was there someone ta- caring for him?
                      [dec]
Patient: = oh, there was:. there was a very ni:ce son,
          [raises head slightly and nods]
          my nephew, y'see. he cared for his father,
          [nods]   [nods]
          all along (   )
                      [dec]
Doctor: but did one need: ... to bathe him? to take
          him to the bathroom?
                      [acc]
Patient: I don't quite remember, doctor, =
          [looks to the right briefly and faces
          doctor; shakes head briefly]

Doctor: =you don't know.
                 [acc]
Patient: I don't quite remember. (1.1)
                 [looks down]
                           [acc]
Doctor: mmm. (3.5) are you religious? ...
Patient: I am a devoted Catholic. ..
                 [looks at doctor; nods and smiles]
                 a devo::ted Catholic,
                 [acc]
                 〈I ha- I have-〉 I have a lot of faith,
                 [series of nods]
                           [dec]
                 I'm ve:ry faithful. ...
                 [long nod]
                 this is very important, right doctor. ...
                 [long nod]
Doctor: /mmm./
Patient: faith is a very important thing, right.
                 I'm very faithful.=
                 [series of nods]
                           [acc]
Doctor: you never- .. never had another religion?
                 always a Catholic?
Patient: no. always a Catholic. (1.3)
                 [shakes head]
Doctor: you go to church?
Patient: I like going to church very much.
                 [nods and looks downward]
                 I like going to church very much. (5.1)
                 [looks down and looks up]
                           [dec]
Doctor: are you having some pro:blems now? ...
                 feeling that something isn't
                 still quite right? ....
Patient: ⌐no, I think that now everything is fine,
                 doctor. ...
                 [looks down to the right; looks up at
                 doctor and raises head slightly to the
                 left]
                           [dec]
Doctor: you had complained .. of a weakness in your=
                 =arms /remember?=
Patient: =yeah, in my hands, doctor, in my hands.
                 [raises head slightly and nods] |
Doctor: ∟ what's it like,
                 this weakness? ..
                           [acc]
Patient: ⌐it's it's that I don't feel much
                 my han:ds

          [looks at both hands, raises hands, closes
          hands inward]

Patient: .. see. =
          [looks at the doctor, opens and shuts hands]

Doctor: = you can't make any movements?
          [moves hands, rests hands on armchair]

Patient: yeah. I can't (   )
          [shakes head, looks at doctor]

Doctor: what do you feel when =
        = you're about to make a movement?

Patient: I have difficulty,
        doctor. =
          [raises head and nods]

Doctor: = do you eat by yourself?

Patient: what?

Doctor: do you eat by yourself? (1.3)

Patient: (no:, these-)
          [looks down and slightly to the right; raises
          head and eyes and looks at doctor]
              [dec]

Doctor: or must someone help you eat? =

Patient: = these days my sister helped me, y'know. =
          [raises her head and nods]
                   [acc]

Doctor: = 'cause you can't ... hold the spoon by
        yourself? you can't raise the spoon? /what is
        it?/

Patient: I can't because of my <u>hands</u>, y'know, doctor.
        .. this problem.
          [raises head slightly, then pulls head back]
              [acc]

Doctor: yes, but what do <u>you feel</u> when you try to eat
        by yourself? (2.0)

Patient: I have difficulty. (1.3)
          [looks away, to the right and downward;
          looks at the doctor]
              [dec]

Doctor: but the <u>difficulty</u> is in the strength needed
        to rai-) raise <u>the spoon</u>? (1.3) or is it that
        you can't reach your mouth? =

Patient: = no, it's to raise the fork. =
          [raises her head and nods]

Doctor: = is it? =

Patient: = /it's/ to raise the fork. (2.0)
          [series of nods]

Doctor: /make this movement, like this./ (3.8)
          [patient imitates doctor's gestures and raises both hands; turns arms
          outward, with hands closed; doctor touches
          patient's left arm; patient looks at left

arm; doctor takes hand away; and patient
opens hands and looks at them]

Doctor: [acc]
are you feeling ... you are not feeling =
= anything now, are you? =

Patient: = no. (1.5)
[looks at doctor, places hands back on
armchair and resumes baseline position]

[camera with focus on both participants; both
are in baseline position]
                 [acc]
Doctor: and to go to the bathroom, do you also need
someone to help? ....
                 [dec]
Patient: yes. to zip up my pants, (y'know /not very/)
[series of nods]
Doctor: ⌊ /you also can't =
= do it yourself./

Patient: yeah, I can't. (2.0)
but I think I'm much better now,
[series of nods]
y'know doctor, thank God

Doctor: do you think you're feeling better now than
you were a few days ago?
[moves hands in "explaining" gestures]

Patient: oh:, I AM. =
                 [long nod]
Doctor: = rea:lly? =
Patient: = I think I'm much better. =   .
[long nods]
Doctor: = what do you think is better?
                 [acc]
what- how were you feeling then,
[shifts body postures, first to left, and
then to right; similar hand movements]
and how is it different now? (1.1)
                 [acc]
Patient: ⌐well, now I feel more inclined to do things,
y'know,
[nods; moves her head right and left;
makes pointing gesture with her hands]
more interest in life. (2.1)
[raises head and nods]
[acc]

Doctor: you weren't feeling this way before?
[shakes head]
[dec]
Patient: no, /I wasn't./ =
[shakes head]

                              [acc]
Doctor: =/no?/ what were you /feeling?/
                  [dec]
Patient: no, ⌐because of ill:ness, y'know doctor,
                         | [nods]
Doctor: └   mmm.
          [lowers her head and nods]
Patient: one gets very upset, y'know. (1.5)
                              [nods]
                  [acc]
Doctor: /mmm./ have you been able to swallow again?=
          [nods]   [raises right hand and points to
          throat; follows with hand
          gesture pointing to stomach]
Patient: =oh:, yes, /quite well/=
          [long nod]   [series of nods]
Doctor: =you were having problems, .. remember? ....
Patient: ⌐no, I always could swallow well, doctor,
                         [series of nods]
Doctor: //really?//
Patient: /always swallowed (food) well./
          [series of nods] |
Doctor: └so what was happening=
          =that you couldn't ... eat? ...
          [makes same hand gestures as above]
          the food wouldn't go down? ....
          [resumes baseline position]
Patient: no, the food always went down well ... always.
                  [nods] |
Doctor: └ really?
                              [nods]
Patient: /always./ (2.0)
          [nods]
Doctor: do you see well?=
          [raises and lowers head]
Patient: =I see-, no, I use glasses.=
          [nods; pulls head back; smiles]
Doctor: =/you use glasses./=
          [hand movements: tightens hands together;
          relaxes and tightens hands again]
Patient: =I use glasses. ...
          [nods]   [smiles]
                  [acc]
Doctor: for a long time? ....
          [moves backward, turns body to the right,
          left hand on left thigh; smiles]
Patient: for many years. ....
                  [smiles]
                         [acc]
Doctor: //mmm.// and with walking, you're also not

          having any problems?
          [gestures with right hand]

Patient: no, I'm not, ... /no, I'm not./ (3.0)
          [smiles]

Doctor: //mmm.//
          [series of nods]
          what do you intend to do, ... when you leave
          this place? (1.9)
          [turns head slightly to the right]

Patient: ⌐to go on with my life, right.
          [smiles and turns head slightly to right;
          looks down, then looks up, turns head to
          left]
              [acc]
          I won't work as a saleswoman anymore, y'know
          doctor, ...
              ⌊dec⌋
          cause I'm ti:red,
          I've decided to retire, y'know .... .
             [long nod]   [smiles]

Doctor: mmm.

Patient: ⌐I'll go on living with my sis:ter, (1.2)
                       [smiles]
          ⟨there's only the three of us⟩
                [slight nod]
          she is ve:ry kind, /y'know./
          [long nod]

Doctor: ⌊ mmm.

Patient: so, ⟨we'll⟩ go on living together the three
          of us .... [nods]   [nods]

Doctor: what do you usually do, ... /well when you're
          home?/ (1.5)
          [shifts position: bends slightly forward, with
          both hands on the chair, raises her head]
                     [acc]

Patient: ⌐I always do some se:wing, any little thing
          to kill time,⌐y'know doctor. (1.8)
          [turns head slightly to the right, looks
          downward, then looks at doctor and
          nods]

Doctor: ⌊mmm. and your son, do you have a
          lot of con:tact with him (or)?
          [turns head slightly to the right; raises and
          lowers head]

Patient: oh, yes. I am crazy about my son.
          [series of short head shakes]
          (he) is my on:ly child.
          [short nod; brings her head forward]
          I'm crazy about him, Doctor
          Edna.

```
                      [acc]
             I'm really crazy about him. (1.8)
             [shakes her head]      [looks down]
Doctor:      your son is from your marriage, isn't he? =
                      [acc]
Patient:     = he is, from my-

                               [acc]
Doctor:                      └ you were married. =
Patient:     = ⟨I was married.⟩
             [long nod]
                      [dec]
Doctor:      how long? .... // were you ma-//
Patient:                    └I was married for twelve
             years. ....
Doctor:      mmm.
Patient:     I separated after twelve years. (1.5)
                            [long nod]
                      [acc]                    [dec]
Doctor:      you're the one who asked for a separa::tion =
             [short nod; short head movement]
             = or was it your husband? =
Patient:     = ⌐no, 'cause I found out.
             there was a huge betrayal, y'know doctor. ...
             my self-esteem- ... I got very hurt,
             [series of nods]
Doctor:      [nods]
                      [acc]
Patient:     so much so I separated from him. ...
             [series of nods]
             I was the one who wanted the separation,
             y'know. =
Doctor:      = mmm. =
Patient:     = he didn't even wan:t, and all that.
                               [nods]
                      [dec]
             but oh: ... It was a very serious situation,
             doctor. (1.5)
             [looks away, to the right and down; looks up
             and faces the doctor]
             there really had to be a separation, y'know. =
             [shakes her head]
                      [acc]
Doctor:      = and why did you only have one child? ....
             [doctor shifts position: folds both hands
             together, bends slightly forward and turns
             head slightly to right; bends further
             forward]
Patient:     ⌐because (it didn't),
             [moves torso backward, raises head and right
             hand, turns hand outward]
             I didn-, I suffered a lot,
```

[gestures with hand, gestures with head toward the left,
facing the doctor]
I thought childbirth was terrible =
           [shakes head]
= the pain, ... y'know,
Doctor: [nods and moves slightly backward]
          [acc]
Patient: **so that afterward then I had a procedure so =**
        = that I wouldn't have any more (children),
        [smiles, lowers head slightly]
           [dec]
        I avoi:ded it.
          [nod]
Doctor: **/you were afraid to have children./ =**
        [short nods]
Patient: **= yes. (1.7) because the pain is terrible,**
       |nods|
       isn't it, doctor. (1.3)
Doctor: **//mmm mmm//**
       [nods]
Patient: **/I don't know/ do you have children? (2.0)**
       [nods, bends forward and smiles]
Doctor: **/⁗⁗⁗./**
       [short nod]
Patient: **do you have children? =**
       [bends further forward, to right; smiles]
Doctor: **= /yes, I do./ =**
       [nods]   [bends more, elbows touch thighs,
                    hands folded tighter]

Patient: **= yes, then you know that it is a terrible**
       pain, right. the pain of childbirth is-

Doctor: ⌈ **then, because of that, you did =**
       = not want any- =
       [raises torso up against the chair, raises
       her head and bends slightly forward]
Patient: **= /yes, it was, it was/ because of that that I =**
       = did not want any more. (1.8)
       [series of nods, looks away to the right and
       down, long nod]
       because of the pain. (2.7)
       [looks away]
                 [acc]
Doctor: **//mmm, mmm.//** ⌈**and your son:,**
       [gestures with arms, opening up]
       do you- uhm::, often go out with him or he
       comes to see you::? ...
       [gestures with hands]
Patient: **he comes to see me, I visit him:. (1.3)**
       [short nod]

Doctor: and your granddaughter. do you <u>see</u> her
          frequently?
          [moves torso slightly backward and forward;
          gestures with hand]
Patient: oh, yes <u>ve:ry</u> much. I am crazy about my=
          =little granddaughter. (1.2)
          [smiles]
                            [acc]
          she is a dar::ling young lady, y'know.
          she is sixteen years old. she is a darling.
              [nods]   [short nods]
                  [acc]
Doctor: /mmm, mmm./ so now- you ... are feeling well?
          [folds hand together]
Patient: I am, doctor. I'm feeling quite well, thank=
          [raises head slightly, long nod and smiles]
          =God.=
Doctor: =do you think you can go home and:: take care
          of your things?=
          [raises her head slightly; looks up at
          patient; series of nods]
Patient: =oh: yes, I think so, quite well. (1.3)
          [long nod]   [smiles]
Doctor: //mmm, mmm.//
          [nods]
Patient: quite well. ....
          [series of nods]
Doctor: so, O.K., Dona Jurema, ... we'll still talk
          (before you go). O.K.
                        [nods]
Patient: yes, yes, doctor. .... I'm at your disposal.
          [nods and smiles]
Doctor: /so, O.K., (come over here with me.)/
          [patient motions to get up, doctor holds
          patient's left arm, patient gets up, then
          doctor gets up, still holding patient's left
          arm, and walks patient to the door]
Patient: /so ( ) my illness ( )
Doctor: (wait a little bit over there, O.K.)

Note

1. In this interview the doctor and the patient keep their sitting positions and shift minimally from what Schefflen calls "baseline postures" (1973:29). For the discharge interview it corresponds to their initial postural arrangement. Chapter 2 provides a full description.

REFERENCES

Aitchison, J. 1987. *Words in the Mind*. Oxford: Basil Blackwell.

Akiskal, H. S., and V. R. Puzantian. 1979. "Psychotic Forms of Depression and Mania." *Psychiatric Clinics of North America* 2:419–39.

Almeida, L. Q. 1987. "Clinical Interpretation and the Reframing of Experience: Evidence from Therapeutic Discourse." Ph.D. diss., Georgetown University.

Andreasen, N. C. 1979a. "The Clinical Assessment of Thought, Language, and Communication Disorders: The Definition of Terms and Evaluation of Their Reliability." *Archives of General Psychiatry* 36:1315–21.

———. 1979b. "Thought, Language, and Commmunication Disorders." *Archives of General Psychiatry* 36:1325–30.

Andreasen, N. J. C., Ming T. Tsuang, and A. Canter. 1974. "The Significance of Thought Disorder in Diagnostic Evaluations." *Comprehensive Psychiatry* 15, no. 1,27–34.

Andreasen, N. J. C., and P. S. Powers. 1974. "Overinclusive Thinking in Mania and Schizophrenia." *British Journal of Psychiatry* 125:452–56.

Arieti, S. 1974. *Interpretation of Schizophrenia*. New York: Basic Books.

Astrachan, B. M., M. Harrow, D. Adler, L. Brauer, A. Schwartz, C. Schwartz, and G. Tucker. 1972. "A Checklist for the Diagnosis of Schizophrenia." *British Journal of Psychiatry* 121: 529–39.

Atkinson, M. 1979. "Prerequisites for Reference." In *Developmental Pragmatics,* ed. by Elinor Ochs and Bambi B. Schieffelin, 229–50. Cambridge: Cambridge University Press.

Atkinson, J. M., and J. Heritage, eds. 1984. *Structures of Social Action*. Cambridge: Cambridge University Press.

Austin, J. L. [1962] 1975. *How to Do Things with Words*. Cambridge, Mass: Harvard University Press.

Bartlett, F. C. 1932. *Remembering*. Cambridge: Cambridge University Press.

Basso, K. H. [1970, 1972] 1979. "To Give Up on Words: Silence in Western Apache Culture." In *Language and Social Context,* ed. P. P. Giglioli, 67–86. New York: Penguin.

Bates, E., and B. MacWhinney. 1982. "Functionalist Approaches to Grammar." In *Language Acquisition: The State of the Art,* ed. Eric Wanner and Lila R. Gleitman, 173–218. Cambridge: Cambridge University Press,

———. 1979. "A Functionalist Approach to the Acquisition of Grammar." In *Developmental Pragmatics,* ed. E. Ochs and B. B. Schieffelin, 167–211. New York: Academic Press.

Bateson, G. [1972] 1981. "A Theory of Play and Fantasy." In *Steps to an Ecology of Mind,* 177–93. New York: Chandler. Reprint. New York: Ballantine.

Bateson, G., D. D. Jackson, J. Haley, and J. H. Weakland. 1956. "Towards a Theory of Schizophrenia." *Behavioral Science* 1:251–64.

Becker, A. L. 1982a. "Beyond Translation: Aesthetics and Language Description." In *Contemporary Perceptions of Language: Interdisciplinary Dimensions*. Georgetown University Round Table on Languages and Linguistics 1982, ed. H. Byrnes, 124–38. Washington, D.C.: Georgetown University Press.

———. 1982b. "On Emerson on Language." In *Analyzing Discourse: Text and Talk*. Georgetown University Round Table on Languages and Linguistics 1981, ed. D. Tannen, 1–11. Washington, D.C.: Georgetown University Press.

———. 1979. "Text-building, Epistemology, and Aesthetics in Javanese Shadow Theatre. In *The Imagination of Reality,* ed. A. L. Becker and Aram Yengoyan, 211–43. Norwood, N.Y.: Ablex.

Benson, D. F. 1973. "Psychiatry Aspects of Aphasia." *British Journal of Psychiatry* 123: 555–56.

Bernstein, B. 1960. "Review of the Lore and Language of School Children by I. and P. Opie." *British Journal of Sociology* 11:178–81.

Bleuler E. [1911] 1950. *Dementia Praecox; or the Group of Schizophrenias*. New York: International University Press.

Brown, G., and G. Yule. 1983. *Discourse Analysis*. Cambridge: Cambridge University Press.

Brown, P., and S. Levinson. [1978] 1979. "Universals in Language Usage: Politeness Phenomena." In *Questions Politeness: Strategies in Social Interaction,* ed. E. Goody, 56–289. Cambridge: Cambridge University Press.

Brown, R., and Albert Gilman. [1972] 1979. "The Pronouns of Power and Solidarity." In *Language and Social Context,* ed. Paolo Giglioli, 252–82. Harmondsworth, England: Penguin.

Button, G., and N. Casey. 1984. "Generating Topic: The Use of Topic Initial Elicitors." In *Structures of Social Action: Studies in Conversation Analysis,* ed. J. M. Atkinson and J. Heritage, 167–90. Cambridge: Cambridge University Press.

Byrne, P. S. and B. E. L. Long. 1976. *Doctors Talking to Patients: A Study of the Verbal Behavior of General Practitioners Consulting in Their Surgeries*. Southampton, England: Hobbs.

Cameron, N. A. 1947. *The Psychology of Behavior Disorders*. Boston: Houghton Mifflin.

———. [1944] 1964. "Experimental Analysis of Schizophrenic Thinking." In *Language and Thought in Schizophrenia,* ed. J. S. Kasanin. Berkeley: University of California Press.

Chacon Jurado Filho, L. 1986. *Cantigas de Roda—Jogo, Insinuação e Escolha*. Campinas, Brazil: Unicamp.

Chafe, W. 1986. "How We Know Things about Language: A Plea for Catholicism." In *Language and Linguistics: The Interdependence of Theory, Data, and Application*. Georgetown University Round Table on Languages and Linguistics 1985, ed. Deborah Tannen and James E. Alatis, 214–25. Washington, D.C.: Georgetown University Press.

———. 1979. "The Flow of Thought and the Flow of Language." In *Syntax and Semantics,* Vol. 12, *Discourse and Syntax,* ed. T. Givón. New York: Academic Press.

———. 1976. "Givenness, Contrastiveness, Definiteness, Subjects, Topics and Point of View." In *Subject and Topic,* ed. C. Li and S. Thompson, 25–55. New York: Academic Press.

Chaika, E. O. 1977. "Schizophrenic Speech, Slips of the Tongue, and Jargonaphasia: A Reply to Fromkin and to Lecours and Vanier-Clement." *Brain and Language* 4:464–75.

———. 1974. "A Linguist Looks at 'Schizophrenic' Language." *Brain and Language* 1, 257–76.

Chapman, J. D. 1966. "The Early Symptoms of Schizophrenia." *British Journal of Psychiatry,* 122:225–51.

Chapman, L. J. and J. P. Chapman. 1973. *Disordered Thought in Schizophrenia.* Englewood Cliffs, N.J.: Prentice-Hall.

Charniak, E. 1975. "Organization and Inference in a Frame-like System of Common Sense Knowledge. In *Theoretical Issues in Natural Language Processing,* ed. R. Schank and B. L. Nash-Weber, 42–51. Cambridge, Mass.: Bolt, Beranek, and Newman.

Chenail, R. J. 1991. *Medical Discourse and Systemic Frames of Comprehension.* Norwood, N.J.: Ablex

Cicourel, A. V. 1983. "Language and the Structure of Belief in Medical Communication." In *The Social Organization of Doctor-Patient Communication,* ed. S. Fisher and A. Dundas-Todd, 221–39. Washington, D.C.: The Center for Applied Linguistics.

Clayton, P., F. N. Pitts, and G. Winokur. 1965. "Affective Disorder: IV. Mania." *Comprehensive Psychiatry* 6:313–22.

Cohen, B. D. 1978. "Referent Communication Disturbances in Schizophrenia." In *Language and Cognition in Schizophrenia,* ed. S. Schwartz, 1–34. New York: Erlbaum.

Coulthard, M. [1977] 1981. *An Introduction to Discourse Analysis.* London: Longman.

Duranti, A. 1986. "The Audience as Co-author, An Introduction." In *The Audience as Co-author.* ed. A. Duranti and D. Brenneis. Special issue of *Text* 6, no. 3:239–47.

Durbin, M., and R. L. Marshall. 1977. "Speech and Mania: Syntactic Aspects." *Brain and Language* 4:208–18.

Erickson, F. 1982. "Money Tree, Lasagna Bush, Salt and Pepper: Social Construction of Topical Cohesion in a Conversation among Italian-Americans." In *Analyzing Discourse: Text and Talk.* Georgetown University Round Table on Languages and Linguistics 1982, ed. D. Tannen, 43–70. Washington, D.C.: Georgetown University Press.

Erickson, F., and W. Rittenberg. 1987. "Topic Control and Person Control: A Theory Problem for Foreign Physicians in Interaction with American Patients." *Discourse Processes* 10:401–15.

Erickson, F., and J. Shultz. 1982. *The Counselor as Gatekeeper: Social Interaction in Interviews.* New York: Academic Press.

———. 1977. "When Is a Context? Some Issues and Methods in the Analysis of Social Competence." *The Quarterly Newsletter of the Institute for Comparative Human Development* 1, no. 2:5–10.

Falk, J. 1979. "The Conversational Duet." Ph.D. diss., Princeton University.

Fasold, R. 1990. *Sociolinguistics of Language.* Cambridge: Basil Blackwell.

Feldstein, S., and J. Jaffe. 1963. "Schizophrenic Speech Fluency: A Partial Replication and Hypothesis." *Psychological Reports* 13:775–80.

Ferguson, C. A. [1977] 1979. "Baby Talk as a Simplified Register." In *Talking to Children,* ed. C. E. Snow and C. A. Ferguson, 209–35. Cambridge: Cambridge University Press.

Fillmore, C. J. 1981. "Pragmatics and the Description of Discourse." In *Radical Pragmatics,* ed. P. Cole, 143–66. New York: Academic Press.

———. 1976. "The Need for a Frame Semantics within Linguistics." In *Statistical Methods in Linguistics,* 5–29. Stockholm: Skriptor.

———. 1974. "Pragmatics and the Description of Discourse." In *Pramatik II,* ed. S. Schmidt, 83–104. Fink.

Firbas, J. 1974. "Some Aspects of the Czechoslovak Approach to the Problems of Functional Sentence Perspective." In *Papers on Functional Sentence Perspective,* ed. F. Danes. Prague: Academia.

Fisher, S. 1984. "Institutional Authority and the Structure of Discourse." In *Discourse Processes* 7, no. 2:201–24.

———. 1983. "Doctor/Patient Talk: How Treatment Decisions Are Negotiated in Doctor/Patient Communication." In *The Social Organization of Doctor-Patient Communication,* ed. S. Fisher and A. D. Todd, 135–57. Washington, D.C.: Center for Applied Linguistics.

———. 1982. "The Decision-Making Context: How Doctors and Patients Communicate." In *Linguistics and the Professions,* ed. R. Di Pietro, 51–97. Hillsdale, N.J.: Ablex.

Flor-Henry, P. 1976. "Lateralized Temporal-Limbic Dysfunction and Psychopathology. In *Origins and Evolutions of Language and Speech,* ed. S. R. Harnad, H. D. Steklis, and J. Lancaster. Annals of the New York Academy of Sciences, Vol. 280. New York: The New York Academy of Sciences.

Foucault, M. [1975, 1977] 1987. *Discipline and Punish—The Birth of the Prison.* Paris: Gallimard. Reprint. London: Penguin.

Frake, C. 1977. "Plying Frames Can Be Dangerous: An Assessment of Methodology in Cognitive Anthropology." *The Quarterly Newsletter of the Institute for Comparative Human Development* 1, no. 3:1–7.

Frankel, R. M. 1984. "From Sentence to Sequence: Understanding the Medical Encounter through Microinteractional Analysis." *Discourse Processes* 7, no. 2:135–70.

———. 1983. "The Laying On of Hands: Aspects of the Organization of Gaze, Touch, and Talk in a Medical Encounter." In *The Social Organization of Doctor-Patient Communication,* ed. S. Fisher and A. D. Todd, 19–54. Washington, D.C.: Center for Applied Linguistics.

Fromkin, V. A. 1980. *Errors in Linguistic Performance: Slips of the Tongue, Ear, Pen, and Hand.* New York: Academic Press.

———. 1975. "A Linguist Looks at 'A Linguist Looks at Schizophrenic Language.'" *Brain and Language* 2:498–503.

———. 1973. "The Non-anomalous Nature of Anomalous Utterances." In *Speech Errors as Linguistic Evidence,* ed. V. A. Fromkin, 215–43. The Hague: Mouton.

Garfinkel, H. [1972] 1986. "Remarks on Ethnomethodology." In *Directions in Sociolinguistics,* ed. J. J. Gumperz and D. H. Hymes, 301–24. New York: Holt, Rinehart & Winston. Reprint. Oxford: Basil Blackwell.

Garfinkel, H. 1956. "Conditions of Successful Degradation Ceremonies." *American Journal of Sociology* 61.

Givón, T. 1983. "Topic Continuity in Discourse: A Quantitative Cross-Language Study." In *Typological Studies in Language,* vol. 3, ed. T. Givón. Amsterdam: J. Benjamins.

Goffman, E. 1981a. "Footing." In *Forms of Talk,* 124–59. Philadelphia: University of Pennsylvania Press.

———. 1981b. "Replies and Responses." In *Forms of Talk*, 5–77. Philadelphia: University of Pennsylvania Press.

———. 1981c. *Forms of Talk*. Philadelphia: University of Pennsylvania Press.

———. 1974. *Frame Analysis*. New York: Harper & Row.

———. [1967] 1982. *Interaction Ritual*. New York: Anchor Books. Reprint. New York: Random House.

———. 1961. *Asylums*. New York: Anchor Books.

Gonçalves, J. C. 1984. "Topical Development in the Acquisition of Portuguese as a Second Language in Classroom Interaction and Naturalistic Discourse." Ph.D. diss. Georgetown University.

Gottschalk, L. A., and G. C. Gleser. 1964. "Distinguishing Characteristics of the Verbal Communications of Schizophrenic Patients." In *Disorders of Communication*, ed. D. McRioch and E. A. Weinstein. Baltimore: Williams & Wilkins.

Grice, H. P. 1975. "Logic and Conversation." In *Syntax and Semantics*. Vol. 3, *Speech Acts*, ed. P. Cole and J. L. Morgan, 41–58. New York: Academic Press.

Grimshaw, A. D. 1990a. "Research on Conflict Talk: Antecedents, Resources, Findings, Directions." In *Conflict Talk: Sociolinguistic Investigations of Arguments in Conversation*, ed. A. D. Grimshaw, 280–324. Cambridge: Cambridge University Press.

Grimshaw, A. D., ed. 1990b. *Conflict Talk: Sociolinguistic Investigations of Arguments in Conversation*. Cambridge: Cambridge University Press.

Gruzelier, J. H. 1978. "Bimodal States of Arousal and Lateralized Dysfunction in Schizophrenia: Effects of Chlorpromazine." In *The Nature of Schizophrenia: New Approaches to Research and Treatment*, ed. L. C. Wynne, R. I. Cromwell, and S. Matthysse. New York: Wiley.

Gumperz, J. J. 1986. "Interactional Sociolinguistics in the Study of Schooling." In *The Social Construction of Literacy*, ed. J. Cook-Gumperz, 45–68. Cambridge: Cambridge University Press.

———. 1984. "The Retrieval of Sociocultural Knowledge in Conversation." In *Language in Use*, ed. J. Baugh and J. Sherzer, 127–38. Englewood Cliffs, N.J.: Prentice-Hall.

———. 1982. *Discourse Strategies*. Cambridge: Cambridge University Press.

———. 1977. "Sociocultural Knowledge in Conversational Inference." In *Linguistics and Anthropology*. Georgetown University Round Table on Languages and Linguistics 1977, ed. Muriel Saville-Troike, 191–211. Washington, D.C.: Georgetown University Press.

Halliday, M., and R. Hassan. 1976. *Cohesion in English*. London: Longman.

Harrison, P. A. 1983. *Behaving Brazilian*. Rowley, Mass.: Newbury House.

Harrow, M., M. Silverstein, and J. Marengo. 1983. "Disordered Thinking." *Archives of General Psychiatry* 40:765–71.

Harrow, M., L. S. Grossman, M. L. Silverstein, and H. Y. Meltzer. 1982. "Thought Pathology in Manic and Schizophrenic Patients." *Archives of General Psychiatry* 39:665–71.

Harrow, M., and D. Quinlan. 1977. "Is Disordered Thinking Unique to Schizophrenia?" *Archives of General Psychiatry* 34, no. 1:15–21.

Hoyle, S. 1988. "Boy's Sportscasting Talk: A Study of Children's Language Use." Ph.D. diss. Georgetown University.

Hymes, D. 1974. "Ways of Speaking." In *Explorations in the Ethnography of*

Speaking, ed. R. Bauman and J. Sherzer, 433–51. Cambridge: Cambridge University Press.

James, W. 1950. *Principles of Psychology,* vol. 2. New York: Dover.

Jefferson, G. 1984. "On Stepwise Transition from Talk about Trouble to Inappropriately Next-Positioned Matters." In *Structures of Social Action,* ed. J. Maxwell Atkinson and J. Heritage, 191–222. New York: Cambridge University Press.

Jefferson, G. 1972. "Side Sequence." In *Studies in Social Interaction,* ed D. Sudnow, 294–337. New York: Free Press.

Johnston, M. H., and P. S. Holzman. 1979. *Assessing Schizophrenic Thinking.* San Francisco: Jossey-Bass.

Johnstone, B. 1984. "Repeating Yourself: Discourse Paraphrase and the Generation of Language." *Proceedings of the Eastern States Conference on Linguistics,* 250–59.

Kasanin J. S., ed. [1944] 1964. *Language and Thought in Schizophrenia.* New York: Norton.

Keenan, E., and B. B. Schieffelin. 1976. "Topic as a Discourse Notion." In *Subject and Topic.* ed. C. N. Li, 335–84. New York: Academic Press.

Kendon, A. 1981. *Non-verbal Communication, Interaction, and Gesture.* The Hague: Mouton.

———. 1979. "Some Emerging Features of Face-to-Face Interaction Studies." *Sign Language Studies* 22:7–22.

Kirshenblatt-Gimblett, B. 1976. *Speech Play.* Philadelphia: University of Pennsylvania Press.

Kraepelin, E. [1919] 1925. *Dementia Praecox and Paraphrenia.* Edinburgh: E & S Livingstone.

Kress, G. [1985] 1989. *Linguistic Processes in Sociocultural Practice.* Oxford: Oxford University Press.

Labov, W. 1972. "The Transformation of Experience in Narrative Syntax." In *Language in the Inner City,* 354–96. Philadelphia: University of Pennsylvania Press.

Labov, W., and D. Fanshel. 1977. *Therapeutic Discourse.* New York: Academic Press.

Laing, R. D. [1967] 1974. *The Politics of Experience and the Bird of Paradise.* Middlesex, England: Penguin.

Lakoff, R. 1981. "Schizophrenia as Communication." *Semiotica* 34, no. 3/4:355–74.

Levinson, S. C. 1983. *Pragmatics.* Cambridge: Cambridge University Press.

Li, C. N., and S. A. Thompson. 1976. "Subject and Topic: A New Typology of Language." In *Subject and Topic,* ed. C. N. Li. New York: Academic Press.

Lipkin, K. M., J. Dyrud, and G. G. Meyer. 1970. "The Many Faces of Mania." *Archives of General Psychiatry* 22:262–67.

McDermott, R. P., and H. Tylbor. 1983. "On the Necessity of Collusion in Conversation." *Text* 3, no. 3:277–97.

MacKinnon, R. A., and R. Michels. 1971. *The Psychiatric Interview in Clinical Practice.* Philadelphia: W. B. Saunders.

McQuown, N. E., G. Bateson, R. L. Birdwhistell, H. W. Brosen, and G. F. Hockett. 1971. "The Natural History of an Interview." Microfilm Collection of Manuscripts in Cultural Anthropology, Joseph Regenstein Library, University of Chicago, Chicago.

Mandler, J. M. 1979. "Categorial and Schematic Organization in Memory." In *Memory Organization and Structure,* 259–99. New York: Academic Press.

Manning, P. K. 1980. "Goffman's Framing Order: Style as Structure." In *The View from Goffman,* ed. J. Ditton, 252–83. New York: St. Martin's.

Martin, J. R., and S. R. Rochester. 1975. "Cohesion and Reference in Schizophrenic Speech." In *The First LACUS Forum,* ed. A. Makkai and V. Makkai, 302–11. Columbia, Mo.: Hornbeam Press.

Maynard, D. W. 1982. "Person-description in Plea Bargaining." *Semiotica* 42, no. 2/48 195–213.

———. 1980. "Placement of Topic Changes in Conversation." *Semiotica* 30, no. 3/4:263–90.

Maynard, D., and D. II. Zimmerman. 1984. "Topical Talk, Ritual and the Social Organization of Relationships." *Social Psychology Quaterly* 47, no. 4:301–16.

Mehan, H. 1990. "Oracular Reasoning in a Psychiatric Exam: The Resolution of Conflict in Language." In *Conflict Talk,* ed. A. D. Grimshaw, 160–77. Cambridge: Cambridge University Press.

———. 1979. *Learning Lessons: Social Organization in the Classroom.* Cambridge, Mass: Harvard University Press.

Minsky, M. 1975. "A Framework for Representing Knowledge." In *The Psychology of Computer Vision,* ed. P. H. Winston. New York: McGraw-Hill.

Mishler, E. G. 1984. *The Discourse of Medicine: Dialectics of Medical Interviews.* Norwood, N.J.: Ablex

Ochs, E. 1979. "Transcription as Theory." In *Developmental Pragmatics,* ed. E. Ochs and B. B. Schieffelin, 43–72. New York: Academic Press.

Ochs, E., and B. B. Schieffelin, eds. 1979. *Developmental Pragmatics.* New York: Academic Press.

Paget, M. A. 1983. "On the Work of Talk: Studies in Misunderstandings." In *The Social Organization of Doctor-Patient Communication,* ed. S. Fisher and A. D. Todd, 55–74. Washington, D.C.: Center for Applied Linguistics.

Philips, S. O. 1976. "Some Sources of Cultural Variability in the Regulation of Talk." *Language in Society* 5.81–96.

Pittenger, R. E., C. F. Hockett, and J. J. Danehy. 1960. *The First Five Minutes: A Sample Microscopic Interview Analysis.* Ithaca, N.Y.: P. Martineau.

Polanyi, L. 1979. "So What's the Point?" *Semiotica* 25, no. 3/4:207–41.

Pontes, E. 1981. "Da Importância do Tópico em Português." Paper presented at the Annual Linguistics Meeting, 1981, Catholic University of Rio de Janeiro.

Price-Williams, D., and S. Sabsay. 1979. "Communicative Competence among Severely Retarded Persons." *Semiotica* 26, no. 1/2:35–63.

Reiser, D. E., and A. K. Schroder. [1980] 1984. *Patient Interviewing: The Human Dimension.* Baltimore: Williams & Wilkins.

Ribeiro, B. T. 1993. "Framing in Psychotic Discourse." In *Framing in Discourse,* ed. D. Tannen. New York: Oxford University Press.

———. 1991. "Papéis e Alinhamentos no Discurso Psicótico." In *Cadernos de Estudos Lingüísticos 20—Sociolingüística,* ed. G. M. Oliveira e Silva and F. Tarallo, 113–38. Campinas, Brazil: Unicamp.

———. 1991b. "Esquemas de Conhecimento e Quadros Interacionais no Discurso Psicótico." Paper presented at the 2d International Meeting on the Philosophy of Language, August 4–8, Center for Logic, Epistemology and History of Science at Unicamp, State University of Campinas, Brazil.

Rochester, S. R., and J. R. Martin. 1979. *Crazy Talk*. New York: Plenum Press.

Rochester, S. R., J. R. Martin, and S. Thurston. 1977. "Thought-Process Disorder in Schizophrenia: The Listener's Task." *Brain and Language* 4:95–114.

Rosenberg, S. D., and G. J. Tucker. 1976. "Verbal Content and the Diagnosis of Schizophrenia." Paper presented at the 29th Annual Meeting of the American Psychiatric Association, Florida.

Rumelhart, D. E. 1975. "Notes on a Schema for Stories." In *Representation and Understanding: Studies in Cognitive Science*, ed. D. G. Bobrow and A. Collins. New York: Academic Press.

Sacks, H. 1972a. Unpublished transcribed lecture, no. 5. School of Social Science, University of California, Irvine.

———. [1972b] 1988. "On the Analyzability of Stories by Children." In *Directions in Sociolinguistics—The Ethnography of Communication*, ed. J. J. Gumperz and D. Hymes, 325–45. Oxford: Basil Blackwell.

———. 1971. Unpublished transcribed lecture, March 11. School of Social Science, University of California, Irvine.

Sacks, H., E. Schegloff, and G. Jefferson. 1978. "A Simplest Systematics for the Organization of Turn-taking in Conversation." In *Studies in the Organization of Conversational Interaction*, ed. J. Schenkein, 7–55. New York: Academic Press.

Sacks, H., E. Schegloff, and G. Jefferson. 1974. "A Simplest Systematics for the Organization of Turn-taking for Conversation." *Language* 50:696–735.

Salzinger, K., S. Portnoy, and R. S. Feldman. 1978. "Communicability Deficit in Schizophrenics Resulting from a More General Deficit." In *Language and Cognition in Schizophrenia*, ed. S. Swartz, 35–53. Hillsdale, N.J.: Lawerence Erlbaum.

Schank, R., and R. Abelson. 1977. *Scripts, Plans, Goals, and Understanding: An Inquiry into Human Knowledge Structures*. Hillsdale, N.J.: Lawrence Erlbaum.

Scheflen, A. E. 1973. *Communicational Structure: Analysis of a Psychotherapy Transaction*. Bloomington, Ind.: Indiana University Press.

———. 1972. *Body Language and the Social Order*. Englewood Cliffs, N.J.: Prentice-Hall.

Schegloff, E. A. 1982. "Discourse as an Interactional Achievement: Some Uses of 'Uh Huh' and Other Things that Come between Sentences." In *Analyzing Discourse: Text and Talk*. Georgetown University Round Table on Language and Linguistics 1981, ed. D. Tannen, 71–93. Washington, D.C.: Georgetown University Press.

———. 1972a. "Notes on Conversational Practice: Formulating Place." In *Studies in Social Interaction*, ed. D. Sudnow, 75–119. New York: Free Press.

———. [1972b] 1988. "Sequencing in Conversational Openings." In *Directions in Sociolinguistics*, ed. J. J. Gumperz and D. Hymes, 346–80. Oxford: Basil Blackwell.

Schegloff, E., and H. Sacks. 1973. "Opening Up Closings." *Semiotica* 4:283–327.

Schiffrin, D. [1988] 1989. "Conversation Analysis." In *Linguistics: The Cambridge Survey*. Vol. 4, *Language: The Socio-cultural Context*, ed. F. J. Newmeyer, 251–76. Cambridge: Cambridge University Press.

———. 1987a. *Discourse Markers*. Cambridge: Cambridge University Press.

———. 1987b. "Sociolinguistic Approaches to Discourse: Toward a Synthesis and Expansion." Paper presented at NWAVE XVI, October 24. University of Texas, Austin.

———. 1985. "Conversational Coherence: The Role of 'Well.'" *Language* 61:640–67.

———. 1984. "Jewish Argument as Sociability." *Language in Society* 13:311–35.

Schultz, J., S. Florio, and F. Erickson. 1982. "Where's the Floor?" In *Ethnography and Education,* ed. P. Gilmore and A. A. Glatthorn, 88–123. Washington, D.C.: Center for Applied Linguistics.

Scollon, R. 1979. "A Real Early Stage: An Unzippered Condensation of a Dissertation on Child Language." In *Developmental Pragmatics,* ed. E. Ochs and B. B. Schieffelin, 215–28. New York: Academic Press.

Searle, J. R. 1969. *Speech Acts.* Cambridge: Cambridge University Press.

Sheehan, S. [1982] 1983. *Is There No Place on Earth For Me?.* Boston: Houghton Mifflin. Reprint. New York: Vintage Books.

Shuy, R. 1983. "Three Types of Interference to an Effective Exchange of Information in the Medical Interview." In *The Social Organization of Doctor-Patient Communication,* ed. S. Fisher and A. D. Todd, 189–202. Washington, D.C.: Center for Applied Linguistics.

———. 1982. "Topic as the Unit of Analysis in a Criminal Law Case." In *Analyzing Discourse: Text and Talk.* Georgetown University Round Table on Languages and Linguistics 1981, ed. D. Tannen, 113–26. Washington, D.C.: Georgetown University Press.

———. 1981. "Can Linguistics Evidence Build a Defense Theory in a Minimal Case?" *Studia Linguistica* 35.

———. 1974. "Problems in Communication in the Cross-cultural Medical Interview." *Working Papers in Sociolinguistics* 19. Austin: University of Texas.

Snow, C. E. and C. A. Ferguson. [1977] 1979. *Talking to Children.* Cambridge: Cambridge University Press.

Steward, S. 1978. *Nonsense.* Baltimore: The Johns Hopkins University Press.

Streeck, J. 1985. *Social Order in Child Communication: A Study in Microethnography.* Philadelphia: John Benjamins.

———. 1984. "Embodied Contexts, Transcontextuals, and the Timing of Speech Acts." *Journal of Pragmatics* 8:113–37.

Sullivan, H. S. 1954. *The Psychiatric Interview.* New York: Norton.

———. [1944] 1964. "The Language of Schizophrenia." In *Language and Thought in Schizophrenia,* ed. J. S. Kasanin, 4–16. New York: Norton.

Tannen, D. 1990. *You Just Don't Understand: Women and Men in Conversation.* New York: Morrow.

———. 1989. *Talking Voices.* Cambridge: Cambridge University Press.

———. 1987a. "Repetition and Variation as Spontaneous Formulaicity in Conversation." *Language* 63, no. 3:574–605.

———. 1987b. "Repetition in Conversation as Spontaneous Formulaicity." *Text* 7, no. 3:215–43.

———. 1986. *That's Not What I Meant!* New York: Morrow.

———. 1985. "Frames and Schemas in the Discourse Analysis of Interaction." *Quaderni di Semantica* 6, no. 2:313–21.

———. 1984. *Conversational Style: Analyzing Talk among Friends.* Norwood, N.J.: Ablex.

———. 1979. "'What's in a Frame?' Surface Evidence for Underlying Expectations." In *New Directions in Discourse Processing*, ed. R. Freedle, 137–81. Norwood, N. J.: Ablex.

Tannen, D., and C. Wallat. 1987. "Interactive Frames and Knowledge Schemas in Interaction: Examples from a Medical Examination/Interview." *Social Psychology Quarterly* 50, no. 2:205–16.

———. 1986. "Medical Professionals and Parents: A Linguistic Analysis of Communication across Contexts." *Language in Society* 15:295–312.

Vachek, J. 1966. "Some Historical Aspects of the Prague School." In *The Linguistic School of Prague*. Bloomington, Ind.: Indiana University Press.

van Dijk, T. A. 1982. "Episodes as Units of Discourse Analysis." In *Analyzing Discourse: Text and Talk*. Georgetown University Round Table on Languages and Linguistics 1981, ed. D. Tannen, 177–95. Washington, D.C.: Georgetown University Press.

———. 1977. *Text and Context*. London: Longman.

Venneman, T. 1975. "Topic, Sentence Accent, and Ellipsis: A Proposal for Their Formal Treatment." In *Formal Semantics of Natural Language,* ed. E. L. Keenan, 313–27. Cambridge: Cambridge University Press.

Watzlawick, P., J. H. Beavin, and D. D. Jackson. 1967. *The Pragmatics of Human Communication*. New York: Norton.

West, C. 1984. "Medical Misfires: Mishearings, Misgivings, and Misunderstandings in Physician-Patient Dialogues." *Discourse Processses* 7, no. 2:107–34.

———. 1983. "Ask Me No Questions . . . An Analysis of Queries and Replies in Physician-Patient Dialogues." In *The Social Organization of Doctor-Patient Communication,* ed. S. Fisher and A. Dundas Todd, 75–106. Washington, D.C.: Center for Applied Linguistics.

West, C., and D. H. Zimmerman. 1982. "Conversation Analysis." In *Handbook of Methods in Nonverbal Behavior Research,* ed. K. Scherer and P. Ekman, 506–41. New York: Cambridge University Press.

Willis, P. [1977] 1981. *Learning to Labor: How Working Class Kids Get Working Class Jobs*. Farnborough, England: Saxon House. Reprint. New York: Columbia University Press.

Wills, D. D. [1977] 1979. "Participant Deixis in English and Baby-talk." In *Talking to Children,* ed. C. E. Snow and C. A. Ferguson, 271–95. Cambridge: Cambridge University Press.

Winograd, T. 1972. *Understanding Natural Language*. New York: Academic Press.

Winokur, G. W., P. J. Clayton, and T. Reich. 1969. *Manic-Depressive Illness*. St. Louis: Mosby.

Wolfenstein, M. 1954. *Children's Humor: A Psychological Analysis*. Glencoe, Ill.: Free Press.

Wykes, T., and J. Leff. 1982. "Disordered Speech: Differences between Manics and Schizophrenics." *Brain and Language* 15:117–24.

INDEX